CONTEMPORARY ISSUES IN TRANSPHOBIC HATE AND PREJUDICE

Bringing together international research and perspectives on bias, prejudice, and hatred towards transgender communities, this collection explores the ways in which transphobia manifests across different times and spaces, addressing an important contemporary issue and filling the current gap in hate studies literature.

This book comes at a crucial time, in which gender identity has become a divisive political tool, contributing to a social climate in which transgender people have become legitimate targets for suspicion, discrimination, and hate. Exploring contemporary debates surrounding transphobic hate crime, the book focuses on understanding transphobic hate crime, examining criminal justice and policy responses, analysing spaces and places where transphobia manifests, and delving into discourse, representation, and construction of transgender identities. Showcasing a diversity of research from across the criminological disciplinary landscape and through research that deploys an innovative array of methodological approaches, this book seeks to contribute to the growing canon of academic research into experiences of transphobic hate crime and provides important insights at a time of unprecedented political, social, and direct threats to trans people's lives.

Presenting research that is both important and innovative, *Contemporary Issues in Transphobic Hate and Prejudice* will be of great interest to students and scholars working within the disciplines of Criminology, Sociology, Gender Studies, Law, Media Studies, and Queer Studies.

Ben Colliver is an Associate Professor of Criminology at Birmingham City University, UK.

Jane C. Healy is a Visiting Fellow in Criminology at Bournemouth University, UK.

Katie McBride is a Criminologist and Associate Head of School at the University of Plymouth, UK.

Gina Gwenffrewi is a lecturer and researcher in culture and media through the prism of Trans and Queer Studies at the University of Edinburgh.

Queering Criminology and Criminal Justice

Edited by Matthew Ball, Queensland University of Technology
Angela Dwyer, University of Tasmania
Vanessa Panfil, Old Dominion University

Research into the criminal justice experiences of lesbian, gay, bisexual, transgender, and queer (LGBTQ+) people has grown significantly in recent years, particularly under the label of 'queer criminology'. Criminologists and criminal justice scholars are increasingly responding to the historical exclusion of LGBTQ+ people and their lack of representation in criminal justice studies and policies.

This series explores LGBTQ+ issues in relation to crime, criminology, and criminal justice, including: LGBTQ+ victimisation and offending; theoretical and conceptual developments required to ensure criminology better represents LGBTQ+ people; and studies into the experiences of LGBTQ+ people in relation to criminal justice agents, institutions, and practices.

Queering Criminology and Criminal Justice serves as a focal point around which the field of queer criminology can develop and allows a diverse array of researchers globally (including those from the global South) to discuss a variety of criminological topics. It also aims to reinforce the importance of queer and intersectional critiques to criminology more broadly and act as a point of reference for criminologists outside of queer criminology, as well as criminal justice agents/LGBTQ+ service providers seeking to develop more inclusive, representative, and diverse understandings and practices.

Contemporary Issues in Transphobic Hate and Prejudice
Transforming the Narrative
Edited by Ben Colliver, Jane C. Healy, Katie McBride, and Gina Gwenffrewi

For more information about this series, please visit: https://www.routledge.com/Queering-Criminology-and-Criminal-Justice/book-series/QCCJ

CONTEMPORARY ISSUES IN TRANSPHOBIC HATE AND PREJUDICE

Transforming the Narrative

Edited by Ben Colliver, Jane C. Healy, Katie McBride, and Gina Gwenffrewi

Routledge
Taylor & Francis Group
LONDON AND NEW YORK

Designed cover image: Shutterstock

First published 2026
by Routledge
4 Park Square, Milton Park, Abingdon, Oxon OX14 4RN

and by Routledge
605 Third Avenue, New York, NY 10158

Routledge is an imprint of the Taylor & Francis Group, an informa business

British Library Cataloguing-in-Publication Data
A catalogue record for this book is available from the British Library

ISBN: 9781032932156 (hbk)
ISBN: 9781032931982 (pbk)
ISBN: 9781003564928 (ebk)

DOI: 10.4324/9781003564928

Typeset in Sabon
by KnowledgeWorks Global Ltd.

CONTENTS

LIST OF CONTRIBUTORS

Joanna Ashcroft is a full time PhD student at the University of Portsmouth, UK.

Grayson Bartels is a Criminology PhD candidate and Tutor at the University of Edinburgh, UK.

Rowenia Bender is a Researcher at the Center for Criminological Research Saxony in Chemnitz, Germany.

Aaron Bielejewski is a Sociologist and Criminologist at the Center for Criminological Research Saxony in Chemnitz, Germany.

Ben Colliver is an Associate Professor of Criminology at Birmingham City University, UK.

Sarah Connelly is a Lecturer in Criminology at the University of Sunderland, UK.

Ioannis Dimitrakopoulos is a Lecturer in Criminology at Arden University, UK.

Marta Pérez-Fernández is a PhD student in Law at the University of Edinburgh, UK.

Gina Gwenffrewi is a lecturer and researcher in culture and media through the prism of Trans and Queer Studies at the University of Edinburgh.

Jane C. Healy is a Visiting Fellow in Criminology at Bournemouth University, UK.

Aileen Krumma is a Psychologist and Researcher at the Center for Criminological Research Saxony in Chemnitz, Germany.

Brendan Lantz is an Associate Professor of Criminology and Criminal Justice and Director of the Hate Crime Research and Policy Institute at Florida State University, USA.

Katie McBride is a Criminologist at the University of Plymouth, UK.

Ewa Milczarek is an Assistant Professor at the Faculty of Law and Administration, University of Szczecin, Poland.

James Pickles is a Senior Lecturer in Criminology at the University of Brighton, UK.

Anika Radewald is a Researcher at the Center for Criminological Research Saxony in Chemnitz, Germany.

Amrik Singh Roudh is a PhD student at Bournemouth University, UK.

Deliah Wagner is a Researcher at the Center for Criminological Research Saxony in Chemnitz, Germany.

Kristin Weber is a Researcher at the Center for Criminological Research Saxony in Chemnitz, Germany.

Marin R. Wenger is an Associate Professor in the College of Criminology and Criminal Justice at Florida State University, USA.

1

INTRODUCTION: NAMING VIOLENCE, RESISTING ERASURE – TRANSPHOBIA AND THE POLITICS OF HATE

Ben Colliver, Katie McBride, and Gina Gwenffrewi

Introduction

In recent years, transgender and gender-diverse communities have gained unprecedented visibility, grassroots activism has grown in scope and visibility, and cultural conversations about gender have in some cases expanded across global contexts. Yet alongside this visibility, we have witnessed a concurrent and intensifying wave of transphobia – manifested in law, media, politics, and on the streets (Desjardins and Hepburn, 2025; Martino and Kuhl, 2024). Trans people, particularly trans women, non-binary individuals, and people at the intersections of multiple marginalised identities, face a growing spectrum of hostility, including threats, harassment, and targeted violence (Colliver, 2021). Meanwhile, trans masculine people – particularly young people – find themselves and the gender-affirming care they require the target of 'insidious concerns' that deny their agency and dismiss their trans subjectivity, within the quasi-misogynistic frame that they need to be saved from themselves (Elster, 2022). Transphobia is not simply a lingering prejudice of the past – it is arguably a defining feature of our current moment.

This collection is the culmination of a conference hosted by the British Society of Criminology Hate Crime Network in June 2023 at Bournemouth University that addressed transphobic hate crime. The event brought together academics, practitioners, and activists to reflect on the extent of transphobic hate crime scholarship, activism, and policy developments. However, even since June 2023, there have been significant changes in policy and practice that affect trans people. There have been positive developments for trans people across some areas of Western Europe, including the Self-Determination Act of 2024 in Germany, allowing for the legal self-identification of trans people,

DOI: 10.4324/9781003564928-1

including a 'diverse' option to reflect those who identify outside of the gender binary. Similar legislation was enacted in Finland and Spain in 2023 and in Sweden in 2025.

However, there have also been a number of legal rollbacks globally. A number of countries, including Russia, Bulgaria, and Hungary, have introduced legislation and policy that prevents legal recognition of a trans person's gender. In the US, over 20 states have banned trans people from participating in school sports based on their gender identity, and in particular most of those states have focused on the banning of transgender women and girls' participation. In 2025, Iowa removed legislation that prevented discrimination in housing and employment based on gender identity and also abolished the ability for individuals to amend the sex markers on their birth certificates. In the United Kingdom, following the Cass Review (Cass, 2024), an indefinite ban on providing puberty blockers to under 18s was enacted. Following this, in 2025 the Supreme Court ruled that for the purposes of the Equality Act, trans women were not to be regarded legally as women, a verdict that days later prompted the UK government and its watchdog the Equality and Human Rights Commission (EHRC) to announce blanket bans on trans people's access to the single-sex spaces aligned to their self-identified gender (Good Law Project, 2025b). At the time of writing, the EHRC is in the process of producing statutory guidance that is likely to entrench this interpretation. In the words of the Good Law Project, these post-Supreme Court ruling developments in the UK 'shamefully deny the reality of trans existence and will lead to daily humiliation for trans people' (Good Law Project, 2025a).

The contemporary crisis: Understanding the current legal, social, and political context of anti-trans hate

The publication of this collection occurs at a historically critical juncture for transgender rights globally. As we write in 2025, empirical evidence demonstrates an unprecedented escalation in both legislative restrictions targeting transgender communities and documented levels of anti-trans violence. This convergence of factors creates what the Human Rights Campaign characterises as an epidemic of violence occurring alongside systematic legislative rollbacks (Human Rights Campaign, 2024).

Official data from legislative tracking organisations reveals the unprecedented scope of current anti-trans legislative efforts. The Trans Legislation Tracker, which monitors anti-LGBTQ+ legislation across the United States, documents 942 bills under consideration in 2025 that would negatively impact trans and gender non-conforming people (Trans Legislation Tracker, 2025). This represents the fifth consecutive record-breaking year for such legislation, following 2024's unprecedented introduction of 88 bills at the federal level alone.

Research by the Williams Institute at UCLA School of Law, recognised nationally for its rigorous, independent research methodology and cited by the US Supreme Court in landmark cases (Williams Institute, 2024), demonstrates the population-level impact of these legislative restrictions. Their analysis reveals that 93% of transgender youth aged 13–17 in the United States, representing an estimated 280,300 young people, live in states that have passed or proposed laws restricting fundamental rights including healthcare access, educational participation, and facility usage (Williams Institute, 2024). Human Rights Watch, applying international human rights monitoring standards, documents that since 2021, 25 states have enacted comprehensive bans on gender-affirming healthcare for transgender youth, disrupting medical access for over 100,000 young transgender people (Human Rights Watch, 2025). These restrictions extend beyond healthcare to encompass what Human Rights Watch characterises as systematic attempts to erase trans life through coordinated policy initiatives.

Federal Bureau of Investigation (FBI) hate crime statistics provide the most comprehensive official data on anti-transgender violence in the United States. FBI data demonstrates a consistent upward trajectory in gender identity-motivated hate crimes, increasing from 307 reported offences in 2021 to 547 in 2023, representing a 78% increase over two years (FBI, 2024). Notably, the 2023 figure includes 401 specifically anti-transgender incidents and 146 targeting gender non-conforming individuals.

The Human Rights Campaign's systematic tracking of fatal violence against transgender individuals, which employs broader inclusion criteria than legal hate crime definitions, documented 36 transgender and gender-expansive people killed in the 12-month period between Transgender Day of Remembrance 2023 and 2024, with 30 deaths occurring in the 2024 calendar year alone (Human Rights Campaign, 2024). This data aligns with global monitoring by Transgender Europe (TGEU), whose Trans Murder Monitoring project documented 350 trans and gender-diverse people murdered globally between October 2023 and September 2024, representing one of the highest annual death tolls since systematic monitoring began in 2008 (TGEU, 2024b).

In England and Wales, Home Office statistics demonstrate persistently high levels of anti-transgender hate crime, with 4,780 offences recorded in 2023/24, representing only a marginal decline from 4,889 offences in 2022/23 (UK Home Office, 2024). Williams Institute research using National Crime Victimization Survey data reveals that transgender people are over four times more likely than cisgender people to experience violent victimisation, including rape, sexual assault, and aggravated assault (Williams Institute, 2022).

TGEU's comprehensive annual mapping of transgender rights across Europe and Central Asia, which tracks legislative developments in 54 countries across 32 areas of trans-specific legislation, provides authoritative documentation of regional trends. For the first time in the 13-year history of this monitoring project, TGEU reports that setbacks in human rights of trans people across Europe and Central Asia now clearly outweigh progress (TGEU, 2024a). This regression includes three countries, Russia, Bulgaria, and Hungary, implementing complete bans on legal gender recognition, representing what TGEU characterises as a strategic assault on fundamental freedoms, equality, democracy, and on Europe itself.

The UK context demonstrates how supposedly evidence-based policy reviews can facilitate rights' rollbacks. Following publication of the Cass Review in April 2024, itself subject to extensive academic critique regarding methodological limitations and potential bias (Horton, 2024; FGEN, 2024), the UK government implemented an indefinite ban on puberty blockers for under-18s. NHS England subsequently reported that no new prescriptions of gender-affirming hormones have been issued to minors in the year following the Review's publication, despite such treatments not being explicitly banned (NHS England, 2025). Evidence of the harms of the puberty-blocker ban on trans children and young people are beginning to emerge, however, with 'very serious adverse effects, less than a year after its imposition, including sharply declining mental health, increased depression, social isolation, anxiety, stress, self-harm, school avoidance and suicide ideation' (Kennedy, 2025: 1).

The April 2025 UK Supreme Court ruling in *For Women Scotland v The Scottish Ministers* further undermined transgender rights by determining that sex in the Equality Act 2010 refers exclusively to biological sex assigned at birth (UK Supreme Court, 2025). United Nations human rights experts have expressed concern that this ruling risks entrenching legal uncertainty and undermining the rights of transgender persons in all aspects of life, and may justify exclusionary policies that further stigmatise and marginalise an already vulnerable population (UN Office of the High Commissioner for Human Rights, 2025).

Academic analysis reveals the coordinated, transnational nature of contemporary anti-trans mobilisation. Research documents how organisations such as the Heritage Foundation, the principal architects of Project 2025's anti-trans agenda in the USA, promote restrictive legislation across multiple jurisdictions. Such well-resourced think tanks receive proposals from illiberal actors in Poland and Hungary on shaping European Union policy (Quinan, 2025). This coordination represents what TGEU describes as concerted efforts of anti-gender and anti-rights movements that instrumentalise and vilify trans people to push wider anti-democratic political agendas.

Longitudinal polling data demonstrates concerning shifts in public attitudes toward transgender rights. YouGov polling in the UK shows increased scepticism towards transgender rights across the board, with support for allowing people to socially identify as a different gender declining from 55% in 2022 to 49% in 2024 (YouGov, 2025). This attitudinal shift extends to younger demographics previously supportive of transgender rights, suggesting the effectiveness of coordinated disinformation campaigns.

This comprehensive analysis of official statistics, peer-reviewed research, and systematic monitoring data reveals transgender communities facing an unprecedented convergence of legislative hostility, documented violence, and shifting public sentiment. As TGEU observes, this represents more than just a crisis for trans communities, but rather a broader crisis of democracy and fundamental rights requiring rigorous academic analysis capable of illuminating underlying mechanisms whilst centring affected communities' experiences (TGEU, 2024a).

This collection emerges not merely as an academic exercise, but as an essential intervention providing analytical tools for understanding how transphobic hate operates across individual, institutional, and structural levels. The empirical evidence presented here demonstrates the urgent necessity for scholarship that can both document these phenomena and contribute to evidence-based responses promoting justice, equality, and safety for transgender and gender-diverse communities globally.

Naming the problem: Beyond individualised understandings of transphobia

Defining identities in a way that is reflective of individual experiences is difficult. However, the definition provided by Hines (2010) is commonly drawn on in the academic literature, in which she notes the term transgender is:

> a range of gender experiences, subjectivities and presentations that fall across between or beyond stable categories of 'man' and 'woman'. Transgender includes gender identities that have, more traditionally, been described as 'transsexual', and a diversity of genders that call into question an assumed relationship between gender identity and presentation and the 'sexed' body.
>
> *(Hines, 2010: 1)*

This definition of 'transgender' is especially valuable in that it recognises gender expressions that exist between and beyond the binary categories of 'man' and 'woman'. However, we acknowledge that the term itself is subject to debate, both within and across gender-diverse communities. Monro (2003) highlights the complexities surrounding the use of transgender as an 'umbrella term', arguing that while the term's broad inclusivity brings visibility to a wide range of identities, it risks overlooking the distinct needs, experiences, and interests of the varied groups it seeks to encompass. Accordingly, each chapter in this collection provides the definition of this term utilised for the authors' own research and/or analysis.

Transphobia is commonly defined as the irrational fear, hatred, or aversion towards transgender and gender non-conforming people (Hill, 2002). Similar to homophobia and other forms of prejudice, the term denotes both individual-level bias and systemic discrimination. However, critics argue that framing transphobia as an 'irrational fear' is reductive and risks pathologising prejudice rather than addressing its social and political roots (Serano, 2007). As several contributors to this volume argue, transphobia operates across multiple levels: interpersonal, institutional, cultural, and structural; in these latter cases, potentially taking the form of what Amery and Mondon call 'organised transphobia' (2024). It is embedded in the policing of gender (Doan, 2010; Browne, 2004), in medical gatekeeping (Ashley, 2019), and in education (Siegel, 2019).

Transphobia may manifest in various ways. Microaggressions – everyday slights and invalidations – are another form of transphobia that frequently go unnoticed or unaddressed. Nadal et al. (2012) developed a taxonomy of transphobic microaggressions, including misgendering, exoticisation, and denial of trans experiences. Such behaviours, while less overt than physical violence or hate speech, cumulatively impact mental health and social inclusion (McLemore, 2015). More visible manifestations of transphobia may be in a range of criminal behaviours, commonly referred to as 'hate crimes' or 'bias crimes'. Whilst there is no legal consensus internationally as to what constitutes a hate crime, academically it is broadly understood as a criminal offence motivated by hostility or prejudice toward a person based on their actual or perceived membership in a particular social group (Iganski and Levin, 2015). These groups typically include race, religion, sexual orientation, disability, and gender identity, although protected characteristics vary by jurisdiction. In this context, a transphobic hate crime refers to offences motivated by prejudice against transgender people.

Overview of collection

The opening section of this collection, 'Understanding Identities and Transphobia', explores how trans identities are constructed, contested, and regulated in different social and cultural contexts. These chapters trace the genealogies of transphobia, interrogate the language through which trans people are made intelligible or illegible, and critique the epistemological foundations of hate crime categorisations. This section sets the groundwork for the volume, establishing transphobia as a multifaceted and deeply embedded social force.

In *Chapter Two*, Colliver critically examines the complex realities of transphobic hate crime by analysing the hierarchical structures that inform societal, institutional, and individual conceptualisations of victimisation. Employing empirical data derived from qualitative interviews with transgender and non-binary participants, Colliver demonstrates that prevailing perceptions of legitimate victimhood are significantly shaped by dominant discourses – most notably the emphasis on 'stranger danger' and the prioritisation of physical violence. Utilising a queer theoretical framework in conjunction with critical realism, the analysis foregrounds the ways in which microaggressions and non-physical forms of abuse – frequently enacted by individuals within the victim's immediate social networks, such as family members or friends – are systematically trivialised or disregarded in both public narratives and criminal justice responses. The research highlights the pervasive underreporting of transphobic hate crimes and the consequent marginalisation of transgender perspectives. In doing so, it calls for a more expansive and inclusive understanding of victimisation – one that interrogates dominant hierarchies and legitimises the diverse and often overlooked experiences of trans individuals.

Chapter Three critically examines the rise and evolution of anti-trans activism in the United Kingdom, contextualising it within broader global movements opposing gender diversity and LGBTQ+ rights. Drawing from feminist history, legal precedents, media analysis, and international human rights commentary, Pickles traces the shift from early trans-exclusionary radical feminist discourses to the contemporary mainstreaming of gender-critical activism. The chapter highlights how anti-trans rhetoric, framed as concern for women's rights or biological realism, has gained traction across political, media, and academic domains. Through a detailed analysis of actors, organisations, and strategies, the chapter explores how these discourses – often cloaked in the language of reasonableness – contribute to the systemic marginalisation of trans people. Pickles also documents international condemnation of the UK's role in advancing trans-hostile narratives and underscores the coordinated global funding and ideological networks sustaining anti-gender movements.

In *Chapter Four*, Connelly explores the compounded marginalisation faced by young transgender and non-binary individuals in the United Kingdom through an intersectional framework. Focusing on the convergence of age and gender identity, the chapter interrogates how public discourse, legal structures, and media narratives co-construct these identities as both politicised and vulnerable. Connelly analyses the impact of cultural debates, healthcare policy, and legal recognition on young trans and non-binary lives, highlighting systemic inequalities that limit agency, access, and citizenship. Key themes include the erasure of young voices in political and medical decision-making, the exclusionary nature of age-related legal frameworks, and the weaponisation of safeguarding discourse against gender-diverse youth. Through intersectional analysis, the chapter illustrates how these overlapping axes of identity intensify social exclusion and harm, underscoring the need for inclusive reform and more equitable representations in public discourse and policy.

The second section of this collection, 'Global Patterns in Policy and Practice', explores how transgender identities and experiences of hate are dealt with through policy and within the criminal justice system. The objective of this section is to explore manifestations of transphobia in democratic institutions and policy-making. The section draws upon international case studies in Poland, Germany, the US, and the UK to provide insights into the ways in which transphobic discourses are tethered to political narratives which lead to institutional manifestations of prejudice against transgender identities. The social inequalities that this perpetuates are demonstrated through the examples drawn from within the criminal justice systems of England and Wales, Poland, Germany, and the United States.

In *Chapter Five*, Gwenffrewi engages with the multivalent concept of prison abolition, to the overlapping themes of structural racism and transphobia. Drawing on a mix of film studies and textual analysis, the chapter uses as its frame the documentary *Free CeCe!* (2018), about the experience of American trans woman of colour CeCe McDonald and her ordeal within the US prison industrial complex, including her incarceration in a men's prison. The analysis includes a study of the vectors of class, racism and homophobia/transphobia that contributed to McDonald's prior experience of oppression and the subsequent incarceration; McDonald's commitment to prison abolition activism; and a deconstruction of some of the different ways prison abolition and justice are understood by different contributors. This latter aspect reflects the apparent lack of a consensus around abolitionism but also the significance of racism in discussions about it, and the broader discussions about the diversity of structural oppression that some trans communities in particular experience.

Focusing on jury processes, in *Chapter Six* Singh examines juror bias against transgender victims in hate crime trials in England and Wales, with a focus on the impact of jury composition and inter-group contact on verdict outcomes. Drawing on empirical data from three large-scale mock-jury studies (N=1623), it investigates whether imagined inter-group contact can reduce transprejudice and improve verdict fairness. The findings reveal that LGBT+ representative juries, or juries simulated with inter-group contact exposure, significantly reduced victim blame and transprejudice while increasing guilty verdicts, perceived victim suffering, and support for sentence enhancements. The chapter situates these results within broader discussions of structural stigma, institutional exclusion from jury service, and legal reform, arguing that current jury recruitment practices systematically disadvantage LGBT+ communities, particularly transgender people. Policy recommendations include adopting more inclusive juror selection processes based on international models and embracing imagined contact as an effective prejudice reduction strategy. By highlighting the ethical, legal, and psychological benefits of representative juries, the chapter makes a strong case for reforming jury systems to ensure greater fairness in hate crime trials.

In *Chapter Seven*, Milczarek investigates the intersection of transphobic hate crime and the rise of illiberal democracy in Poland, highlighting how political, legal, and societal mechanisms collectively foster discrimination against transgender individuals. The chapter explores how right-wing populism instrumentalises anti-LGBTQ+ sentiment – particularly transphobia – to consolidate power, construct national identity, and reinforce traditionalist norms. Drawing on legal analysis, policy developments, and court judgments, the chapter illustrates the systemic marginalisation of transgender people through hate speech, legislative gaps, and symbolic acts such as 'LGBTQ+-free zones'. It further examines the role of media and political rhetoric in legitimising hostility, as well as the psychological and social impact of discrimination on the transgender community. The chapter concludes by underscoring the urgent need for legal reforms, international accountability, and inclusive public discourse to counteract the escalating climate of hate and safeguard human rights in contemporary Poland.

In *Chapter Eight*, Lantz and Wenger examine fatal violence against transgender individuals in the United States, with a specific focus on bias-motivated homicides. Drawing on data from the Tracking Transgender Homicide in America project, the authors present one of the first comprehensive quantitative analyses comparing transphobic hate crimes with other homicides involving transgender victims. Through logistic regression and detailed case studies, the chapter identifies critical distinctions in victim profiles, circumstances of the crimes, and systemic responses – highlighting the prevalence of homelessness, survival sex work, and deadnaming by police. It argues that these crimes must be understood through an intersectional and symbolic interactionist lens, revealing how broader social forces, institutional failures, and legislative gaps contribute to patterns of targeted violence. The authors call for enhanced legal protections, improved data collection, and culturally competent responses to ensure justice for transgender victims and to reduce systemic harm.

This section of the collection closes with *Chapter Nine* in which Weber and colleagues present findings from a large-scale, cross-sectional survey examining public attitudes toward transphobic hate crime in Germany. Drawing on data from over 3,300 participants in the HaSteX study, the authors explore how transphobic attitudes, political orientation, intergroup contact, and diversity beliefs shape support for police intervention in hate crimes against transgender individuals. Despite increasing visibility of transgender people, the findings highlight persistent gaps in public empathy, political recognition, and institutional protection. The study underscores the critical role of public discourse, media representation, and interpersonal experience in shaping societal responses to anti-trans violence in contemporary Germany.

In the third section of this collection, 'Space, Place, and Transphobia', the focus is on the diversity of spaces and places within which experiences of transphobia, prejudice, and hate manifest and how these contribute to a wider environment of fear for transgender and other gender-diverse people. The objectives of this section are to highlight the infiltration of transphobic discourse and hate into every corner of our existence. The section elucidates experiences drawn from, firstly, workplace settings, exploring the protective and avoidance strategies that are actively deployed by transgender people to protect themselves and their livelihoods; and secondly, online spaces, where hate crimes target transgender and other gender-diverse people by exposing personal details, leaving them exposed to attack online and in-person. Finally, this section critically considers queer dating apps as 'safe' spaces by illuminating the impacts of microaggressions and horizontal transphobia through the rejection of non-heteronormative identities.

In *Chapter Ten*, McBride draws on qualitative life-story interviews with trans women in England and Wales. This chapter positions the workplace as a key site of *silent violence*, where cisnormative organisational cultures reproduce hate through microaggressions, administrative exclusion, and, at the extreme, sexual assault. Employing Žižek's notion of symbolic violence, Berlant's 'cruel optimism', and insights from Critical Hate Studies, McBride shows how neoliberal imperatives of individual responsibility compel trans employees to self-silence, 'cover', and endure precarity in pursuit of professional legitimacy. Three rich case studies illuminate the continuum of harm: Bird's thwarted job search and moment of retaliatory violence; Jenny-Anne's outing, harassment, and dismissal despite exemplary performance; and Julie's coerced compliance during a work-related sexual assault abroad. Collectively, they reveal how legal protections are undercut by managerial inaction, media scapegoating, and the 2025 enshrinement of 'gender-critical' belief, which further legitimates exclusion. The chapter therefore calls for structural transformation that moves beyond performative diversity to challenge the cisnormative logics embedded in contemporary labour markets.

In *Chapter Eleven*, Pérez-Fernández and Bartels examine the phenomenon of doxxing – deliberate online exposure of personal information – as a mechanism of harm disproportionately targeting transgender individuals. Drawing on digital zemiology and queer criminology, the authors argue for a reconceptualisation of online space as real and consequential, challenging the traditional divide between online and offline harms. They outline the importance of digital spaces for trans communities as sites of identity formation, support, and belonging, while highlighting how doxxing and trolling exploit these same spaces to delegitimise and endanger. Through theoretical analysis and personal narrative, the authors show that doxxing not only invades privacy but constitutes a form of non-corporeal violence with tangible psychological, social, and physical impacts. Ultimately, they advocate for legal, institutional, and cultural shifts that recognise the legitimacy of online harms, urging more nuanced and responsive frameworks that centre the lived experiences of marginalised communities in digital spaces.

The focus of *Chapter Twelve* is on microaggressions faced by transgender, non-binary, and gender non-conforming individuals on Grindr, a widely used LGBTQ+ dating app. Dimitrakopoulos examines the subtle yet harmful nature of these microaggressions and reveals how – through misgendering, fetishisation, and rejection – they reinforce cisnormative ideals, contribute to existential harm, and act as mechanisms of conformity and social control. Using a harm-based framework and microaggression theory, the chapter situates these behaviours within broader systems of marginalisation and prejudice in queer spaces. It concludes with calls for greater awareness, policy scrutiny, and future research into intersectional harms and the policing of gender non-conformity in digital dating environments.

The final section of this collection, 'Discourse, Representation, and Construction', seeks to explore media and online discourses, representations, and constructions of transgender identities. The key objectives of this section are to elucidate the ways in which transgender identities have been constructed within the traditional media and online as a threat and illuminate the insidious nature of the hate that ensues. It considers the role of public discourse that has resulted from the UK government's proposals to amend the Gender Recognition Act (GRA) and to review its position on the banning of so called 'conversion' therapy to exclude transgender people. Specifically, it looks at how transphobia has manifested online and generated a new hateful rhetoric that presents transgender people (women in particular) as posing a danger to others.

Chapter Thirteen by Gwenffrewi examines the burden of representation experienced by trans women in the UK, in the case of convicted rapist and trans woman Isla Bryson. This media and political furore in 2023 became both a delegitimising talking point about the hypothesised threat constructed around trans women as well as the justification for the tightening of regulations allowing trans women prisoners in women-only prisons. The chapter's content analysis of media coverage reveals the media's propensity to conflate such isolated acts as Bryson's with trans women more generally, including the supposed threat of the passing of Gender Recognition Act (GRA) reform, despite the disconnection between GRA reform and the processes involved in decision-making about housing trans women prisoners. The chapter concludes that there exists structural bias against trans women in media representations, including the perpetuation of harmful stereotypes, with implications for the safety, dignity, and rights of trans women in the public sphere.

In *Chapter Fourteen*, Ashcroft investigates the rise in transphobic online hate following the 2018 proposed amendments to the Gender Recognition Act (GRA). Drawing on 20,833 UK-based tweets from 2017 to 2022, the study employs Natural Language Processing (NLP) to analyse language patterns, trending topics, and term frequency. Findings reveal a significant increase in anti-transgender rhetoric – particularly targeting trans women – across themes of biology, women's spaces, and perceived threats to children. Language was often politicised and moralistic, echoing far-right narratives, and high-profile figures like J.K. Rowling were shown to have notable influence on discourse spikes. Despite some positive sentiment, abusive and stigmatising terms such as 'trans ideology.' 'mutilating children', and 'bloody pronouns' proliferated. This study evidences an acceleration in online hate correlating with socio-political developments, highlighting urgent implications for policy, platform governance, and support services for the transgender community.

In the concluding chapter of this collection, Healy revisits the spectrum of harm, hatred, Othering. and abuse that trans communities experience, drawing on similarities with Hollomotz's continuum of violence, and positioning these experiences as symbolic of a justice void that overwhelms every aspect of trans people's lives. This chapter synthesises the major themes and insights developed throughout the volume, presenting a critical overview of the contemporary landscape of transphobic hate, harm, and systemic injustice. Ultimately, this concluding chapter makes a call to action: for a broader, more inclusive understanding of harm, and for legal, academic, and activist frameworks that challenge cisnormative assumptions and affirm the lived realities of trans people. The collection as a whole represents a powerful intervention into trans studies and hate crime scholarship, standing as both testimony and resistance in the face of rising anti-trans hostility.

References

Amery, F., and Mondon, A. (2024). Othering, peaking, populism and moral panics: The reactionary strategies of organised transphobia. *The Sociological Review, 73*(3), 680–696.

Ashley, F. (2019). Gatekeeping hormone replacement therapy for transgender patients is dehumanising. *Journal of Medical Ethics, 45*(7), 480–482.

Browne, K. (2004). Genderism and the bathroom problem: (re)materialising sexed sites, (re)creating sexed bodies. *Gender, Place and Culture: A Journal of Feminist Geography, 11*(3), 331–346.

Cass, H. (2024). Independent review of gender identity services for children and young people: Final report. https://cass.independent-review.uk/home/publications/final-report/

Colliver, B. (2021). *Reimagining Hate Crime: Transphobia, Visibility and Victimisation.* London: Palgrave Macmillan.

Desjardins, B. and Hepburn, T. (2025). The gender agenda's agenda: How 'tabloid media sensationalist scumbag [s]' mobilize affect to promote transphobia. *Sociological Inquiry*. Online First. https://doi.org/10.1111/soin.70001

Doan, P. L. (2010). The tyranny of gendered spaces – reflections from beyond the gender dichotomy. *Gender, Place and Culture: A Journal of Feminist Geography*, *17*(5), 635–654.

Elster, M. (2022). Insidious concern: Trans panic and the limits of care. *Transgender Studies Quarterly*, *9*(3), 407–424.

FBI (2024). Crime in the United States, 2023: Hate crime statistics. https://www.fbi.gov/how-we-can-help-you/more-fbi-services-and-information/ucr/hate-crime

FGEN (2024). Letter from academics concerned about The Cass Review. *Feminist and Gender Studies Network*, 18 April. https://feministgenderequality.network/letter-from-academics-concerned-about-the-cass-review/

Good Law Project (2025a). Help us challenge the Supreme Court's judgment on trans rights. https://goodlawproject.org/crowdfunder/supreme-court-human-rights-for-trans-people/

Good Law Project (2025b). Trans inclusion after the Supreme Court decision: FAQs. https://goodlawproject.org/resource/trans-inclusion-after-the-supreme-court-decision-faqs/

Hill, D. B. (2002). Genderism, transphobia, and gender bashing: A framework for interpreting anti-transgender violence. In B. Wallace and R. Carter (Eds.), *Understanding and Dealing with Violence: A Multicultural Approach*. California: Sage Publications, 113–136.

Hines, S. (2010). Introduction. In S. Hines and T. Sanger (Eds.), *Transgender Identities: Towards a Social Analysis of Gender Diversity*. New York: Routledge, 1–22.

Horton, C. (2024). The Cass Review: Cis-supremacy in the UK's approach to healthcare for trans children. *International Journal of Transgender Health*, 1–25.

Human Rights Campaign (2024). *An Epidemic of Violence Against the Transgender and Gender-Expansive Community in the United States: The 2024 Report*. Washington, DC: Human Rights Campaign Foundation.

Human Rights Watch (2025). *'They're Ruining People's Lives': Bans on Gender-Affirming Care for Transgender Youth in the US*. New York: Human Rights Watch.

Iganski, P. and Levin, J. (2015). *Hate Crime: A Global Perspective*. London: Routledge.

Kennedy, N. (2025). Harming children: the effects of the UK puberty blocker ban. *Journal of Gender Studies*, 1–17.

Martino, W. and Kuhl, D. (2024). Epistemic injustice and violence in times of resurgent anti-trans backlash, emboldened white supremacist rhetoric and far-right extremism. *Discourse: Studies in the Cultural Politics of Education*, *45*(5–6), 599–613.

McLemore, K. A. (2015). Experiences with misgendering: Identity misclassification of transgender spectrum individuals. *Self and Identity*, *14*(1), 51–74.

Monro, S. (2003). Transgender politics in the UK. *Critical Social Policy*, *23*(4), 433–452.

Nadal, K. L., Skolnik, A., and Wong, Y. (2012). Interpersonal and systemic microaggressions towards transgender people: Implications for counselling. *Journal of LGBT Issues in Counselling*, *6*, 55–82.

NHS England (2025). Adult gender services review update. 15 March.

Quinan, C. L. (2025). From criminalisation to erasure: Project 2025 and anti-trans legislation in the US. *Punishment & Society*, *27*(1), 108–127.

Serano, J., (2007). *Whipping Girl: A Transsexual Woman on Sexism and the Scapegoating of Femininity*. California: Seal Press.

Siegel, D. P. (2019). Transgender experiences and transphobia in higher education. *Sociology Compass*, *13*(10).

TGEU (2024a). *Trans Rights Index & Map 2024*. Berlin: Transgender Europe.
TGEU (2024b). *Trans Murder Monitoring 2024*. Berlin: Transgender Europe.
Trans Legislation Tracker (2025). 2025 anti-trans bills tracker. https://translegislation.com
UK Home Office (2024). *Hate Crime, England and Wales, 2023/24*. London: Home Office Statistical Bulletin.
UK Supreme Court (2025). *For Women Scotland Ltd v The Scottish Ministers* [2025] UKSC 11.
UN Office of the High Commissioner for Human Rights (2025). UN experts warn of legal uncertainty and rights implications following UK Supreme Court ruling. Press Release, 9 May.
Williams Institute (2022). *Transgender People over Four Times More Likely Than Cisgender People to be Victims of Violent Crime*. Los Angeles: Williams Institute at UCLA School of Law.
Williams Institute (2024). *The Impact of 2024 Anti-Transgender Legislation on Youth*. Los Angeles: Williams Institute at UCLA School of Law.
YouGov (2025). Where does the British public stand on transgender rights in 2024/25? 11 February.

SECTION I

Understanding Identities and Transphobia

2

TRANSGRESSING SOCIAL 'NORMS': UNDERSTANDING TRANSPHOBIA AND HOSTILITY AGAINST GENDER-DIVERSE COMMUNITIES

Ben Colliver

Introduction

Transphobic hate crime represents a deeply troubling and pervasive form of violence rooted in prejudice against transgender and gender non-conforming individuals. Such acts not only target individuals but also reinforce systemic inequalities and societal marginalisation. Despite growing academic interest in the oppression of transgender individuals (Concannon, 2022; Jamel, 2018), much of the existing literature on hate crime continues to prioritise extreme manifestations of violence, often overlooking the more nuanced and everyday forms of victimisation experienced by transgender communities. This focus not only skews public and institutional perceptions of hate crime but also perpetuates the invisibility of non-physical and micro-level victimisation within these discourses.

This chapter draws upon empirical data to conceptualise different hierarchies that exist in relation to understanding transphobic hate crime. The first hierarchy addressed in the chapter relates to perpetrators; the chapter interrogates how societal and institutional narratives, such as 'stranger danger', shape perceptions of legitimate victimhood, influencing both individual reporting behaviours and broader systemic responses. The second hierarchy that is interrogated relates to offence type, reflecting on how physical violence may be understood as a 'legitimate' form of victimisation. In doing so, it aims to contribute to a more inclusive understanding of hate crime, emphasising the need for policy and practice to address the full spectrum of victimisation towards transgender individuals.

For this chapter, the definition of 'transgender' provided by Hines (2010: 1) is used, in which Hines notes that the term transgender describes

> a range of gender experiences, subjectivities and presentations that fall across, between or beyond stable categories of 'man' and 'woman'. Transgender

DOI: 10.4324/9781003564928-3

> includes gender identities that have, more traditionally, been described as 'transsexual', and a diversity of genders that call into question an assumed relationship between gender identity and presentation and the 'sexed' body.

This definition of 'transgender' is intended to acknowledge gender expressions that exist outside the binary framework of 'man' and 'woman'. However, the term itself is not without controversy. As Monro (2003) observes, the expansive use of 'transgender' as an umbrella term risks eliding significant differences in the experiences, needs, and political interests of diverse gender non-conforming groups. Such inclusivity, while aiming to foster solidarity, may inadvertently obscure specific forms of marginalisation faced by particular subgroups. The abbreviated term 'trans' is also used as a similarly broad descriptor.

Understanding violence against trans people

Violence against transgender people has most commonly been explored within hate crime scholarship (Colliver, 2021; Jamel, 2018). This scholarship has primarily focused on either microaggressions (Nadal et al., 2016; Wright et al., 2024) or more socially recognisable forms of victimisation such as physical violence. Sue et al. (2007) define microaggressions as everyday verbal and non-verbal actions, including insults, snubs, and slights, which may be intentional or unintentional. These behaviours convey negative or harmful messages to individuals or groups based on their membership in a particular minority category. The pervasive nature of microaggressions is widely recognised as contributing to significant adverse outcomes for those targeted (Brondolo et al., 2008; Szymanski et al., 2008). These effects can manifest as mental health challenges and hinder access to essential services such as healthcare, education, and other social systems, which frequently become sites of further victimisation. However, research on microaggressions predominantly examines non-criminal acts or incidents where criminality remains ambiguous, such as anti-social behaviour, name-calling, and harassment (Keels et al., 2017; Roffee and Waling, 2016).

Sue et al. (2007) identify three primary categories of microaggressions that individuals may encounter: microassaults, microinsults, and microinvalidations. Of these, microinsults and microinvalidations are often described as occurring outside the perpetrator's conscious awareness and are argued to be potentially the most harmful to victims. Microinsults are characterised by explicit denigrations, including verbal and non-verbal forms of abuse, such as name-calling and social exclusion. Microinvalidations, on the other hand, involve behaviours and comments that dismiss, negate, or invalidate the lived experiences of minority groups. These two categories align with the general understanding of microaggressions as non-criminal acts.

Microassaults, by contrast, are defined as conscious expressions of biased beliefs or attitudes that manifest through verbal abuse and discriminatory actions. Sue (2010: 3) expands upon this definition by introducing the concept of 'extreme forms of microassaults', which may encompass behaviours such as bullying, social isolation, physical violence, hate speech, and even anti-LGBTQ+ legislation. The inclusion of physical violence within the framework of microaggressions presents a conceptual contradiction. Specifically, the term 'microaggression' implies actions of lesser severity compared to more overt or extreme forms of aggression. The prefix 'micro' suggests that the behaviours it encompasses should be relatively minor in scale and impact. Consequently, the lack of definitional precision and ambiguity surrounding what constitutes 'physical violence' as an extreme microaggression raises significant challenges for research investigating microaggressions experienced by marginalised communities.

Scholars have suggested that prior studies on hate crime have inadvertently established a hierarchical framework, wherein different types of hate crime are ranked in terms of severity (Rose and Mechanic, 2002). In this hierarchy, acts of physical and sexual violence are often the focus of investigation compared to other forms of hate crime. This is evident in several studies where participants have been asked to indicate the 'most serious' incident they have experienced (Rose and Mechanic, 2002: 16) or to explain when they have felt most at risk of 'physical danger' (Herek et al., 1999: 201). As a result, participants are typically constrained to discussing a single incident, despite potentially having experienced multiple occurrences. This approach often compels participants to prioritise one specific incident, frequently guided by research questions that emphasise terms such as 'violence' and 'physical danger'. Meyer (2010) argues that such research methodologies perpetuate the hierarchical categorisation of hate crime incidents, with verbal abuse frequently positioned at the lower end of the spectrum. This approach to researching hate crime also contributes to the conceptualisation of hate crime as being singular, isolated incidents, rather than appreciating physically violent forms of victimisation as one element of a wider system of oppression.

The focus on physically violent incidents of victimisation is reinforced by sensationalised media headlines. As Hall et al. (1978: 68) argue, 'any crime can be lifted into news visibility if violence becomes associated with it ... Violence represents a basic violation of the person ... It thus represents a fundamental rupture in the social order'. It is therefore unsurprising to find that although the victimisation of trans people is scarcely reported, when it is covered in mainstream media, it primarily focuses on the sexual or physical victimisation of victims. News headlines such as 'Boys arrested after woman stabbed in "hate crime"' (Morris, 2024) reinforce perceptions that hate crime victimisation manifests in the most extreme forms of physical violence. This is unsurprising, as Jewkes (2015) highlights the specific elements that crime stories must possess to be deemed 'newsworthy', which include elements such as physical violence, sexual content, and the presence of risk. The media reinforce dominant ideologies and narratives that become naturalised as 'common sense' (Gitlin, 1978). Consequently, hate crimes that do not involve physical or sexual violence are less likely to gain public visibility, thereby influencing societal perceptions of what constitutes a 'legitimate' hate crime. Arguably, the media depict violent stories disproportionately to their actual frequency. Despite dominant media frameworks depicting hate crime as being physically violent, Home Office (2024) reports indicate that 55% of recorded hate crimes are non-physically violent.

Media representations of hate crime also perpetuate 'stranger danger' narratives that reinforce ideas that legitimate incidents of hate crime occur in public spaces, perpetrated by someone 'unknown' to the victim. Indeed, it has been argued that much early hate crime scholarship concluded that hate crime was overwhelmingly perpetrated by strangers (Mason, 2005). However, other research has highlighted the high prevalence of transphobic victimisation that occurs in private, perpetrated by friends, family, and others who are known to the victim (Colliver and Jamel, 2023; Kuehnle and Sullivan, 2001). The focus on physically violent victimisation or non-criminal acts of microaggression means that forms of victimisation such as verbal abuse, harassment, and property offences are overlooked and conceptualised as discrete, unrelated incidents. Instead, as will be demonstrated in this chapter, the victimisation of trans people is better understood as a continuum of victimisation.

Chakraborti (2015: 1746) argues that it is unequal power relations 'that reinforce the dominant position of the powerful and the marginal position of the "other"'. As such, hate crime acts as a

> mechanism of power and oppression, intended to reaffirm the precarious hierarchies that characterise a given social order. It attempts to re-create simultaneously the threatened (real or imagined) hegemony of the perpetrator's group and the 'appropriate' subordinate identity of the victim's group. It is a means of marking both the Self and the Other in such a way as to re-establish their 'proper' relative positions, as given and reproduced by broader ideologies and patterns of social and political inequality.
>
> *(Perry, 2001: 10)*

Perry provides a comprehensive analysis to enhance our understanding of identity-based violence, emphasising the complex interaction between individual victimisation and broader societal structures and processes. Central to this phenomenon is the pervasive influence of social, cultural, and political frameworks, which create conditions conducive to the perpetuation of such violence. Perry highlights the role of social hierarchies, and how these hierarchies assign power and privilege dependent on an individual's positioning across a number of social hierarchies. Victimisation, in this context, serves a dual function: it reinforces the subordinate status of trans communities within these hierarchies, while simultaneously consolidating cisnormativity. Regarding transgender individuals, violence can be interpreted as a form of 'gender policing', whereby individuals are marginalised for deviating from traditional gender norms and roles (Colliver, 2021; Perry, 2001).

Doan (2010: 635) offers a complementary perspective, asserting that transgender individuals confront the 'tyranny of gender' when they challenge dominant societal expectations surrounding gendered behaviour in Western contexts. This oppression becomes evident when heteronormative and hegemonic standards are imposed, enforcing binary gender identities and expressions. The existence of transgender individuals thus disrupts the presumed natural congruence between physical embodiment and lived gender experiences. Expanding on this, Browne (2004) highlights that violence and abuse often arise from the perceived incongruity between an individual's affirmed gender identity and societal interpretations of their gender presentation. This phenomenon, referred to as 'genderism', involves hostile judgements directed at gender non-conforming bodies. Butler (as cited in Tourjée, 2015) further contends that transgender women are often perceived as having rejected masculinity, thereby exposing the inherent instability of masculine constructs.

Methodology and theoretical approach

The research project outlined in this chapter adopts a distinctly queer theoretical and methodological approach. Queer perspectives are fundamentally oriented toward disrupting heteronormativity and challenging the predominance of heterosexual and cisgender frameworks within academic research and discourse (Browne and Nash, 2010). In alignment with a social constructivist perspective on gender, queer approaches critically interrogate biological essentialist conceptions of sex and gender (Perreau, 2016). Mainstream criminology, as argued by Dwyer et al. (2016), continues to exhibit heteronormative tendencies, often marginalising LGBTQ+ individuals within research agendas. At the time this data was collected (2016–2018), there was a dearth of criminological literature dedicated to exploring transphobic hate crime. By centring transgender lives, this project sought to address a significant gap in academic literature. Historically, research on anti-LGBTQ+ violence has been dominated by cisgender gay men as participants (Jones and Newburn, 2001), leading to a marked underrepresentation of transgender voices and a limited understanding of the distinct forms of victimisation they face. At its essence, queer perspectives in criminology seek to challenge normative frameworks and generate novel ways of understanding the experiences of LGBTQ+ individuals in relation to criminal justice systems

(Dwyer et al., 2016). As Browne and Nash (2010: 7) claim, queer scholarship 'in its contemporary form is anti-normative and seeks to subvert, challenge and critique a host of taken for granted "stabilities" in our social lives'. This research project extends the existing body of work on transphobic hate crime through a queer lens, critically engaging with and challenging the dominant narratives in hate crime scholarship.

Methodologically, this research project was also shaped by queer perspectives. Whilst drawing heavily from feminist methodologies, queer approaches strive to uncover '"queer" cracks in the heteronormative façade' (Green, 2002: 522). Given that queer theoretical frameworks critique the assumptions relating to the presumed stability of relationships between gender identity, gender expression, and the sexed body, qualitative research methods are often employed within queer scholarship (Plummer, 2003). The qualitative interview data discussed in this chapter was gathered as part of a doctoral research project designed to explore the experiences of transgender individuals. This qualitative component formed one aspect of a mixed-methods study, which also included 396 online surveys, 32 semi-structured interviews, and a discourse analysis of 1,756 comments extracted from YouTube videos addressing the contentious topic of gender-neutral toilets (Colliver, 2018). Data collection and analysis occurred through 2016–2018. The overarching aim of this research was to highlight the lived reality for transgender and non-binary people's experiences of transphobic victimisation. The semi-structured interviews centred on participants' encounters with discrimination and violence driven by hostility and prejudice. While initial questions focused on less severe incidents, often referred to as 'micro-crimes' (Colliver, 2021), the discussions naturally expanded to encompass more severe forms of violence, including physical and sexual victimisation.

The data obtained from the semi-structured interviews were analysed thematically, following the six-step framework outlined by Braun and Clarke (2006). The approach to analysis reflects a critically realist approach, aiming to explore and report participants' experiences, meanings, and lived realities. Unlike a constructionist approach – which, as Braun and Clarke (2006: 9) suggest 'examines the ways in which events, realities, meanings, experiences and so on are the effects of a range of discourses operating within society' – a critical realist approach acknowledges that while participants construct their own subjective realities, these constructions are interwoven with the social structures in which they operate. Importantly, this perspective does not assume a singular, objective truth but recognises the coexistence of multiple, interrelated subjective understandings, each carrying equal authenticity (Ussher, 1999). By adopting this approach, the analysis transcends micro-level interactions, enabling a broader exploration of how social structures influence individual experiences (Crinson, 2001).

The research design adhered strictly to the ethical guidelines outlined in the British Society of Criminology's *Statement of Ethics* (2015). A total of 32 interviews were conducted, and the participant sample was diverse in terms of age, gender, race, sexuality, religion, and disability status. 11 participants were transgender men, 14 participants were transgender women, and 7 participants identified outside of the gender binary. All participants identified as transgender, in alignment with the definition provided at the beginning of this chapter. The participants' ages ranged from 17 to 67 years, with a mean age of 32 years. Regarding ethnicity, the majority of participants (54.8%) identified as White British. The remainder of the sample comprised individuals from a range of ethnic backgrounds, including Black British (10%), British Asian (3.2%), Black African and White British (3.2%), Black Caribbean and White British (3.2%), White American (3.2%), South American (3.2%), Bangladeshi (3.2%), White European (3.2%), Irish Traveller (6.4%), Thai (3.2%), and Pakistani (3.2%). Additionally, participants reported a variety of religious affiliations, including Christianity, Islam, and Sikhism. While all participants were able to communicate in English, levels of fluency varied. For most participants, English was their first language; however, four participants reported speaking English as a second language.

It is important to note that the data utilised in this chapter was collected between 2016–2018 and therefore may not fully reflect the current social, legal, and political context surrounding transphobic hate crime. Over the past decade, public attitudes, policy frameworks, and legal definitions related to transgender rights and hate crime have evolved significantly, and are therefore not reflected in participants' narratives herein. The historical nature of the data raises concerns regarding changes in reporting practices and data-recording standards. Increased awareness of transphobia, shifts in police training, and the introduction of new guidelines may have influenced how transphobic incidents are perceived, reported, and categorised today compared to a decade ago.

Hierarchies of hate

Hierarchies operate on multiple levels, both consciously and unconsciously. These hierarchies contribute to varying degrees of social awareness regarding specific forms of victimisation, with some forms receiving greater attention while others remain marginalised. This differential awareness influences not only the experiences of victims but also societal perceptions at large. Such dynamics have significant implications for whether individuals recognise their victimisation as criminal, which subsequently affects the likelihood of reporting incidents to law enforcement. Furthermore, an individual's expectations, predictions, and assumptions about how authorities might respond to their victimisation play a critical role in shaping their decision on whether an incident is deemed 'worthy' of being reported. Participant data is now drawn upon to demonstrate the ways in which participants conceptualised their experiences of transphobic hate crime.

Hierarchies of perpetrators

Christie's (1986) concept of the 'ideal victim,' particularly in the context of 'stranger danger', serves as a foundational framework in understanding participants' perceptions of their victim status. For transgender individuals, experiences of victimisation perpetrated by friends or family members challenge traditional conceptualisations of victimhood, rendering the criminality of such events as ambiguous. This phenomenon has been discussed in the literature on familial and domestic violence and abuse (Corteen et al., 2016), where the existence of a visible relationship with the perpetrator obscures the classification of victimisation as criminal, thereby undermining the recognition of the victim's status. Consequently, Christie's notion of the ideal victim – characterised by the absence of a prior relationship with the perpetrator – appears to influence participants' narratives of victimisation involving known offenders. It follows that transphobic victimisation within familial or domestic contexts is likely to be significantly underreported due to the contested legitimacy of victim status in these situations.

An example of this is provided by Deena, a 34-year-old, who reflected on her experience of physical violence by her father and expresses that she 'didn't really consider it to be a hate crime, or any crime, because they were family'. Deena frames her understanding within the context of love, respect, and a desire not to disappoint her family further. Values such as love, loyalty, and respect are often central to victims' perceptions of their own victimisation. Victimisation by family members is frequently difficult to categorise as a 'hate crime', even when the criminal nature of the act is acknowledged. This difficulty arises because 'hate' directly opposes the core values most commonly associated with the concept of 'family' as understood by participants. It is important to note that while family units may not always provide a safe or 'loving' environment, they are often conceptualised this way as a result of dominant social frameworks. As Bushra, a 29-year-old woman, explains:

> No, I did not [consider it to be a hate crime]. I know that it was a crime. I know it is illegal to hurt people, but I did not think it was a hate crime. It was my family, my family I know they loved me, but I brought shame and disgrace to them.

For Bushra, the violence she experienced when she disclosed her trans identity to her family came from her father and brothers. When participants described experiences of abuse by family members and friends, notions of self-blame are commonly invoked. In this context, self-blame contributes to the understanding of abuse as not being hate-motivated. Bushra is explicitly aware that her victimisation was criminal, yet her feelings of self-blame lead her to override the identification of her family members as perpetrators of crime.

Media narratives that perpetuate the concept of 'stranger danger' are clearly reflected in participants' narratives and their perspectives on risk. 'Stranger danger' serves as an intrinsic element in the way risk is perceived and evaluated, and it has concrete implications for how individuals engage with everyday life. This framing shapes participants' understanding of safety and influences their behaviours and decisions in various contexts. Rose, a 67-year-old trans woman, explains that the fear of strangers is rooted in the mystery of how strangers 'will react' to trans people. This perspective was echoed by Sam, a 31-year-old trans man, who spoke about the 'power of the unknown' and the associated risks with unfamiliar situations. Despite recounting incidents of severe physical abuse by family members, perceptions of risk were still predominantly framed in terms of the 'unknown'. This highlights the profound influence of 'stranger danger' and its deep integration into society's understanding of criminal victimisation. Consequently, victimisation is most commonly feared from 'socially recognisable perpetrators', rather than those who may have committed violence but are less publicly acknowledged as perpetrators, such as family and friends.

For some participants who felt responsible for their own victimisation, there was also a sense of unawareness regarding what constitutes a hate crime and the perception that, as identified by Sam, it was 'just family dealing with it in the way they know how'. In this context, the identity of the perpetrator as a family member may become their master status (Hughes, 1945) making it challenging to recognise them as a perpetrator due to the pre-existing relationship. It is crucial to acknowledge the difficulties in identifying a family member as a perpetrator, as this can impact whether incidents are reported to the police. Deena, who chose not to report her experience, reflects on whether her decision would have been different if the perpetrator had been a stranger.

> If it was a stranger, or someone I didn't know, or a random person on the street, I definitely would have reported it. So my family being family, that is a definite reasons why I didn't do anything about it.

The role of 'family' plays a central part in how victims interpret their experiences and decide whether to pursue criminal justice. However, it is not solely a desire to avoid bringing additional 'trouble' to the family that shapes reporting decisions. For some participants, the familial status of the perpetrator led to the perception that the police would not recognise the incident as criminal. In these cases, the involvement of family in the perpetration of hate crimes reframed the victimisation as a 'domestic situation', leading to victims perceiving their victimisation as falling outside the scope of police intervention. This reframing diminishes the perceived severity of the incident, effectively stripping it of its criminality and reducing its recognition as a hate crime.

Christie's (1986) concept of the 'ideal victim', which posits that specific conditions must be met for an individual to be recognised as a 'legitimate' victim, suggests that many instances of victimisation experienced by transgender individuals remain unacknowledged. Research indicates that trans communities face disproportionately high levels of family rejection, relationship breakdowns, and discrimination or abuse in employment compared to cisgender individuals (Durso and Gates, 2012; METRO Charity, 2014). While these events may not inherently constitute abuse, they often occur in contexts where abuse and victimisation are present. Given that family rejection, relationship breakdowns, and workplace discrimination frequently involve perpetrators with pre-existing relationships to the victim, the resulting victimisation is less likely to be perceived as legitimate. Addressing these barriers to recognising victimisation is crucial, as the failure to identify such incidents as legitimate crimes has a significant impact on reporting behaviours. This contributes to the underreporting of transphobic hate crimes, highlighting the need for practical interventions to support victims and improve their access to justice.

Hierarchy of offence type

Based on participant narratives, there also exists a hierarchy of behaviours in which the criminality of some behaviours, such as physical violence, is more socially recognisable. It is important to understand the hierarchical nature of victimisation, as it has material consequences that relate to the underreporting of hate crime. Having previously written around the concept of 'micro-crime' victimisation (Colliver, 2021), these experiences can be described as particular forms of criminal victimisation in which the criminality of such acts may be less socially recognisable, including acts such as verbal abuse and harassment. The type of victimisation experienced by transgender individuals significantly shapes their understanding and conceptualisation of their own victimhood. A distinct hierarchy of victimisation emerges, where physical and sexual violence are regarded as 'legitimate' and 'authentic' forms of harm, while micro-crime victimisation is often dismissed as 'wasting police time'. This hierarchical perception is not unique; globally, crimes are commonly ranked, with the most serious offences eliciting the most punitive responses and less severe crimes perceived as less consequential (Cogan, 2002). Forms of victimisation such as verbal abuse, harassment, and online abuse are frequently considered unworthy of police attention. Reporting these types of incidents is sometimes viewed as diminishing the legitimacy, authenticity, and validity of more 'serious' victimisations, such as physical violence.

These concerns may be compounded by more recent legislative changes to the recording of 'non-crime hate incidents' (NCHI), following the judgement made in the case of *Miller v The College of Policing* (2021). In June 2023, a revised Code of Practice, accompanied by updated guidance, was introduced to promote a more proportionate and pragmatic approach to the recording of NCHIs. The new framework is intended to ensure that the recording of NCHIs occurs only where it is necessary and justified, thereby mitigating the risk of placing excessive administrative demands on police services and protecting individuals' rights to freedom of expression. This is particularly concerning given that research demonstrates a significant proportion of victimisation targeting transgender individuals falls into what might be classified as 'low-level' offences, including verbal abuse, harassment, and online victimisation (Chakraborti et al., 2014; METRO Charity, 2014). Consequently, the ranking and prioritisation of crimes have a profound impact on the likelihood of victims reporting their experiences to the police. This underscores the need to challenge these hierarchies to ensure that all forms of victimisation are taken seriously and addressed appropriately.

When defining and discussing hate crimes, participants often referenced offences such as assault, actual bodily harm (ABH), and grievous bodily harm (GBH), frequently emphasising that the most severe manifestation of hate could result in the 'murder of a trans person'. This highlights how the hierarchy of offence types permeates both social and individual understandings of crime and victimisation, placing physical violence at the forefront of discussions about hate crime. Physical and sexual violence are thus more socially recognisable as forms of victimisation. This is not to suggest that verbal abuse, harassment, and online abuse lack social visibility; however, they are less readily identified as criminal victimisation. The disparity in recognition underscores the need to broaden societal and institutional understandings of hate crimes to encompass non-physical forms of abuse, which are often significant in the experiences of marginalised groups such as transgender individuals.

The lack of seriousness associated with micro-crime victimisation was often reinforced through interactions with the police, in which incidents of verbal abuse in public, harassment, and online abuse were regularly recorded as 'hate incidents' rather than as criminal offences. As Dilip, a 45-year-old man described:

> One time I went to the police to report that someone had been following me down the street calling a 'dirty tranny' and wouldn't leave me alone. The police said it was a hate incident not a crime, so there was nothing they could do about it. They made a note and stuff, but that was it. So, I don't think verbal abuse like that is a hate crime.

The experience described by Dilip was a recurring theme across the interviews, with police interactions playing a significant role in shaping individuals' perceptions of their own victimisation. While physical violence dominated as the most socially recognised and legitimate form of victimisation, some participants acknowledged that non-physically violent offences, such as harassment and verbal abuse, were criminal and reportable. This acknowledgment indicates a perception of criminality associated with non-violent offences, challenging the established hierarchy of victimisation. However, even when victims recognise verbal abuse, harassment, and online abuse as criminal, the response from the police can lead them to reconceptualise their victimisation as non-criminal. As a result, future incidents of a similar nature are less likely to be reported. This dynamic not only perpetuates underreporting but also impacts an individual's ability to process their experience of victimisation. Victims may endure the psychological and emotional effects of victimisation but struggle to reconcile these feelings due to an inability to recognise their experiences as 'legitimate'.

Wider societal frameworks that confer legitimacy to specific forms of victimisation significantly shape individuals' understanding of their own experiences. These perceptions are not unfounded, as policing scholarship has demonstrated that policing interests have historically focused on 'crime fighting' rather than 'helping people' (Charman, 2020). Bowling (1999) outlines the 'hierarchy of police relevance' which indicates a hypothetical set of values that police officers use, sometimes subconsciously, other times consciously, in their response to different incidents. Bowling (1999) refers to 'good crime' as unambiguous criminal offences with a 'good' victim and a 'good' perpetrator, and those that offer the prospect of a 'good' arrest being made that leads to a successful prosecution.

As Greer and Reiner (2012) argue, the media play a central role in amplifying violent crime, with news outlets frequently selecting stories that dramatise interpersonal violence because they are perceived to attract larger audiences. This emphasis marginalises forms of victimisation that are less visually sensational but equally damaging, such as psychological abuse, coercive control, and hate-motivated harassment. Walklate (2011) highlights that the 'hierarchy of victimisation' privileges victims of physical violence, often rendering the experiences of those subjected to non-violent harms invisible within both public discourse and policy agendas. Consequently, societal preoccupation with physical violence sustains a narrow understanding of victimhood, obscuring the broader realities of harm and vulnerability experienced by many victims in contemporary society. Garland (2001) has further argued that modern crime control strategies are shaped by a culture of control in which visible bodily harm becomes a political and symbolic site for reaffirming social order. By foregrounding spectacular violence, media outlets and political actors sustain a punitive populism that sidelines more complex, systemic forms of harm, particularly those affecting already marginalised groups.

The findings of this chapter underscore the complexities surrounding transphobic hate crime and the systemic barriers that hinder its recognition and reporting. By examining the intersection of societal hierarchies, familial relationships, and the enduring influence of 'stranger danger' narratives, this work highlights the pervasive impact of dominant frameworks in shaping perceptions of legitimate victimhood. These frameworks not only marginalise non-physical forms of victimisation, such as micro-crimes, but also reinforce a social and institutional devaluation of trans lives. Participants' experiences reveal that the hierarchical nature of victimisation perpetuates the underreporting of hate crimes, particularly those involving known perpetrators or subtle, yet harmful, acts of discrimination. The normalisation of micro-crimes, coupled with inadequate institutional responses, further complicates trans individuals' ability to process and validate their experiences of victimisation.

Conclusion

The hierarchical nature of hate crime victimisation has been examined, revealing that transgender individuals conceptualise the legitimacy of their experiences based on their position within various social hierarchies. Participants reported a wide range of victimisation experiences perpetrated by family members, friends, and community members. This research contributes to the literature that critiques dominant narratives of 'stranger danger' in hate crime victimisation. However, this is not to suggest that strangers are not perceived as a potential threat or responsible for some instances of victimisation. Rather, it challenges the assumption that victims are always interchangeable and lack a prior relationship with the offender. Notions of 'stranger danger' significantly influence transgender individuals' decisions about reporting hate crime incidents. Victimisation by family, friends, or colleagues is less likely to be viewed as criminal, even in cases involving physical or sexual violence, further complicating the recognition and reporting of such offences.

A key theme emerging from participants' interviews is the concept of socially conscious and recognisable victimisation, which significantly influences how transgender individuals perceive their own experiences of harm. This theme is closely tied to the hierarchical nature of hate crime victimisation. Transphobic micro-crimes are often less socially recognisable compared to dominant conceptualisations of hate crimes, making it challenging for victims to establish legitimate victim status. This may stem from the inability of less 'extreme' forms of victimisation to capture public imagination or meet societal expectations of newsworthy crime narratives. Such perceptions have profound implications for how transgender individuals view their victimisation and whether they regard it as legitimate or worthy of police attention.

To address these issues, it is imperative to deconstruct the hierarchies of victimisation that prioritise physical violence and 'ideal victim' constructs. This requires a concerted effort to broaden societal and institutional understandings of hate crime, ensuring that all forms of transphobic victimisation are acknowledged and addressed. Moreover, fostering a critical engagement with the structural conditions that produce these hierarchies can contribute to more inclusive policies and practices, ultimately enhancing the visibility and validity of trans experiences within hate crime discourse.

References

Bowling, B. (1999). *Violent Racism: Victimisation, Policing and Social Context.* Oxford: Oxford University Press.

Braun, V. and Clarke, V. (2006). Using thematic analysis in psychology. *Qualitative Research in Psychology*, *3*(2), 77–101.

British Society of Criminology. (2015). *Statement of Ethics* [Online]. Available at: http://www.britsoccrim.org/ethics/ [Accessed: 3 December 2024].

Brondolo, E., Brady, N., Thompson, S., Tobin, J.N., Cassells, A., Sweeney, M. (2008). Perceived racism and negative affect: Analyses of trait and state measures of affect in a community sample. *Journal of Social and Clinical Psychology*, *27*, 150–173.

Browne, K. (2004). Genderism and the bathroom problem: (Re)materialising sexed sites, (re)creating sexed bodies. *Gender, Place and Culture*, *11*(3), 331–346.

Browne, K. and Nash, J. (2010). Queer methods and methodologies: An introduction. In J. Nash and K. Browne (Eds.), *Queer Methods and Methodologies: Intersecting Queer Theories and Social Science Research*. Farnham, Surrey: Ashgate Publishing Limited, 1–24.

Chakraborti, N. (2015). Re-thinking hate crime: Fresh challenges for policy and practice. *Journal of Interpersonal Violence*, *30*(10), 1738–1754.

Chakraborti, N., Garland, J., and Hardy, S. (2014). *The Leicester Hate Crime Project: Findings and Conclusions*. Leicester: University of Leicester.

Charman, S. (2020). Making sense of policing identities: the 'deserving' and the 'undeserving' in policing accounts of victimisation, *Policing and Society*, *30*(1), 81–97.

Christie, N. (1986). The ideal victim. In E. Fattah (Ed.), *From Crime Policy to Victim Policy*. London: Macmillan, 17–30.

Cogan, J. (2002). Hate crime as a crime category worthy of policy attention. *American Behavioral Scientist*, *46*(1), 173–185.

Colliver, B. (2018). *The Normalcy of Hate: A Critical Exploration of Micro-Crimes Targeting Transgender People*. Unpublished doctoral thesis. London: Kingston University. Available at: https://researchinnovation.kingston.ac.uk/en/publications/the-normalcy-of-hate-a-critical-exploration-of-micro-crimes-targe-2 [Accessed: 31 October 2025].

Colliver, B. (2021). *Reimagining Hate Crime: Transphobia, Visibility and Victimisation*. London: Palgrave Macmillan.

Colliver, B., Coyle, A., and Silvestri, M. (2019). The 'online othering' of transgender people in relation to 'gender neutral toilets'. In K. Lumsden and E. Harper (Eds.), *Online Othering: Exploring Digital Violence and Discrimination on the Web*. London: Palgrave Macmillan, 215–238.

Colliver, B. and Jamel, J. (2023). Internalised homophobia or externalised transphobia: Violence against transgender women in a sexual or romantic context. In J. Mercer and M. McGlashan (Eds.), *Toxic Masculinity: Men, Meaning and Digital Media*, 110–128.

Concannon, L. (2022). Protecting difference: A discussion on transphobic and homophobic hate crime in the Irish context. *Critical Social Policy*, *42*(3), 490–509.

Corteen, K., Morley, S., Taylor, P., and Turner, J. (2016). *A Companion to Crime, Harm and Victimisation*. Bristol: Policy Press.

Crinson, I. (2001). A realist approach to the analysis of focus group data. Paper presented at the 5th Annual IACR Conference, Roskilde University, Denmark, August 17–19.

Doan, P. (2010). The tyranny of gendered spaces: Reflections from beyond the gender dichotomy. *Gender, Place and Culture*, *17*(5), 635–654.

Durso, L. and Gates, G. (2012). *Serving our Youth: Findings from a National Survey of Services Providers Working with Lesbian, Gay, Bisexual and Transgender Youth who are Homeless or at Risk of Becoming Homeless*. Los Angeles: The Williams Institute.

Dwyer, A., Ball, M., and Crofts, T. (2016). Queering Criminologies. In A. Dwyer, M. Ball, and T. Crofts (Eds.), *Queering Criminology*. London: Palgrave Macmillan, 1–14.

Galupo, M. P., Krum, T. E., Hagen, D. B., Gonzalez, K. A., and Bauerband, L. A. (2014). Disclosure of transgender identity and status in the context of friendship. *Journal of LGBT Issues in Counseling*, *8*(1), 25–42.

Garland, D. (2001). *The Culture of Control: Crime and Social Order in Contemporary Society*. Chicago: University of Chicago Press.

Ghazi-Tehrani, A. and Kearns, E. M. (2020). Biased coverage of bias crime: Examining differences in media coverage of hate crimes and terrorism. *Studies in Conflict and Terrorism*, *46*(8), 1283–1303.

Gitlin, T. (1978). Media sociology: The dominant paradigm. *Theory and Society*, *6*(2), 205–253.

Green, A.I. (2002). Gay but not queer: Toward a post-queer study of sexuality. *Theory and Society*, *31*(4), 521–545.

Greer, C. and Reiner, R. (2012). Mediated mayhem: Media, crime, criminal justice. In M. Maguire, R. Morgan, and R. Reiner (Eds.), *The Oxford Handbook of Criminology* (5th ed.). Oxford: Oxford University Press, 245–278.

Hall, S. Critcher, C., Jefferson, T., Clarke, J. and Roberts, B. (1978). *Policing the Crisis: Mugging, the State and Law and Order*. London: Macmillan.

Herek, G., Gillis, J., Cogan, J., and Glunt, E. (1999). Hate crime victimization among lesbian, gay and bisexual adults: Prevalence, psychological correlates and methodological issues. *Journal of Interpersonal Violence*, 12(2), 195–215.

Home Office (2024). *Hate Crime, England and Wales, Year Ending March 2024*. London: Home Office

Hughes, E. C. (1945). Dilemmas and contradictions of status. *The American Journal of Sociology*, *50*(5), 353–359.

Jamel, J. (2018). *Transphobic Hate Crime*. London: Palgrave Macmillan.

Jewkes, Y. (2015). *Media and Crime* (3rd ed.). London: Sage Publications

Jones, T. and Newburn, T. (2001). *Widening Access: Improving Police Relationships with 'Hard-to-Reach' Groups*. London: Home Office.

Keels, M., Durkee, M., and Hope, E. (2017). The psychological and academic costs of school-based racial and ethnic microaggressions. *American Educational Research Journal*, *54*(6), 1316–1344.

Kuehnle, K. and Sullivan, A. (2001). Patterns of anti-gay violence: An analysis of incident characteristics and victim reporting. *Journal of Interpersonal Violence*, *16*, 928–943.

Mason, G. (2005). A picture of hate crime: Racial and homophobic harassment in the United Kingdom. *Current Issues in Criminal Justice*, *17*(1), 79–95.

McDevitt, J., Balboni, J., Garcia, L., and Gu, J. (2001). Consequences for victims: A comparison of bias – and non-bias-motivated assaults. *American Behavioral Scientist*, *45*(4), 697–713.

METRO Charity. (2014). *Youth Chances: Summary of First Findings*. London: METRO Charity.

Meyer, D. (2010). Evaluating the severity of hate-motivated violence: Intersectional differences among LGBT hate crime victims. *Sociology*, *44*(5), 980–995.

Monro, S. (2003). Transgender politics in the UK. *Critical Social Policy*, *23*(4), 433–452

Morris, J. (2024). Boys arrested after woman stabbed in 'hate crime'. *BBC News*, 3 July. Available at: https://www.bbc.co.uk/news/articles/cgl7rxgg37xo [Accessed: 5 December 2024].

Nadal, K. L., Whitman, C. N., Davis, L. S., Erazo, T., and Davidoff, K. C. (2016). Microaggressions toward lesbian, gay, bisexual, transgender, queer, and genderqueer people: A review of the literature. *The Journal of Sex Research*, 53(4–5), 488–508.

Perreau, B. (2016). *Queer Theory: The French Response*. Stanford: Stanford University Press.

Perry, B. (2001). *In the Name of Hate: Understanding Hate Crimes*. London: Routledge.

Plummer, K. (2003). Queers, bodies and postmodern sexualities: A note on revisiting the 'sexual' in symbolic interactionism. *Qualitative Sociology*, *26*(4), 515–530.

Roffee, J. and Waling, A. (2016). Rethinking microaggressions and anti-social behaviour against LGBTIQ+ youth. *Safer Communities*, *15*(4), 190–201.

Rose, S. M., and Mechanic, M. B. (2002). Psychological distress, crime features, and help-seeking behaviors related to homophobic bias incidents. *American Behavioral Scientist*, *46*(1), 14–26.

Sue, D. W. (2010). Microaggressions, marginality, and oppression: An introduction. In D. W. Sue (Ed.), *Microaggressions and Marginality: Manifestation, Dynamics, and Impact*. New Jersey: John Wiley and Sons Inc, 1–13.

Sue, D. W., Capodilupo, C. M., and Holder, A. M. B. (2007). Racial microaggressions in the life experience of Black Americans. *Professional Psychology: Research and Practice*, *39*, 329–336.

Szymanski, D. M., Kashubeck-West, S., and Meyer, J. (2008). Internalized heterosexism. *Counselling Psychologist*, *36*, 510–524.

Tourjée, D. (2015). Why do men kill trans women? Gender theorist Judith Butler explains. *Vice*, 16 December. Available at: https://www.vice.com/en/article/z4jd7y/why-do-men-kill-trans-women-gender-theorist-judith-butler-explains [Accessed: 23 November 2024].

Ussher, J. M. (1999). Women's madness: A material–discursive–intra-psychic approach. In D. Fee (Ed.), *Psychology and the Postmodern: Mental Illness as Discourse and Experience*. London: Sage Publications, 207–230.

Walklate, S. (2011). *Handbook of Victims and Victimology*, London: Routledge.

Walters, M. (2011). A general theories of hate crime? Strain, doing difference and self-control. *Critical Criminology*, *19*, 313–330.

Wang, L-I (2022). Reframing hate. *The Journal of Criminal Law & Criminology*, *112*(4), 847–873.

Wright, T., Lewis, G., Greene, T., Pearce, R., and Pitman, A. (2024). The association between microaggressions and mental health among UK trans people: A cross-sectional study. *Social Psychiatry and Psychiatric Epidemiology*, *60*(5), 1211–1225.

3

ANTI-TRANS ACTIVISM: AN OVERVIEW

James Pickles

Introduction

The rise of anti-trans activism has grown significantly in recent years. What was once a set of ideological disagreements over the nature of womanhood has evolved into an expansive anti-trans movement that seeks to roll back trans rights and institutionalise exclusionary policies. This movement encompasses a range of actors – including self-identified 'gender-critical' feminists, conservative politicians, and far-right nationalists – who, despite differing ideological foundations, share a common goal: the restriction of trans inclusion in law and society (Graff and Korolczuk, 2021; Bassi and LaFleur, 2022).

Before proceeding, it is important to establish how this chapter approaches certain terminological and methodological concerns. When discussing 'gender-critical' beliefs, a term preferred by those holding these views and recognised in UK legal contexts through the Forstater case, I acknowledge both their legal status and their contested nature. Throughout this chapter, I critically examine anti-trans rhetoric, which often employs harmful and dehumanising tropes. While I necessarily reference such rhetoric to analyse it, I do so with careful framing that does not legitimise unfounded claims. Following Thurlow's (2022) taxonomy, I distinguish between various forms of trans-hostile perspectives, from the uninformed to the deliberately antagonistic, with particular attention to how claims of 'reasonableness' and 'just asking questions' often mask deeper exclusionary aims. This approach allows for a thorough examination of anti-trans activism while maintaining an ethical commitment to trans dignity and human rights principles.

Coinciding with these very public debates is a growing activism aimed to shape public opinions over trans inclusion and acceptance. The 2023 British

DOI: 10.4324/9781003564928-4

Social Attitudes Survey highlights a notable decline in public support for trans individuals since 2019 (Clery, 2023) and findings from the National Centre for Social Research (2021) indicate that while Britain has generally become more accepting of non-traditional family structures, diverse sexual relationships, and abortion over the past four decades, attitudes toward transgender people appear to diverge from this broader trend. The survey (Clery, 2023) shows a drop of 23 percentage points in the share of people who believe transgender individuals should be able to amend the sex on their birth certificate: a decrease from 53% to 30%. Further, the proportion of respondents who describe themselves as 'not at all prejudiced' against transgender individuals has also decreased from 82% to 64% since 2019. These trends mirror the increasing visibility of gender-critical discourse in political and media spaces (Mediatique, 2020), where trans people are frequently portrayed as a threat to women's rights, children's safety, and biological reality (Billard, 2023). Such narratives, often framed as 'reasonable concerns' about biology or fairness (Thurlow, 2024a), contribute to a climate where trans identities are pathologised, delegitimised, and subject to growing legal and social restrictions.

This chapter examines the historical and contemporary landscape of anti-trans activism in the UK, tracing the ideological evolution from trans-exclusionary radical feminism ('TERF') in the 1970s to its contemporary rebranding as gender-critical feminism. While gender-critical advocates present their arguments as safeguarding women's rights, their rhetoric frequently mobilises exclusionary tropes that dehumanise trans people; framing trans women as predatory men, trans men as confused lesbians, and non-binary people as a trend or ideological contagion (Thurlow, 2024a). Thurlow's (2024a) expansion on Serano's (2018) taxonomy of trans-hostile perspectives offers a useful framework for understanding this movement's internal distinctions, and is discussed further below.

The chapter begins with an overview of anti-trans activism, situating the UK gender-critical movement within the broader context of global anti-gender discourse (Bassi and LaFleur, 2022). It then traces the historical evolution of trans-exclusionary feminism, illustrating how early radical feminist critiques of gender essentialism were repurposed to justify contemporary opposition to trans rights. It examines the mainstreaming of anti-trans narratives through political institutions, media platforms, and legal frameworks, highlighting the mechanisms through which gender-critical discourse has gained legitimacy. The chapter concludes by reflecting on the implications of these ideological shifts for trans rights and inclusion, underscoring the urgent need to resist the normalisation of anti-trans rhetoric. Through this chapter, a critical analysis of the rise of gender-critical activism in the UK is presented, situating it within the broader landscape of anti-gender politics while interrogating the strategies and discourses that sustain trans exclusion in contemporary society. Finally, this chapter uses Sally Hines' working definition of transgender and uses the short-term trans throughout:

> The term 'transgender' denotes a range of gender experiences, subjectivities and presentations that fall across, between or beyond stable categories of 'man' and 'woman.' 'Transgender' includes gender identities that have, more traditionally, been described as 'transsexual,' and a diversity of genders that call into question an assumed relationship between gender identity and presentation and the 'sexed' body.
>
> *(Hines, 2010: 1)*

Histories of anti-trans activism

Since 2019, activism opposing trans rights and what is often labelled as 'gender ideology' or 'transgender ideology' has gained substantial visibility in mainstream media, surfacing frequently on major news channels and entertainment talk shows (Shaw, 2022). Demonstrations have been held across major UK cities, with speakers advocating for various anti-trans or trans-exclusionary beliefs, ideologies, and policies (Elliards, 2023). While trans-exclusionary politics itself is not new, scholars exploring its historical evolution point out that the widespread public attention given to trans issues, the frequent coverage of anti-trans views in established media, and the formation of trans-exclusionary organisations on social media platforms are relatively recent developments (Hines, 2020). These factors contribute to today's intense and often hostile discourse surrounding trans people.

Trans-exclusionary politics has origins in certain strands of radical feminist theory, rooted in a small subset of voices within feminist discourse. Janice Raymond's *The Transsexual Empire* (1979) is frequently referenced as an early foundational text, framing trans women as appropriators of female identity who, in her view, infiltrate women's spaces to perpetrate male violence. British radical feminists, such as Sheila Jeffreys, also advanced trans-exclusionary perspectives, positing that transgender activism is 'deeply problematic from a feminist perspective' and arguing that transsexuality represents a human rights violation (Jeffreys, 1997: 55). Citing Raymond's work, Jeffreys warns of the 'transsexing' (sic) of lesbians, arguing that sex reassignment surgery is a form self-harm or mutilation, and believes that transsexuality endangers the feminist pursuit of women's liberation by reinforcing gender dichotomies; the cornerstone of male dominance (Jeffreys, 1997: 71). Although cisgender lesbians are sometimes assumed to lead trans-exclusionary activism, studies show that the majority of cisgender lesbians support trans-inclusive frameworks (e.g., Lamble, 2024; Rogers, 2024; Tate and Pearson, 2016; Worthen, 2022). Nevertheless, tensions exist between certain feminist and lesbian activist circles and trans-inclusive politics.

Reflecting on early feminist anti-trans positions, MacDonald (1998) suggests that trans perspectives could contribute valuable insights into understanding gender-based oppression. Similarly, other prominent scholars at the time, like Kessler and McKenna (1978), analysed 'transsexualism' without engaging in trans-exclusionary politics. Rather, they aimed to explore how trans experiences could deepen understandings of gender as a performance and of the power dynamics inherent within gender constructs, specifically regarding women's liberation. Scholars documenting this history note how 'mainstream feminist thought has generally seen the relationship between feminism and trans phenomena as a locus for enquiry into the construction and manifestation of gender relations and systems' (Pearce et al., 2020: 683) rather than an inherent conflict.

The emergence of a prominent UK gender-critical movement, hostile toward trans inclusivity, can be traced back to a 2018 public consultation on potential revisions to the Gender Recognition Act (GRA), initiated by then-Prime Minister Theresa May (see Bassi and LaFleur, 2022; Billard, 2023; Hines, 2020; Pearce et al., 2020). The GRA currently allows trans individuals to amend the sex marker on their birth certificate, though the process has been criticised as invasive, costly, and bureaucratic, in that it requires trans individuals to live in their gender for two years and obtain a medical diagnosis of gender dysphoria (Hines, 2013). The consultation proposed simplifying this process by allowing self-identification via legal witness, rather than requiring medical diagnosis, a proposal which was met with support from LGBTA+ groups but also raised opposition and galvanised a new opposing political agenda. Groups such as Woman's Place UK, Fair Play for Women, and, later, the LGB Alliance emerged in the UK, forming a vocal trans-exclusionary activist network with a substantial online presence as well as involvement in political lobbying on trans rights. Critics often refer to these groups as 'TERF' (trans-exclusionary radical feminist) organisations (Hines, 2020; Pearce et al., 2020), a term that circulated widely online (Billard, 2023). These groups are also frequently referred to as 'gender critical' in mainstream press coverage (Shaw, 2022). Prominent figures began to openly support these groups and were in turn labelled as leading TERF figures, including Jeffreys, journalists Julie Bindel, Sonia Sodha, Suzanne Moore, and Sarah Ditum, athlete Sharon Davies, activist Kellie-Jay Keen, lawyer Allison Bailey, and author J. K. Rowling, among many others, who broadly argue that trans womanhood is illegitimate and a fiction aimed at undermining women's spaces (Bassi and Lafleur, 2022: 314). Many of these figures often reject or ridicule the label TERF as a derogatory moniker, preferring to identify (although not all these figures do) as gender-critical activists. The term has also been criticised as overly broad, as many trans-exclusionary advocates, such as Kellie-Jay Keen, do not identify as radical feminists or gender-critical feminists. In fact, Keen has explicitly rejected the label of 'feminist' entirely

(Keen, @ThePosieParker, Twitter/X, 8 July 2023) and often disengages from feminist scholarship entirely (Fahs, 2024).

From TERF to gender critical

Leading figures who provide commentaries critical of trans women and of trans politics, such as journalist Suzanne Moore, argue that '"Terf" is the ultimate slur against women. It's woman-hating, ageist and designed to silence those who wants to speak out. People who use it show an inability to think – and listen' (Moore, 2023). Rejecting the 'TERF' acronym and distancing themselves from traditional radical feminist frameworks, proponents of anti-trans or exclusionary perspectives generally identify as supporting 'gender-critical' beliefs. Gender-critical beliefs have legal protections following a successful tribunal case brought by activist Maya Forstater. Although initially unsuccessful, Forstater brought claims of discrimination and victimisation against her employer after her contract was not renewed due to her public critiques towards proposed changes to the GRA (2004) and her stated intentions to misgender trans people. The judge initially ruled that her gender-critical beliefs were not protected in law as they failed the fifth component of the 'Grainger criteria', which states a belief must be 'worthy of respect in a democratic society, be not incompatible with human dignity and not conflict with the fundamental rights of others'. Her appeal against the initial ruling was, however, successful, setting a precedent that

> gender-critical beliefs can be protected from discrimination under the Equality Act 2010 ... The EAT said this 'does not mean that those with gender-critical beliefs can 'misgender' trans persons with impunity' and noted that acts of harassment and discrimination against trans people in the workplace are also prohibited by the Equality Act.
>
> *(Brione, 2022: n.p.)*

Whilst these beliefs do have protections, gender-critical and trans-exclusionary activists propagate a range of assertions that often go beyond seeing biological sex as immutable. For instance, Phipps posits that cis women's safety is constructed as under threat by trans women: experiences of sexual violence are 'mobilised by trans-exclusionary feminists alongside a construction of trans women as predatory, dangerous and essentially male' (Phipps, 2017: 310). Billard (2023: 238) agrees that gender-critical rhetoric frequently frames trans women as 'predators invading women's spaces', positioning them as 'biologically male'.

Common unsubstantiated arguments made by gender-critical and trans-exclusionary activists also include the notion that trans advocacy 'grooms' young people (a claim critiqued by Serano, 2022), and that it promotes a 'social contagion' (Keen, 2023) that supposedly sways vulnerable children into embracing what they call 'gender ideology'. They frame transgender healthcare for youth as inherently harmful, equating it with 'medical mutilation', and argue that trans identities fundamentally threaten and potentially erase the recognition of cis women's experiences and identities (Ashley, 2020; Billard, 2023; Jones and Slater, 2020; Hines, 2020; Serano, 2020). Notably, such arguments are represented via alternative media, such as blog posts, op-eds, and online essays, rather than through traditional academic venues, as scrutinised by Zanghellini (2020).

Serano (2022: n.p., original emphasis) critiques these harmful claims, arguing that

> ... those who hurl the word 'groomer' at LGBTQ+ people in this manner typically do so without a shred of evidence that the targeted person has engaged in such activities. While anti-trans/LGBTQ+ campaigners may frame their interventions in terms of 'safeguarding children', they rarely if ever express similar concern over *actual cases* of grooming and CSA (child sexual abuse), the overwhelming majority of which are perpetrated by cis-hetero men who are family members or close acquaintances of the child.

For those seeking further exploration of legally recognised gender-critical beliefs, references to foundational analyses can be found in works by Hotine (2021), Williams (2020), and Zanghellini (2020), all of which critique the medical, philosophical, and sociological implications of this discourse. While these beliefs have legal protections, it is crucial to acknowledge the documented harms to trans people resulting from gender-critical activism, including increased social stigma, barriers to healthcare access, and deteriorating mental health outcomes (Hughto et al., 2021; Ashley, 2020; Jones and Slater, 2020). Importantly, gender-critical discourse has found common ground with conservative anti-gender movements, particularly those driven by neo-conservative and religious agendas (Gusmeroli, 2024). An examination by Libby (2022) of materials from conservative evangelical groups, such as Focus on the Family and Family Policy Alliance, reveals a near-identical rhetoric to that of gender-critical or anti-gender advocates, with both groups labelling trans identities as dangerous, predatory, or unnatural. Libby finds that 'because evangelicals draw so heavily on trans-exclusionary radical feminist and gender-critical writing about sex and gender, their conception of sex dimorphism is almost identical.' She goes on to argue:

> that the rhetorical and citational scaffolding of these documents mirrors earlier evangelical responses to gay rights activism and the broader LGBTQIA movement ... The sources quoted are typically alarmist, outdated, one-sided, and at odds with broader scientific and medical communities.

> However, what is unique in these specifically anti-transgender statements is the inclusion of trans-exclusionary radical feminist and 'gender-critical' writing as representative of the 'feminist' perspective on transgender issues.
> *(Libby, 2022: 426)*

As part of a broader political campaign, the framing of trans identities as a threat is therefore deployed to intensify a perceived battle of ideas over gender constructionism and biological essentialism. While gender-critical activists often present their concerns in terms of 'just asking questions' or raising 'reasonable concerns,' their rhetoric frequently goes beyond this public framing. For example, prominent gender-critical author Kathleen Stock has claimed that trans-inclusive policies represent 'a belief system that's implicated in the erasure of women as a type of person conceptually, which has knock-on effects for women in relation to single-sex spaces' (quoted in Shaw, 2022: 773). Gender-critical activists argue that left unchecked, this so-called 'trans ideology' could undermine the biological distinctions that they believe are central to women's identities and rights. For example, the organisation Sex Matters (2025: n.p.) argues:

> In recent years people have been called 'hateful' simply for making ordinary, everyday statements about what it means to be male or female. Public bodies and private entities are silencing and punishing lawful speech about sex and gender as 'transphobic': people have been removed from social media platforms, had websites and social media forums shut down, been bullied and harassed at work, lost jobs, and been arrested, questioned and prosecuted for communications offences.

This characterisation, however, contrasts sharply with academic analyses documenting what Kennedy (2022) terms the 'mirroring dynamic' of anti-trans activism, wherein accusations often reflect the behaviour of those making them. Recent trends show major social media platforms like Twitter/X removing trans-inclusive policies while permitting discourse that delegitimises trans identities (Akrivos, 2024). Similarly, the Office for Students, in the UK, imposed a £500,000 penalty on Sussex University for attempting to create a trans-inclusive campus climate (Bettergarcia et al., 2024), suggesting that institutional power has frequently been leveraged against trans inclusion rather than in support of it.

The rise of anti-trans activism and its entry into mainstream discourse in the UK and the US are part of a larger cultural and political conflict. Tudor (2023: 290) argues 'these attacks come from a variety of actors, ranging from the far right including both the conservative mainstream and Christian fanatics to liberals or traditionally left-wing institutions like strands within socialist parties, trade unions and certain strands of feminism.' Indeed, many leading figures of anti-trans activism comes from traditional left thinkers, e.g., Julie Bindel, Selina Todd, Suzanne Moore, etc.

This coalition of anti-trans, gender-critical, and religious-right perspectives constitutes what Bassi and LaFleur (2022) describe as post-fascist feminism, a movement that is grounded – in contrast with diverse strands of radical feminist thought from the 1970s onwards (Pearce et al., 2020) – in essentialist ideas of womanhood (Williams, 2020) and finds alignment with conservative politics. Extensive media coverage has further amplified this perspective, with both print and broadcast outlets often adopting a hostile stance toward trans issues. The resulting moral panic about trans people is inflamed by constant media exposure from high-profile gender-critical commentators, who have considerable reach on public social media platforms and arguably have sway in both media and policy circles. Shaw (2022: 772) notes that

> academics rarely feature in the media unless a breakthrough discovery is achieved, usually in the realms of science, the environment or health. One academic, Kathleen Stock, is an exception … Prof Stock has featured in multiple stories in the right-wing British press including The Times, The Daily Telegraph, The Daily Mail, and The Express, all of whom are uncritically sympathetic of her.

Combining media, politics and rhetoric

Bassi and Lafleur (2022) trace this coalition of discourses to campaigns led by right-wing organisations that have increasingly relied on issues of gender and sexuality to energise their constituencies. Lee Anderson, former Deputy Chairman of the UK Conservative Party, infamously remarked in early 2023 that the next general election should be fought on a platform of 'culture wars and trans debate' (Colbert, 2023: n.p.). Such rhetoric has gained traction at the highest levels of government, with then-Prime Minister Rishi Sunak openly deriding opposition leaders for an inability to 'define a woman' while ignoring the presence of Brianna Ghey's mother on the parliamentary estate – a mother mourning her trans daughter murdered earlier that year (Courea, 2024). Statements like these show how anti-trans sentiments have permeated mainstream politics, directly impacting legislative moves to alter the Equality Act (2010) in order to limit trans access to single-sex spaces (Schofield, 2024).

The mainstreaming of anti-trans viewpoints by influential figures, legacy media, and populist politicians has led to a climate in which hostility toward trans individuals is increasingly normalised. Much of this is reflective of Hall et al.'s (1978) conceptualisation of a moral panic, understood as 'a spiralling process of media exaggeration, public outcry, and state response that amplifies social anxieties, leading to increased policing and repressive laws' (Hall et al., 1978: 223). This climate of fear and suspicion has influenced public sentiment, leading to decreased support for trans rights and rising rates of transphobic violence (Clery, 2023). Indeed, the UK government's own hate crime report from 2022–2023 made clear that 'transgender issues have been heavily discussed by politicians, the media and on social media over the last year, which may have led to an increase in these offences, or more awareness in the police in the identification and recording of these crimes' (Home Office, 2023: n.p.).

Arguably, the heightened rhetoric can create a social environment in which anti-trans hostility can flourish unchecked. Thurlow (2024a) provides a taxonomy for understanding varying degrees of trans-hostile perspectives, distinguishing between the uninformed, the antagonistic, and the 'trans suspicious' – those who claim to support certain trans protections but seek to differentiate 'legitimate' trans identities from perceived activist agendas. Thurlow observes that many gender-critical advocates position themselves as merely concerned about issues of biology and common sense, creating a rhetoric of 'reasonableness' that often masks deeper exclusions, where anti-trans advocacy is reframed as 'pro-woman' and trans erasure as 'realism about biology'.

In the absence of comprehensive criminological studies examining the profiles of anti-trans hate crime perpetrators, Thurlow's categories provide a useful lens for conceptualising the kinds of sociocultural forces driving increased anti-trans hostility. The alignment between religious and gender-critical positions, the media's role in shaping moral panics (Hall et al., 1978), and the legitimisation of gender-critical views in government discourse across both Conservative and Labour administrations all contribute to the hostile social backdrop against which these prejudices are allowed to grow. The Labour government, after taking office in 2024, also engaged with gender-critical advocates like J. K. Rowling to discuss potential revisions to gender recognition processes (Walker et al., 2024) demonstrating that leading gender-critical figures can gain direct access to policymakers. The current climate, thus, requires urgent scholarly and social attention to mitigate these impacts and to counter the exclusionary narratives that have gained a foothold in both policy and public opinion.

International concern for anti-trans activism in the UK

The rise of gender-critical activism in the UK has been noted as contributing to the decline in rights for trans people by several international bodies, such as the United Nations and the European Council, based on assessments made by independent experts representing these bodies. Indeed, rising anti-trans activism has been a feature of their reports into general human rights and LGBTA+ rights more broadly. These are significant developments in which the UK's position is addressed within the international community on human rights generally and trans rights specifically, as presented below.

In 2021, the General Rapporteur to the Parliamentary Assembly of the Council of Europe, Fourat Ben Chikha, published a comprehensive report on combating rising hate against LGBTA+ people in Europe. He noted that anti-LGBTA+ hate speech was entwined, more generally, with anti-gender discourse, and that this was often at the heart of dismantling and attacking trans rights, notably within the United Kingdom. The report stated 'there is a direct link between heteronormativity and heterosexism, on the one hand, and the growing anti-gender and gender-critical movements' (Parliamentary Assembly, 2022: 7), and Point 52 of his report specifically discussed the United Kingdom as a nation where anti-trans rhetoric, has gained 'baseless and concerning credibility, at the expense of both trans people's civil liberties, and women's (sic), and children's rights' (Parliamentary Assembly, 2022: 14).

> It is also becoming increasingly difficult for individuals and organisations to publicly affirm young trans people without being subject to hostility and disproportionate questioning from wider society. The 'gender-critical' movement, which wrongly portrays trans rights as posing a particular threat to cisgender women and girls, has played a significant role in this process.
>
> *(Parliamentary Assembly, 2022: 1)*

Chikha's report details several challenges facing trans and non-binary people in the UK. Notably, it references the 2021 IDAHOT Forum, where the then-UK Minister for Equalities, Kemi Badenoch – who, at the time of writing, is the current leader of the UK Conversative Party – stated, in contradiction with international human rights standards with respect to the rights of trans people, 'We do not believe in self-identification'. Such rhetoric is being used to roll back the rights of trans and non-binary people and is contributing to growing human rights problems (Parliamentary Assembly, 2022: 1). According to Chikha, the gender-critical movement has played a central role in misrepresenting trans rights as a threat to cisgender women and obstructing reforms to the Gender Recognition Act (e.g., Bindel, 2023). This concurs with observations made by other writers (see Hines, 2019, 2020; Thurlow, 2024a, 2024b). The calls to roll back trans rights, arguably, has deeper implications for human rights more generally.

Dunja Mijatović, the Commissioner for Human Rights from the European Council, visited the United Kingdom in 2022 to assess the overall landscape of human rights. She condemned the then Conservative government by observing that generally there is 'an increasingly antagonistic attitude by the UK government towards human rights, and verbal attacks on lawyers and organisations defending human rights' (Mijatović, 2022: 6). Senior ministers in the Conversative government at the time had made several calls to withdraw from the European Human Rights Convention (Elgot, 2023) and frequently engaged in what has been described in both the UK and the US as the politics of culture wars, especially over trans issues (Castle, 2019), despite opinions showing that trans issues are relatively low down on electoral voting priorities in comparison to views on immigration and asylum seekers (Ipsos, The Policy Institute, King's College London, 2023).

International figures in the Parliamentary Assembly of the Council of Europe have further condemned the rising anti-LGBTA+, and specifically anti-trans, rhetoric in the political and media sphere in the United Kingdom (Parliamentary Assembly, 2022). The Council of Europe Commissioner for Human Rights noted that the rights of trans people are being deliberately framed as 'diametrically opposed to the rights of (cis) women and other lesbian, gay, and bisexual people through the use of stereotypes and unfounded prejudices about trans people. In particular, trans people are erroneously conflated with sexual predators, using unfounded notions of "predatory determinism"'(Parliamentary Assembly, 2022: 21); a harmful narrative that assumes trans people, especially trans women, pose an inherent threat to the safety of cisgender people, particularly women and children, by attributing malicious intent to their gender identity solely on the basis of being transgender (Parliamentary Assembly, 2022). The Commissioner specifically expressed concern that trans people were being used for electoral purposes by parliamentarians who employ deliberately inflammatory and dehumanising rhetoric as 'wedge issues' to turn the status of trans people into a 'culture war' (Parliamentary Assembly, 2022: 21; Castle, 2019). Her first recommendation on the issue was for 'government representatives and parliamentarians to refrain from stigmatising and harmful discourse against LGBTA+ people, and especially trans people, including promoting narratives that frame trans people as a threat' (Parliamentary Assembly, 2022: 24).

Similarly, Independent Expert to the United Nations, Victor Madrigal-Borloz, also produced a report (United Nations General Assembly, 2024) based on his visit to the United Kingdom in 2023. The report raised a variety of concerns on the widespread toxic political discourse relating to trans people and their rights.

> During the visit, the Independent Expert received information about thousands of articles spreading misinformation and witnessed first-hand the casual appropriation by top-level political actors of rhetoric closely associated with the questioning of legal protections based on gender reassignment. The following is a key example: 'what is a woman?', a question that, in the social and political context, is commonly asked by 'gender-critical' actors to challenge the legal recognition of trans women under the law of the United Kingdom and to mock trans women.
>
> *(United Nations General Assembly, 2024: 9)*

Similar to Commissioner Mijatović's observations, the report noted that the UK news media frequently perpetuates harmful stereotypes of trans people, drawing again on stereotypes of predatory determinism by often portraying trans people as inherently dangerous to other groups in society; and often employing homophobic and transphobic rhetoric to do so. This negative framing, compounded by abusive language from politicians, has, in the Independent Expert's view, amplified hate speech on social media, which he correlates with a surge in harassment, threats, and bias-motivated violence, including hate crimes in the UK (Home Office, 2023).

Such anti-trans narratives are increasing and legitimising the deterioration in the quality of trans lives internationally. This can most recently be seen in the cascade of executive orders issued by President Donald Trump in the USA. The 'Executive Order Defending Women from Gender Ideology Extremism and Restoring Biological Truth to the Federal Government' (The White House, 2025) uses many of the tropes about trans people already highlighted in this chapter. The order employs inflammatory language that mischaracterises trans women as 'men' who 'self-identify as women' to gain access to women's spaces; a harmful claim that has been repeatedly debunked by research showing no evidence of increased safety risks in inclusive spaces (Serano, 2020). The order falsely frames trans existence as an 'effort to eradicate the biological reality of sex' that 'fundamentally attack[s] women'; rhetoric that employs what Thurlow (2024a) identifies as a common tactic of positioning trans rights as inherently opposed to women's rights (Hines, 2020). This executive order represents a concerning codification of anti-trans rhetoric into official government policy.

Section 2 of the executive order outlines that '... It is the policy of the United States to recognize two sexes, male and female. These sexes are not changeable and are grounded in fundamental and incontrovertible reality. Under my direction, the Executive Branch will enforce all sex-protective laws to promote this reality' (The White House, 2025), before going on to provide definitions of sex as male and female. Critics and observers of the global anti-gender movements have expressed concern over this networked attempt to bring in such legislation – particularly as this specific executive order defines female and male as 'person[s] belonging, at conception', to the sex produced at cellular level, which seemingly outlines fetal personhood, thus raising concerns over the subsequent impact on abortion rights (Sherman, 2025).

The global networked funding of anti-gender activism and narratives from far-right stakeholders has also raised concern from international human rights bodies. The European Parliamentary Forum for Sexual and Reproductive Rights published a wide-reaching report in 2021 exploring the funders who are against human rights for sexual and reproductive health in Europe. The report (European Parliamentary Forum, 2021) compiled financial data from 2009–2018 from 50 anti-gender actors operating within Europe and found that anti-gender initiatives were heavily funded, organised, and unified. Following analysis of this data, it concludes that

> anti-gender funders from the US, Russia, and Europe, while primarily active in their respective geographies, interact with each other in transnational settings such as the WCF and PNfV … The picture that emerges is of a transnational community of like-minded religious extremists and related alt- and far-rights actors making strategic funding decisions across international borders.
>
> *(European Parliamentary Forum, 2021: 78)*

Importantly, the report makes clear that due to the nature of 'dark money' being hidden from declaration through a variety of means – with the intention of influencing political elections, public discourse, and public policy – the data scrutinised is only the 'tip of the iceberg'. The forum found that USD707.2 million was funnelled in to anti-gender purposes from a restricted group of 54 organisations between 2009 and 2018, across the United States, Europe and the Russian Federation. Funders comprised of NGOs, right-wing think tanks, religious organisations, and political parties, including:

> USD81.3 million originates from 10 actors in the United States, either NGOs or conservative think tanks from the US Christian Right. These 10 actors, in turn, benefit from funding from a series of conservative US foundations which are themselves the product of US conservative billionaires who have close connections with the US Republican Party and the US alt-and far-right.
>
> *(European Parliamentary Forum, 2021: 7)*

Further, the Russian Federation accounts for a further USD188.2 million, originating from two Russian oligarchs, Vladimir Yakunin and Konstantin Malofeev, with historical links to far-right political parties. Finally, the report states that 'at least four Russian government agencies operating internationally account for additional, yet unspecified, financial support to anti-gender mobilisations globally' (European Parliamentary Forum, 2021: 7).

Europe is the epicentre of anti-gender funding, making up the 'largest share of antigender funding in Europe, standing at USD437.7 million' (European Parliamentary Forum, 2021: 7). The report identifies nearly 20 private foundations engaged in specific anti-gender mobilisation in Europe, including new transnational NGO alliances, a pan-European anti-abortion federation, pan-European fascist parties; and further connections between a European-level Christian political party, an ultra-conservative social media platform, and 'a set of inter-related pseudo-Catholic, far-right actors' (European Parliamentary Forum, 2021: 7).

Public funding is increasingly co-opted by these movements. The report concludes that these movements seek to erode gender equality and human rights while advancing an illiberal agenda that undermines pluralist democracy and regulated market economies. Their activities represent both an ideological campaign fuelled by anti-gender rhetoric and a broader effort to reshape societal norms and governance towards the right of the political spectrum, a move which can be seen reflected in President Trump's aforementioned executive orders (The White House, 2025). These executive orders align closely with the Heritage Foundation's Project 2025 blueprint, a comprehensive policy agenda that specifically targets trans rights (Heritage Foundation, 2023). Thus, it is not just ideological frameworks and gender-critical publications that are utilised collaboratively across the evangelical right and anti-gender activists, as highlighted by Libby (2022), but it is also the financial investment into the movements that are networked and coordinated with the aim of shaping media and political discourse. Challenging anti-trans politics in Britain demands confronting its cross-political nature and examining the shared factors that bridge these divergent strands across the political spectrum in order to build effective movements of resistance

Conclusions

The systemic challenges faced by trans individuals are shaped by a complex network of intersecting forces, including the rise of anti-transgender movements, hostile media narratives, and an increasingly toxic sociopolitical climate. These forces are not isolated but part of a coordinated global effort to undermine the dignity, rights, and safety of trans people. Anti-gender movements, though often obscured, are well-funded and strategically organised, transcending national borders to influence public policy and sow division. By framing trans existence as a threat to societal norms, such movements exploit cultural anxieties and perpetuate deeply ingrained biases to justify their positions, fostering an environment where transphobia can flourish.

The UK serves as a stark example of this phenomenon, with the rise of anti-trans rhetoric and the disproportionate influence of the gender-critical movement drawing significant international concern. Gender-critical activists have shaped public policy debates and media coverage, creating a hostile climate that not only endangers trans individuals domestically but also emboldens similar efforts globally. The normalisation of anti-trans rhetoric in British politics and media has inspired conservative and far-right groups elsewhere, amplifying efforts to roll back trans rights. Donald Trump's 2025 executive orders reinforcing binary gender definitions reflect a broader international trend of eroding equality and inclusion mechanisms. International human rights organisations have condemned this development, highlighting its far-reaching consequences for social justice.

References

Akrivos, D. (2024). Editorial standards in transgender reporting: How do the UK press regulators navigate complaints and controversies? *Communication Law*, *29*(2), 38–58.

Ashley, F. (2020). A critical commentary on 'rapid-onset gender dysphoria'. *The Sociological Review*, *68*(4), 779–799. https://doi.org/10.1177/0038026120934693

Bassi, S., and LaFleur, G. (2022). Introduction: TERFs, gender-critical movements, and postfascist feminisms. *TSQ*, 9(3), 311–333.

Bettergarcia, J., Crone, C., Herry, E., and Ali, B. (2024). Centering the margins: Reimagining resilience and resistance for transgender and nonbinary people of color. *Journal of Social Issues*, *80*, 896–919.

Billard, T. J. (2023). 'Gender-critical' discourse as disinformation: Unpacking TERF strategies of political communication. *Women's Studies in Communication*, *46*(2), 235–243. https://www.tandfonline.com/doi/abs/10.1080/07491409.2023.2193545

Bindel, J. (2023). Scotland's gender recognition bill would have harmed women. *AlJazeera*, 3 February. Available at: https://www.aljazeera.com/opinions/2023/2/3/scotlands-gender-recognition-bill-would-have-harmed-women [Accessed: 5 May 2023].

Brione, P. (2022). Employment Tribunal rulings on gender-critical beliefs in the workplace. House of Commons Library (online). Available at: https://commonslibrary.parliament.uk/employment-tribunal-rulings-on-gender-critical-beliefs-in-the-workplace/ [Accessed: 1 April 2025].

Castle, J. (2019). New fronts in the culture wars? Religion, partisanship, and polarization on religious liberty and transgender rights in the United States. *American Politics Research*, *47*(3), 650–679.

Clery, E. (2023). British Social Attitudes 40: Public Views on Transgender Rights and Identity. London: National Centre for Social Research,

Colbert, L. (2023). Lee Anderson's culture wars: How the Conservative Party is flirting with far-right hate to appeal to its base. *Byline Times*, 15 February. Available at: https://bylinetimes.com/2023/02/15/lee-andersons-culture-wars-how-the-conservative-party-is-flirting-with-far-right-hate-to-appeal-to-its-base/ [Accessed: 30 April 2025].

Courea, E. (2024). Sunak refuses to apologise to Brianna Ghey's father over PMQs trans jibe. *The Guardian*, 8 February. Available at: https://www.theguardian.com/politics/2024/feb/08/rishi-sunak-refuses-apologise-brianna-ghey-father-pmqs-trans-jibe [Accessed: 30 April 2025]

Elgot, J. (2023). Tory MPs to push for UK exit from European Convention on Human Rights. *The Guardian*, 5 February. Available at: https://www.theguardian.com/politics/2023/feb/05/tory-mps-to-push-for-uk-exit-from-european-convention-of-human-rights [Accessed: 2 April 2025].

Elliards, X (2023). Who is Posie Parker? The anti-trans founder of Standing for Women. *The National*, 4 February. Available at: https://www.thenational.scot/news/23299549.posie-parker-anti-trans-founder-standing-women/ [Accessed: 21 January 2025].

European Parliamentary Forum. (2021). *Tip of the Iceberg: Religious Extremist Funders against Human Rights for Sexuality and Reproductive Health in Europe 2009–2018*. Brussels: EPF.

Fahs, B. (2024). The urgent need for radical feminism today. *Signs: Journal of Women in Culture and Society*, *49*(2), 479–497.

Graff, A., and Korolczuk, E. (2021). *Anti-Gender Politics in the Populist Moment*. London: Routledge.

Gusmeroli, P. (2024). Is gender-critical feminism feeding the neo-conservative anti-gender rhetoric? Snapshots from the Italian public debate. *Journal of Lesbian Studies*, *28*(3), 382–399.

Hall, S., Critcher, C., Jefferson, T., Clarke, J., and Roberts, B. (1978). *Policing the Crisis: Mugging, the State, and Law and Order*. London: Palgrave Macmillan.

Hines, S. (2010). Introduction. In S. Hines and T. Sanger (Eds.), *Transgender Identities: Towards a Social Analysis of Gender Diversity*. New York: Routledge, 1–24.

Hines, S. (2013). *Gender Diversity, Recognition and Citizenship: Towards a Politics of Difference*. London: Palgrave Macmillan.

Hines, S. (2019). The feminist frontier: On trans and feminism. *Journal of Gender Studies*, *28*(2), 145–157.

Hines, S. (2020). Sex wars and (trans) gender panics: Identity and body politics in contemporary UK feminism. *The Sociological Review*, *68*(4), 699–717.

Home Office (2023). Hate crime, England and Wales, 2022 to 2023 second edition. Available at: https://www.gov.uk/government/statistics/hate-crime-england-and-wales-2022-to-2023/hate-crime-england-and-wales-2022-to-2023 [Accessed: 6 January 2025].

Hotine, E. (2021). Biology, society and sex: Deconstructing anti-trans rhetoric and trans-exclusionary radical feminism. *JNDS*, *2*(3), 1–5.

Hughto, M. W. J., et al. (2021). Negative transgender-related media messages are associated with adverse mental health outcomes in a multistate study of transgender adults. *LGBT Health*, *8*(1), 32–41.

Human Rights Watch (2020). Joint statement on the rights of trans people in the UK. 17 May. Available at: https://www.hrw.org/news/2020/05/17/joint-statement-rights-trans-people-uk [Accessed: 1 November 2024].

Ipsos, The Policy Institute, King's College London (2023). Woke vs Anti-woke? Culture War Divisions and Politics. London: Ipsos.

Jeffreys, S. (1997). Transgender activism: A lesbian feminist perspective. *Journal of Lesbian Studies*, 1(3–4), 55–74.

Jones, C., and Slater, J. (2020). The toilet debate: Stalling trans possibilities and defending 'women's protected spaces'. *The Sociological Review*, *68*(4), 834–851. https://doi.org/10.1177/0038026120934697

Judiciary of England and Wales (2024). *Rex v Scarlett Jenkinson & Eddie Ratcliffe: Sentencing Remarks of Mrs Justice Yip DBE*. Manchester: Manchester Crown Court.

Keen, K. J. (2023). LBC - Kellie-Jay v James O'Brien. Available at: https://www.youtube.com/watch?v=W_Jiq1KPBAY&t=2s&ab_channel=Kellie-JayKeen [Accessed: 1 April 2025].

Kennedy, N. (2022). Anti-trans activists are using 'mirror propaganda'. Here's how to spot it. *OpenDemocracy*, 5 December. Available at: https://www.opendemocracy.net/en/5050/anti-trans-transphobia-gender-critical-mirror-propaganda/[Accessed: 30 April 2025].

Kessler, S. J., and McKenna, W. (1978). *Gender: An Ethnomethodological Approach*. Chicago: University of Chicago Press.

Lamble, S. (2024). Confronting complex alliances: Situating Britain's gender critical politics within the wider transnational anti-gender movement. *Journal of Lesbian Studies*, *28*(3), 504–517.

Lewis, J., and Fraser, M. R., (1996). Patches of grief and rage: Visitor responses to the NAMES project AIDS Memorial Quilt. *Qualitative Sociology*, *19*, 433–451.

Libby, C. (2022). Sympathy, fear, hate: Trans-exclusionary radical feminist and evangelical Christianity. *Transgender Studies Quarterly*, *9*(3), 425–442.

MacDonald, E. (1998). Critical identities: Rethinking feminism through transgender-politics. *Atlantis*, *23*(1), 3–11.

Mediatique (2020). *Examining Trends in Editorial Standards in Coverage of Transgender Issues*. London: Independent Press Standards Organisation.

Mijatović, D. (2022). *Commissioner for Human Rights of the Council of Europe: Report Following Her Visit To the United Kingdom From 27 June to 1 June 2022*. Strasbourg: Council of Europe.

Moore, S. (2020). Women must have the right to organise. We will not be silenced. *The Guardian*, 2 March. Available at: https://www.theguardian.com/society/commentisfree/2020/mar/02/women-must-have-the-right-to-organise-we-will-not-be-silenced [Accessed: 25 September 2025].
Moore, S. (2023). 'Terf' is the ultimate slur against women. *The Telegraph*, 8 June. Available at: https://www.telegraph.co.uk/women/life/terf-ultimate-slur-against-women-transphobia-feminism/ [Accessed: 25 September 2025].
Paceley, M. S., et al. (2021). 'I didn't come here to make trouble': Resistance strategies utilized by transgender and gender diverse youth in the Midwestern US. *Youth*, *1*, 29–46.
Parliamentary Assembly (2021). Combating rising hate against LGBTI people in Europe. Available at: https://assembly.coe.int/LifeRay/EGA/Pdf/TextesProvisoires/2021/20210921-RisingHateLGBTI-EN.pdf [Accessed: 14 November 2024].
Pearce, R., Erikainen, S., and Vincent, B. (2020). TERF wars: An introduction. *The Sociological Review*, *68*(4), 677–698. https://doi.org/10.1177/0038026120934713
Perry, B., and Alvi, S. (2012). 'We are all vulnerable': The in terrorem effects of hate crimes. *International Review of Victimology*, *18*(1), 57–71.
Phipps, A. (2017). Sex wars revisited: A rhetorical economy of sex industry opposition. *Journal of International Women's Studies*, *18*(4), 306–320.
Pickles, J. (2021). Sociality of hate: The transmission of victimization of LGBT+ people through social media. *International Review of Victimology*, *27*(3), 311–327.
Raymond, J. G. (1979). *The Transsexual Empire: The Making of the She-Male*. Boston: Beacon Press.
Rogers, B. A. (2024). TERFs aren't feminists: Lesbians stand against trans exclusion. *Journal of Lesbian Studies*, *28*(1), 24–43. https://doi.org/10.1080/10894160.2023.2252286
Schofield, K. (2024). 'Don't call it culture wars': Kemi Badenoch clashes with journalist over single-sex spaces. *Huffington Post*, 1 May. Available at: https://www.huffingtonpost.co.uk/entry/dont-call-it-culture-wars-kemi-badenoch-clashes-with-journalist-over-single-sex-spaces_uk_6631ef97e4b0849b2edd86fb [Accessed: 20 January 2025].
Serano, J. (2018). Thoughts about transphobia, TERFs, and TUMFs. Available at: https://juliaserano.medium.com/thoughts-about-transphobia-terfs-and-tumfs-b77a18c1a225 [Accessed: 1 April 2025].
Serano, J. (2020). Autogynephilia: A scientific review, feminist analysis, and alternative 'embodiment fantasies' model. *The Sociological Review*, *68*(4), 763–778.
Serano, J. (2022). Anti-trans 'grooming' and 'social contagion' claims explained. Available at: https://juliaserano.medium.com/anti-trans-grooming-and-social-contagion-claims-explained-a511a93b042f [Accessed: 1 April 2025].
Sex Matters (2025) Freedom of speech. Available at: https://sex-matters.org/where-sex-matters/freedom-of-speech/ [Accessed: 25 November 2025].
Shaw, D. (2022). A tale of two feminisms: Gender critical feminism, trans inclusive feminism and the case of Kathleen Stock. *Women's History Review*, *32*(5), 768–780.
Sherman, C. (2025). Trump's executive order on gender uses language pointing to 'fetal personhood'. *The Guardian*, 23 January. Available at: https://www.theguardian.com/us-news/2025/jan/23/trump-executive-order-fetal-personhood [Accessed: 23 January 2025].
Tate, C. C., and Pearson, M. D. (2016). Toward an inclusive model of lesbian identity development: Outlining a common and nuanced model for cis and trans women. *Journal of Lesbian Studies*, *20*(1), 97–115. https://doi.org/10.1080/10894160.2015.1076237
The Guardian (2020). Differing perspectives on transgender rights [Letter]. 4 March. Available at: https://www.theguardian.com/society/2020/mar/04/differing-perspectives-on-transgender-rights [Accessed: 25 September 2025].

The Heritage Foundation (2023). *Mandate for Leadership: The Conservative Promise, Project 2025*. P. Dans and S. Groves (Eds.). Washington, DC: The Heritage Foundation.

The White House (2025). Defending women from gender ideology extremism and restoring biological truth to the federal government. Available at: https://www.whitehouse.gov/presidential-actions/2025/01/defending-women-from-gender-ideology-extremism-and-restoring-biological-truth-to-the-federal-government/ [Accessed: 27 January 2025].

Thurlow, C. (2024a). From TERF to gender critical: A telling genealogy? *Sexualities*, *27*(4), 962–978.

Thurlow, C. (2024b). Sisters, it's been a while! The emotional pull of the lesbian 'gender critical' movement and a failure of solidarity. *Journal of Lesbian Studies*, *28*(1), 161–174.

Tudor, A. (2023). The anti-feminism of anti-trans feminism. *European Journal of Women's Studies*, *30*(2), 290–302.

United Nations General Assembly (2024). *Visit to the United Kingdom of Great Britain and Northern Report of the Independent Expert on Protection against Violence and Discrimination Based on Sexual Orientation and Gender Identity*. V. Madrigal-Borloz and Human Rights Council (Eds.). New York: United Nations General Assembly.

Walker, P., Adu, A., and Brooks, L. (2024). JK Rowling agrees to meeting with Labour about gender transition policy. *The Guardian*, 24 June. Available at: https://www.theguardian.com/politics/article/2024/jun/24/labour-gender-transition-recognition-process-trans [Accessed: 25 September 2025].

Williams, C. (2020). The ontological woman: A history of deauthentication, dehumanization, and violence. *The Sociological Review*, *68*(4), 718–734.

Worthen, M. G. F. (2022). This is my TERF! Lesbian feminists and the stigmatization of trans women. *Sexuality & Culture*, *26*, 1782–1803. https://doi.org/10.1177/2158244020927029

Zanghellini, A. (2020). Philosophical problems with the gender-critical feminist argument against trans inclusion. *Sage Open*, *10*(2). https://doi.org/10.1177/2158244020927029

4

AN INTERSECTIONAL LENS ON THE EXPERIENCES OF YOUNG TRANSGENDER AND NON-BINARY PEOPLE IN THE UK

Sarah Connelly

Introduction

Entrenched in discourse that covers the definition of identities, access to certain spaces, safeguarding, and overarching narratives of risk, gendered identities continue to sit at the forefront of public debate (Colliver et al., 2019; Human Dignity Trust, 2019). From public appeals around terminology within the Equality Act 2010 to the most recent rulings within the Supreme Court, re-emerging discussions on conversion therapy, and claims around 'harmful' support for young people, the existence of transgender and non-binary support has once again risen in public interest (Mermaids, n.d.). Current narratives around trans and non-binary bodies evidence that gendered bodies continue to be a contested aspect of the social world (Stonewall, 2018; The Trevor Report, 2022). When focusing on the relationship of gender and age, further inequalities are visible for young trans and non-binary populations. At the centre of this debate sits the experiences of young trans and non-binary populations whose choices and visibility vary depending on how gender and age are understood as both silos and as intersecting facets of a person's identity.

Intersectionality, a term coined by Crenshaw (1989), calls for analyses of identity to engage with the fact that identities are multifaceted, rather than singular dimensions of self. Through this movement, away from a singular axis understanding to a recognition of intersecting identities, a more in-depth understanding of how the compounding of identities can further impact experiences can be created, in this case in relation to gender and age. This chapter aims to re-introduce the relationship between gender and age through an intersectional lens to promote the further understanding of the current human rights situation across the United Kingdom and provide considerations

DOI: 10.4324/9781003564928-5

around the barriers faced when both gender and age intersect within a British context. It will examine how social bodies are constructed and represented, and what this can mean for the group of people affected. This chapter does not seek to challenge age restrictions but instead highlights the need to recognise politicised identities.

The chapter begins with an introduction to the visibility of trans and non-binary people within the UK. It then frames the body, mapping gender and age onto it as social categories, as well as introducing the theoretical lens of intersectionality (Crenshaw, 1989). Intersectionality is then applied to cultural and public discourse, healthcare, citizenship, political debates, and tabloid coverage across the time span of 2020–2025 to illustrate how young gender-fluid minorities sit at an intersection that is often overlooked.

Visibility and existence of trans and non-binary people in the UK

Before delving into the human's rights situation of the UK and the intersections that are actively compounded, it is important to first introduce and contextualise the visibility of trans and non-binary people. The terms 'transgender' and 'non-binary' are used to identify and understand gender identities. In the UK, the two identities can be seen as umbrella terms to encompass a range of gender identities.

Gender identity and visibility

The term 'transgender' itself can offer varying levels of inclusivity and expression of identity, and varies from being used in relation to a person wishing to transition to another gender identity, or to more broadly referring to the rejection of the gender identity assumed at birth (Rainbow Project, n.d.). Non-binary, however, describes sitting outside of traditional descriptions of masculinity and femininity (Stonewall, n.d.). Each offers a fluid understanding to gender identity as opposed to traditional ideologies of gender performativity and identification. Whilst cisgendered bodies are typically established as the norm across societal structures and values, a signifier of difference is assigned to those who do not fit this mould. This construction of difference can lead to significant implications in relation to (in)visibility within society, misrepresentation, or further marginalisation (Colliver and Silvestri, 2022). Visibility of gender-fluid populations also leads to its own set of obstacles. As trans and non-binary identities gain further visibility, discourse leads to contentious debates for identities that do not fit the heteronormative framework that is ingrained in Western cultures.

The uncertainties around gender diverse bodies have been documented over time. From questions around meaning, changes to public and private spaces, sport, to more overarching and sometimes oversimplified question of

'Who is trans and what do we mean by this?', uncertainty and scrutiny exists towards gender-fluid populations, and what their existence may mean to cisgender populations (Stonewall, 2024). Although the UK has experienced increases in trans visibility and cohesion, this has also led to increases in hostility, as celebrating agency has led to tensions around gendered expectations (Berlin and Brice, 2022). In 2021 for instance, Home Office statistics indicate that 2,630 people had reported being a victim of a hate crime due to being transgender. The Government Equalities Office followed this up to show that 88% of people do not report such hate crimes, and another 48% were dissatisfied with the police response when reporting (Stop Hate UK, n.d.), leading to further ambiguity in regards to the impacts of such visibility.

Gender identity and the Census 2021

In 2021, the Office for National Statistics gathered and reported trans populations in its first rendition of the Census that included two voluntary questions on gender identity. This was a historic development and movement in the UK since previous iterations resulted in gaps in representative data on such populations. The Census obtained 45.7 million responses, and of those 262,000 participants answered 'No' when asked 'Is the gender you identify with the same as your sex registered at birth?' (Office for National Statistics, 2021). In this recent performance of national reporting, 48,000 (0.10%) of the population identified as trans men, another 48,000 (0.10%) identified as trans women, 30,000 (0.06%) identified as non-binary, and a further 18,000 (0.4%) selected a gender identity not disclosed (Office for National Statistics, 2021). In addition, it was found that 118,000 people (0.24%) reported to not identifying with their birth sex but did not complete the additional section to identify their gender identity. The report noted these estimates came with ambiguity due to reliance on self-reporting, yet still demonstrated development in the collection of national statistics.

Challenges in representation

To contextualise this in terms of the intersection between gender and age, however, the Census 2021 only documents and reports participants who are 16 years of age and older, meaning any person under 16 years and identifying as transgender or non-binary would not be documented. Whilst every household is obligated to take part, the report cannot determine that every person documented has been documented correctly. This may come down to a multitude of reasons including a young person being at the early stages of recognition, narratives of 'kids being kids', but also the potential of non-gender-affirming spaces where a young person may not feel comfortable or able to identify how they feel with a caregiver (The Human Rights Campaign Foundation, n.d.; The

Trevor Report, 2021). Once we apply and consider age around young people and identity, statistics can somewhat shift in representation.

Data outside of national datasets further document levels of discrimination and uncertainty faced by young trans and non-binary populations, and when focusing solely on trans and non-binary young people, visibility is matched with narratives of discrimination and harm. The World Health Organization for example identified suicide as a critical health problem in 2021, with a rise in younger populations in the UK. Outside of this, young trans and non-binary young people have also been identified to be at a greater risk of suicide compared to cisgender populations (The Trevor Report, 2021, 2024), yet this issue is not addressed as a priority in relation to governmental initiatives to safeguard young populations. Additional reports further support this narrative, highlighting lasting impacts of discrimination faced by younger populations and impacts on feelings of belonging and overall wellbeing (YouGov, 2021; The Trevor Report, 2021, 2024). Whilst charity responses have grown to protect and advocate, public and political agendas have taken an alternative route, leading to a further polarisation of the topic and leaving an ongoing challenge in regards to understanding the underrepresentation of this population in relation to their visibility, experiences, and needs.

Framing bodies, identities, and the intersection

The human body was once understood as corporeal, a physical entity where value was ascribed from medical disciplines and arguably medicalised from birth (Shilling, 2003; Nettleton, 2020). Entwined in health narratives and changes to medical advancements, the body was understood as something to treat, to fix, or to essentially manage. Harm to a body within this context would be understood as a physical injury or illness that impacted the body's health (Conrad, 1985; Nettleton, 2020). Whilst the body was a missing element of earlier grand theories, this has not impacted the historical relationships between problematised bodies and societal values.

Gendered bodies

Gendered bodies were once understood as a natural given and were entangled in ideologies that saw gender identity to be an outcome of a person's biological sex rather than something that is constructed through autonomy. This naturalisation of gender created an essentialist connotation around the existence and construction of gendered identities (Butler, 2004), leading to a binary framework for how people should act with their bodies. Biomedical discourses have long dominated the understanding of gendered bodies (Bordo, 1995), shaping how women's bodies have been medicalised and regulated in relation to behaviours. Additionally, studies into how heteronormativity influences the way bodies are understood, particularly in relation to gendered performativity and sexuality, evidence how entrenched social and physical bodies are within gendered assumptions (Foucault, 1976, 2020). Experiences of health and the body can also be seen as hierarchical, socially constructed, and a stratified aspect of human existence, shaped within society and fashioned by powerful institutions and cultural normalities (Klawiter, 2004).

The move to the 'social body', however, documents how understandings of the body began to change in relation to social dimensions and factors. Shilling's (2003) work analysed the shift to the 'social body' and how through a sociological exploration, the body can be understood as something that is influenced and shaped by society and its expectations, as well as physical and health factors. In this way, agency of the body was emphasised in relation to how people navigate societal expectations and structures, whether this be through embodying social norms and values, or resisting such social structures. The relationship between 'harm' and 'bodies' changes in this context, as behaviours and rejections of socialised norms attached to the body are understood as injurious to society rather than an act of agency. Research into rejections to social order, norms, and socialisation have evidenced how bodies can also be used as signifiers of social ostracism. Butler (1990) reiterated the meaning that gender performativity held within Western cultures in relation to how seriously the rejection of heteronormativity could be. She highlighted how harm has changed in meaning, referring to the person being harmful for not following social cues. This also furthered the questioning of ongoing essentialist connotations of the 'right' body and the 'Othered' body, leading the social body to be a contested and highly politicised site within day-to-day society (Lawler, 2008). In relation to the social body, this evidences how meaning attached to the body is powerful. Internally guised, identity formulates commodities, which alienate the 'Other', and in turn is related and associated with discourse around harm and risk. Gender, as a concept, can be perceived as a social structure (Connell, 1987). This is echoed across a range of work by gender theorists, including De Beauvoir's (1949) work on gender being socially constructed, Goffman's (1963) emphasis on construction through interactions and performances, and Butler's (1990) work on *doing* gender.

Gendered bodies can now be understood as socially constructed aspects of society, as well as active agents in the inequalities faced in everyday life. Societal understandings have moved on from seeing the body as only a physical attribute, yet regulatory practices and negotiations of the 'right' body continue to manifest. In recent years, sociological contributions have focused upon the meaning of gender in relation to achieving political recognition and medical intervention (Hines, 2007) – for example, works exploring the political and medical ideologies that are mapped upon trans bodies, creating a singular hierarchy of needs, and thus challenging the fluidity of non-binary gendered practices (Butler, 2004).

Constructions of age and the body

The framing of the social body can impact how it is understood, performed, and legitimised within discourse. Age can play a significant role in how bodies are governed and adds additional layers to consider in relation to agency and autonomy. 'Young people' can be understood as an umbrella term, used as a broad category but often shifting in regards to who this encompasses and embedded in narratives of safeguarding. In the UK, a child is defined to be anyone who has not yet reached their 18th birthday and someone who should be protected (Office of the United Nations High Commissioner for Human Rights, 1989; NSPCC Learning, 2023). The age of consent in relation to a person choosing and consenting to medical treatment is 16 years old, unless that person has been identified as not meeting levels of competence, awareness, and intelligence (Mental Capacity Act, 2005; NHS, n.d.). Despite this, the age of criminal responsibility is 10 years old and the age to vote in the UK is between 16 and 18 years old, showing how the construct can vary dependent on context and how bodies are interpreted. The framing varies, yet themes of vulnerability, autonomy, and regulation remain. Entwined in legal definitions, the framing of age can impose expectations and access to autonomy.

Barry (2005) argues that young people are frequently unheard in society, evidenced by an absence of spaces where their voices can be acknowledged and a lack of legislation that directly addresses the unique challenges they face, and that this contributes to a form of institutional ageism. While young people struggle to have their voices heard, those who are gender-fluid face an even greater challenge. Though age and gender carry different meanings, they similarly shape and control how the body is perceived and managed, with both being socially constructed forces that regulate individual autonomy.

Adolescence is a particularly sensitive time-point for younger generations in relation to social and emotional growth, and is additionally under-researched when intersecting with gender non-conformity (Spivey and Prinstein, 2018). It is a time where tension between finding a sense of self and gaining autonomy balance with societal expectations around identity politics. This tension leads to young people becoming inherently vulnerable due to entanglement between autonomy, needs for safeguarding, and how this may impact agency. Youth-focused policies aim to empower young people but often overlook how the intersection of age with other characteristics, such as gender identity, can hinder this empowerment.

The intersection

The categories of gender and age both have a significant effect on how the body is constructed and regulated. However, young trans and non-binary populations form a group who sit within these themes and at intersections of agency, autonomy, and regulation. In this sense, it is vital to understand how the two categories compound together rather than look at them in isolation. At a time where inequalities and social injustice seem to be unwavering, issues of inequality do not stand in isolation. Inequalities are interconnected and exist outside of our own agency when thinking about bodies and identities. Inequalities exist within social and political structures. As Hill Collins (2019: 1) points out, 'social inequality seems as durable as ever'. In relation to gender and age, this underscores how such systems can and will continue to impact how marginalised groups experience society, as well as how this will be understood and navigated. There is a need for a deeper understanding and examination of how such inequalities can compound and enforce barriers and injustice.

As previously mentioned, a singular axis approach to understanding inequality does not provide an in-depth analysis into the powerful structures and processes of inequality that exist within society. Intersectionality highlights the oversights across multiple structural factors of inequalities (Hill Collins, 2019). Intersectional thinking allows theory to move past seeing and understanding bodily categories as silos and enabling an inquiry which considers the intersection and compounding of two or more identities, whilst also considering the socio-political agency at play too. Intersectional lenses to social problems provide a critical form of inquiry and praxis (Hill Collins, 2019), as the compounding of two or more social categories can be examined in relation to the socio-political contexts they sit within. When applying an intersectional lens, the intersection between age and gender highlights a unique set of challenges.

Themes of autonomy, agency, and regulated bodies exist across both categories but when entangled together, there is a need to explore how the compounding of the two categories interacts with existing social structures and contexts. Trans people have continued to receive interest across political, social, and cultural spaces for years (Hines, 2007), whilst discourse around young gender-fluid populations continues to be a highly debated topic and has evolved across the UK significantly since 2022. It is clear that trans and non-binary populations have become politicised. Existing across institutional and public domains, the compounding of identities between gender and age has continued to be a topic of focus, yet the intersection and relationship between how the two categories interrelate has been missed from the mainstream discourse. The next section explores discourse across 2020–2025 and applies an intersectional lens to better understand the impact on young trans lives.

Legal discourse: Legal frameworks and impacts

Whilst gender fluidity remains at the forefront of global perspectives (Human Dignity Trust, 2019), the United Kingdom has continued a steady decline in attitudes towards trans rights between 2019 and 2024 (National Centre for Social Research, 2024). Whilst amendments and reforms to legislation and policy exist in the United Kingdom (for example the Gender Recognition Act, 2004; the discussions and rulings involving the Equality Act, 2010; Annex L in the Police and Crime Evidence Act), concerns of protection, discrimination, and transphobia are still prevalent for trans and non-binary populations across England, Northern Ireland, Scotland, and Wales. For instance, the Equality Act (2010) aims to protect individuals from discrimination based on a range of characteristics, including 'sex' and 'gender reassignment'. However, the Act's protections are limited for non-binary and gender-fluid young people, and as of 2025, now include the questioning of the meaning around the term 'sex' in relation to trans women. The politicisation of trans and non-binary populations has created significant debates and controversy within political and legal discourse, which serves to either protect or marginalise these groups.

The Gender Recognition Act (GRA) of 2004 enables transgender people to apply for legal recognition of their gender identity and allows for an amendment of their official documents. Individuals must be at least 18 years old, provide evidence of living in alignment with their desired gender for at least two years, and present a medical diagnosis of gender dysphoria from two independent practitioners. Although the GRA has facilitated significant changes in access to citizenship, applying an intersectional lens reveals that these provisions disproportionately disadvantage younger trans and non-binary individuals. A study conducted by TransActual (2021), involving nearly 700 trans people in the UK, revealed the significant barriers faced by this demographic. Participants ranged in age from 18 to 74, and 78% reported being unable to access legal identification that matched their gender identity. Furthermore, 65% expressed a desire for identity documentation that recognises non-binary as a valid gender category. In 2022 however, the UK government launched a public consultation to assess the role of self-identification and medical diagnosis within the legal recognition process (Stop Hate, n.d.). Although the consultation suggested several areas for reform, no significant changes to the law have yet occurred. In Scotland, the Gender Recognition Reform Bill was introduced in 2022, aiming to simplify the process and reduce waiting times. The Bill has since been passed by the Scottish Parliament and awaits Royal Assent (The Scottish Parliament, n.d.).

These findings underscore the gap in legal recognition and the challenges faced by gender-fluid individuals. The GRA also discriminates against young trans individuals who would not be able to meet the age threshold (Hines, 2007), particularly those under the age of 18, who may encounter compounded difficulties in accessing healthcare and legal recognition. Young trans and non-binary voices are also often absent and overlooked in political conversations, with some of this population too young to vote (Mermaids, 2024), although the voting age is changing to 16 before the next general election in the UK (Clarke, 2025).

Citizenship and health

Legal and political discourse can act as an indicator to understand how a group is valued in relation to citizenship and access, with legislative frameworks in the UK shaping both inclusion and exclusion to citizenship and healthcare for populations. Central to these discussions is the concept of citizenship, a mechanism to access means. Legal recognition of gender plays a pivotal role in how demographic groups are visible in society and protected under the law, where a lack of gender recognition can have broader implications in terms of visibility and social inclusion (Hines, 2013). This lack of recognition can directly impact healthcare, and without legal recognition, trans and non-binary populations may encounter significant barriers.

The Cass Review (2024) found that services available to children within the healthcare system are often designed for adults, leaving young people disadvantaged. There has also been a considerable increase in gender identity referrals in recent years, raising questions about the adequacy of support, long waiting times, and care for young people in gender identity clinics. Investigations into gender and age as intersecting categories remain under-researched, with insufficient data on how these factors interact (Cass, 2024). As well as experiencing delays and barriers to access healthcare, young transgender individuals may also experience discrimination through not being taken seriously by their GP or other medical professionals, or experiencing medical staff with little to no understanding of the referral procedures (Teti et al., 2021). Davy et al.'s (2022) work furthered this with their findings outlining inconsistencies in care, knowledge and practice.

The long waiting times reported by the Tavistock and Portman NHS Foundation Trust (Department of Health and Social Care Media Centre, 2024) were not isolated but connected to broader issues within the healthcare system. These failures reiterate the need for further research and reform, as well as for the acknowledgment of the intersectionality between gender and age in these critical areas. Instead, impacts on young people included restrictions on puberty blockers (Department of Health and Social Care, 2024), the Cass Review's (2024) recommendations for change, and the closure of Tavistock (Department of Health and Social Care, 2024; Mermaids, 2022b; Tavistock and Portman NHS Foundation Trust, n.d.).[1] For example, the Cass Review urged for a fundamentally different model in response to trans healthcare, queries of how decision-making happens within cis-normative spaces has been highlighted in relation to this closure (Horton, 2024).

From this, it is clear that transitioning young people may not receive adequate support until they are 18 or older, and for non-binary young people, there is limited legal protection or recognition as the focus remains on binary gender transitions. This highlights an urgent need for further inclusive reform. Returning to an earlier point raised on access to healthcare and age, when applying an intersectional lens to this, there is a clear disparity in how young trans populations will experience and access healthcare. In addition, the Equality Act does not fully protect non-binary young people, highlighting the need for legal frameworks to better reflect the diversity of gender identities within society (Fairburn et al., 2022).

Cultural debates and public discourse

Cultural debates are far from *just* abstract explorations of life. Exploring the media representations of groups and how they are encoded with meaning through digital spaces provides a lens to how certain demographics are presented and to an extent understood within society. These representations across cultural discourse are far from neutral. They are sites of struggle where presentations of identities are lenses into how society and structures shape and see people (Hall, 2013). The politicisation of trans and non-binary bodies features across cultural and media spaces, often in the form of stories that provoke interest or fear, with a history of some media outlets producing stories that include themes of deception and gender fraud (Hines, 2019, 2020). Between 2020 and 2025, there was a mix of both positive and negative representations. In 2022–2023, media attention largely focused on disputes between the charities Mermaids[2] and the LGB Alliance[3] and the tribunal that took place in November 2022. Accusations made in the media included suggestions that the documentation produced by Mermaids had 'hidden messages' and 'agendas' (Wakefield, 2022) and promoted a gender ideology that encourages minors to transition without further assessment. As the two sides critiqued one another, the overall dispute intensified existing tensions within the LGBTQ+ community on the inclusion of transgender people. Although this argument consisted of discussions of harms towards children, little was stated around how these disputes could harm young gender-fluid people. In 2022, Mermaids paused their public-facing support services – a clear impact of heightened political and legal pressures. The pause was to protect the staff at Mermaids from harassment across their channels, and led to young people losing access to a space for support. For reference, the 2022 review of the charity highlighted their work supporting over 8000 people in one year across calls, web chat, and group forums (Mermaids, 2022a).

Encoding ideologies in media representations

Themes across online spaces during 2022 included headlines with phrases such as: 'anti-trans', 'offensive homophobic conspiracy', 'removal of charitable status', and 'difficult and problematic issues' (Wakefield, 2022; Walker, 2023; Harris, 2022). Other examples include articles that report on calls to amend laws to restrict anyone under the age of 18 in the UK undergoing any form of gender reassignment surgery (Daly, 2023), citing concerns regarding young people making irreversible decisions and later regretting them. Whilst NHS guidance refers to a young person needing to be 16 years old to consent to medical intervention, providing they have the capacity to do so, this is often not applied in such circumstances.

Through these headlines, ideological meanings can be encoded and decoded (Hall, 2013). These codes signify tension and ambivalence on trans-inclusion. When applying an intersectional lens, for young trans and non-binary demographics, such meanings can have profound impacts. When analysing the ideological meanings shared within such reports, discourse reveals an underlying age-based assumption for trans youth and informed decisions regarding gender identity. Again, the entanglement of gender, age, and the theme of capacity further compound one another.

Intersectional impact

Trans and non-binary young people are often erased from public discourse, and are voiceless as a result. TransActual's 2021 survey of 697 trans people in the UK found that 97% of research participants reported being negatively impacted by the digital media. When examining the impact of transphobia created or existing within media spaces, 97% experienced this via digital and print media (TransActual, 2021). A significant number (85%) also reported that the transphobic rhetoric in the UK that occurs in the media had impacted factors such as mental health and their treatment by family members, co-workers, and friends. This evidences the significant impact that normalised stigma and politicisation of identities across public spaces is having on young trans people and that this can detrimentally affect their mental health.

Political debates and tabloid coverage

Lastly, the representation of trans and non-binary young people will be explored in relation to public discourse surrounding political leaders within the UK and the coverage from tabloid media. Between 2020 and 2025, a range of gender-affirming and gender-critical events occurred within the public eye. Representations across these public spaces can highlight broader ideological blueprints, which can impact experience, visibility, and overall citizenship of young trans and non-binary people. Yet, public views differ between those who view trans rights as a 'culture war' and those who show little or no attention to the debate (YouGov, 2022).

Whilst certain British 'broadsheet' newspapers are deemed respectable places of information and truth, Montiel-McCann's (2022) work prompts us to remember the power systems and productions of knowledge at play in these media outlets. Broadsheets hold a 'unique position for reproducing hegemonic discourse by appearing to be the most rooted in epistemological truth and, hence, offering a "reflection" of society devoid of the bias shown in the tabloids' (Montiel-McCann, 2022: 2693).

Drawing on cultural hegemony, Montiel-McCann (2022) discusses the normative versions of gender through Western cultures where heteronormative, white, able bodies are perceived to be the norm through existing social structures, encoded information, and representations evident in popular culture (Hall, 2013). Akrivos (2022) also discusses the role of journalism in British politics in setting/(re)constructing public agendas and social realities of contexts and people, leading to the creation of a space where constructions of lives and identities are publicly encoded and decoded, defined, received, critiqued, and negotiated.

The deviant and problematised 'Other' is also not a new phenomenon in Western popular cultures, and whilst constructed and ever-changing, its impacts are heavy and real. Throughout these ongoing debates and discussions of rights and access, few representations or discussions consider the impact that such public debates may have on the communities who are being discussed. Trans and non-binary populations have a long history of being ridiculed for not 'fitting' into heteronormative norms and values. Bringing together two marginalised and arguably silenced groups who meet at this intersection, this chapter implores for us to consider how this attention may impact young trans and non-binary people in relation to being at the centre of a culture war. Trans youth sit at an intersection of gender and age, where each compounds how decision-making and agency can be understood. This exists outside of cultural debates and can be seen across political discourse too. Between 2020 and 2025, some political parties framed trans and non-binary populations as undermining economic productivity and cohesion. The Reform UK party for example refer to the conversation around trans rights as 'woke', 'divisive', and 'harmful' (Perry, 2024). This rhetoric diminishes the lived experiences of trans people and contributes to the polarisation of the group.

Political discourse has furthered debates on gender identity. Media responses to these debates also include coverage of former Prime Ministers' stances on trans rights in relation to protecting children from 'harmful' ideologies (Roger, 2024) and continue to polarise the conversation around trans identities. This framing of trans rights as a threat to societal norms contributes to the erasure of trans youth's voices, further marginalising them in both the political and public contexts.

Constructions of Othering are evident here, with growing literature that examines the Othering of gender-diverse bodies and how the media present them. Research into British journalism and how it either contributes to the marginalisation or allyship to this demographic is under-researched and under-developed (Montiel-McCann, 2022). Applying an intersectional analysis here can further understanding of the layered impacts of such debates, and lead to broader implications in terms of how gender and age interplay across political, social, and cultural discourse. Framing and allowing discourse that present trans rights as a threat to social cohesion not only erases the lived experiences of young trans people from the debate but further marginalises and normalises such stigma and discrimination. This conflict fosters misunderstanding and detachment, making it harder for people to empathise with or fully engage in the realities faced by trans individuals. This can be seen in recent travesties such as the murder of Brianna Ghey (Vaughan, 2024), as well as within the collective narratives evidenced throughout the data presented above.

Conclusion

Across cultural, political, and social discourse, trans and non-binary youth are positioned as harmful or harmed in relation to transitioning. Crenshaw's (1989) framework enables a deeper analysis into the discrimination, marginalisation, and harm experienced by this demographic. Through poorer access to healthcare, limited options around citizenship until the age of 18, and ongoing politicised and harmful language evidenced across cultural and public spaces, an interlocking system of inequality is demonstrated for this demographic of young people in the UK. Gender identity and age as intersecting categories can influence how a body can be understood and regulated, with implications and assumptions around agency and capacity. When reframing harm, the cultural, political, and social discourse can be understood to position this demographic in a potentially harmful intersection with limited access to support, citizenship, and a sense of belonging. Through intersectionality, the structures, regulations, and barriers faced evidence how risk discourse can cause harm. Therefore, this chapter pushes for a reconsideration of how harm is framed in relation to this demographic.

The politicisation of gender-diverse experiences and rights through public debate and legislative changes has had a longstanding domino effect, as evidenced in recent political debates. Age is a lost contributor in the gender debate but by applying an intersectional lens, Hill Collins' (2019) understanding of social problems illustrates the impact of political and cultural narratives which further compound the marginalisation of trans and non-binary populations. There is an absence of lived experienced voices and community led initiatives in legal, political, and medical contexts when considering trans people (Todd, 2025). Regardless of which side of the 'culture war' a person attaches themselves to, the narratives and impacts do not add up.

It is essential to pause and confront such biases and dispel some of the often-prominent narratives communicated through digital spaces on trans and non-binary identities. Concerns of 'harming' children by providing access to conversations and interventions around gender fluidity are positioned as a push for further safeguarding of younger populations. However, as outlined by the various charity sector reports mentioned previously, such narratives are doing quite the opposite. Young trans and non-binary people sit at this intersection and are harmed through such discourse which feeds into daily life. The United Nations Convention on the Rights of the Child (Office of the United Nations High Commissioner for Human Rights, 1989) states that every child should know and understand their rights, including the protection of their identity, access to health services, and a freedom of expression. This is not evident in the literature and media discourses presented herein. Although the Convention does not refer to gender identity in these examples, the overarching goal to safeguard and protect young people is lost and abandoned if young people feel voiceless, marginalised, and in some cases demonised.

Notes

1 The Tavistock and Portman NHS Foundation Trust was the UK's oldest and longest established gender identity development service. Accepting referrals from across the UK, the clinic provided support through multi-disciplinary teams to provide holistic and gender-affirming care. The service did, however, face scrutiny due to varying concerns.

2 Mermaids is a UK based charity that was founded in 1995. The charity works to support young trans people (11–25 years old). Their strategy includes a range of services including direct support services, youth advocacy, policy and campaigns, and training and education.

3 The LGB Alliance is a registered charity founded in 2019. The charity works to enhance the rights of lesbian, gay, and bisexual people (not including transgender people). Work includes highlighting discrimination, protecting children, campaigning against self-ID laws, and promoting free speech for same-sex attracted people who experience discrimination based on their sexual orientation.

References

Akrivos, D. (2022). Transgender reporting in the British press: Editorial standards and discursive harms in the post-Leveson era. *Journal of Media Law*, *14*(2), 406–441. doi: 10.1080/17577632.2022.2153216.

Bachman, C. L., and Gooch, B. (2018). *LGBT in Britain Trans Report.* YouGov. Stonewall. Available at: https://files.stonewall.org.uk/production/files/lgbt_in_britain_-_trans_report_final.pdf?dm=1724230505 [Accessed: 26 September 2025].

Barry, M. (2005). *Youth Policy and Social Inclusion: Critical Debates with Young People*. London: Routledge.

BBC (2024a). Rishi Sunak faces calls to apologise over trans jibe to Starmer at PMQS. Available at: https://www.bbc.co.uk/news/uk-politics-68229785 [Accessed: 12 December 2024].

BBC (2024b). What are the parties saying about women's rights and gender identity? Available at: https://www.bbc.co.uk/news/articles/c4nng2j42xro [Accessed: 12 December 2024].

Berlin, S., and Brice, S. (2022). The ontopolitics of gender as transindividual relation. In: C. Cremin (Ed.), *Deleuze, Guattari and the Schizoanalysis of Trans Studies*. London: Bloomsbury, 9–34.

Bordo, S. (1995). *Unbearable Weight: Feminism, Western Culture, and the Body*. California: Berkeley: University.

Butler, J. (1990). *Gender Trouble: Feminism and the Subversion of Identity*. New York: Routledge.
Butler, J. (2004). *Undoing Gender*. New York: Routledge.
Cass, H. (2024). The Cass Review. Independent review of gender identity services for children and young people. Available at: https://cass.independent-review.uk/home/publications/final-report/ [Accessed: 26 September 2025].
Children's Commissioner (2024). Press release: Over a quarter of a million children still waiting for mental health support. https://www.childrenscommissioner.gov.uk/blog/over-a-quarter-of-a-million-children-still-waiting-for-mental-health-support/ [Accessed: 26 September 2025].
Clarke, J. (2025, 17 July). How will votes at 16 and changes to voter ID work? *BBC News*. https://www.bbc.co.uk/news/articles/cm2lgnze013o
Colliver, B. (2021). Claiming victimhood: Victims of the 'transgender agenda'. In: J. Bailey, A. Flynn, and N. Henry (Eds.), *The Emerald International Handbook of Technology-Facilitated Violence and Abuse*. Bingley: Emerald Publishing, 189–204. https://doi.org/10.1108/978-1-83982-848-520211014
Colliver, B., Coyle, A., and Silvestri, M. (2019) The online 'Othering' of transgender and non-binary people. In: K. Lumsden and E. Harmer (Eds.), *Online Othering: Victims of the 'Transgender Agenda' Exploring the Dark Side of the Web*, 215–238. London: Palgrave Macmillan.
Colliver, B., et al. (2022). Intersectional oppression and transgender people's experiences of discrimination. In: J. Healy and B. Colliver (Eds.), *Contemporary Intersectional Criminology in the UK*. Bristol, UK: Bristol University Press, 137–151. https://doi.org/10.51952/9781529215977.ch009
Colliver, B., and Silvestri, M. (2022). The role of (in)visibility in hate crime targeting transgender people. *Criminology & Criminal Justice*, *22*(2), 235–253. https://doi.org/10.1177/1748895820930747
Connell, R. (1987). *Gender and Power: Society, the Person, and Sexual Politics*. Cambridge: Polity Press in association with Blackwell Publishers Ltd.
Conrad, P. (1985). The meaning of medication: Another look at the compliance. *Social Science and Medicine*, 20, 29–37.
Crenshaw, K. (1989). Demarginalizing the intersection of race and sex: A black feminist critique of antidiscrimination doctrine, feminist theory, and antiracist politics. *University of Chicago Legal Forum, 1*, 139–167. https://scholarship.law.columbia.edu/faculty_scholarship/3007
Daly, P. (2023). Liz Truss to propose law banning trans women from single-sex spaces. *Independent*, 3 December. Available at: https://www.independent.co.uk/news/uk/politics/liz-truss-males-single-sex-spaces-b2457602.html [Accessed: 13 December 2024].
Davis, S. (2023). *Queer and Trans People of Colour in the UK: Possibilities for Intersectional Richness*. London: Routledge. https://doi.org/10.4324/9780429437694
Davy, Z., Benson J., and Barras, A. (2022). Shared care and gender identity support in primary care: The perspectives and experiences of parents/carers of young trans people. *Health*, *28*(2), 235–252. https://journals.sagepub.com/doi/10.1177/13634593221138616
De Beauvoir, S. (1949). *The Second Sex* (2nd ed.). Translated by H. M. Parshley. New York: Vintage Books.
Department of Health and Social Care (2024). Ban on puberty blockers to be made indefinite on expert's advice. Press Release. Gov.uk. Available at: https://www.gov.uk/government/news/ban-on-puberty-blockers-to-be-made-indefinite-on-experts-advice#:~:text=Puberty%20blockers%20for%20the%20treatment,will%20be%20reviewed%20in%202027 [Accessed: 8 April 2025].
Department of Health and Social Care Media Centre (2024). Puberty blockers: What you need to know. Available at: https://healthmedia.blog.gov.uk/2024/12/11/puberty-blockers-what-you-need-to-know/ (Accessed: 10 October 2025).

Equality Act (2010). Available at: legislation.gov.uk/ukpga/2010/15/contents [Accessed: 07 April 2025].
Fairburn, C., Barton, C., Pyper, D., and Lipscombe, S. (2022). Non-binary gender recognition: Law and police. Research Briefing. Available at: https://commonslibrary.parliament.uk/research-briefings/cbp-9515/
Foucault, M. (1976). Selections from the history of sexuality. In J. Appleby, E. Covington, D. Hoyt, M. Latham, and A. Sneider (Eds.), *Knowledge and postmodernism in historical perspective*. London: Routledge.
Foucault, M. (2020). *Discipline and punish: The birth of the prison*. Translated by A. Sheridan. London: Penguin Books.
Goffman, E. (1963). *Stigma: Notes on the Management of the Spoiled Identity*. Englewood Cliffs, NJ: Prentice Hall
GOV.UK (2021a). Banning conversion therapy. Available at: https://www.gov.uk/government/consultations/banning-conversion-therapy/banning-conversion-therapy [Accessed: 26 September 2025].
GOV.UK (2021b). Conversion therapy: An evidence assessment and qualitative study. Available at: https://www.gov.uk/government/publications/conversion-therapy-an-evidence-assessment-and-qualitative-study/conversion-therapy-an-evidence-assessment-and-qualitative-study#executive-summary [Accessed: 17 December 2024].
GOV.UK (2021c). UK to host its first global LGBT conference. Available at: https://www.gov.uk/government/news/uk-to-host-its-first-global-lgbt-conference [Accessed: 26 September 2025].
Government Equalities Office (2018). Trans people in The UK. Available at: https://assets.publishing.service.gov.uk/media/5b3a478240f0b64603fc181b/GEO-LGBT-factsheet.pdf [Accessed: 26 September 2025].
Hall, S. (2013). The work of representation. In: S. Hall, J. Evans, and S. Nixon (Eds.). *Representation* (2nd ed.). London: Sage, 1–13.
Harris, J. (2022). Mermaids' attempt to shut gay charity 'profoundly homophobic', tribunal hears. *The Telegraph*, 8 November. Available at: https://www.telegraph.co.uk/news/2022/11/08/mermaids-attempt-shut-gay-charity-profoundly-homophobic-tribunal/ [Accessed: 8 April 2025].
Hill Collins, P. (2019). *Intersectionality as Critical Social Theory*. Durham: Duke University Press. https://doi.org/10.1515/9781478007098
Hines, S. (2007). *TransForming Gender: Transgender Practices of Identity, Intimacy and Care*. Bristol, UK: Policy Press.
Hines, S. (2013). *Gender Diversity, Recognition and Citizenship: Towards a Politics of Difference*. London: Palgrave Macmillan.
Hines, S. (2019). The feminist frontier: On trans and feminism. *Journal of Gender Studies*, *28*(2), 145–157.
Hines, S. (2020). Sex wars and (trans) gender panics: Identity and body politics in contemporary UK feminism. *The Sociological Review (Keele)*, *68*(4), 699–717. https://doi.org/10.1177/0038026120934684
Home Office (2021). *Hate crime, England and Wales, 2020 to 2021*. Available at: https://www.gov.uk/government/statistics/hate-crime-england-and-wales-2020-to-2021/hate-crime-england-and-wales-2020-to-2021 [Accessed: 8 April 2025].
House of Commons (2022). Non-binary gender recognition: Law and policy. Available at: https://commonslibrary.parliament.uk/research-briefings/cbp-9515/#:~:text=No%20legal%20recognition,to%20female%20or%20vice%20versa [Accessed: 26 September 2025].
Horton, C. (2024). The Cass Review: Cis-supremacy in the UK's approach to healthcare for trans children. *International Journal of Transgender Health*, 1–25. https://doi.org/10.1080/26895269.2024.2328249

Human Dignity Trust (2019). *Injustice Exposed. The Criminalisation of Transgender People and Its Impacts*. London: Human Dignity Trust. Available at: https://www.humandignitytrust.org/wp-content/uploads/resources/Injustice-Exposed-the-criminsalisation-of-trans-people.pdf [Accessed: 26 September 2025].

Klawiter, M. (2004). Breast cancer in two regimes: The impact of social movements in illness experience. *Sociology of Health and Illness*, *26*(6), 845–874.

Lawler, S. (2008). *Identity: Sociological Perspectives*. Cambridge: Polity Press.

LGB Alliance (2025). Our purpose. Available at: https://lgballiance.org.uk/purpose/ [Accessed: 8 April 2025].

Mental Capacity Act (2005). Available at: https://www.legislation.gov.uk/ukpga/2005/9/contents (Accessed: 10 October 2025).

Mermaids (2022a). Mermaids 2022: Year in review: Our highlights of 2022. Available at: https://mermaidsuk.org.uk/news/mermaids-2022-year-in-review/ [Accessed: 8 April 2025].

Mermaids (2022b). Tavistock closure: Your questions answered. Available at: https://mermaidsuk.org.uk/news/tavistock-closure-your-questions-answered/ (Accessed: 10 October 2025).

Mermaids (2024). *Strategy 2024 – 2027* [Strategy report]. Available at: https://www.mermaidsuk.org.uk/wp-content/uploads/2024/02/Mermaids-Strategy-2024-2027.pdf [Accessed: 8 April 2025].

Mermaids (n.d.). *Trans Youth Manifesto*. Available at: https://mermaidsuk.org.uk/transyouthmanifesto/ [Accessed: 8 April 2025].

Mind (2022). *Conversion 'Therapy' Ban: Legislating to Protect the Mental Health of the LGBTQIA+ Community*. Available at: https://www.mind.org.uk/media/tcsjaimo/conversion-therapy-ban-legislating-to-protect-the-mental-health-of-the-lgbtqia-community-december-2022.pdf [Accessed: 8 April 2025].

Montiel-McCann, C. S. (2022). 'It's like we are not human': Discourses of humanisation and Otherness in the representation of trans identity in British broadsheet newspapers. *Feminist Media Studies*, *23*(6): 2962–2978. https://www.tandfonline.com/doi/full/10.1080/14680777.2022.2097727

National Centre for Social Research (2024). Five years of unprecedented challenges | The impact of the 2019 – 2024 Parliament on Public Opinion. Available at: https://natcen.ac.uk/publications/british-social-attitudes-41-five-years-unprecedented-challenges [Accessed: 1 April 2024].

Nettleton, S. (2020). *The Sociology of Health and Illness* (4th ed.). Cambridge: Polity Press.

NHS (n.d.). Children and young people: Consent to treatment. Available at: https://www.nhs.uk/conditions/consent-to-treatment/children/ [Accessed: 4 May 2023].

NSPCC Learning (2023). Children and the law: Definitions of a child. Available at: https://learning.nspcc.org.uk/child-protection-system/children-the-law#definitions-of-a-child [Accessed: 21 May 2023].

Office for National Statistics (2021). Gender identity, England and Wales: Census 2021. Available at: https://www.ons.gov.uk/peoplepopulationandcommunity/culturalidentity/genderidentity/bulletins/genderidentityenglandandwales/census2021 [Accessed: 26 September 2025].

Office of the United Nations High Commissioner for Human Rights (1989). Convention on the Rights of the Child. Treaty no. 27531. United Nations Treaty Series, 1577, 3–178. Available at: https://treaties.un.org/doc/Treaties/1990/09/19900902%2003-14%20AM/Ch_IV_11p.pdf [Accessed: 3 November 2025].

Perry, S. (2024, 5 July). Reform UK's divisive manifesto takes aim at 'transgender ideology' and 'pronoun swapping'. *Pink News*. https://www.thepinknews.com/2024/07/05/reform-uk-manifesto-nigel-farage-trans-lgbtq-election/ [Accessed: 3 November 2025].

Rainbow Project (n.d.). What we do: What do we mean by trans or non-binary? Available at: https://www.rainbow-project.org/what-we-do-mean-by-trans-or-non-binary/ [Accessed: 8 April 2025].

Rogers, A. (2024). Liz Truss 'furious' after MPs accused of blocking transgender reform bill. *Sky News*, 15 March. Available at: https://news.sky.com/story/liz-truss-furious-after-mps-accused-of-blocking-transgender-reform-bill-13095370 [Accessed: 13 December 2024].

Shilling, C. (2003) *The Body and Social Theory* (2nd ed.). London: Sage.

Spivey, L. A., and Prinstein, M. J. (2018). A preliminary examination of the association between adolescent gender nonconformity and suicidal thoughts and behaviors. *Journal of Abnormal Child Psychology*, *47*(4), 707–716. doi:10.1007/s10802-018-0479-6.

Stonewall (2018). Trans hub. Available at: https://www.stonewall.org.uk/resources/lgbtq-hubs/trans-hub/the-truth-about-trans#:~:text=Within%20this%2C%20the%20number%20of,people%20in%20England%20and%20Wales [Accessed: 26 September 2025].

Stonewall (2024). Public attitudes towards trans people. Research briefing. Available at: https://files.stonewall.org.uk/production/files/polling_on_trans_people.pdf?dm=1724230509 (Accessed 10 October 2025).

Stonewall (n.d.). List of LGBTQ+ terms. Available at: https://www.stonewall.org.uk/resources/list-lgbtq-terms#:~:text=N-,Non%2Dbinary,man'%20or%20'woman [Accessed: 8 April 2025].

Stop Hate UK (n.d.). Transgender hate crime. Available at: https://www.stophateuk.org/about-hate-crime/transgender-hate/ [Accessed: 8 April 2025].

Tavistock and Portman NHS Foundation Trust (n.d.). Gender identity clinic (GIC). Available at: https://tavistockandportman.nhs.uk/services/gender-identity-clinic-gic/ (Accessed: 10 October 2025).

Teti, M., Kerr, S., Bauerband, L. A., et al. (2021). A qualitative scoping review of transgender and gender non-conforming people's physical healthcare experiences and needs. *Frontiers in Public Health*, *9*, 598455.

The Human Rights Campaign (n.d.). Transgender children and youth: Understanding the basics. Available at: https://www.hrc.org/resources/transgender-children-and-youth-understanding-the-basics [Accessed: 26 September 2025].

The Scottish Parliament (n.d.). Gender Recognition Form (Scotland) Bill. Available at: https://www.parliament.scot/bills-and-laws/bills/s6/gender-recognition-reform-scotland-bill#:~:text=Reform%20(Scotland)%20Bill-,Gender%20Recognition%20Reform%20(Scotland)%20Bill,is%20their%20%E2%80%9Cacquired%20gender%E2%80%9D.&text=The%20Bill%20was%20introduced%20on%202%20March%202022 [Accessed: 26 September 2025].

The Trevor Report (2021). The Trevor Report national survey. Available at: https://www.thetrevorproject.org/survey-2021/ [Accessed: 26 September 2025].

The Trevor Report (2022). 2022 national survey on LGBTQ youth mental health. Available at: https://www.thetrevorproject.org/survey-2022/ [Accessed: 26 September 2025].

The Trevor Report (2024). 2024 United Kingdom survey on the mental health of LGBTQ+ young people. Available at: https://www.thetrevorproject.org/survey-international/uk/2024/en/ [Accessed: 26 September 2025].

Todd, J. (2025). Exploring young trans and non-binary people's strategies and spaces for navigating marginality in the United Kingdom: A novel resilience, resistance, and restoration framework. *Annals of the American Association of Geographers*, *115*(6), 1309–1325. https://doi.org/10.1080/24694452.2025.2478258 [Accessed: 3 November 2025].

TransActual (2021). Trans lives survey 2021: Enduring the UK's hostile environment. Available at: https://transactual.org.uk/wp-content/uploads/TransLivesSurvey2021.pdf [Accessed: 26 September 2025].

Trans Kids Deserve Better (n.d.). Available at: https://transkidsdeservebetter.org/ [Accessed: 26 September 2025].

Vaughan, H. (2024). Brianna Ghey: How teenagers with a thirst for death and murder plotted killing on their phones. *Sky News*, 2 February. Available at: https://news.sky.com/story/brianna-ghey-how-teenagers-with-a-thirst-for-death-and-murder-plotted-killing-on-their-phones-13033534 [Accessed: 8 April 2025].

Wakefield, L. (2022). Anti-trans LGB Alliance accuses trans charity Mermaids of an 'offensive homophobic conspiracy'. *Pink News*. Available at: https://www.thepinknews.com/2022/11/08/lgb-alliance-mermaids-tribunal-charity-commission/ [Accessed: 8 April 2025].

Walker, P. (2023). Key takeaways from Rishi Sunak's 7,500-word Tory conference speech. *The Guardian*, 4 October. Available at: https://www.theguardian.com/politics/2023/oct/04/key-takeaways-rishi-sunak-tory-conference-speech [Accessed: 13 December 2024].

World Health Organization (2021). *Suicide Worldwide in 2019: Global Health Estimates*. Available at: https://apps.who.int/iris/bitstream/handle/10665/341728/9789240026643-eng.pdf [Accessed: 26 September 2025].

YouGov (2021). International survey: How supportive would Britons be of a family member coming out? Available at: https://yougov.co.uk/international/articles/37846-international-survey-how-supportive-would-britons- [Accessed: 26 September 2025].

YouGov (2022). Where does the British publish stand on transgender rights in 2022? Availableat:https://yougov.co.uk/society/articles/43194-where-does-british-public-stand-transgender-rights-1 [Accessed: 26 September 2025].

SECTION II

Global Patterns in Policy and Practice

5

PRISON ABOLITION AND THE CASE OF CECE MCDONALD

Gina Gwenffrewi

Introduction: Transness, policing and the prison industrial complex in the USA

Few issues signify the class-based and race-based divergence within and between trans communities in the Anglophone Global North like policing and the prison industrial complex, with the responding current political campaigns around prison abolition and defunding the police. Conceived by the social historian Mike Davis (1995), the notion of a prison industrial complex encompasses the increasing commercialisation of the prison sector in the 1990s and its emergence 'as a major economic and political force' (A. Davis, 2003: 84). A racialised element to the prison industrial complex has also been identified by Black historians such as Angela Davis and Michelle Alexander, who see it as manifesting the most recent iteration of the eugenicist Jim Crow's persecution of Black and brown Americans via policing and imprisonment. This includes in relation to its re-iterative exploitation of a supply of a cheap, disempowered form of labour, and the targeting of Black and brown lives as a means of continued racialised marginalisation, political scapegoating, and economic exploitation. As Angela Y. Davis (2003) says of the current iteration, arguably initiated by the 1994 Crime Bill of President Bill Clinton and Senator Joe Biden among other nominally left-of-centre Democrat politicians, the prison industrial complex involves not only cross-party ideals of law enforcement and incarceration but 'an array of relationships linking corporations, government, correctional communities, and media' (A. Davis, 2003: 84).

Regarding trans lives, Elias Walker Vitulli has observed how the 'words, lives, and experiences' of imprisoned trans and gender non-conforming

DOI: 10.4324/9781003564928-7

people 'are rarely part of trans studies conversations' (Vitulli, 2014: 162–164). At a mainstream level, former Human Rights Campaign spokesperson and now Democrat Senator Sarah McBride makes no mention of the prison industrial complex in her homonormative memoir *Tomorrow Will Be Different* (2018). Janet Mock similarly occludes it from her talkshow circuit as well as her memoir *Redefining Realness* (2014), while devoting two pages critical of mass incarceration in her 331-page, career- and romance-focused *Surpassing Certainty* (2018). Conversely, both Mock and McBride cite anti-carceral Stonewall veterans as inspirations, for example McBride referencing Marsha P. Johnson (McBride, 2018), and Mock claiming abolitionist campaigner Miss Major Griffin-Gracy as a mentor (Mock, 2016). This vocal identification that briefly name-checks iconography during interviews or literary passages arguably sanitises and obscures the violence, visceral anti-establishment discourse, and most importantly the radical ideas, used to challenge the status quo by such historic but also romanticised figures. It does little, for example, to highlight a major component of the activism of Johnson, Griffin-Gracy, and Sylvia Rivera, and the grassroots organisation that Johnson and Rivera helped form in 1970, the Street Transvestite Action Revolutionaries (STAR). Their nine-point manifesto includes demands directly addressing enduring issues of institutional police violence and discrimination, the dynamic of political sovereignty, and the reliance of US society on the implicitly eugenicist incarceration of its most vulnerable citizens:

> The immediate end of all policy harassment and arrest of transvestites and gay street people, and the release of transvestites and gay street people from all prisons and all other political prisoners ... We want a revolutionary peoples' government, where transvestites, street people, women, homosexuals, blacks, puerto ricans, indians, and all oppressed people are free, and not fucked over by this government who treat us like the scum of the earth and kills us off like flies, one by one, and throws us into jail to rot.
>
> *(Lewis, 2017: 76–77)*

Researching this period of anti-carceral-focused Queer and Trans People of Colour (QTPOC) activism, Abram Lewis describes how another US-based movement of the time, Transexual Action Organization (TAO), 'centred critiques of policing, incarceration, and other forms of state violence' with a simultaneous, anti-assimilationist rejection of strategies 'that sought to build better relationships with law enforcement' (2017: 62). Class and race appear to have been contributing factors to the membership of these organisations, with Lewis noting how 'TAO and STAR were arguably the most successful at developing an intersectional, coalition-based politics that centred especially vulnerable trans populations ... composed of low-income and homeless transfeminine people of color, immigrants, and sex-workers' (2017: 60–61).

Their legacy, including in relation to abolitionism, can be seen not in the lifestyle narratives of Mock or the homonormative policy focus of McBride, but in the radical transfeminism of trans theorists and activists in North America such as Dean Spade, Eric Stanley, and Tourmaline, and organisations like the Trans and Intersex Justice Project and the Sylvia Rivera Law Project. Thus, the grassroots activists connected to these latter organisations, nameless by the standards of celebrity trans visibility, are the closest inheritors to the legacy of Johnson, Rivera, et al. They either inhabit or work at the margins of a society policed by discriminatory law enforcement and delineated by the structural conditions of poverty and other related inequalities such as unaffordable housing and unstable, inadequately paid employment; conditions that cannot be repaired by visibility alone.

Rarely do trans figures emerge from these socio-economic margins to receive mainstream attention, while signifying the coming together of issues of policing and incarceration in relation to class and race in the Stonewall tradition, like CeCe McDonald. Arrested in 2011 following an attack upon her by white supremacists, during which in the act of self-defense McDonald killed one of her assailants, McDonald's case initially attracted local support from a community movement led by members of the local Minneapolis-based Trans Youth Support Network (TYSN), who were already familiar with McDonald and in turn formed the 'CeCe Support Committee'. This grassroots base ultimately led to national and international attention as McDonald awaited trial over several months in solitary confinement in a men's prison. Eventually sentenced to 41 months in a men's prison and released on parole after 19 months, McDonald has since emerged as a vocal advocate of the prison abolition movement in the US. With the exception of a few high-profile magazine interviews (Erdely, 2014), the central resources that recount McDonald's experiences include her blog posts on her carceral experiences on a Wordpress website and a documentary. These sources focus on the events surrounding her incarceration and the structural issues related to them, with substantial segments of her personal life absent. Building thematically on these writings is the documentary *Free CeCe!* (2018), about the case and McDonald's subsequent involvement in abolitionist and trans-rights activism. Directed and produced by Jac Gares, and with Laverne Cox as executive producer and interviewer, the film centres McDonald while including interviews with legal experts, academics, activists, and members of McDonald's family. Gares (2025) describes the film as exploring 'the role of race, class and gender' as well as highlighting 'the large number of voices questioning the prison industrial complex and seeking to undo it'. The film is worthy of analysis both as an account of McDonald's harrowing experience of the prison industrial complex, and as a case study in the construction of documentary film-making about the dispossessed, in this case through the amplification of the voice of a trans woman of colour fighting multiple forms of structural oppression.

Voice/s of the community in *Free CeCe!*

With McDonald's experience of incarceration being central to the documentary, it can be argued that *Free CeCe!* exemplifies a tradition of documentary film-making about marginalised voices in the neoliberal age. Michael Chanan highlights the emergence of this new paradigm that stresses themes of social justice, including for Black Americans:

> the result [is] that the Civil Rights movement, which began to take shape in the 1950s, held out the promise of a separate politics which succoured the idea of black pride, with corresponding cultural implications. Eventually this would produce new modes of black film-making, both fiction and documentary.
>
> *(2007: 242)*

The development of these new modes of documentary-making, in keeping with the neoliberal ethos of individualism, has been met either with excitement or caution. Sujatha Fernandes analyses the neoliberal-inflected, curated personal stories of ostensibly dispossessed voices which 'shift the focus away from structurally defined axes of oppression and help to defuse the confrontational politics of social movements' (Fernandes, 2017, p. 2) – arguably recognisable in the carefully curated, apolitical brand of Janet Mock. Michael Renov, however, also recognises the powerful potential of new modes of autobiographical documentaries, contrary to the self-promotion and occlusion of social critiques that can occur, for an individualism that melds with community action:

> It is not at all surprising that much current autobiography has been produced at the margins of commercial culture by feminists, gays, people of color, and mavericks of every stripe. Contrary to critics who view this outpouring as reactionary – the individualist backlash against movement solidarity or the acting out of unbridled solipsism – the work is frequently engaged in community building and is deeply dialogic. This other may be the family as in the case of 'domestic ethnography' or members of a community linked by racial memory or elected affinity. Tonally, the work is tremendously diverse – celebratory, elegiac, solemn, delirious – but it is almost always affirmational of a self culturally specific and publicly defined.
>
> *(2004: xvi–xvii)*

Renov concludes that, 'the autobiographical impetus I am describing has infused the documentary tradition with a much-needed vitality and expanded its vernacular.'

Arguably, *Free CeCe!* can be viewed as a reflection of Renov's optimistic position, a semi-autobiographical trans story inclusive of family reconciliation and community-based camaraderie, but also one addressing institutional racism via a host of informed voices. Accordingly, perhaps in keeping with the normative-defying nature of a queer text, it produces a sometimes conceptually dis-unified amalgam of separate 'community' voices and competing priorities, while generating a tension against the narrative of the individual. On this latter point, McDonald both occupies the documentary's centre stage but does not restrict it from other voices and the larger context that the film attempts to connect with. This includes McDonald's experience of mass incarceration in connection to broader movements, contrary to the rhetoric of meritocracy and freedom synonymous with homonational, neoliberal ideology. Or as Chanan says of the neoliberal-age, social-justice-focused documentary generally: 'Here we find a dialectic that moves back and forth between personal and social identity, the self-inscription of the film-maker in an act of self-assertive presence, and the re-interpretation of historical imagery by recontextualising it' (2004: 243).

Free CeCe!, then, consistent with the dichotomy identified by Chanan, and inclusive of a semi-biographical mode that shares screen time with Queer and Black activist communities and accompanying critical traditions, combines both personal story and a broader critique of mass incarceration. This is in relation to Black and QTPOC experience, and in turn McDonald's voice vies with a flurry of accompanying others.

In the first half, these voices include TYSN's chief executive Katie Burgess, who leads the community organising to raise public awareness of McDonald's plight. She is interviewed along with a series of legal experts on either side of the trial's divide. Additional voices come in the form of recordings of McDonald being misgendered on the news. Mediating the interviews and threading together the disparate voices is high-profile trans actress Laverne Cox, making clear her identification with McDonald. Yet the voices pluralise further in the second half: family members within domestic settings vie for time with experts on Black history, Queer history, and/or the prison industrial complex, such as Angela Davis, Tourmaline, and Eric Stanley. Community organisers Isa Noyola of El/La Para Translatinas and Lourdes Ashley Hunter of the Trans Women of Color Collective then become the focus of the camera's gaze at, respectively, a shrine in San Francisco for murdered trans women of colour, and a public square demonstration in New York City. The number of voices indicates that the 'discursive coherence' of the transgender voice, previously 'a necessary strategy to combat logics of pathologization' (Anastasia, 2014: 262), gives way to a reformulation, different to the tightly curated, much-documented, individual-focused transitioning trans narrative.

Perhaps signalling the confidence, or the necessary plurality of McDonald's intersectional experience of oppression, the pluralised voice of *Free CeCe!* accords with Andrew Anastasia's recognition of how, 'As transgender studies approaches its second iteration, claiming our discursive voice is less urgent.' Anastasia notes the impact of this second iteration where the trans woman's voice and the transgender cause are less unified or connected: 'Trans* voices can fail to make sense in spectacular ways when our voices no longer provide adequate evidence for the bodies that emit them' (Anastasia, 2014: 263). Anastasia's notion of a conflict between voice and body is an intriguing one, and one way of understanding the pluralisation of a discursive voice in *Free CeCe!* These voice(s) – those that share time with McDonald's own in the documentary – are pivotal to McDonald's experience if we are to make sense of it. The individualised, curated personal storytelling template identified by Fernandes is replaced by a more communitarian, politicised mode.

The difficulty in balancing an individual story with social critique involving several intersectional strands is, however, also arguably a reason for its lukewarm reception by certain film critics during the film's showing at various film festivals. On the one hand, *Free CeCe!* is praised by the LA Film Festival's reviewer Christopher James for its 'moving and interesting' representation of the personalised narrative surrounding McDonald (James, 2016), as well as for the significance of the issues it raises. As Imogen Hay said at the film's showing at the Scottish Queer International Film Festival, the audience had appeared to gather 'not so much to view a film, but to address transphobia, racism and expose the horrors of the American prison system' (Hay, 2017). Hay's observation indicates another of the documentary's functions beyond entertainment: *Free CeCe!* can be said to work as a rallying point for communities of activists and sympathisers to gather around. According to Hay (2017), irrespective of the film's success as a form of entertainment, '... it is difficult to criticize the experience of this film, the conversations it brought up far surpassed seeing the experience as only a screening.'

Conversely, *Free CeCe!*'s value as a communitarian text does appear to undermine its impact if Hay's position is indicative of some critical reaction. Hay (2017) also claims, for example, 'I struggled to follow the path of the documentary, and this lack of focus within the film prompted me to lose mine as a viewer.' On the issue of coherence and the melding of personalisation and larger contexts, James similarly describes an awkward balancing act for the documentary, with *Free CeCe!* being 'at odds with itself. It wants to tell the story of CeCe but it also wants to be a grander examination of the plight of the transgender community as a whole.'

Arguably, this pattern of criticism highlights the challenge of crafting a single, coherent transgender narrative around a subject faced with, and keen to discuss, multiple forms of structural inequalities. Yet it also appears to reflect McDonald's own necessary intentions for the documentary in departing from either an activist-based, single-issue focus or an individualised, apolitical gender-transition narrative, and putting instead her abolitionist-based activism at the forefront of her story, while interspersing it with fragments of a transitioning arc and slice-of-life narrative. Rejecting the idea, in one post-documentary interview, of developing her status as celebrity or brand, McDonald says:

> If I'm a public personality or whatever the case may be, that wasn't my intention. What I am is a black trans woman who is an activist, who is fighting to help the most marginalized, the most targeted ... I'm not trying to produce some public image, or be a 'celebritay,' or any of that.
>
> *(2017: 34)*

By this apparent determination to pluralise the voice and extend the camera's focus beyond the film's subject, as stated in subsequent interviews, McDonald arguably answers some of the questions asked by Kate Nash in her analysis of issues of trust in documentary film-making. Nash for example says,

> Since the truth of the documentary is no longer guaranteed, the documentary-maker's gaze must be interrogated in order to draw attention to the process by which the social actor is transformed into the documentary subject. The concern of such analysis is to interrogate the power of representation. Who is represented in the documentary, who represents them and with what effect?
>
> *(2010: 22)*

Thematically, and in response to these questions, McDonald's input appears to be substantial in what the film both includes and omits. By contrast to the documentary's focus on mass incarceration, for example, the interview with *Rolling Stone* magazine (Erdely, 2014) – uncharacteristically for McDonald in relation to many of her other interviews – appears far more typical of the focus on personal, linear narrative, with harrowing details of McDonald's 'lost' years during adolescence. These accounts are largely absent from both the documentary and interviews such as the one in *Mask Magazine* when McDonald is accompanied by activist and campaigner Katie Burgess (Burgess, 2015), or the one with Griffin-Gracy in the TPOC archival anthology *Trap Door* (2017), where the focus is much more on structural racism, poverty, and mass incarceration. In this respect, McDonald's additional media output is useful for responding to another of Nash's concerns, namely how 'the participant very rarely has a space from which to speak about their involvement in the documentary.' McDonald's supplementary output suggests that the documentary is aligned with her own priorities in terms of narrative.

Abolitionist themes in *Free CeCe!*

It can be argued that the documentary's narrative complexity stems from the multiple issues produced by the McDonald case. This includes the issue of violence against trans women of colour by civilians, but also violence against trans women of colour by the prison industrial complex. Hay's (2017) review reflects a potential conflict with these issues:

> The film seemed not to know what it wanted to be. Was it an expose of the American prison system? A retelling of CeCe's story and its importance? A history of political campaigns to support transgender people? It left me with many moral questions: the justification of carrying a weapon and 'protecting yourself' was presented in a very troubling way, such as in a rally where a woman [in New York, from members of the Trans Women Of Color Collective] shouted to a crowd to carry scissors and to 'use your nails' to fight back, almost seeming to call on more violence in response to transphobia which, as the film already addressed, kills people. In this way, it complicated the issue for me as a viewer. I could see what they were going for, but I still found the way in which things were described as morally questionable.

Hay's discomfort arguably reflects the uncertain waters that are being charted with this documentary in relation to the conceptualising of prison abolition. For example, outside of the documentary and on this potentially underdeveloped topic, scholar and co-founder of the Black Lives Matter movement Patrisse Cullors notes: 'The historical context of abolition is minimally understood, either in today's social movements or in US society more broadly' (2019: 1684). Cullors, in turn, does advocate for the kind of ideas implicit in what is being expressed by McDonald and others throughout the documentary, as a starting point to a more complex discussion on alternative modes of justice. These ideas include, for example, the need 'to abolish prisons, policing, and militarization, which are wielded in the name of "public safety" and "national security"'(Cullors, 2019: 1686). Yet Cullors also addresses, at the next level, the idea of 'reparative justice into our vision for society and community building in the twenty-first century.' Cullors articulates some personalised examples of restorative justice that includes the notion that 'Abolition seeks out restorative practices for all, even when that implies working with the perpetrator of said violence' (Cullors, 2019: 1688). Cullors, as a former victim of abuse, then details an example where, through careful mediation over a period of time, she confronts and establishes a dialogue with the perpetrator of the abuse. She describes this engagement as 'challenging, heart-wrenching, and awkward. But most of all, our meeting was healing. Incredibly healing' (Cullors, 2019: 1694). This sensitive issue of engaging in processes of reparative justice arguably represents the next step in discussions on prison abolition and alternative forms of healing and justice. However, it is entirely absent in *Free CeCe!*. This is most apparent with the extremely limited references to the perpetrators of the original hate crime against McDonald, particularly Molly Shannon Flaherty, who appears to have instigated the original violence by physically assaulting McDonald while also using verbally racist and transphobic abuse. She is later jailed for six months for assault (*Free CeCe*, 2018: 13.06). Arguably, her absence in the documentary reveals a missing 'other half' to a sufficiently developed debate on abolition and reparative justice, as Cullors discusses it, with its implications for both the victim and the perpetrator of hate crimes.

The documentary instead skirts the issue of alternative modes of justice before settling on the well-evidenced argument that McDonald was wrongly imprisoned due to the nature of the trial and the implicitly racist and transphobic attitudes that shaped the prosecution and trial overall. Yet this notion of wrongful arrest is subtly different to the issue of abolitionism, even as the two subjects potentially intersect in McDonald's case. The fleeting nature of this intersection is underlined by the documentary's subsequent movement away from abolitionist ideas about alternative, restorative justice, to a more substantial focus on racism and gender-policing involved in both the prison industrial complex and the family.

On abolition and restorative justice, the documentary briefly interviews trans abolitionist and scholar Eric Stanley, who, like Cullors, suggests a need to discuss alternatives to carceral justice. Stanley asks, 'I think that something that abolition really allows us to do is imagine an entirely different way of relating to each other. What would it mean, what would real justice look like? What would real accountability look like? What would real healing actually feel like to us?' (*Free CeCe*, 2018: 68.06). These questions, in alignment with Cullors' similar reflections, might have been the platform for a deeper exploration of restorative justice as a replacement for carceral justice, linking McDonald too to her original white-supremacist assailant Molly Shannon Flaherty. In turn, they might also have led to pragmatic reflections, similar to those made by Cullors and the Black Lives Matter movement, on defunding the police and finding alternative restorative/transformative treatments for social, psychological, and economic causations and situations in relation to racism and transphobia. At this juncture, *Free CeCe!* might have stabilised around this narrative and become a documentary focused on abolitionism. However, Stanley's questions are left unanswered.

Instead, the documentary shifts its focus to violence against trans women of colour via an interview in the documentary's second half with the mother of Black trans woman Islan Nettles, who was killed in a transphobic attack. The interview focuses on the need to protect trans women of colour from violence (*Free CeCe*, 2018: 73.08), and is discernibly different from Stanley's rhetorical questions, with nothing mentioned about the sensitive issue of alternative forms of treatment for and engagement with violent offenders – including perpetrators of hate crime – against innocent and marginalised people. Separate media coverage of the killing, not referred to in the documentary, in fact highlights how Nettles' parents believe the killer's 12-year sentence for second-degree manslaughter is 'too lenient' (McKinley, 2016). As mentioned in Hay's (2017) critique of the film, the documentary deviates towards the understandable rage of TWOC communities on violence against trans women of colour, as expressed during a public protest. Exemplifying the point made by Hay, however, it is unclear whether the documentary is calling for the prison industrial complex to be shut down, or to protect trans women of colour, for example with additional hate crime legislation. Complicating this issue further is a contribution by film-maker and trans woman of colour Tourmaline, in alignment with Stanley, calling for people to 'challenge the economy of outrage' and to reject the creation of 'disposable lives' through carceral justice. The documentary shifts from expressions of outrage to calls for challenging an economy of outrage without distinguishing between the two.

Prison abolition at a conceptual level in *Free CeCe!*, therefore, as noted by film critic Marlon Wallace, is arguably rendered by these sometimes competing segments to 'just a talking point' (Wallace, 2016). Another major 'talking point' raised in the documentary, as referred to briefly by McDonald, concerns racism within highly resourced, white-centred, mainstream LGBTQI+ organisations. McDonald briefly makes the statement about racism towards the end of *Free CeCe!*, to audience applause, when she is shown speaking publicly at an event. The point is left unexplored, however, and with only the evidence of the documentary for support, this isolated statement is confusing and narratively dissatisfying, given that the only white LGBTQI+ activists we see referenced in the film are Leslie Feinberg, Katie Burgess, Eric Stanley, and legal specialist Chase Strangio. Each of them is shown advocating passionately on behalf of McDonald, with Feinberg briefly incarcerated for her graffiti in support of McDonald on the walls of Minneapolis county jail, while Burgess devotes considerable effort as the organiser of the CeCe Support Committee for McDonald. This is not to question McDonald's claim, however. Outside of the documentary, in a preceding event titled 'Socialism 2014', McDonald engages in an insightful discussion on how one of the most highly resourced LGBTQI+ organisations in the US, the Human Rights Campaign, failed to provide public support for her during her incarceration. McDonald's exchange with the conference chair is a revealing indication of the way mainstream LGBTQI+ organisations appear to distance themselves from issues of racism, poverty, and the prison industrial complex, as they did in the case of CeCe McDonald:

> *Conference chair*: Now, most mainstream larger LGBT groups didn't get involved in your case, groups like the Human Rights Campaign. Why do you think that is, CeCe, and what would you say to them?
>
> *McDonald*: [I would tell them to] 'Fuck off' (Audience laughter) And I say that because I had a really strong support system, the CeCe Support

> Committee, all of you who literally donated and spent time writing letters, and I couldn't give a fuck less about the Human Rights Campaign, cos guess what, I still overcame my obstacle with or without them ... If you don't want to support that, then your existence is really irrelevant.
>
> *(McDonald, 2014: 24.46–27.00)*

I would argue that, while risking overwhelming the documentary further, the insight provided by this exchange at 'Socialism 2014' would have benefited *Free CeCe!*, by connecting intersecting issues of racism and LGBTQI+ activism in relation to McDonald's experience, as briefly raised by her. Instead, talk of abolition splinters into an array of issues, each one deserving substantial focus in its own right, but none receiving the development they require.

Where the documentary succeeds most convincingly, in relation to debates on carceral justice, is the simple exposure of prison's inhumanity as well as its particular harms to incarcerated trans women. From the beginning of *Free CeCe!*, it is evident that McDonald's transness is managed and framed in relation to the justice system in ways that are detrimental to her mental health, her safety, and her ability to get justice. In the latter case, this begins with the media coverage, where the news reports replayed in the documentary reveal the bias of suppressing her trans identity, for example, 'St Paul man arrested in fatal stabbing at bar ... A twenty-three year-old man was arrested on suspicion of murder' (*Free CeCe*, 2018: 1.55). McDonald's prison-related narrative similarly highlights the ideological dominance of cisheteropatriarchy, with the systematic attempt to occlude her transness, partly by establishing prohibitions exempt to other prisoners. As McDonald says,

> They still view us as men, and they feel like we aren't entitled to those things that women have ... That I couldn't wear my clothes a certain way ... shorts, or ... that accentuates my body ... or curves ... A lot of things that they did to take away my transness, and turn me into a man ... so I can fit in or be safe.
>
> *(Free CeCe, 2018: 39.43)*

The regime McDonald endures in prison conforms to studies elsewhere, reflecting trans women's experiences in men's prisons. More broadly, it undermines the notion of either a trans-friendly paradigm or a justice system that does anything other than debilitate those in its control. Consistent with McDonald's reflections in *Free CeCe!*, trans abolitionist campaigners Janetta Johnson and Toshio Meronek, for example, note how,

> Inside, trans women are routinely referred to using male pronouns. This verbal anti-trans violence, which many trans girls experienced outside, only gets worse inside prison. If someone lived as a woman prior to prison,

> misgendering them feels like an attack, and their basic instinct is to get ready to fight. This feeling of always having to be on the defensive is mentally and physically draining.
>
> *(2015: 262–263)*

The effect of various prison prohibitions on McDonald's mental health, in alignment with the broader analysis by Johnson and Meronek (2015), are reflected in McDonald's recollection, 'It was really depressing ... I feel like they tried to make you hate yourself as someone who's not conforming' (*Free CeCe*, 2018: 42.29). One particular situation that appears to have affected an already traumatised McDonald during her trial involves her being placed in solitary confinement for three months prior to her actual sentence, officially for her own safety as a trans woman in danger from the male prisoners. The documentary suggests the solitary confinement affected her mental health during this time, arguably exacerbating her own trauma and desperation, and in turn affecting the outcome of the trial via the inconsistent evidence she initially gives under investigation (*Free CeCe*, 2018: 23.11). Johnson and Meronek (2015: 262) note how solitary confinement of trans women is a common occurrence, ostensibly presented as a means of protecting the trans prisoner but effectively punishing them for their gender non-conformity:

> A study of California inmates found that 59 percent of trans women held in men's prisons were sexually abused, vs. 4 percent of non-trans prisoners. Reporting these assaults can elicit retaliation, including time in solitary confinement, which is justified by prison administrators as a 'safety measure' for the good of the trans person.

Overall, *Free CeCe!* can be said to succeed as a case study in consolidating other research by revealing the inadequacy of existing institutions to cater for trans identities. In relation to abolitionist themes, this is problematic, in that it suggests the solution might be for prisons to better accommodate trans female identity, a reformist response hardly in keeping with the general abolitionist position of McDonald and the theme of *Free CeCe!*. Again, more time and case studies focused on the inherent violence of prison might have benefitted the abolitionist position referenced in the documentary. Yet to return to Renov's (2004) appraisal of new forms of autobiographical documentaries, *Free CeCe!* also encapsulates how 'Tonally, the work is tremendously diverse – celebratory, elegiac, solemn, delirious – but it is almost always affirmational of a self culturally specific and publicly defined' (2004: xvii). In this vein, *Free CeCe!*'s value as a documentary related to abolitionism can also be seen as providing a platform for subsequent discussions, rather than producing solutions. True to Renov's (2004) broader observation, 'the work is frequently engaged in community building and is deeply dialogic.' The issue of coherence and multiple strands is arguably a necessity for this dynamic, and at the very least, a dialogue with the audience is established to address the point made by Cullors outside of the documentary. Cullors, for example, says, 'The historical context of abolition is minimally understood, either in today's social movements or in US society more broadly' (2019: 1684). *Free CeCe!* arguably embodies this confusion of subtly different ways of understanding the abolitionist concept.

The gaze of CeCe McDonald: Self-actualisation, solidarity and the question of 'whose feminism is it anyway?'

On Kate Nash's urging of how 'the documentary-maker's gaze must be interrogated', we also see parallels with Stefanie van de Peer's adaptation of Gaze theory in relation to feminist documentary making in the developing world. This includes, according to van de Peer, 'conceptions of the reciprocity of an intersubjective look between spectator, subject and director that results – through the unfolding of histories and stories enfolded by subject-positions – into a feminist solidarity' (2017: 3). The Gaze of CeCe McDonald, streamed through the visual medium of a documentary constructed by multiple participants, is resultingly complex. Ultimately, however, the documentary has McDonald at its centre, and a subject's arc is portrayed with a Gaze that acquires increasing confidence and prestige in the public realm as the documentary continues with a discernible arc involving the subject. Simultaneously, the anti-neoliberal themes underscore how a personal arc, one involving a process of self-actualisation, can be depicted without it becoming an example of neoliberal-themed, curated storytelling. In this respect, McDonald's arc embodies the position stated by bell hooks, who on the importance of self-actualisation within solidarity-based movements, says:

> Certainly, collective black female experience has been about the struggle to survive in diaspora. It is the intensity of that struggle, the fear of failure (as we face daily the reality that many black people do not and are not surviving) that has led many black women thinkers, especially within feminist movement, to wrongly assume that strength in unity can only exist if difference is suppressed and shared experience is highlighted … [but] Opposition is not enough. In that vacant space after one has resisted there is still the necessity to become – to make oneself anew.
>
> *(1992: 51)*

Free CeCe! appears to recognise the significance of self-actualisation within a broader activist setting, as articulated by hooks. In the construction of the personal arc, McDonald's initial reflections are in a casual setting, with McDonald dressed in sweat pants, tank top, and plastic sandals in a suburban location.

The overall look is unremarkable; she could be anyone. A shift then occurs as the events of her incarceration are described and analysed, before the documentary climaxes, first with McDonald having become a stylishly attired public speaker, and then as the subject of an art exhibition called 'Whose Feminism Is It Anyway?' The protagonist's final scene captures a symbolic transformation, concluding in the prestigious setting of the fine arts.

The symbolism of transformation into an articulate and politicised speaker on social justice is consolidated by the recurring symbol of the phoenix, which McDonald adopts for an elaborate tattoo to celebrate her freedom (*Free CeCe*, 2018: 56.49). This personal sentiment is re-affirmed towards the documentary's end at the gallery in which the exhibition 'Whose Feminism Is It Anyway?' takes place. McDonald again describes her identification with the mythical bird,

> This creature embodies resilience, it embodies me throughout my transitioning ... I am a person who overcame these tribulations that people thought were going to keep me down. I refuse to become a statistic. I refuse to become another victim. I refuse to let someone determine my life.
>
> *(Free CeCe, 2018: 85.00)*

Community, solidarity, and a demand for social change are encompassed in the significations of the exhibition at the film's end. Dressed in a shining toga with a pair of wings emerging from her back, McDonald's depiction is subversively resonant of the national female – and white – personification of the United States, Columbia, as represented by the symbol of the Hollywood film studios. In the documentary footage, additional poses show McDonald holding a flamed torch, and in another image, a ribbon stating 'visibility is not enough'. The image of McDonald at this climax is in fact from a collection of three 'transgendered women activists 'committed to direct action and civil disobedience' (Bowers, 2016). These appear to occupy centre stage in a photo installation titled 'Trans Liberation'. The three trans women '[stand] in powerful poses', a hammer hanging ominously from McDonald's belt, while the other trans models hold a rifle and a brick, respectively. Overall, the exhibition, with its slogans of solidarity and TWOC focus, appears to challenge the white-centred and middle-class cisgendered structuring of feminism in the Anglophone Global North, in reflection of Alison Phipps' observation that 'White and privileged women dominate mainstream feminism' (2020: 6).

The combination of a symbol of liberty with a rejection of the neoliberal-aligned conception of trans liberty, namely visibility, contrasts with the position advocated separately by McBride and Mock. For example, in *Redefining Realness*, Mock says, 'I believe that telling our stories, first to ourselves and then to one another and the world, is a revolutionary act ... I hope that my being *real* with you will help empower you to step into who you are and encourage you to share yourself with those around you' (2014: xviii). For Mock perhaps most of all, visibility and the sharing of narratives will arguably liberate trans women of colour in an act of individual empowerment. For McDonald, in this final image of the documentary especially, the individualised connection with the phoenix and the idea of rebirth is balanced with a call to arms for feminist solidarity. As well as the claim of personal resilience, she says, 'We need to learn to stick with each other. Stick up for each other. Empower each other as women. To move with our heads held high' (*Free CeCe*, 2018: 85.00).

The title of the exhibition, 'Whose Feminism Is It Anyway?', in consolidation of this theme, connects to the tradition of radical feminism within trans studies too. It shares, for example, the position expressed by trans feminist Emi Koyama, herself following in a tradition that questions the inclusiveness and unity of feminism in the Anglophone Global North. Koyama analyses the relationship between feminism and trans identity and how the terms 'feminism' and 'sisterhood' exclude 'racial equality, economic justice and freedom of gender expression' (2020: 737). In *Free CeCe!*, the invocation of an intersectional, Black feminism highlights the connection of the documentary's central theme with the one addressed by Koyama. In alignment with Koyama's essay, McDonald ends the documentary challenging a middle-class and white-centred mainstream feminism and LGBTQI+ politics. Simultaneously, she subverts the implicitly white iconography of the US. Dressed in the elegant shining toga, she has replaced an originally white-centred symbol for the USA with one re-imagined as a trans woman of colour, offering a new iconography of the racially oppressed for the country.

Conclusion

CeCe McDonald's story is part of a bigger picture involving social movements that demand structural changes to the USA's classist and racist neoliberal society. The iconography of the Stonewall rioters Marsha P. Johnson, Sylvia Rivera, and Miss Major Griffin-Gracy is significant here. Since her emergence as a public figure, McDonald has consistently advocated for their application in relation to a number of forces at play. One is the potential impact of class in alignment with race, another is the gatekeeping that decides who gets to be seen in mainstream discourse. It is also worth noting Mock's statement, 'I have been held up consistently as a token, as the "right" kind of trans woman (educated, able-bodied, attractive, articulate, heteronormative)' (2014: xvii). To this list of characteristics, one can add ideological conformity. In this respect, the divide between McDonald and more lifestyle-focused and neoliberal-aligned trans celebrities exemplifies, to a degree, an analysis by Slavoj Žižek on the 'discourse of 'resistance' (2012: 84), regarding how in 'late capitalism ... political struggle proper is transformed into the cultural struggle for the recognition of marginal identities and the tolerance of differences' with an accompanying 'tension between content and form' (Žižek, 1999: 262). Mock and McBride, in their Clintonian moderation, can be said to exemplify the triumph of form, or style, over content. McDonald, by contrast, embodies in her activism and through *Free CeCe!* a coalitional, communitarian project of numerous voices, one that subordinates the cult of the exceptional individual while combining resistance with ideas for structural change.

References

Alexander, M. (2012). *The New Jim Crow: Mass Incarceration in the Age of Colorblindness*. New York: The New Press.

Anastasia, A. (2014). Voice. *Transgender Studies Quarterly*, *1*(1–2), 262–263.

Bowers, A. (2016). Whose feminism is it anyway? https://www.andrewkreps.com/exhibitions/andrea-bowers/exhibition-views

Burgess, K. (2015). CeCe McDonald and Katie Burgess discuss prisoner support. Interview with Hanna Hurr. The Fling Issue, *Mask Magazine*. July.

Chanan, M. (2007). *The Politics of Documentary*. London: British Film Institute.

Cullors, P. (2019). Abolition and reparations: Histories of resistance, transformative justice, and accountability. *Harvard Law Review*, *132*(6), 1684.

Davis, A. Y. (2003). *Are Prisons Obsolete?* New York: Seven Stories Press.

Davis, M. (1995) Hell factories in the field: A prison-industrial complex. *The Nation*, *260*(7), 229–234.

Erdely, S. R. (2014). The Transgender Crucible. *Rolling Stone*. 30 July.

Fernandes, S. (2017). *Curated Stories: The Uses and Misuses of Storytelling*. New York: Oxford University Press.

Free CeCe! (2018). Directed by Jacqueline Gares, featuring CeCe McDonald. Jac Gares Media.

Gares, J. (2025). *Free CeCe!* documentary. https://www.freececedocumentary.com

Hay, I. (2017). Film review: Free CeCe! – in association with the Scottish Queer International Film Festival. *Qmunicate*. 25 October.

hooks, b. (1992). Is Paris burning? In hooks, b. (Ed.), *Black Looks: Race and Representation*. Boston, MA: South End Press, 145–156.

James, C. (2016). LA Film Festival review: 'Free CeCe' powerfully chronicles transgender movement. 3 June.

Johnson, J., and Meronek, T. (2015). Custody's long shadow: Reentry support as abolitionist work. In E. A. Stanley and N. Smith (Eds.), *Captive Genders: Trans Embodiment and the Prison Industrial Complex*. Edinburgh: AK Press, 261–268.

Koyama, E. (2020). Whose feminism is it anyway? The unspoken racism of the trans inclusion debate. *The Sociological Review Monographs*, *68*(4), 735–744.

Lewis, A. J. (2017). Trans history in a moment of danger: Organizing within and beyond 'visibility' in the 1970s. In R. Gossett, E. Stanley, and J. Burton (Eds.), *Trap Door: Trans Cultural Production and the Politics of Visibility*. Boston, MA: MIT Press, 57–90.

McBride, S. (2018). *Tomorrow Will Be Different: Love, Loss, and The Fight for Trans Equality*. New York: Crown Archetype.

McDonald, C. (2014). The struggle for trans liberation: A conversation with CeCe McDonald. Socialism 2014 [event]. *WeAreManyMedia*. 21 August. youtube.com/watch?v=emx5iHwbPOg.

McDonald, C. (2017). Cautious living: Black trans women and the politics of documentation.' In R. Gossett, E. Stanley, and J. Burton (Eds.), *Trap Door: Trans Cultural Production and the Politics of Visibility*. Boston, MA: MIT Press, 23–38.

McKinley, Jr., J. C. (2016, 19 April). Man sentenced to 12 years in beating death of transgender woman. *The New York Times*. https://www.nytimes.com/2016/04/20/nyregion/man-sentenced-to-12-years-in-beating-death-of-transgender-woman.html
Mock, J. (2014). *Redefining Realness: My Path to Womanhood, Identity, Love, and So Much More*. New York: Atria Books.
Mock, J. (2016). Janet Mock discusses her HBO documentary, 'The Trans List'. *Build Series*. https://www.youtube.com/watch?v=PgXqNiFAqRE
Mock, J. (2018). *Surpassing Certainty: What My Twenties Taught Me*. New York: Atria Books.
Nash, K. (2010). Exploring power and trust in documentary: A study of Tom Zubrycki's Molly and Mobarak. *Studies in Documentary Film*, 4(1), 21–33.
Phipps, A. (2020). *Me, Not You: The Trouble with Mainstream Feminism*. Manchester: Manchester University Press.
Renov, M. (2004). *The Subject of Documentary*. Minneapolis: University of Minnesota Press.
Van de Peer, S. (2017). *Negotiating Dissidence: The Pioneering Women of Arab Documentary*. Edinburgh: Edinburgh University Press.
Vitulli, E. W. (2014). Prison industrial complex in the United States. *Transgender Studies Quarterly*, *1* (1–2), 162–164.
Wallace, M. (2016). Movie review – Free CeCe (Portland Film Festival). *The M Report*. 31 August.
Žižek, S. (1999). *The Ticklish Subject: The Absent Centre of Political Ontology*. London: Verso.
Žižek, S. (2012 [2002]). *Welcome to the Desert of the Real*. London: Verso.

6

ADDRESSING JURY STIGMA TOWARDS TRANSGENDER VICTIMS OF HATE CRIMES

Amrik Singh Roudh

Introduction

At the time of writing, only race and religion are provided with extra protection under aggravated hate crime laws in England and Wales, with higher sentence maxima (Sentencing Council Guidelines, 2019). The Law Commission (2020) proposed that the characteristics of transgender identity, sexual orientation, and disability should be included to achieve parity and to reflect the extra harm experienced by victims from these groups. Aggravated hate crime offences have sentence maxima of at least two years, i.e., above the powers of magistrate courts, who can only deal with offences carrying a maximum of six months custody. Therefore, under the new proposals, transphobic, homophobic, biphobic, and disability aggravated hate crimes would involve trials by jury in Crown Courts. However, LGBT+ people are under-represented in UK juries, largely due to jurors being invited solely from the electoral register and also due to the fact that they experience significantly higher rates of mobility issues, unemployment, and homelessness (Lever, 2017). For this chapter, transgender is defined according to Scottish Law, i.e., an umbrella term which includes (a) transvestism, transsexualism, and intersexuality, (b) those that have changed their gender, and (c) any other gender identity that is not the standard male or female gender identity. This is inclusive of people with non-binary or gender-queer genders, or those who are agender, as well as any individuals who do not identify with the sex or gender they were assigned at birth.

US and Canadian studies with mock-jurors have shown significantly higher levels of stigma towards transgender victims compared to cisgender victims, which is also associated with significantly lower conviction rates (Ellingwood

DOI: 10.4324/9781003564928-8

et al., 2022; Miller and London, 2021). However, no mock-jury studies have explored prejudice towards transgender victims (transprejudice) based on UK hate crime laws, although jurors are required to be unbiased (Daly and Pattenden, 2005). Furthermore, there are no solution-focused studies investigating any prejudice reduction strategies. This chapter draws on research which sought to address these gaps by exploring prejudice reduction via inter-group contact. In a series of three mock-juror studies (N = 1623), the research compared the prejudice reduction effects of inter-group contact on jury-eligible participant decisions in mock-jury groups described as LGBT+ diverse, with cisgender-heterosexual control groups. A transphobically aggravated hate crime case scenario was designed to show evidence of guilt based on UK hate crime laws (Sentencing Council Guidelines, 2019).

This chapter will show how both transprejudice and victim blame levels were significantly lower towards the transgender female victim in LGBT+ representative groups compared to non-LGBT+ representative groups, while guilty verdicts, agreement with hate crime laws, defendant blame, and perceived victim suffering were all significantly higher. The findings have implications for homophobic and biphobic hate crime trials via direct inter-group contact effects and could also help boost the participation of minorities in jury service and public trust in the jury system.

Evidence and impact of mock-juror prejudice against transgender victims

To date, there is a dearth of research, with only six studies that have explored the impact of mock-juror bias or stigma towards transgender victims of hate crimes (Ringger, 2021). Blackham (2006) found that amongst their sample of 120 US participants, the rape of a transgender victim was rated as less serious than the rape of a victim with an unknown gender, and a transgender victim was rated more blameworthy. Thomas et al. (2016) identified that transprejudice predicted victim blame more for a transgender victim of grievous bodily harm compared to a (gender-unspecified) control victim amongst 311 US mock-jurors. However, as their study did not specify participants be jury-eligible, it is difficult to compare their findings with mock-juror studies.

Miller and London (2021) recruited 368 jury-eligible, US-based community volunteers and had them read a summary of an alleged child sexual abuse case between a male teacher and an adolescent victim. When the victim was described as cisgender compared to transgender, mock-jurors were more likely to convict the defendant and rate the defendant less credible and the victim more credible. Michalski et al. (2022) found their US mock-jurors (N = 233) rendered more lenient verdicts and increased victim blame in their transgender condition compared to their control condition. However, their case scenario was that of attempted murder with an outdated transgender panic defence, making it difficult to generalise to the majority of hate crimes.

Ellingwood et al. (2022) recently showed a victim's sexual and gender identities can result in significant differences in verdicts using an alleged aggravated sexual assault case. Mock-jurors (375 Canadian undergraduates) delivered significantly more guilty verdicts when the victim was male or female compared to transgender male (transgender female identity was not addressed in their research), although findings are not generalisable to non-sexual crimes, particularly under the different English and Welsh jury systems and laws. Finally, Carter et al. (2023), amongst their sample of 223 US undergraduates, found male mock-jurors perceived rape against transgender male or female victims as significantly less severe, which negatively impacted on the rate of not guilty verdicts compared to a cisgender male or female. However, no studies have tested any prejudice reduction strategies in the context of mock-jury research. The research in this chapter explored participant transprejudice levels towards transgender victims in heterogeneous and homogenous mock-jury groups and the impact on guilty verdicts.

The additional benefits of diverse juries

Studies on public opinions in the US have shown the general public view verdicts and especially convictions of minority defendants as more legitimate when juries contain minority jurors (Ellis and Diamond, 2003; Wilkenfeld, 2004). In a New Zealand study, Young et al. (2001) concluded that the diversity of knowledge, perspectives, and personal experiences of more representative juries enhanced the common sense and competency of a jury as the fact-finders – a finding that can also be extrapolated to UK juries.

Mock-jury studies comparing racially diverse juries, to ensure representation of minorities, have been shown to reduce racial bias in verdicts and improve group cooperation during deliberation (Sommers, 2006). Compared to all White juries, racially diverse juries deliberated longer, made fewer mistakes, and focused more on the facts of the case. Race, gender, and ethnic diversity have also been shown to increase the quality of discussions and decisions, enhancing innovation and problem-solving (Kirchmeyer and Cohen, 1992). Where these characteristics overlap in victims with intersecting identities, there could be even greater benefits with such diverse juries.

Furthermore, Lever (2017) argued that diverse juries would also positively impact on the way cases are treated by the police and the criminal justice system (CJS). Currently, under-represented juries are the norm in England and Wales, with research needed to explore how they may result in injustice to victims of crimes in terms of unfairly lower conviction rates. Sommers (2006) found mock-jurors in racially diverse groups were more receptive to discussing bias than jurors in all-White juries, even when the

Black jurors were not active in deliberations (Sommers and Adekanmbi, 2008). Sommers (2006) had 200 community mock-jurors deliberate on the trial of a Black defendant and found White mock-jurors in diverse juries: cited more case facts; made fewer errors; were more amenable to discussions regarding racism; and even prior to any discussions, were more lenient towards the Black defendant, showing that the effects of diversity do not just occur due to information exchange.

Ellis and Diamond (2003) studied 320 jury-eligible members of the public and found that in the racially diverse juries, mock-jurors: delivered more accurate decisions; made fewer inaccurate statements during deliberations; spent more time deliberating; discussed a wider range of facts and perspectives; rated the homogeneous jury as less fair when the verdict was guilty; corrected each other's factual inaccuracies more often; and outperformed all-White juries on all deliberation measures.

Although the advantages observed in these studies were based largely on racially diverse juries, we can generally expect jury decisions to be fairer in diverse juries compared to homogenous juries as these effects occurred even when the minority jurors were not active in deliberations (Sommers and Adekanmbi, 2008) suggesting inter-group contact effects. More diverse juries and increased jury diversity have also been recommended as a solution to reduce the problem of juror bias (Levinson and Young, 2009).

Additionally, Carbone and Plaut (2013) have argued that diverse juries help reflect the voices of a community and stimulate psychological and behavioural benefits for those who participate, supporting their civic identity. Jury service can engender a sense of civic pride and satisfaction analogous to having the right to vote in elections (Carbone and Plaut, 2013). According to Gastil et al. (2010), an invitation to undertake jury service can garner a sense of political efficacy and the belief that one is competent and their participation matters, which can potentially translate into other forms of political participation (Langton and Cohen, 2005). Consolini (1992) also showed that jury participation can encourage those that have been historically alienated and marginalised more into public life and discourse.

Despite all these advantages, the problem remains that LGBT+ people are under-represented in UK juries as a consequence of solely using the electoral register for recruiting potential jurors. This constitutes institutional stigma (Hatzenbuehler, 2016), i.e., an unjust recruitment policy that denies and fails to protect the equal rights of minorities to equal jury participation, and of victims to experience less biased and fairer verdicts in more representative juries. Individuals of different minority backgrounds sometimes process the same information in different ways, often reaching different conclusions, hence procedures that exclude certain groups can result in partiality (Adams and Lane, 1998).

In many countries, these difficulties seem to have a particularly acute impact on transgender people who, despite their over-representation in trials as defendants, are under-represented as jurors, as well as lawyers, judges, and court staff (Israel, 1998). Jury selection has become a political and legal struggle for African-Caribbean, South Asian, and other minority groups in Britain (Enright, 1991). Asian, African, and Native American minorities in the US have also challenged their under-representation on juries (Alschuler, 1995).

Inadequate jury diversity also undermines the appearance of justice (Ellis and Diamond, 2003) and ultimately confidence in the CJS. According to Rawls (2005), fulfilling public duties, especially those as important as jury service and the doing of justice, confirms one's status as a full member of society and as a trusted member of one's community. The judicial system is meant to reflect judgements as a community and to bind communities collectively and individually, to promote solidarity and social cohesion. This is not possible 'if, however unintentionally, significant numbers of our population have little if any chance of contributing to those decisions themselves, or of seeing others like them doing so, either' (Lever, 2017: 6). One of the main advantages of trials by jury is the greater scope for democratic participation that they create, which is lost in homogenous juries. The research in this chapter considered one approach to addressing this.

Inter-group contact as a prejudice reduction strategy

Promoting positive inter-group contact (Allport et al., 1954) is one of the most effective prejudice reduction methods (Pettigrew et al., 2011) particularly for prejudice towards LGBT+ people (Paluck et al., 2021). A plethora of research shows inter-group contact reduces stigma towards a wide range of marginalised identities, including all five hate crime identities in England and Wales; race, religion, sexual orientation, gender identity, and disability (Cotten-Huston and Waite, 1999; Lemmer and Wagner, 2015; Marinucci et al., 2021; Pettigrew and Tropp, 2006; Pettigrew et al., 2011; Smith et al., 2019).

Positive inter-group contact lowers prejudice by identifying salient commonalities with outgroup members and reducing inter-group anxiety and threat (Stephan and Stephan, 1985); by reducing uncertainty (Blascovich et al., 2001); by reducing negative stereotypes and increasing trust (Lee et al., 2014); by enhancing knowledge about the outgroup; and by increasing empathy and perspective-taking (Swart et al., 2011). Therefore, this research also explored the wider impact of inter-group contact on participants' evaluations of victim blame, perceived victim suffering, and support for transgender hate crime laws.

White et al. (2014) explored religious inter-group bias with Christian and Muslim participants, showing that inter-group stigma was reduced in the experimental conditions with effects lasting over a year. West et al. (2017) showed contact with transgender people was also associated with decreased transphobia and with increased support for transgender civil rights. Through the use of two unique national surveys, Tadlock et al. (2017) showed the positive influence of contact with transgender people on attitudes about transgender people and transgender rights (Acker, 2017). Despite these positive and encouraging findings, to date, very little research has examined whether contact with transgender individuals can reduce the high levels of stigma directed toward transgender people (Paluck et al., 2021). However, this experimental procedure is limited as many people lack outgroup experience or contact with the transgender community and are more likely to benefit from secondary transfer effects to reduce their prejudices.

Secondary transfer effects of inter-group contact

Pettigrew (2009) described secondary transfer effects as the phenomenon of generalisation of positive attitudes transferred to additional stigmatised outgroups not necessarily involved in the original contact encounter. Norton and Herek (2013, N = 2281) reported higher ratings of transgender people on a 'feeling thermometer' by cisgender subjects who reported past contact with gay and lesbian people, providing evidence for secondary transfer effects between sexual and gender minorities. Norton and Herek (2013) reasoned that since gay, lesbian, and transgender people are stigmatised for a common reason, often associated with violating male and female gender norms, increasing contact with gay and lesbian people will transfer into less prejudice towards transgender people.

The effect of contact with homosexuals has been found to transfer and lower stigma towards transgender people (Hoffarth and Hodson; 2018; Tadlock et al., 2017). Tee and Hegarty (2006) conducted a study in the UK with 151 undergraduate students, showing prior contact with gay and lesbian people was also a significant predictor for support of transgender civil rights via secondary transfer effects.

Imagined inter-group contact

One of the most significant recent advances in the field of inter-group contact is the finding that simply *imagining* a positive inter-group contact can also have some of the same benefits of *actual* inter-group contact. The imagined contact task asks participants to simply close their eyes and for two minutes imagine talking to a specified outgroup member where the interaction is positive, relaxed, and comfortable (Harwood et al., 2011). Research shows this can evoke the same emotional, cognitive, and behavioural effects experienced in actual inter-group interactions (Hewstone and Swart, 2011). A meta-analysis of imagined contact studies (Miles and Crisp, 2014) showed statistical support for both prejudice reduction and increasing intentions to behave positively towards specified outgroups. Imagined contact with gay individuals has also been shown to reduce prejudice towards transgender people (Hoffarth and Hodson, 2018).

An increasing number of studies have shown that imagined contact: reduces inter-group bias and improves both explicit and implicit outgroup attitudes (Miles and Crisp, 2014; Turner et al., 2007); promotes the projection of positive traits onto the outgroup (Stathi and Crisp, 2008); reduces stereotype threat (Abrams et al., 2008); and reduces inter-group disgust (Hodson et al., 2015). Furthermore, these effects also generalise from an individual outgroup member to the whole outgroup (Stathi et al., 2011) and benefit people with higher levels of prejudice most (West et al., 2017). Research also shows the longitudinal effectiveness of imagined contact in severe forms of discrimination (Vezzali et al., 2020). Moreover, imagined contact has the advantages of being an inexpensive and practical experimental means of reducing inter-group prejudice and is especially useful where direct contact is difficult or unethical to set up (Turner et al., 2007).

The current research

In this chapter's study, the impact of secondary transfer effects of imagined contact with a gay male juror or a heterosexual male juror on transprejudice levels towards a transgender female victim in four transphobic hate crime cases is presented. Findings are part of a PhD project, completed in 2024 (Singh, 2025).

Measuring transprejudice via the social distance measure

Bogardus's (1938) social distance measure was chosen as the measure of transgender stigma as this has been widely applied and adapted to examine attitudes toward LGB+, and transgender people specifically (Hinrichs and Rosenberg, 2002). This is a 6-item, 6-point Likert scale measuring desired social distancing levels from LGBT+ individuals. Social distancing levels have been found to be related to prejudicial and negative attitudes towards LGBT+ people (Kushnirovich, 2020), and are also commonly used internationally as a proxy measure for stigma (Mathias et al., 2018) as well as a proxy measure of transgender stigma (Tompkins et al., 2015). Research has reaffirmed the scale's reliability, validity, and merits (Parrillo and Donoghue, 2005). Orosz et al. (2016) recently showed the scale has good internal consistencies concerning LGBT+ groups (α pre-test measure = 0.90; α post-test measure = 0.94). Winter et al. (2009) adapted the social distancing scale to measure the prejudicial and social distancing attitudes of 841 undergraduates towards transgender women in seven countries, including the UK. Furthermore, King et al. (2009) also found that decreased social distance was also associated with increased support for

TABLE 6.1 Design of study 1, showing the experimental groups (1–4) and control groups (5–8)

Group	*Offence: Common assault or actual bodily harm*	*Type of offence: Aggravated or base*	*Imagined contact: Gay male or heterosexual male*
1	Common assault	Aggravated	Gay Male
2	Common assault	Base	Gay Male
3	Actual bodily harm	Aggravated	Gay Male
4	Actual bodily harm	Base	Gay Male
5	Common assault	Aggravated	Hetero Male
6	Common assault	Base	Hetero Male
7	Actual bodily harm	Aggravated	Hetero Male
8	Actual bodily harm	Base	Hetero Male

equal opportunities, for transgender civil rights, and anti-discrimination laws, making this measure well suited to hate crime research.

Design

The mixed (between and within subjects) design resulted in eight groups as shown in Table 6.1. The within-subjects factor was pre-test and post-test social distance levels.

Procedure

In study one only, all participants were also initially asked to complete the pre-test social distance measure (Bogardus, 1938).

Step 1: Participants completed the imagined contact task (adapted from the methodology of Harwood et al., 2011) for their assigned group (imagined contact with a gay male juror or a heterosexual male juror). Participants were asked to imagine they were part of a mock-jury with a gay male or heterosexual male juror by imagining sitting next to them in the jury room and having a short positive conversation with them.

Step 2: Next, participants were shown the crime vignette relevant to their assigned groups (common assault [CA] or actual bodily harm [ABH] case summary). The victim was described as a transgender woman.

Step 3: Participants were asked a manipulation check question (to check participants had read the gender of the victim) and then had to answer the verdict question as guilty or not guilty for their assigned offence type (aggravated or base).

Step 4: Finally, participants were required to complete the remaining measures:

victim blame, defendant blame, perceived victim suffering, the sentence enhancement agreement measure, and the post-test social distance measure.

Findings

Imagined contact with a gay male juror showed significantly reduced post-test transprejudice levels in all four offence groups (common assault, aggravated common assault, actual bodily harm, and aggravated actual bodily harm). Imagined contact with a heterosexual male juror showed no significantly reduced post-test transprejudice levels in any of the four offence groups. Figure 6.1 shows the data for the offence of common assault.

Impact on guilty verdict rates

The chi-square analysis also showed participants delivered more guilty verdict rates in all four gay male imagined contact groups, compared to the heterosexual male imagined contact groups, although this was only significantly higher for the offence with the lowest maximum sentence (common assault).

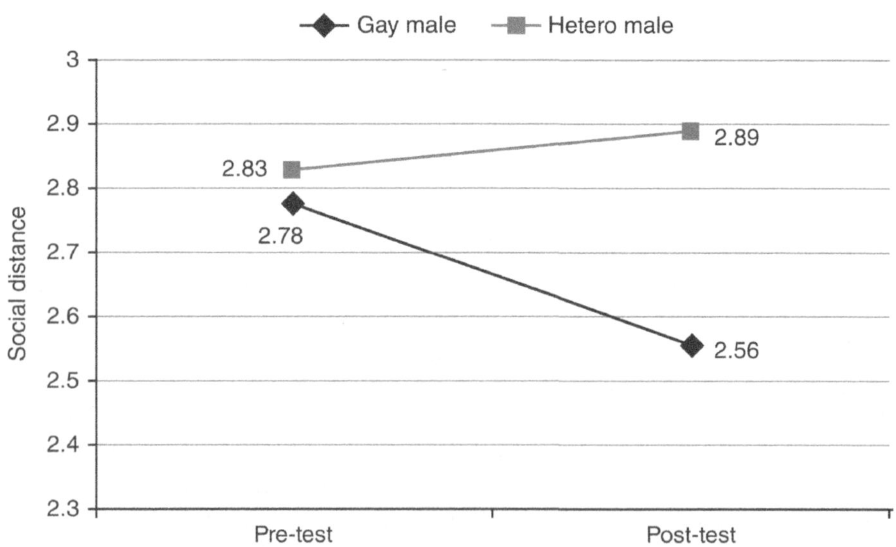

FIGURE 6.1 Within-subject social distance levels towards transgender women.

TABLE 6.2 Impact of imagined contact with a gay male juror compared to a male juror on measures in the base offences

Measure of the base offences	*Finding*
Common assault	
Sentence enhancement	Significantly higher
Perceived victim suffering	Significantly higher
Actual bodily harm	
Defendant blame	Significantly higher
Sentence enhancement agreement	Significantly higher
Perceived victim-suffering	Significantly higher
Victim blame	Significantly higher

Table 6.2 shows the wider impact of imagined contact on the measures in the base offences.

A follow up study corroborated the effects observed herein, in that social distance scores were also found to be significantly lower in both the gay male (pro-victim and pro-defendant) jury foreperson groups compared to the corresponding heterosexual male jury foreperson groups. A further third study also showed that social distance was again found to be significantly lower in the gay female groups, compared to the corresponding female pro-victim and pro-defendant groups. Participants delivered significantly higher guilty verdict rates in the pro-victim, gay female group compared to the pro-victim, female group.

Discussion

This research found that participant transprejudice was significantly lower in the gay groups compared to the heterosexual groups (N = 1623) and that guilty verdict rates were also significantly higher. Based on these findings, juror prejudice towards a transgender female victim of such hate crimes could be expected to be significantly lower in an LGBT+ diverse jury compared to a non-LGBT+ diverse jury, and verdicts fairer as a result. These are two of the most significant benefits of having more LGBT+ diverse juries, particularly in such sensitive hate crime cases. Similarly, Tompkins et al. (2015) showed that imagined contact with transgender individuals resulted in participants showing a similar significant post-test level increase in their willingness to socially engage with transgender individuals, as shown in this study via imagined contact with a gay co-mock-juror.

The transgender population comprises around 15% of the LGBT+ community (UK Census, 2021) therefore juries are significantly more likely to have a cisgender LGB+ juror rather than a transgender juror. Moreover, this research shows that such effects can start to occur within a relatively short time-frame, following the commonly employed imagined contact task (Crisp et al., 2009) which took approximately 20 minutes to complete. Additionally, 9% of participants identified as LGBT+, so for 91% of participants in the control groups, imagined contact with the heterosexual male did not constitute inter-group contact and therefore, as expected, there were no prejudice reduction effects in the control groups.

When juries are under-representative of minority groups, this keeps juridic power in the hands of majority groups and denies minority groups an opportunity to voice their opinions and perspective and decreases their chances of accessing fair justice. Furthermore, not only do the public have more confidence in diverse juries (Ellis and Diamond, 2003) but they have been shown to make fairer decisions via increased perspective-taking by other jurors (Sommers and Adekanmbi, 2008). Juror verdicts should be as unbiased as possible and these findings support the need for more LGBT+ representative juries in LGBT+ hate crime cases and cases involving victims with such intersecting characteristics. The findings of this study positively support the inclusion of more LGBT+ representative juries, which could help reduce the higher attrition rates in jury service noted amongst minority groups.

Although this study only specifically measured social distance towards transgender women, it is likely that such imagined contact could also significantly increase participants' willingness to socially engage with transgender men and LGBT+ individuals generally. In line with inter-group contact research, such effects would be expected to also have direct inter-group effects of stigma reduction if the victim was gay and the target of a homophobic or biphobic hate crime or victim of a non-hate crime. Across two studies (N = 242 and 172), Fitzgerald et al. (2023) recently showed contact with gay and lesbian people reduced prejudice toward transgender individuals indirectly through lower prejudice towards both gay and lesbian people.

Moreover, Pettigrew and Tropp's (2006) meta-analyses reviewed 515 inter-group contact studies involving 250,000+ participants, revealing that 94% of these studies reported a negative correlation between contact and prejudice ($r = -0.22$), and under Allport et al.'s (1954) optimal conditions the strength of this relationship increased to $r = -0.29$. Furthermore, such effects typically generalise to the whole outgroup, other scenarios, other outgroups, and universally across nations, genders, and age groups (Pettigrew et al., 2011). The more recent meta-analysis by Paluck et al. (2021) also confirmed a reliable overall effect size of $d = 0.22$ for face-to-face contact on reducing LGBT + prejudice, which was more than twice the effect size for racial prejudice ($d = 0.10$).

It is important not to overlook the fact that during this research, the pre-test transprejudice levels of the majority of the participants in the gay groups was shown to have been significantly reduced. Future research employing such imagined inter-group contact with co-mock-jurors is also likely to yield such secondary benefits whilst conducting mock-jury research, therein adding to the ethical advantages.

Additional findings included significantly higher sentence enhancement agreement levels and perceived victim suffering ratings in the gay groups compared to the heterosexual males. Higher victim suffering scores are especially relevant in the context of hate crime research given research shows hate crime victims suffer more than non-hate crime victims, for example often experiencing higher levels of depression, nervousness, anger, difficulty concentrating, fear, and feeling unsafe (McDevitt et al., 2002).

Flores et al. (2018) also found that reducing transphobia was associated with increased public support for transgender rights, which could also explain the increased agreement with sentence enhancement laws observed in the LGBT+ groups showing reduced transphobia. Participants or jurors agreeing more with such key sentence enhancement hate crime laws is in itself a huge benefit of LGBT+ diverse juries and could also help reduce jury nullification incidents. Diverse juries have also been shown to be better in several other aspects for both minority victims and defendants compared to homogenous juries (Cornwell and Hans, 2011).

Since 1981, however, the practice in England and Wales has been to randomly select jurors by computer from the electoral register only. However, this has been shown to lead to juries that are un-representative of their local community and minority group defendants and victims (Lever, 2017) as minority groups are less likely to be on the local electoral lists from which jurors are invited for jury service (Thomas and Balmer, 2007). Despite numerous US courts also declaring that racially diverse juries are superior to White-only juries (Wilkenfeld, 2004), minorities continue to be systematically under-represented on juries in the US and the UK. The causal factors are institutional stigma and discrimination (Lever, 2017; Wilkenfeld, 2004). The UK is one of the few countries that still selects jurors from a single register.

The largest UK study on ethnic representation within juries was undertaken by Thomas (2017) and found that the most significant factors predicting whether a summoned juror would serve on a jury were income and employment. The employed were noted to be over-represented among serving jurors and the retired and the unemployed under-represented. Transgender people are also around 14 times more likely to be homeless (Albert Kennedy Trust, 2018) so we would expect transgender people to be significantly under-represented in UK juries.

The Equality Act (2010) gave transgender people legal protection against discrimination for the first time in the UK. However, the continued practice of sending out jury summons based solely on the electoral register discriminates against transgender people as they are less likely to be on the electoral register due to significantly higher rates of homelessness, unemployment, and mobility issues. A survey by Stonewall (2018) of 871 transgender and non-binary people reported homelessness figures to be as high as 25% amongst transgender people in the UK, which would also make it difficult for a quarter of this group to receive any summons for jury service or to be on electoral registers used for compiling jury lists. The UK could benefit from adopting the more modern international models for juror selection based on multiple lists.

Policy recommendations based on international models

Electoral lists are not representative of communities, and jury selection solely from the electoral roll unfairly disadvantages minority groups further (Darbyshire et al., 2002). Critics have argued that the Juries Act (1974) should be amended so that the electoral roll is merged with other lists such as Driver and Vehicle Licensing lists, Department for Work and Pensions lists, and/or mobile phone subscriber lists (Darbyshire et al., 2002). Almost half a century ago in the US, Kairys et al., (1977) showed how minorities were under-represented on juries due to selection from a single list (voters' list). The Uniform Jury Selection and Service Act (1968) adopted in most US states made the use of multiple lists mandatory. There have been several legal challenges to the lack of ethnic mix on juries, and recommendations to government to alter both the summoning process and the empanelling of juries in order to achieve greater ethnic representation in the UK (Thomas, 2017).

Therefore, there is very little value in extending hate crime laws to additional characteristics when UK jury selection procedures fail to provide fair and representative juries for victims based on these protected characteristics. Legal challenges to the lack of gender, disability, religious, and sexual orientation mix of juries is required to achieve greater representation and to ensure parity with ethnic mix, particularly given intersecting characteristics. This is more important than ever now in the light of the Law Commission (2020) proposal to extend hate crime laws to additional characteristics.

Over 30 years ago, the Runciman Commission (1993) proposed that a jury include at least three members from the same ethnicity as the defendant and victim in racially sensitive cases. In 2001, Lord Justice Auld further recommended that in sensitive cases there should be a special modified jury selection protocol to ensure at least three minority jurors are chosen.

These recommendations have never been implemented despite jury decision-making studies showing evidence of mock-juror verdicts being biased according to all five hate crime characteristics. A modern approach is thus required – one that is in line with international models and that produces more diverse juries via multiple registers to promote the equal inclusion of marginalised groups in jury service. If and when such measures are embraced, they are likely to be piecemeal based on ethnicity and therein create further disparities.

Jury selection methods need to be modified to create more balanced juries, in sensitive cases at a minimum. According to a recent UK Census (ONS, 2021), 9% of the adult population in London identify as LGBT+. This equates to an average of one (1.08) LGBT+ juror in every 12-member jury in London and as high as 1.5 LGBT+ jurors in some areas. Around 350,000 jurors are summoned each year for jury service so, given the size of the UK LGBT+ population of around 1.5 million, this should be easily achievable by adjusting the empanelling allocation procedure following random selection from multiple lists. For example, in LGBT+ hate crime cases the computer system could randomly select two jurors from the pool of LGBT+ jurors available and randomly select ten other jurors from the general pool of available jurors. In exceptional circumstances, a judge also has the power to compose a more mixed jury (Thomas, 2008) and judges should be encouraged to utilise this power in sensitive hate crime cases to enhance trial fairness given the multifarious advantages of diverse juries.

More diverse juries would also provide more opportunities for inter-group contact. To show genuine commitment to equality, diversity, and inclusion and to reduce juror bias, there is an urgent need to adopt a modern jury selection procedure that ensures juries are more representative and fairer for transgender people.

References

Abrams, D., Crisp, R. J., Marques, S., Fagg, E., Bedford, L., and Provias, D. (2008). Threat inoculation: Experienced and imagined intergenerational contact prevents stereotype threat effects on older people's math performance. *Psychology and Aging*, *23*(4).

Acker, G. (2017). Transphobia among students majoring in the helping professions. *Journal of Homosexuality*, *64*(14), 2011–2029.

Adams, E. S. and Lane, C. J., (1998). Constructing a jury that is both impartial and representative: Utilizing cumulative voting in jury selection. *NYUL Review*, *73*, 703.

Albert Kennedy Trust (2018). LGBT youth homelessness. https://www.taipawb.org/wp-content/uploads/2018/07/LGBT-Youth-Homelessness-A-UK-National-scoping-of-cause-prevalence-response-and-outcome.pdf

Allport, G. W., Clark, K., and Pettigrew, T. (1954). *The nature of prejudice*. Reading, MA: Addison-Wesley Publishing Company.

Alschuler, A. W. (1995). Racial quotas and the jury. *Duke Law Journal*, *44*, 704–743.

Blackham, J. (2006). *Public perceptions of crime severity and attributions of victim blame toward transgender victims of sexual assault*. Fresno: Alliant International University.

Blascovich J., Mendes, W. B., Hunter, S. B., Lickel, B., and Kowai-Bell, N. (2001). Perceiver threat in social interactions with stigmatized others. *Journal of Personality and Social Psychology*, *80*, 253–267.

Bogardus, E. (1938). Social distance and its practical applications. *Sociology and Social Research*, 22, 462–476.

Carbone, C. S., and Plaut, V. C. (2013). Diversity and the civil jury. *William & Mary Law Review*, *55*, 837.

Carter, L. M., Goodmon, L. B., Urs, M., and Rutledge-Jukes, H. (2023). The effects of victim gender identity, juror gender, and judicial instructions on victim blaming, crime severity ratings, and verdicts in sexual assault trials. *Journal of Homosexuality*, *70*(6), 1187–1224.

Consolini, P. M. (1992). *Learning by doing justice: Jury service and political attitudes* (Doctoral dissertation). Berkeley: University of California.

Cotten-Huston, A. L., and Waite, B. M. (1999). Anti-homosexual attitudes in college students: Predictors and classroom interventions. *Journal of Homosexuality*, *38*, 117–133.

Cornwell, E. Y., and Hans, V. P. (2011). Representation through participation: A multilevel analysis of jury deliberations. *Law and Society Review*, *45*(3), 667–698.

Crisp, R. J., Stathi, S., Turner, R. N., and Husnu, S. (2009). Imagined intergroup contact: Theory, paradigm and practice. *Social and Personality Psychology Compass*, *3*(1), 1–18.

Daly, G., and Pattenden, R. (2005). Racial bias and the English criminal trial jury, *Cambridge Law Journal*, *64*(3), 678–710.

Darbyshire, P., Maughan, A., and Stewart, A. (2002). What can we learn from published jury research? Findings for the Criminal Courts Review 2001. *Criminal Law Review*, 970–980.

Ellingwood, H., Pica, E., Pozzulo, J., and Schultheis, E. (2022). The influence of victim sexual orientation, gender, and gender identity on mock jurors' judgments. *Journal of Police and Criminal Psychology*, *38*, 461–468.

Ellis, L., and Diamond, S. S. (2003). Race, diversity, and jury composition: battering and bolstering legitimacy. *Chicago-Kent Law Review*, *78*(3), 1033–1058.

Enright, S. (1991). Multi-racial juries. *New Law Journal*, 141(6513), 992–996.

Fitzgerald, H. N., Owen, C. K., and Shook, N. J. (2023). Fringe benefits: Secondary transfer effects of lesbian, gay, and bisexual contact on transgender prejudice. *Current Psychology*, *43*, 3548–3561.

Flores, A. R., Haider-Markel, D. P., Lewis, D. C., Miller, P. R., Tadlock, B. L., and Taylor, J. K. (2018). Challenged expectations: Mere exposure effects on attitudes about transgender people and rights. *Political Psychology*, *39*(1), 197–216.

Gastil, J., Deess, E. P., Weiser, P. J., and Simmons, C. (2010). *The jury and democracy: How jury deliberation promotes civic engagement and political participation*. Oxford: Oxford University Press.

Harwood, J., Paolini, S., Joyce, N., Rubin, M., and Arroyo, A. (2011). Secondary transfer effects from imagined contact: Group similarity affects the generalization gradient. *British Journal of Social Psychology*, *50*(1), 180–189.

Hatzenbuehler, M. L. (2016). Structural stigma: Research evidence and implications for psychological science. *American Psychologist*, *71*(8), 742–751.

Hewstone, M., and Swart, H. (2011). Fifty-odd years of inter-group contact: From hypothesis to integrated theory. *British Journal of Social Psychology*, *50*, 374–386.

Hinrichs, D. W., and Rosenberg, P. J. (2002). Attitudes toward gay, lesbian, and bisexual persons among heterosexual liberal arts college students. *Journal of Homosexuality*, *43*, 61–84.

Hodson, G., Dube, B., and Choma, B. (2015). Can (elaborated) imagined contact interventions reduce prejudice among those higher in intergroup disgust sensitivity (ITG-DS)? *Journal of Applied Social Psychology*, *45*, 123–131.

Hoffarth, M. R., and Hodson, G. (2018). When intergroup contact is uncommon and bias is strong: The case of anti-transgender bias. *Psychology & Sexuality*, *9*(3), 237–250.

Israel, M. (1998). Ethnic bias in jury selection in Australia and New Zealand. *International Journal of the Sociology of Law*, *26*(1), 35–54.

Kairys, D., Kadane, J., and Lehoczky, J. P. (1977). Jury representativeness: A mandate for multiple source lists. *California Law Review*, *65*, 776.

King, M. E., Winter, S., and Webster, B. (2009). Contact reduces transprejudice: A study on attitudes towards transgenderism and transgender civil rights in Hong Kong. *International Journal of Sexual Health*, *21*(1), 17–34.

Kirchmeyer, C., and Cohen, A. (1992). Multicultural groups: Their performance and reactions with constructive conflict. *Group and Organization Management*, *17*(2), 153–170.

Kushnirovich, N. (2020). Is negative the new positive? Secondary transfer effect of exposure to LGBT portrayals in TV entertainment programs. *Journal of Applied Social Psychology*, *50*(2), 115–130.

Langton, L., and Cohen, T. (2005). U.S. Dept. Of Justice, Bureau of Justice Statistics special report, No. NCJ223851, civil bench and jury trials in state courts.

Law Commission (2020, September). Hate crime laws, a consultation paper (250). https://www.report-it.org.uk/files/law_commission_consultation_hate-crime-final-report.pdf

Lee, Y. T., Ottati, V. C., Lin, C., and Chan, S. X. (2014). How are Asian Americans seen and evaluated? Examining ethnic stereotypes and their cultural complexity. *Cross-Cultural Communication*, *10*(2), 98–111.

Lemmer, G., and Wagner, U. (2015). Can we really reduce ethnic prejudice outside the lab? A meta-analysis of direct and indirect contact interventions. *European Journal of Social Psychology*, *45*(2), 152–168.

Lever, A. (2017). Democracy, epistemology and the problem of all-white juries. *Journal of Applied Philosophy*, *34*(4), 541–556.

Levinson, J. D., and Young, D. (2009). Different shades of bias: Skin tone, implicit racial bias, and judgments of ambiguous evidence. *West Virginia Law Review*, *112*, 307.

Marinucci, M., Maunder, R., Sanchez, K., Thai, M., McKeown, S., Turner, R. N., and Stevenson, C. (2021). Intimate intergroup contact across the lifespan. *Journal of Social Issues*, *77*(1), 64–85.

Mathias, K., Kermode, M., Goicolea, I., Seefeldt, L., Shidhaye, R., and San Sebastian, M. (2018). Social distance and community attitudes towards people with psycho-social disabilities in Uttarakhand, India. *Community Mental Health Journal*, *54*(3), 343–353.

McDevitt, J., Levin, J., and Bennett, S. (2002). Hate crime offenders: An expanded typology. *Journal of Social Issues*, *58*(2), 303–317.

Michalski, N. D., Bitter, A. N. and Nuñez, N., (2022). 'Trans folks are in the cross-hairs': Jury decision-making and the trans panic defense. *Journal of Interpersonal Violence*, *37*(23–24), NP22453–NP22474.

Miles, E., and Crisp, R. J. (2014). A meta-analytic test of the imagined contact hypothesis. *Group Processes & Intergroup Relations*, *17*(1), 3–26.

Miller, Q. C., and London, K. (2021). Mock jurors' perceptions of child sexual abuse cases involving sexual and gender minority victims. *Psychology of Sexual Orientation and Gender Diversity*, *10*(2), 311–323.

Norton, A. T., and Herek, G. M. (2013). Heterosexuals' attitudes toward transgender people: Findings from a national probability sample of US adults. *Sex Roles*, *68*(11–12), 738–753.

Office for National Statistics (ONS) (2021). *Gender identity*, England and Wales: Census 2021. https://www.ons.gov.uk/peoplepopulationandcommunity/culturalidentity/genderidentity/bulletins/genderidentityenglandandwales/census2021

Orosz, G., Bánki, E., Bőthe, B., Tóth-Király, I. and Tropp, L. R. (2016). Don't judge a living book by its cover: Effectiveness of the living library intervention in reducing prejudice toward Roma and LGBT people. *Journal of Applied Social Psychology*, *46*(9), 510–517.

Paluck, E. L., Porat, R., Clark, C. S., and Green, D. P. (2021). Prejudice reduction: Progress and challenges. *Annual Review of Psychology*, *72*, 533–560.

Parrillo, V. N., and Donoghue, C. (2005). Updating the Bogardus social distance studies: A new national survey. *The Social Science Journal*, *42*(2), 257–271.

Pettigrew, T. F. (2009). Secondary transfer effect of contact: Do intergroup contact effects spread to noncontacted out-groups? *Social Psychology*, *40*(2), 55–65.

Pettigrew, T. F., and Tropp, L. R. (2006). A meta-analytic test of intergroup contact theory. *Journal of Personality and Social Psychology*, *90*(5), 751.

Pettigrew, T. F., and Tropp, L. R. (2008). How does intergroup contact reduce prejudice? Meta-analytic tests of three mediators. *European Journal of Social Psychology*, *38*(6), 922–934.

Pettigrew, T. F. and Tropp, L. R. (2013). Does intergroup contact reduce prejudice? Recent meta-analytic findings. In S. Oskamp (Ed.), *Reducing prejudice and discrimination* (pp. 103–124). Hove, UK: Psychology Press.

Pettigrew, T. F., Tropp, L. R., Wagner, U., and Christ, O. (2011). Recent advances in intergroup contact theory. *International Journal of Intercultural Relations*, *35*(3), 271–280.

Rawls, J. (2005). *A theory of justice*. Oxford: Oxford University Press.

Ringger, C. S. (2021). Attitudinal predictors of juror decisions on gender and sexual minority defendants. *Journal of Homosexuality*, *68*(12), 2047–2074.

Runciman Commission (1993). *The Royal Commission on criminal justice report*. Cmnd 2263.

Sentencing Council Guidelines (2019). Common assault/Racially or religiously aggravated common assault – for consultation only. https://www.sentencingcouncil.org.uk/offences/magistrates-court/item/common-assault-racially-or-religiously-aggravated-common-assault-for-consultation-only/

Singh, A. (2025). *An exploration of the impact of LGBT+ representative mock-juries on mock-juror bias and guilty verdicts in transphobic hate crime cases* (PhD thesis). Bournemouth University.

Smith, C., Davis, J. P., and Roberts, A. (2019). Probative or prejudicial: Biasing effects of background information in police body-worn video evidence on mock-juror decisions in victim-depressed domestic abuse cases. *PsyArXiv*. https://doi.org/10.31234/osf.io/72xwh

Smith, M., (1993, 29 October). Pilot plan to assure that each grand jury has two minorities. *Minneapolis Star Tribune*, p. 6.

Sommers, S. R. (2006). On racial diversity and group decision making: Identifying multiple effects of racial composition on jury deliberations. *Journal of Personality and Social Psychology*, *90*(4), 597–612.

Sommers, S. R., and Adekanmbi, O. O. (2008). Race and juries: An experimental psychology perspective. *Critical Race Realism: Intersections of Psychology, Race and Law*, 78–93.

Stathi, S., and Crisp, R. J. (2008). Imagining intergroup contact promotes projection to outgroups. *Journal of Experimental Social Psychology*, *44*(4), 943–957.

Stathi, S., Crisp, R., and Hogg, M. (2011). Imagining intergroup contact enables member-to-group generalization. *Group Dynamics: Theory, Research, and Practice*, *15*(3), 275–284.

Stephan, W. G., and Stephan, C. W. (1985). Intergroup anxiety. *Journal of Social Issues*, *41*, 157–175.

Stonewall (2018). *LGBT in Britain – Trans report*. https://www.stonewall.org.uk/resources/lgbt-britain-trans-report-2018

Swart, H., Hewstone, M., Christ, O., and Voci, A., (2011). Affective mediators of intergroup contact: A three-wave longitudinal study in South Africa. *Journal of Personality and Social Psychology*, *101*(6), 1221–1238.

Tadlock, B. L., Flores, A. R., Haider-Markel, D. P., Lewis, D. C., Miller, P. R., and Taylor, J. K. (2017). Testing contact theory and attitudes on transgender rights. *Public Opinion Quarterly*, *81*(4), 956–972.

Tee, N., and Hegarty, P. (2006). Predicting opposition to the civil rights of trans persons in the United Kingdom. *Journal of Community & Applied Social Psychology*, *16*(1), 70–80.

Thomas, C. (2008). Exposing the myths of jury service. *Criminal Law Review*, 6, 415.

Thomas, C. A. (2017). Ethnicity and the fairness of jury trials in England and Wales 2006-2014. *Criminal Law Review*, *2017*(11), 860–876.

Thomas, D. M., Amburgcy, J., and Ellis, L. (2016). Anti-transgender prejudice mediates the association of just world beliefs and victim blame attribution. *International Journal of Transgenderism*, *17*, 176–184.

Thomas, C. A., and Balmer, N. J. (2007). *Diversity and fairness in the jury system*. Ministry of Justice. https://www.ucl.ac.uk/laws/sites/laws/files/diversityfairness.pdf

Tompkins, T. L., Shields, C. N., Hillman, K. M. and White, K. (2015). Reducing stigma toward the transgender community: An evaluation of a humanizing and perspective-taking intervention. *Psychology of Sexual Orientation and Gender Diversity*, *2*(1), 34.

Turner, R. N., Crisp, R. J., and Lambert, E. (2007). Imagining intergroup contact can improve intergroup attitudes. *Group Processes & Intergroup Relations*, *10*(4), 427–441.

UK Census (2021). 2021 census: What do we know about the LGBT+ population? https://commonslibrary.parliament.uk/2021-census-what-do-we-know-about-the-lgbt-population/

Uniform Jury Selection and Service Act (1968). Mississippi and Indiana, Code, Section, 13–5–8(1).

Vezzali, L., Birtel, M. D., Di Bernardo, G. A., Stathi, S., Crisp, R. J., and Cadamuro, A. (2020). Don't hurt my outgroup friend: Imagined contact promotes intentions to counteract bullying. *Group Processes and Intergroup Relations*, *23*(5), 643–663.

West, K., Hotchin, V., and Wood, C. (2017). Imagined contact can be more effective for participants with stronger initial prejudices. *Journal of Applied Social Psychology*, *47*(5), 282–292.

White, F. A., Abu-Rayya, H. M., and Weitzel, C. (2014). Achieving twelve-months of intergroup bias reduction: The dual identity-electronic contact (DIEC) experiment. *International Journal of Intercultural Relations*, *38*, 158–163.

Wilkenfeld, J., (2004). Newly compelling: Re-examining judicial construction of juries in the aftermath of Grutter v. Bollinger. *Columbia Law Review*, *104*(8), 2291–2327.

Winter, S., Chalungsooth, P., Teh, Y., Rojanalert, N., Maneerat, K., Wong, Y., and Macapagal, R. (2009). Transpeople, transprejudice, and pathologization: A seven-country factor analytic study. *International Journal of Sexual Health*, *21*, 96–118.

Young, W., Cameron, N., and Tinsley, Y., (2001) New Zealand Law Commission, report 69, 'Juries in criminal trials' (also published as Parliamentary Paper E3169).

7

TRANSPHOBIC HATE CRIME IN ILLIBERAL DEMOCRACIES: A CASE STUDY OF POLAND

Ewa Milczarek

Introduction

Over the past decade, there has been a notable decline in both social satisfaction with democracy and its perceived efficacy globally (Fukuyama, 2015). This trend is coupled with decreasing support for the principles of liberal democracy – characterised by universalism and individualism – and rising endorsement of alternative governance models such as etatism, where the will of the majority often overshadows minority rights (Foa and Mounk, 2016). In this context, countries like Poland and Hungary are increasingly viewed as embracing illiberal democracy (Bień-Kacała, 2020) or even authoritarian populism (Sadurski, 2018). This shift is reflected in changes within the judiciary and other democratic institutions, contributing to the erosion of liberal constitutionalism (Zakaria, 2023) and facilitating the consolidation of power by populist leaders. The crucial element in maintaining the position of populist leaders involves the use of the following mechanisms. Two of them, irrelevant for this discussion, are a control position within their own parties, and using economic operators to raise the funds necessary for the development of their parties and their influence in society by enlarging the vassal system. The third one involves controlling the politics in Poland. Populists create enemies, in this context the European Union, immigrants, left-wing intellectuals, economic liberals, Jews, and sexual minorities (Kubas, 2022).

In Poland, this consolidation of power has exploited various societal divisions, including the stigmatisation of minority groups such as the LGBTQ+ community, and particularly transgender individuals. The term transgender refers to individuals whose gender identity does not align with the sex they were assigned at birth. In the context of this chapter, transgender people are

DOI: 10.4324/9781003564928-9

a marginalised group often facing legal, political, and social discrimination, including hate crimes and institutionalised transphobia. Their rights, recognition, and safety are influenced by national policies, societal attitudes, and international legal frameworks. The exploitation of transphobia for political gain is increasingly evident, manifesting itself in both legal measures and societal attitudes. Specific legislative actions and the creation of 'LGBTQ+-free zones' are examples of how transphobia is institutionalised, exacerbating discrimination and contributing to a climate of fear and hostility.

This chapter explores the dynamics of transphobic hate crimes within the framework of Poland's illiberal democracy. It delves into the specific legal measures aimed at stigmatising transgender individuals and other non-heteronormative people, highlighting how these legal frameworks and societal attitudes interact to foster an environment ripe for transphobic violence. Additionally, it references published research on transphobic crimes, providing a quantitative dimension to the discussion and highlighting the severity and progression of this issue.

The chapter also situates the issue of transphobic violence within an international context, illustrating its relevance in a broader international political discourse. This perspective helps to underline the interconnectedness of transgender rights with global political narratives, emphasising the role of international advocacy and dialogue in addressing and mitigating such human rights abuses. Through a thorough analysis of legislative acts, court judgements, and statistical data, the chapter highlights the multifaceted impact of transphobic violence in Poland, illustrating its profound implications for both the affected individuals and the broader socio-political landscape.

Hate speech in the Polish legal system

Globalisation and integration shape a shared axiological community in democratic states, influencing national law through international standards (Ruczkowski, 2021). In Europe, the EU and the Council of Europe play a key role, balancing national discretion with fundamental legal principles. Poland's 1997 Constitution reflects this European axiological framework, emphasising the rule of law, human rights, equality, and minority rights.

The basic principles establishing the position of an individual in Poland include Art. 32 of the Constitution of the Republic of Poland of 2nd April 1997 (Dz. U. No. 78, item 483), which states that no one may be discriminated against in political, social, or economic life for any reason. Poland has not ratified Protocol No. 12 to the European Convention on Human Rights (ECHR), which introduces a general prohibition of discrimination, however, it is bound by the prohibition of discrimination guaranteed by the ECHR. Protection and guarantees related to protection against discrimination are detailed at the statutory level. The 2010 Equal Treatment Act (Dz. U. No. 254, item 1700) expressly prohibits discrimination on the basis of sexual orientation, but – contrary to the recommendations of the European Commission against Racism and Intolerance (ECRI) – not on the basis of gender identity (CRI[2015]20). One of the manifestations of broadly understood discrimination is hate crime. A bill introducing the criminalisation of such acts was rejected in 2016.

Hate crimes are crimes motivated by intolerance or prejudice towards certain groups within society (OSCE, 2022), including towards transgender people. Transphobia is hostility and negative attitudes towards transgender people or people perceived as belonging to this group, and may manifest itself in behaviour involving different, most often harmful, treatment of these people. Like homophobia, it can take many forms, and transgender people are often victims of homophobia from people who mistakenly treat their gender expression as homosexuality (Makuchowska, Chaber, and Jabłońska, 2013). Transphobic hate violence incorporates verbal, physical, and sexual violence (Jamel, 2017). With transphobic hate crime, it is important to understand the context in which it occurs. Relevant factors include the perceptions of the perpetrator, as well as the extent to which a person is visible as a trans or gender-variant person, along with the trans person's social and environmental circumstances (Turner and Whittle, 2012).

A verbal manifestation of transphobic hate violence is hate speech (de Groot and Immenkamp, 2025). The aim of hate speech is often to attack a specific community, therefore even if hate speech is directed at an individual, they are representative of a group to which – through the attack – certain features are attributed, based on social or biological criteria. In this approach, statements classified as hate speech reduce a given group or person (as a typical representative of such a group) to some collective feature or stereotype that is intended to negatively define that person or group and lead to their humiliation or depreciation in social perception, which, in turn, serves to justify unequal treatment and discrimination of those attacked. Hate speech manifests itself in various types of aggressive linguistic behaviour, such as: discrediting an addressee of a message through offensive and degrading epithets, stigmatising them (understood as social labelling), or degrading their dignity, and may include mockery or blunt criticism (Urbańczyk and Rogalska, 2017).

There is no definition of legal hate speech in either the Polish or EU legal order. Universally binding acts of international law do not contain a generally applicable definition either (Bojanowski, 2021). The definition of hate speech can be found in the Recommendation of the Committee of Ministers of the Council of Europe (R(97)20). Hate speech includes all forms of speech that spread, incite, promote, or justify racial hatred, xenophobia, antisemitism, and other forms of hatred based on intolerance, including discrimination and hostility towards minorities. It also covers all forms of hate-motivated speech, regardless of the means of expression used – including the internet and other means of modern communication.

Even though Polish law does not have a separate regulation regarding hate speech and hate crimes, both phenomena are considered inconsistent with existing Polish law. In the Polish Penal Code (Article 119, Article 256, and Article 257), the use of violence and unlawful threats, incitement to hatred, public insults, and violation of bodily integrity of a person or group of people on grounds of national, ethnic, racial, or religious affiliation are penalised, but the same actions carried out on grounds of sexual orientation or gender identity are not. This legislative gap aligns Poland with several other European countries that also lack explicit hate crime provisions related to gender identity. According to the European Parliamentary Research Service (Immenkamp, 2024), there is a significant variation across EU Member States regarding the characteristics protected under hate crime and hate speech laws. While some states, such as Sweden, Spain, and Malta, have comprehensive legal frameworks that explicitly protect against hate crimes based on sexual orientation and gender identity, others, including Poland, Latvia, and Bulgaria, do not recognise gender identity as a protected category under criminal law.

Since hate speech and other hate crimes based on sexual orientation and gender identity are punishable only to a limited extent (the Polish Penal Code does not indicate these factors as grounds for hate speech), the prosecution of perpetrators must be based on other provisions (including the Code of Misdemeanors) or in a private complaint procedure. This kind of procedure is much more difficult for the injured party as the victims must take personal initiative, including gathering evidence and formulating legal arguments, and also finance their case without any state support. For transgender people who are victims of hate crimes, this may constitute an excessive burden, leading to their repeated victimisation through criminal proceedings themselves (Szeroczyńska and Śledzińska-Simon, 2013). Victims of anti-LGBTQ+ hate crime thus face multiple obstacles in accessing justice. Many rights stemming from Directive 2012/29/EU (the Victims' Rights Directive) are not respected (Godzisz and Rawłuszko, 2018). Persons harmed by hate speech are entitled to commence legal proceedings only if they have been individually insulted. Currently, there are no legal protections against statements that incite hatred or insult the entire LGBTQ+ community.

The analysis of court jurisprudence conducted by the Polish Commissioner for Human Rights indicates that although in some cases the complainants managed to prevent dissemination of content hostile to LGBTQ+ people, the courts usually protect statements that constitute hate speech, which they consider to be subject to freedom of speech (Mazurczak et al., 2019). Moreover, the legal system in Poland itself is insufficiently adapted to the needs of transgender people. They face difficulties resulting from limited access to legal procedures which enable them to confirm their gender identity. In October

2015, President Andrzej Duda vetoed the Gender Reconciliation Act regarding transgender people. The act aimed to introduce a simplified procedure before one specialised court. Currently, transgender people who want to legally confirm their gender still have to rely on a procedure that forces them to sue their parents, who may oppose their demands. Moreover, those who undergo hormone therapy or have undergone surgical procedures have the greatest chance of a favourable decision (and not every transgender person wants to undergo such medical procedures). Self-determination of one's gender identity is not sufficient for the courts. Also, the lack of a law regulating same-sex relationships results in transgender people who are married and would like to align their gender being forced to divorce, even if their relationship is happy (Gierdal et al., 2018). Moreover, identifying as transgender disqualifies one from military service and is classified as a disease or disability (Dz. U. 2024, poz. 466). A high profile example is the case of Laura, a Catalan trans woman, who had custody of her children forcibly removed by the Polish courts. In 2019, when she decided to start her transition, her wife, who did not accept her gender identity, took her two children to Poland. Laura initiated civil and criminal proceedings for the wrongful removal of her children and the Spanish courts found in her favour. Once the case was brought to Poland, following an international return application to the Ministry of Foreign Affairs and the Ministry of Justice, it eventually was brought before the Warsaw Court of Appeal, which rejected the return of the children on the basis that '[the applicant's] acting like a woman would expose them to psychological harm and put them in an intolerable situation that is not natural' (Dz. U. 2024, poz. 466).

Discourses presenting transgender identities as 'unnatural' and potentially harmful to children are rooted in specific social and cultural narratives that have a significant impact on the perception of transgender people. Such narratives often stem from entrenched stereotypes and a lack of knowledge about the diversity of gender identities. In the Polish social context, research shows that the majority of respondents do not personally know any transgender people, which may contribute to the perpetuation of such negative stereotypes (Brown, 2017). An analysis of media discourse in Poland indicates the presence of narratives pathologising transgenderism, which can lead to the dehumanisation of transgender people (Kołodziejek, 2022). Such representations reinforce negative connotations and perpetuate beliefs about the 'unnaturalness' of transgender identities.

Anti-LGBT zones

Anti-LGBT 'zones', also known as 'LGBTQ+ ideology-free zones', refer to some Polish local governments that have declared themselves as areas free from 'LGBTQ+ ideology'. These declarations, which first appeared in 2019, were a symbolic expression of opposition to the promotion of equal rights for LGBTQ+ people. They often included demands to oppose sexual education and end social support for LGBTQ+ people. Although these declarations did not introduce direct legal changes regarding LGBTQ+ people, they expressed a political position denying equality and anti-discrimination activities (Hadel, 2020). At the entrances to areas managed by local governments that have adopted such declarations, signs reading 'LGBTQ+-free zone' appeared.

'LGBTQ+ ideology-free zones' reinforce exclusionary narratives and signal that LGBTQ+ people do not belong. These declarations legitimise discrimination, normalise exclusion, and may encourage harassment. They serve as political tools, appealing to nationalist and conservative ideologies. Ultimately, such measures shape both policy and societal attitudes, deepening marginalisation. LGBTQ+-free zones emerged in response to the Warsaw Municipal Policy for the LGBT+ Community, which promoted support services, anti-violence measures, and representation for LGBTQ+ people. Initiated by the Love Does Not Exclude Association (Stowarzyszenie Miłość Nie Wyklucza), proposed interventions included LGBTQ+ hostels, hate crime monitoring, and school anti-violence programmes. Instead, the presence of these symbolic and inclusive markers visibly entrenches discrimination in public spaces.

Right-wing groups interpreted these positive actions as attempts to undermine the constitutionally guaranteed rights of families and the legal identity of marriage. In response to the 'LGBTQ+ Declaration', the 'Local Government Charter of Family Rights' (Samorządowa Karta Praw Rodzin) was created, prepared by the Ordo Iuris Institute for Legal Culture Foundation (Fundacja Instytut na rzecz Kultury Prawnej Ordo Iuris). This document, which was a model for a local government resolution, included, among other items, prevention of allocation of public funds to projects that undermine the constitutional definition of marriage as a union between a man and a woman. This framing positioned LGBTQ+ identities as inherently oppositional to religious and national values, reinforcing the perception that LGBTQ+ rights threaten the moral and social order.

By casting LGBTQ+ advocacy as an attack on traditional family structures, these policies create a false dichotomy between religious faith and LGBTQ+ inclusion, forcing individuals to choose between the two. This narrative not only fuels societal polarisation but also justifies legal and social discrimination under the guise of protecting cultural and religious heritage. The Charter has become a kind of guideline for declarations and resolutions in opposition to the LGBTQ+ 'ideology', adopted by several dozen local governments – including commune and district councils and voivodeship assemblies. Analysis by Atlas of Hate (Atlas Nienawiści, 2024) indicates that communes, districts, and voivodeships which activists called 'LGBT-free zones' covered approximately one third (31.3%) of Poland's territory and were inhabited by 12.2 million people. These so-called 'LGBT-free zones' in Poland were not just symbolic declarations but functioned as tools of institutional exclusion, legitimising discrimination and fostering a hostile environment for LGBTQ+ individuals (Ploszka, 2022). Research on the anti-LGBTQ+ campaign in

Poland highlights how such declarations contributed to the legal performance of exclusion, signalling that LGBTQ+ individuals do not belong in certain communities and indirectly encouraging discriminatory practices in employment, education, and access to public services (Ploszka, 2022; Bucholc, 2022).

Most of the declarations were prepared according to a standard template, usually stipulating that a given commune is 'free from LGBTQ+ ideology' and intends to fight 'political correctness'. These declarations express support for a family based on traditional values and defence of the education system against LGBTQ+ propaganda, which allegedly threatens the proper development and leads to the sexualisation of the young generation (Declaration of the Małopolska Voivodeship Assembly, 2019). The framing of LGBTQ+ identities as inherently linked to sexualisation reflects a broader pattern of misrepresentation, where LGBTQ+ existence is falsely equated with hypersexuality, reinforcing moral panics and justifying exclusionary policies under the guise of protecting children and traditional values.

There were also declarations to protect entrepreneurs by preventing the 'imposition' of specific criteria on them when selecting employees or contractors, which in practice enabled discrimination against LGBTQ+ people in the workplace. In the resolution of the Rycki District Council we read that they are opposed to, among other items, 'exerting pressure to use the so-called cultural and political correctness (homopropaganda) in many areas of social, political and economic life. We will support teachers, local government officials, entrepreneurs and representatives of other professions in stopping this ideological pressure and homoterror'. The term 'homoterror' frames LGBTQ+ advocacy as a form of coercion or aggression, positioning LGBTQ+ individuals not as marginalised communities seeking equal rights, but as oppressors imposing ideological control, thereby reversing the power dynamic and legitimising discriminatory policies. The resolution also expresses opposition to the 'acceptance of methods and socio-technical measures used by LGBTQ+ activists ... corrupting children, youth and adults, which results in the complete collapse of moral norms and the destruction of the natural and healthy model of family, school and society' (X/40/19).

Such declarations deepened hate speech against the LGBTQ+ community and contributed to an increase in the number of other discriminatory crimes (Ref. CG002(2021)). As a consequence, there has been a deterioration in the individual situation of LGBTQ+ people in these regions (especially young people). In essence, these statements aim to exclude LGBTQ+ people from the local government community (III SA/Lu 312/20).

These declarations were widely criticised both in Poland and internationally as discriminatory and violating human rights (OJ C 255/8; CommDH (2020)27; EUR 37/5882/2022). They were accused of being contrary to the principle of equality before the law and working against the prohibition of discrimination, as well as employee rights and acts of international and EU law. The European Union and other international organisations condemned these declarations, which in some cases resulted in the suspension of European funds for these regions (Krzysztoszek and Mandilara, 2023). In response to international criticism and legal action, some local government units withdrew their declarations, and Polish administrative courts (II SA/Ke 650/19; II SA/Rz 1118/19; II SA/Po 188/20; III SA/Kr 360/20; III SA/Kr 316/20; III SA/Gl 15/20; VIII SA/Wa 42/20; III SA/Lu 7/20; II SA/Rz 27/20) began to invalidate such resolutions, finding them inconsistent with the constitutional principles of equality.

The role of the media and politicians in shaping hate against LGBTQ+ people

According to the Council of Europe (Rec(97)20), 'public authorities and public institutions … have a special responsibility to refrain from statements, in particular to the media, which may reasonably be understood as hate speech … or other forms of discrimination or hatred based on intolerance. Such statements should be prohibited and publicly disavowed whenever they occur.'

Such statements, appearing in the political mainstream, normalise hatred and intolerance, which may lead to their further spread and to building a sense of consent to discriminatory behaviour. The stigmatisation of LGBTQ+ people in Poland is a long-term problem. Transphobic statements made by important public figures which create an atmosphere of hatred and intolerance, were identified in 2007 as among the most important problem areas in the memorandum of the Council of Europe Commissioner for Human Rights (CommDH, 2007). Over the past few years, LGBTQ+ people have come under increasing attack from ruling politicians, religious leaders, and other public figures in Poland. This has come in the form of dangerous and false framing of LGBTQ+ people as a threat to children and as a threat to Christianity (ILGA-Europe, 2020).

Children and young people in Polish schools are particularly vulnerable to anti-LGBTQ+ attacks, stemming from a series of actions aimed at exclusion and stigmatisation of non-heteronormative individuals. Examples include protests organised by conservative groups in front of educational institutions, such as the demonstration by the Życie i Rodzina Foundation outside the II High School in Lublin, opposing the alleged 'genderization' of children (Białach, 2022). Additionally, some schools have implemented bans on wearing LGBTQ+-related symbols, equating them with racist or Nazi content, as was the case at the Jadwiga Grodzka School Complex in Łęczyca (Chrzczonowicz, 2020). Such actions contribute to the marginalisation of LGBTQ+ students, intensifying their sense of alienation and insecurity. The introduction of initiatives promoting acceptance and inclusion, such as 'Rainbow Friday', consequently faced opposition and are often blocked by school administrations under pressure from conservative groups (Ordo Iuris, 2024). The lack of support and acceptance in the school environment can lead to severe mental health issues among LGBTQ+ youth, including depression and suicidal thoughts.

One example of spreading hate speech in Poland involves vans travelling all over the country. Vans (from organisations such as Foundation Pro) regularly incite hateful language against LGBTQ+ persons in Poland by driving around cities, promoting the narrative of an 'LGBTQ+ ideology', and associating LGBTQ+ persons with paedophilia. Loudspeakers broadcast slogans such as 'LGBTQ+ people rape children' and have, on occasion, reportedly been escorted by police vehicles. Citizens have occasionally themselves intervened to stop these vans, as the police take no action to prevent this hate speech (E-005625/2020). In another example, in May 2023, PiS leader Jarosław Kaczyński said that information on LGBTQ+ issues in schools exposes students to 'practices that are certainly harmful to them and may cause serious damage to their psyche'. At the same time, Ombudsman for Children Mikołaj Pawlak said his inspection of LGBTQ+-friendly schools is to protect children from 'criminals' and 'pedophiles'. In a statement, Education Minister Czarnek blamed the spread of 'LGBTQ+ ideology' and 'brainwashing' for the rise of suicide among minors (ILGA-Europe, 2024) (this statement was not supported by any research or statistics). As part of the debate on the first Equality March in Lublin in 2018, the Governor of Lublin posted his statement about the march and its organisers online, defining homosexuality as a 'perversion', 'deviation', and 'degeneration'. The private prosecutor, who was the main and publicly known organiser of the event, accused the Governor of Lublin of defamation, i.e., slander via the mass media, which humiliated him in public opinion and exposed him to the loss of trust needed in his social activities. The district court, although it found that the words used by the Governor were clearly negative terms regardless of the worldview, discontinued the proceedings. In the opinion of the court, punishment in the case would be an attempt to 'change social assessments by means of state coercion' and 'so-called hate speech cannot constitute a gag for freedom of speech'. The court therefore invoked the constitutional freedom of expression, stating that it cannot be a 'censor of public debate', whose participants should also 'adopt the principle of thick skin' and accept painful criticism (III K 936/18).

These examples illustrate how hate speech, microaggressions, and legal interpretations of free speech intersect to maintain structural discrimination. Microaggressions are subtle forms of discrimination, often unconscious or unintentional, that communicate hostile or derogatory messages (Nadal et al., 2016). The normalisation of such rhetoric contributes to a social climate where prejudice is legitimised, making it more difficult for LGBTQ+ individuals to challenge discrimination. As studies show, a high risk of exposure to microaggressions can lead to significant mental health consequences, including stress, anxiety, and internalised stigma (Marchi et al., 2024).

The role of the media in shaping public opinion is extremely important, especially in the context of statements made by public authorities. Media service providers can contribute to both spreading hate speech in the public sphere and limiting it. The Polish Supreme Court (Sąd Najwyższy) pointed out that the term 'propagation' within the meaning of Art. 18(1) of the Broadcasting Act should be understood as 'to spread, popularize some views, ideas, slogans, win someone over to some idea, campaign, etc., contribute to increasing the popularity of something; to proclaim, propagate, popularize, promote' (I KZP 5/02). Although this article does not define the phenomenon of hate speech, it prohibits the presence of content in various radio and television broadcasts that *de facto* contains elements constituting it. In Poland, as in other post-communist countries, the media have a special function (especially in the case of public media) of explaining to people the world around them and situations in which they function as a result of socio-economic changes (Nierenberg, 2007). Hence, the portrayal of transgender people and the entire LGBTQ+ community in the media is so important for shaping social attitudes.

Public and private (television and radio) media, sympathising with the ruling camp or sponsored by it, also have produced hate speech and prejudice against the LGBTQ+ community. Homophobia and transphobia are often treated instrumentally in public debate in order to fuel political disputes (Article 19, 2018). For example, Deputy Minister of Justice, Marcin Warchoł, said that the TVP2's New Year celebration, which featured the group Black Eyed Peas with rainbow armbands, was the 'New Year's Eve of Abnormalities'. The material titled 'Invasion' produced by TVP S.A., in the opinion of the Commissioner for Human Rights, was seen to intensify social hatred towards LGBTQ+ people, violating their dignity, and falsely associating them with paedophilia (XI.505.27.2019.MA).

Examples can also be found within private media, among which the leading voices are church-related stations, including Tadeusz Rydzyk – Radio Maryja and Telewizja Trwam. These particular stations have alleged that LGBTQ+ people pose a threat to the family, nation, state sovereignty, Christianity, children, and even to agriculture (Maszkowski, 2010). Despite complaints about hate speech submitted to the National Broadcasting Council (Krajowa Rada Radiofonii i Telewizji), it refused to initiate proceedings.

The impact of hate speech on LGBTQ+ people

The growing scale of hate speech and microaggressions has led to a deterioration of the situation of LGBTQ+ people in Poland. Research conducted in Poland confirms that in the case of LGBTQ+ people, incidents of prejudice-motivated violence and discrimination that they have been subject to have a significant impact on the experience of minority stress, which leads to greater symptoms of depression, more frequent suicidal thoughts, lower self-esteem, and lower life satisfaction (Mazurczak and Winiewski, 2020). Transgender people are one of the groups most affected by violence within the LGBTQ+ community in Poland. In data produced by Kuta (2021), transgender people were the most likely to suffer physical violence (18.7%) and vandalism (33.3%) of all surveyed groups. The percentage of individuals experiencing verbal violence and threats remained relatively consistent across all groups. For trans people, these figures stand at 59% and 45.9%, respectively. Transgender people also do not report discriminatory incidents for fear of revealing their identity or orientation (PL: 32%, EU average: 21%) and lack of trust in the authorities (PL: 40%, EU average: 21%) (Mazurczak and Winiewski, 2020).

Existing research shows that exposure to hate speech predicted PTSD and depression symptoms. Both effects were mediated by acculturation stress and were significant after controlling for experienced discrimination (Wypych and Bilewicz, 2022). The research on the effect of anti-LGBTQ+ laws in Poland on suicide attempts and fatalities, by applying border-area difference-in-differences models to district-level data, shows that annual suicide attempts increased by 16%, or five attempts per 100k capita, after the enactment of anti-LGBTQ+ statutes. This rise in suicide attempts was most prevalent among men and involved 11 additional suicides per 100k individuals aged 30–49. There was also an increase in suicide attempts in areas that deliberated, but subsequently rejected, anti-LGBTQ+ resolutions, providing evidence that stigmatisation of minority groups leads to declines in this population's mental health (Meyerhoefer, Xue, and Poznańska, 2023).

Although Polish society's attitude towards LGBTQ+ people has gradually improved over the last decade, this trend has reversed in recent years. According to public opinion research published in 2019 by the Public Opinion Research Center (CBOS 90/2019), despite social acceptance of LGBTQ+ groups increasing for many years until 2017 (i.e., when the Law and Justice Party came to power in the country), it has decreased since then. Poland dropped from 33nd in 2015 to 49th place in the 2024 'rainbow index' published annually by the International Lesbian, Gay, Bisexual, Trans and Intersex Association (ILGA-Europe), which reflects the level of respect for the human rights of LGBTQ+ people in 49 European countries (ILGA-Europe, 2020). The lowest rated area of legal protection on the rainbow index is protection against hate crime, the right to respect for family life, and protection against discrimination. Currently, Poland has the worst ranking of all European Union countries.

These trends are also confirmed by the results of research conducted by the EU Agency for Fundamental Rights, which found an increase in prejudice and intolerance towards LGBTQ+ people in Poland. According to a study conducted in 2019, as many as 68% of LGBTQ+ respondents from Poland believe that prejudice and intolerance towards LGBTQ+ people in Poland had increased over the previous five years (EU-LGBTI II). The main reasons for this included negative attitudes and discourse conducted by politicians (88%) and negative changes in the law (51%) (Mazurczak and Winiewski, 2020). The effects of these negative attitudes and discrimination are particularly felt by transgender people, who experience high levels of violence and discrimination. As noted by Godzisz and Pudzianowska (2016), the exclusion of sexual orientation and gender identity from hate crime legislation in Poland perpetuates the notion that some identities are more deserving of legal protection than others, further marginalising LGBTQ+ individuals.

Urgent legal and programmatic actions are needed to protect LGBTQ+ rights in Poland amid rising hatred and violence. The Council of Europe Commissioner urges legal reforms, stricter enforcement of hate speech laws, and recognition of anti-LGBTQ+ prejudice as an aggravating factor in hate crimes. Strengthening anti-discrimination laws is essential for ensuring full legal protection and improving LGBTQ+ living conditions (CommDH (2020)27).

Conclusions

Transphobia in Poland during the populist rule was not only prevalent but also politically and socially instrumentalised. Trans people were framed as disruptive to the social order and systematically denied access to legal recognition. The institutional and political targeting of transgender people reinforces their symbolic role as political scapegoats, exploited to strengthen nationalist rhetoric. More often, it does so indirectly by marginalising and stigmatising minorities in public spaces and reinterpreting existing rights (Kocemba and Stambulski, 2020).

This chapter has discussed the political and social mechanisms used that have fostered intensification of transphobic hate speech, the key aspects of which are:

1. Legislation and politics: In Poland, transphobia is used politically by introducing legislation that stigmatises and marginalises transgender people and other non-heteronormative communities. Examples of such actions include the adoption of local declarations of 'LGBTQ+-free zones', which symbolically, and sometimes practically, exclude these communities from public life. Additionally, the lack of appropriate laws protecting against discrimination based on gender identity increases the legal sanction of transphobia.
2. Public rhetoric of hate: Politicians and other influential public figures often use rhetoric that demonises transgender people, portraying them as a threat to traditional values or social security. Such statements not only reinforce existing prejudices but also legitimise aggressive attitudes and behaviour towards transgender people.

3 Media representation: The media in Poland, especially those controlled by or sympathetic to the previous government, often promote negative images of LGBTQ+ people, including transgender people. Presenting them in a pejorative way contributes to social acceptance of discrimination and violence.
4 Obstacles to access to justice: Transgender people in Poland face numerous obstacles to access justice when they are victims of hate crimes. Legal provisions often do not offer sufficient protection mechanisms, and court procedures can be burdensome and retraumatising for them, discouraging them from reporting crimes.

These mechanisms work together to create an atmosphere in which transphobia is not only tolerated but often encouraged, which has profound and long-lasting effects on the transgender community in Poland. The theoretical constructs of hate (Barth et al., 2023) help to interpret these patterns by framing hate speech as a process of communication rather than individual actions. The systemic approach highlights how hate speech operates within specific communicative contextures, reinforcing exclusionary narratives and legitimising discrimination, as seen in Poland's use of transphobic and homophobic rhetoric to marginalise LGBTQ+ communities. Additionally, the intentionalism and consequentialist perspectives explain how right-wing populists manipulate hate speech for political mobilisation, while its effects normalise violence and restrict access to rights, further embedding discrimination in the socio-political fabric.

Hate crimes and other incidents impact not only the victims themselves because of the immutable and significant aspect of their identity, but also the democratic society and the rule of law, with which an attack on the fundamental principle of dignity and equal rights of all people is incompatible. Effective legal procedures and political stances on hate speech can either fuel discrimination or foster inclusivity, with strict regulations enhancing safety and rights for LGBTQ+ people.

As a first step, it is necessary to introduce direct norms prohibiting hate speech into the legal system and to expand the current definition of hate crimes to explicitly include crimes motivated by bias against gender identity and gender expression. Poland should implement international standards pertaining to the rights of LGBTQ+ people, including the recommendations of the Council of Europe and the judgements of the European Court of Human Rights. This includes express prohibition of discrimination on the basis of gender identity in various areas of society, such as employment, education, access to services (including healthcare), and access to goods and services. Appropriate national regulations and procedures should condemn actions with discriminatory motives. In this way, the state sends a signal to perpetrators of crimes that there is no place for such behaviour in a democratic society (CM/Rec (2010)5).

References

Article 19 (2018). *Polska: Reagowanie na mowę nienawiści*. London: Free Word Centre.

Atlas Nienawiści (Atlas of Hate) (n.d.) https://atlasnienawisci.pl/

Barth, N., Wagner, E., Raab, P., & Wiegärtner, B. (2023). Contextures of hate: Towards a systems theory of hate communication on social media platforms. *The Communication Review*, *26*(3), 209–252. https://doi.org/10.1080/10714421.2023.2208513

Białach S. (2022), *Aktywiści Kai Godek przed szkołą atakują osoby LGBT. Poseł PO zawiadamia policję*. https://wiadomosci.onet.pl/lublin/pikieta-anty-lgbt-przed-szkola-w-lublinie-posel-po-zawiadamia-policje/cm9cwlb

Bień-Kacała, A. (2020). Konstytucjonalizm nieliberalny w Polsce po 2015 roku. In M. Grant (Ed.), *Sądownictwo konstytucyjne: teoria i praktyka*. Warsaw: Wydawnictwo Naukowe UKSW.

Bojanowski, T. (2021). Wybrane prawnokarne aspekty mowy nienawiści w kontekście standardów ochrony wolności słowa. *Prawo W Działaniu*, *47*, 168–186. https://doi.org/10.32041/pwd.4710

Brown, T. (2017) *Opinia Publiczna O Prawach Osób Transpłciowych: Polska*. The Williams Institute. https://williamsinstitute.law.ucla.edu/wp-content/uploads/Public-Opinion-Trans-Poland-Polish-Jan-2019.pdf

Bucholc, M. (2022). The anti-LGBTIQ campaign in Poland: The established, the outsiders, and the legal performance of exclusion. *Law & Policy*, *44*(1), 4–22.

CBOS 90/2019. Stosunek Polaków do związków homoseksualnych. Centrum Badań Opinii Społecznej (CBOS), komunikat nr 90/2019 https://www.cbos.pl/SPISKOM.POL/2019/K_090_19.PDF

Chrzczonowicz, M. (2020). *Uczeń nie może propagować treści rasistowskich, nazistowskich oraz... LGBT. Oko Press*. https://oko.press/uczen-nie-moze-propagowac-tresci-rasistowskich-nazistowskich-oraz-lgbt

CM/Rec (2010)5. Recommendation of the Committee of Ministers to Member States on measures to combat discrimination on grounds of sexual orientation or gender identity.

CommDH (2007). Assessment of the progress made in implementing the 2002 recommendations of the Council of Europe Commissioner for Human Rights, 20 June 2007, paras. 51–57. https://rm.coe.int/16806db77d

CommDH (2020)27. Strasbourg, 3 December 2020. Original version. Memorandum on the stigmatisation of *LGBTI* people in Poland https://rm.coe.int/memorandum-on-the-stigmatisation-of-lgbti-people-in-poland/1680a08b8e

CRI[2015]20. *ECRI report on Poland*. Adopted on 20 March 2015. Published on 9 June 2015. https://rm.coe.int/fifth-report-on-poland/16808b59a0

Declaration of the Małopolska Voivodeship Assembly (2019, 29 April). Nr 1/19, regarding the opposition to the introduction of the 'LGBT' ideology into local government communities.

de Groot, D., and Immenkamp, B. (2025) *Hate speech and hate crime targeting LGBTI people*. European Parliamentary Research Service, Members' Research Service PE 767.219.

Dz. U. No. 78, item 483. The Constitution of the Republic of Poland of 2nd April, 1997.

Dz. U. No. 254, item 1700. Act of 3 December 2010 on implementing certain EU laws on equal treatment.

Dz. U. 2024, poz. 466. Regulation of the Minister of National Defense of 25 March 2024 on determining fitness for military service and the procedure of military medical commissions in these matters.

E-005625/2020. Question for written answer to the Commission Rule 138, vans inciting hate speech against LGBTI persons in Poland https://www.europarl.europa.eu/doceo/document/E-9-2020-005625_EN.html

EU-LGBTI II (2024, 30 April). A long way to go for LGBTI equality. European Union Agency for Fundamental Rights. https://fra.europa.eu/en/publication/2020/eu-lgbti-survey-results

EUR 37/5882/2022. Amnesty International, 'They treated us like criminals' from shrinking space to harassment of LGBTI activists. https://www.amnesty.org/en/documents/eur37/5882/2022/en/

Foa, R., and Mounk, Y. (2016). The democratic disconnect. *Journal of Democracy*, *27*(3), 5–17. https://doi.org/10.1353/jod.2016.0049

Fukuyama, F. (2015). Why is democracy performing so poorly? *Journal of Democracy*, *26*(1), 11–24.

Gierdal, K., Godzisz, P., Knut, P., Makuchowska, M., and Więckiewicz, K. (2018). Rząd PiS to najgorszy rząd dla osób LGBT od '89 roku (report). https://archiwumosiatynskiego.pl/wpis-w-debacie/rzad-pis-to-najgorszy-rzad-dla-osob-lgbt-od-89-roku-raport/

Godzisz, P., and Pudzianowska, D. (2016). Do some identities deserve more protection than others? The case of anti-LGBT hate crime laws in Poland. In J. Schweppe and M. A. Walters (Eds.), *The Globalization of Hate: Internationalizing Hate Crime?* (pp. 174–189). Oxford: Oxford University Press

Godzisz, P., and Rawłuszko, M. (2018). Responding to anti-LGBT hate crimes in Poland: One step forward, two steps back? In P. Godzisz and G. Viggiani (Eds.), *Running Through Hurdles: Obstacles in the Access to Justice for Victims of Anti-LGBTI Hate Crimes in Europe* (pp. 221–243). Warsaw: Lambda.

Hadel M. (2020). Problematyka aksjologicznego nadużycia kompetencji w kontekście tzw. uchwał 'anty-LGBT'. *Rozważania na kanwie aktualnego orzecznictwa sądów administracyjnych. Samorząd Terytorialny*, 12, 7–20.

I KZP 5/02. Resolution of the Polish Supreme Court of March 28, 2002, OSP 2002, No. 12, item 164

II SA/Ke 650/19. Resolution of the Voivodeship Administrative Court in Kielce of September 30, 2019.

II SA/Po 188/20. Resolution of the Voivodeship Administrative Court in Poznań of April 16, 2020.

II SA/Rz 1118/19. Resolution of the Voivodeship Administrative Court in Rzeszów of November 22, 2019.

II SA/Rz 27/20. Resolution of the Voivodeship Administrative Court in Rzeszów of September 8, 2020.

III K 936/18. Decision of the District Court Lublin-Zachód in Lublin of November 6, 2018,

III SA/Gl 15/20. Judgment of the Voivodeship Administrative Court in Gliwice of July 14, 2020.

III SA/Kr 316/20. Resolution of the Voivodeship Administrative Court in Kraków of July 6, 2020.

III SA/Kr 360/20. Resolution of the Voivodeship Administrative Court in Kraków of June 24, 2020.

III SA/Lu 312/20. Dissenting opinion to the Resolution of the Voivodeship Administrative Court in Lublin of February 17, 2021.

III SA/Lu 7/20. Judgment of the Voivodeship Administrative Court in Lublin of August 6, 2020.

ILGA-Europe (2020). https://www.ilga-europe.org/

ILGA-Europe (2024). *Annual review of the human rights situation of lesbian, gay, bisexual, trans, and intersex people covering the period January to December 2023* https://www.ilga-europe.org/sites/default/files/2024/poland.pdf

Immenkamp, B. (2024). *Criminalisation of hate speech and hate crime in selected EU countries*. European Parliamentary Research Service, PE 766.226.

Jamel, J. (2017). Transphobic hate crime on a national and international scale. In J. Jamel (Ed.), *Transphobic hate crime*. Palgrave Hate Studies (pp. 21–40). Cham: Palgrave Macmillan.

Kocemba, K., and Stambulski, M. (2020). Populizm a polityka praw człowieka. *Studenckie Prace Prawnicze, Administratywistyczne I Ekonomiczne*, *31*, 135–156. https://doi.org/10.19195/1733-5779.31.8

Kołodziejek, E. (2022), *Komunikacja inkluzywna. Odpowiedzialność za słowo*, https://etykajezyka.pl/wp-content/uploads/2022/01/ETYKA-JEZYKA-Poradnik-FH-WYDANIE-2.pdf

Krzysztoszek, A., and Mandilara, S. (2023, 18 May). Polish LGBT-free zones won't get EU funding, says French MEP. *Euractiv* https://www.euractiv.com/section/politics/news/polish-lgbt-free-zones-wont-get-eu-funding-says-french-mep/

Kubas, S. (2022). Illiberal democracy in the comparative analysis of Hungary and Poland. *Przegląd Prawa Konstytucyjnego*, *66*(2), 253–267. https://doi.org/10.15804/ppk.2022.02.19

Kuta N. (2021). Sytuacja społeczna osób LGBTA w Polsce 2019–2020. *Tranzycja.pl*. https://tranzycja.pl/publikacje/raport-sytuacja-spoleczna-osob-lgbt-2020-trans-statystyki/#co-raport-sytuacja-spoleczna-osob-lgbta-w-polsce-2019-2020-mowi-o-osobach-trans

Makuchowska M., Chaber A., and Jabłońska, Z. (2013). Ofiary przestępstw z nienawiści'. In L. Mazowiecka (Ed.), *Ofiary przestępstw z nienawiści*. Warsaw: Wolters Kluwer.

Marchi, M., Travascio, A., Uberti. D., De Micheli, E., Quartaroli, F., Laquatra, G., Grenzi, P., Pingani, L., Ferrari, S., Fiorillo, A., Converti, M., Pinna, F., Amaddeo, F., Ventriglio, A., Mirandola, M., and Galeazzi, G. M. (2024). Microaggression toward LGBTIQ people and implications for mental health: A systematic review. *International Journal of Social Psychiatry*, *70*(1), 23–35. doi:10.1177/00207640231194478

Maszkowski, R. (2010). Mowa nienawiści w Radiu Maryja (głos w dyskusji). In A Bodnar, A. Gliszczyńska-Grabias, R. Wieruszewski, and M. Wyrzykowski (Eds.), *Mowa nienawiści a wolność słowa. Aspekty prawne i społeczne*. Warsaw: Wolters Kluwer Polska.

Mazurczak A., Mrowicki M., and Adamczewska-Stachura M. (2019). *The legal situation of non-heterosexual and transgender persons in Poland. Synthesis of the report of the Commissioner of Human Rights*.

Mazurczak, A., and Winiewski, M. (2020). *Długa Droga Do Równości Osób LGBTI Komentarz badawczy i prawny do wyników badania Agencji Praw Podstawowych Unii Europejskiej dotyczących Polski*. Warsaw: Komisja Europejska Przedstawicielstwo w Polsce.

Meyerhoefer, C., Xue, B., and Poznańska, A. (2023). Implications of the decline in LGBT rights for population mental health: Evidence from Polish 'LGBT-free zones'. *NBER Working Paper*. https://doi.org/10.3386/w31702

Nadal, K. L., Whitman, C. L., Davis, L. S., Erazo, T., and Davidoff, K. C. (2016). Microaggressions toward lesbian, gay, bisexual, transgender, queer, and genderqueer people: A review of the literature. *The Journal of Sex Research*, 53(4/5), 488–508.

Nierenberg, B. (2007) *Publiczne przedsiębiorstwo medialne*. Kraków: Wydawnictwo Uniwersytetu Jagiellońskiego, p. 27.

OJ C 255/8 (2021, 29 June). Public discrimination and hate speech against LGBTI people, including LGBTI free zones, European Parliament resolution of 18 December 2019 on public discrimination and hate speech against LGBTI people, including LGBTI free zones (2019/2933(RSP)).

Ordo Iuris (2024). Ofensywa lobby LGBT w polskich szkołach. Ordo Iuris oraz Centrum Życia i Rodziny reagują na 'Tęczowy Piątek'. https://ordoiuris.pl/edukacja/

ofensywa-lobby-lgbt-w-polskich-szkolach-ordo-iuris-oraz-centrum-zycia-i-rodziny-reaguja-na
OSCE (2022). *Hate crime laws: A practical guide* (2nd ed.). Warsaw: OSCE Office for Democratic Institutions and Human Rights.
Ploszka, A. (2022). From human rights to human wrongs. How local government can negatively influence the situation of an individual. The case of Polish LGBT ideology-free zones. *The International Journal of Human Rights*, *27*(2), 359–379.
R(97)20. Recommendation of the Committee of Ministers to Member States on 'hate speech' adopted on 30 October 1997, p. 107.
Ref. CG002(2021). Congress of Local and Regional Authorities, Poland: New Council of Europe report criticizes increasing attacks and discrimination against LGBTI people. https://search.coe.int/directorate_of_communications#{%22CoEIdentifier%22:[%220900001680a16233%22],%22sort%22:[%22CoEValidationDate%20Descending%22]}
Ruczkowski, P. (2021). Aksjologia Konstytucji RP, czyli od wartości do prawa pozytywnego. *Dialogi Polityczne*, *30*, 100–102.
Sadurski, W. (2018). *Poland's constitutional breakdown*. Oxford: Oxford University Press.
Samorządowa Karta Praw Rodzin. (2022). https://kartarodzin.pl/wp-content/uploads/2022/02/SKPR_gmina_digital.pdf
Szeroczyńska, M., and Śledzińska-Simon, A. (2013). Założenia Zmian Prawnych Dotyczących Osób Transpłciowych w Prawie Polskim. In W. Dynarski and K. Śmiszek (Eds.), *Sytuacja prawna osób transpłciowych w Polsce; raport z badań i propozycje zmian* (pp. 198–199). Warsaw: Fundacja Trans-Fuzja.
Turner, L., and Whittle, S. (2012). *Transphobic hate crime in the European Union* (2nd ed.), London: Press for Change, BM Network.
Urbańczyk, M., and Rogalska, E. (2017). Złożoność zjawiska mowy nienawiści w pozaprawnym aspekcie definicyjnym. *Studia Nad Autorytaryzmem I Totalitaryzmem*, *39*(2), 117–135. https://doi.org/10.19195/2300-7249.39.2.8
VIII SA/Wa 42/20. Judgment of the Voivodeship Administrative Court in Warsaw of July 15, 2020.
Warszawska Polityka Miejska Na Rzecz Społeczności LGBT+ (n.d.). https://mnw.org.pl/warszawska-deklaracja-lgbt/
Wypych, M., and Bilewicz, M. (2022). Psychological toll of hate speech: The role of acculturation stress in the effects of exposure to ethnic slurs on mental health among Ukrainian immigrants in Poland. *Cultural Diversity & Ethnic Minority Psychology*, *30*(1), 35–44. https://doi.org/10.1037/cdp0000522
X/40/19. April 30, 2019, the Rycki District Council adopted resolution. Position of the Rycki District Council on stopping gender and 'LGBT' ideology.
XI.505.27.2019.MA (A. Bodnar). https://bip.brpo.gov.pl/sites/default/files/Wyst%C4%85pienie%20do%20Przewodnicz%C4%85cego%20KRRiT%20ws.%20programu%20TVP%20%27Inwazja%27%2C%2018%20listopada%202019%20r.pdf
Zakaria, F. (2023, 2 October). The rise of illiberal democracy. *Foreign Affairs*. https://www.foreignaffairs.com/world/rise-illiberal-democracy

8

FATAL TRANSGENDER HATE CRIMES IN AMERICA: ACCOUNTS FROM A NEWLY ESTABLISHED TRANSGENDER HOMICIDES DATABASE

Brendan Lantz and Marin R. Wenger

Introduction

Homicides targeting transgender people, referring to anyone whose gender identity or gender expression differs from the sex that they were assigned at birth, have reached historically high levels in recent years in America (Fitzgerald, 2017; Lenning, Brightman, and Buist, 2021), increasing by more than 62% between 2019 and 2020, with similar increases thereafter (Lantz, Faulkner, and Mills, 2024). These increases have occurred at such a rate that the American Medical Association (AMA) was prompted to declare fatal attacks against transgender people an 'epidemic' (AMA, 2019). International research has emphasised similar patterns, with evidence indicating that a transgender person is murdered as frequently as every three days (Balzer, 2009). Prior research has noted that many of these instances of fatal violence are hate crimes, or crimes that are motivated by, or at least suspected to be motivated by, bias (Lantz, Faulkner, and Mills, 2024).[1] Yet, fatal violence toward transgender people is extremely understudied (Westbrook, 2022); almost no existing research, moreover, has considered the role that bias motivation might play in structuring differences between such homicides.

This omission is significant, because the examination of differences and similarities between transphobic homicides and non-bias instances of transgender homicide provides for a critical lens through which we can consider the unique theoretical and etiological role of bias in structuring differences in the situational dynamics of transphobic homicide. Bias-motivated homicide and other homicides targeting transgender people may have many characteristics in common, but likely also have etiologically distinct characteristics associated with each type of violence as well. Yet there is virtually no

DOI: 10.4324/9781003564928-10

research applying a theoretical lens to the analysis of variation in transgender homicides that are hate crimes, compared to those that are not.

In its current form, existing literature is unable to even provide basic information about the nature of bias-motivated transgender homicides; this lack of basic information necessarily means that the key features of these violent incidents are not easily understood. Following this, in the current chapter, we address this issue using data from the 'Tracking Transgender Homicide in America' database, a comprehensive nationwide database on deadly violence directed against transgender people which includes data collected since 2010 through extensive open-source data collection methods and maintained by researchers at Florida State University (FSU) (see Lantz, Faulkner, and Mills, 2024). In doing so, we employ quantitative analyses and narrative analyses of several prominent case studies to achieve two primary research aims. First, we conduct a quantitative analysis of transgender homicides, comparing the distinct features of those that are bias-motivated, to those that are not. Second, we apply a narrative case study approach to a selected sample of bias-motivated transphobic homicides to illuminate the unique event trajectories and circumstances under which these homicides took place.

Transgender violence in America

As noted previously, detailed quantitative information on bias-motivated transgender homicide in America is severely lacking. One of the primary reasons for the lack of effective research on bias-motivated transgender homicide has been the critical shortage of data capable of providing insight into this issue (Davies, Tetzlaff-Bemiller, and Drake, 2017; Dinno, 2017; Lenning, Brightman, and Buist, 2021; Lantz, Faulkner, and Mills, 2024; Westbrook, 2022). While the reasons for this lack of data have been discussed at length elsewhere (see Lantz, Faulkner, and Mills, 2024; Westbrook, 2022), one of the primary factors responsible for this omission is the ineffectiveness of tracking gender identity within existing systems that record violent death.

Recent research, however, has taken strides toward better understanding homicides targeting transgender people through other data collection techniques (see Lantz, Faulkner, and Mills, 2024). While such advances are important, it is also critical that we take steps toward understanding variation and heterogeneity in transgender homicide patterns. Much of the existing literature on violence toward transgender people, however, suffers from the presumption that *all* such violence is rooted in transphobic attitudes and motivated by the transgression of gender boundaries. It is true that many incidents of violence targeting transgender populations are, in fact, rooted, implicitly or explicitly, in biased or prejudicial attitudes; but this is not true of all such violence. Transgender people also face violence similar in nature to that of cisgender people including, for example, violence directed at them by family, intimate partners, or simply because of unfortunate circumstances that have nothing to do with the gender identity of the victim. As Lantz, Faulkner, and Mills (2024: 345) put it,

> some violence against transgender people, may be inextricably linked to, and even motivated by, the victim's status as transgender, while other violence may be incidental in that it is directed against a transgender person but independently motivated, while still other forms of violence may not be explicitly motivated by a person's transgender status but still indirectly related to this status through other processes of societal marginalization.

While research on fatal bias-motivated violence toward transgender people is severely limited, there is a more expansive body of research on non-fatal bias violence. Xavier (2000), for example, found that 43% of respondents in a sample of transgender Washington, DC, residents had experienced a victimisation incident; further, roughly 34% of these victims indicated that they felt the crime had been motivated by transphobia, with another 41% indicating they felt the crime was motivated by homophobia. In their national-level survey, Lombardi et al. (2002) found that nearly 60% of respondents reported some type of violence motivated by bias toward their gender identity in their lifetime. These studies aside, little research has specifically focused on the differences between bias crimes and non-bias crimes, and none that we are aware of has specifically focused on differences in fatal violence toward transgender people according to the motivation behind the offence.

Current research: Bias-motivated homicides targeting transgender people

To investigate these differences, this research specifically draws upon a symbolic interactionist framework, which posits that situational dynamics and definitions are socially constructed during the process of interaction, as individuals assess, anticipate, and respond to their environment and the actions of others. Goffman (1959) specifically framed symbolic interactionism within the context of dramatic action, wherein social actors see themselves as acting within a role, while also simultaneously responding to the roles of others; in doing so, Goffman specifically emphasised the importance of social context and interactions in structuring situational outcomes. This framework has been applied by several scholars to the understanding of homicides (see Athens, 1980; Luckenbill, 1977), in both qualitative (Kelley and Gruenewald, 2015) and quantitative contexts (Lantz and Wouters, 2024; Wenger, Lantz, and Pupo, 2024). Specifically, we employ quantitative analyses and narrative analyses of several cases to achieve two primary research aims.

Quantitative differences between bias-motivated transgender homicides and other transgender homicides

To begin, we conduct quantitative analyses examining differences between bias-motivated and non-bias-motivated transgender homicides using data from the Tracking Transgender Homicide in America project. While these data are described in detail elsewhere (see Lantz, Faulkner, and Mills, 2024), we provide a brief overview here. The Tracking Transgender Homicide in America data is held on a comprehensive nationwide database on deadly violence directed toward transgender people dating back to 2010, including detailed quantitative information on victim, perpetrator, and offence characteristics of each violent incident, as well as qualitative narrative information about each case. These data were collected through open-source data collection techniques, including extensive review of media/news reports, police reports, and related sources.

Specifically, we conduct a multivariate logistic regression analysis wherein we predict whether a transgender homicide victimisation incident was bias-motivated, according to a variety of victim and incident characteristics selected based on their demonstrated relevance in previous research on transgender homicide using these data (Lantz, Faulkner, and Mills, 2024; Lantz et al., 2024).[2] Victim characteristics include age (in years), race/ethnicity (Black, Hispanic, or another race), gender (woman or not), and involvement in sex work (yes or no/unknown). Incident characteristics include injury type (gunshot, stab wound, or other), location (on the street, at home, or other), whether an argument preceded the homicide, and whether a robbery was involved. We also include a covariate accounting for the documented presence of deadnaming by law enforcement, a practice wherein the victim is referred to by a non-preferred name, typically matching sex assigned at birth, often the victim's birthname, in order to assess the possibility that the likelihood of this practice differs for bias-motivated homicides, relative to non-bias homicides (see Lantz et al., 2024). Our analysis includes 277 transgender homicide victims.

As seen in Table 8.1, we identify a few key significant differences between fatal bias crimes targeting transgender people and other incidents of fatal violence involving transgender victims. We note that our statistical power is limited by the relatively small sample, so the absence of a significant difference does not mean that a given factor is not important, as it may be significant in a larger sample; we have confidence, however, in those effects that do exhibit significance. First, we observe marginally significant differences by age, such that hate crime victims tend to be younger than non-bias victims ($p < 0.10$). Second, hate crime victims are significantly less likely to be Black, relative to white or other race ($p < 0.01$); we observe no significant difference in the likelihood of bias motivation between incidents involving Hispanic

TABLE 8.1 Likelihood of bias motivation, according to victim and incident characteristics ($N = 277$)

	OR	*C.I.*	*Sig.*
Victim characteristics			
Age	0.946	0.888–1.008	+
Race/ethnicity			
Black	0.098	0.023–.416	**
Hispanic	0.573	0.136–2.412	
Woman	5.799	0.708–47.473	
Sex Work Involvement	3.034	1.071–8.600	*
Incident characteristics			
Injury type			
Gunshot	2.138	0.539–8.478	
Stabbed	0.414	0.075–2.280	
Location			
Street	1.016	0.312–3.311	
Home	2.159	0.680–6.851	
Dispute-related	0.270	0.010–7.273	
Robbery	0.935	0.155–5.632	
Police deadnaming	2.982	1.018–8.733	*
Constant	0.090	0.006–1.367	

Note: Abbreviations: OR=Odds ratio; C.I.=Confidence interval
$+p < 0.10$, $^{*}p < 0.05$, $^{**}p < 0.01$

and incidents involving white or other race victims. Third, we see a strong significant relationship between involvement in sex work and bias motivation, such that hate crimes are significantly more likely to involve victims in sex work, relative to those who have no such history ($p < 0.05$). Finally, we see that police deadnaming is significantly more likely for hate crime victims relative to other victims; this effect is substantial, with the odds of an incident involving deadnaming being bias-motivated almost three times the odds for incidents involving no deadnaming ($p < 0.05$), and will be an important point we return to in our narrative accounts.

Narrative accounts

In the course of our data collections efforts, we have also identified a number of themes that consistently emerge among incidents involving transgender victims of homicide. Here we highlight several cases that exemplify these patterns; we focus, in particular, on narratives involving transgender women, who are the predominant victims in the data.

Neulisa (Alexa) Luciano Ruiz

Neulisa Luciano Ruiz, also known as Alexa, was fatally shot and killed in Toa Baja, Puerto Rico, in February 2020. Alexa was experiencing homelessness – an unfortunately common experience among transgender people, with studies consistently showing that transgender people experience more homelessness and housing insecurity than both cisgender people and other sexual minority populations (The Trevor Project, 2022; Wilson et al., 2020)[3] – when she became the target of a social media post claiming that she was a man using the women's restroom at a McDonald's and that she was using a mirror to 'peep' on people while doing so. Responding law enforcement officers found no proof of the allegations, and the original complainant declined to press charges after learning that Ruiz was unhoused. Nevertheless, the narrative around Alexa spread widely on social media. Shortly after the posts were shared on social media, three young men, Jordany Rafael Laboy Garcia, Christian Yamaurie Rivera Otero, and Anthony Steven Lobos Ruiz, recognised Alexa on the side of the road while they passed by her in a car. The three young men then proceeded to follow her to her car and verbally harass her, before leaving and returning with a paintball gun, which they used to shoot Ruiz repeatedly with paintballs. They recorded each of these actions on their cell phones, sharing the recordings with others, and texting each other to delete them later.

The video, which remained on YouTube for several hours, appeared to show the assailants sexually harassing Ruiz prior to her killing, telling her to 'give me some of that ass'. The threats then escalated from there, with the attackers telling Ruiz they were going to 'shoot her up'. One attacker can be heard saying 'let's spin the tires on this motherfucker,' before another responds with 'you bet I am going to go and shoot him' (misgendering in original quote). While it is unclear whether the assailants that shot Ruiz with paintballs were the same that killed her later that night, Ruiz was later found on the side of the road dead, with multiple gunshot wounds; twelve 9-millimetre bullet casings were found at the scene.

The murder of Alexa Ruiz is one of the clearest examples of 'gender policing' in our data, providing a tragic example of how the act of doing gender in ways that reflect an individual's true identity can turn deadly in social contexts which are otherwise unwelcoming to such behaviour; viewed through a symbolic interactionist perspective, the actions of the perpetrators can be understood as that of actors who otherwise framed their actions as effectively 'policing' the boundaries of acceptable gender-based behaviour (Goffman, 1959). The idea of hate crimes as a form of policing behaviour, for enforcing traditional race- and gender-based hierarchies, was most notably put forth by Perry (2001), who posited that bias crime is a method of policing the behaviour of others that do not subscribe to hegemonic heterosexist social norms. Ruiz was publicly shamed and harassed, both offline and online, for using the bathroom that aligned with her gender identity; the bathroom she used did not, however, align with the perception others had of her gender identity, inciting a violent response to her perceived transgression of traditionally accepted gender norms. We chose to highlight this incident for several other reasons as well. First, the Ruiz killing was rare among the homicides in the Tracking Transgender Homicide data, in that it is one of the few such incidents that was associated with formal hate crime charges, even if those charges were associated with the paintball assault, rather than the murder itself. The presence of video evidence, of course, was fundamental in bringing these charges. Second, this incident highlights the particularly vulnerable social position that Ruiz occupied, which is common among the transgender victims in the data, but unique in comparison to cisgender victims. She was abandoned by her family, who declined requests for a public memorial for Ruiz and had her body cremated without ceremony. She was also experiencing homelessness, an experience shared by many other transgender homicide victims as well (Wilson et al., 2020). Finally, another common theme exemplified by the murder of Ruiz was the blatant misrepresentation and misgendering of the victim by the media. Ruiz was initially referred to as a 'man dressed in a black skirt', a description that is itself layered with transphobia, and a pattern we return to again later. In Ruiz's case, this misrepresentation had profound consequences, provoking her attackers to actively seek her out, and providing a stark example of the tragic impact that such false narratives can have on the lives – and deaths – of transgender women.

Cherry Bush

Cherry Bush lived in Los Angeles and was experiencing homelessness in July 2022 when she was shot and killed because of her gender identity. Authorities charged Eric Antonio Sanchez with her murder, including a hate crime charge. The hate crime charge was facilitated by disparaging comments that Sanchez made publicly based on Bush's perceived gender identity immediately prior to the attack. Very little is known about the circumstances of the killing, other than the fact that Sanchez and Bush had no prior relationship, and Sanchez was reportedly offended by Bush's perceived gender identity.

Like many other victims of transgender homicide, Cherry Bush was misgendered in both media and police reports. Also like many other victims in the Tracking Transgender Homicide database, including Alexa Ruiz, Cherry was experiencing homelessness at the time she was killed. This pattern is worth broader discussion and is in part a product of the disproportionate rates of financial insecurity experienced by transgender and gender non-conforming populations. Wilson et al. (2020), for example, found that more than 8% of transgender adults reported experiencing homelessness at least once in the previous year, a rate that exceeds homelessness rates among cisgender people (1.4%) by a factor of more than six. Research using the National Survey on LGBTQ Youth Mental Health, moreover, estimates lifetime prevalence rates to be higher, such that 38% of transgender girls/women, 39% of transgender boys/men, and 35% of non-binary individuals report experiencing homelessness at some point in their life (The Trevor Project, 2022). Data from the National Alliance to End Homelessness also suggests that rates of homelessness among transgender people are increasing because of a host of factors including familial rejection, victimisation, and discrimination in employment, housing, and other services. Research has also shown that the process of transitioning itself can create employment barriers and is associated with decreased opportunities for employment (Whittle et al., 2007), which has serious impacts on the economic wellbeing of transgender people (Badgett et al., 2007).

Nedra Sequence Morris

Nedra Sequence Morris, a 50-year-old Black transgender woman, was shot and killed in Opa-locka, Florida on 14 May 2022. The perpetrator, Cornelius Bailey, shot Morris inside her car and then abandoned her body in an intersection before disposing of the car and Morris's cell phone in a different location. Advocates in the community, many of whom knew Nedra personally, were vocal that the murder should be investigated as a possible hate crime. What is most notable about this case, other than the profound outpouring of support the victim received from the community, is the way the socio-political context negated the possibility of applying the 'hate crime' label, even if it could be confirmed that Morris was killed because of her gender identity. Put simply, a hate crime charge based on bias toward her gender identity was an impossibility unless it was brought as a federal charge because, at state level, Florida does not include protections for gender identity (or gender) in existing hate crime legislation.

One of the basic tenets of symbolic interactionism, as applied to homicide, is the understanding that the lethal actions of homicide perpetrators represent dramatic action that is the product of the social context in which that action takes place (Goffman, 1959). In this context, the content of state hate crime legislation can be conceptualised as signalling and shaping the broader context of attitudes toward transgender people, defining appropriate and inappropriate behaviour. In other words, if the inclusion of a protected class within a hate crime law signals the social condemnation of violence toward that group, as some scholars have argued (Lantz and Malcom, 2024), then it follows that the omission of that class sends the opposite message: that violence toward transgender people, in this case, is not socially condemned, at least to the same extent that other hate crimes might be. It is perhaps no coincidence that nearly one in five (18%) transgender homicides in the

Tracking Transgender Homicide in America database occurred in two states: Texas (10%) and Florida (8%). These two states not only represent contexts in which gender identity is not included as a protected class in existing hate crime legislation, but also are states in which anti-transgender legislation has proliferated at increasing rates. Individual actions are a function of broader contexts, and while further research is needed, it is critical to consider the effects of such legislative efforts moving forward.

That said, it should also be noted that Texas and Florida are not the only states that fail to protect transgender people in their hate crime legislation. This factor, the omission of gender identity as a protected category from existing hate crime legislation, plays a critical role in limiting responses to bias-motivated violence toward transgender populations in dozens of states across the country. Currently, only 22 states, plus Washington, DC, explicitly enumerate gender identity as a protected category. Yet, hate crimes targeting transgender people, fatal or otherwise, are not confined to those states (or countries) that recognise them as a protected class. Cases such as these highlight the critical need to update and revise existing hate crime legislation to include gender identity as a protected category wherever possible.

Tyianna (Davarea) Alexander and Courtney 'Eshay' Key

Tyianna Alexander, a 28-year-old Black transgender woman who was also known as Davarea by those close to her, was shot and killed in Chicago on 6 January 2021. Tyianna's best friend, Brandon Chris, was in the car with her when she was shot and was also killed. Notably, the killing occurred only weeks after another transgender woman, Courtney 'Eshay' Key, was killed in the same neighbourhood, prompting many to conjecture that the crimes were motivated by bias toward Black trans women, and perhaps committed by the same person or people. Both victims were also killed in similar fashion, shot in the head and left for dead. Although it would later come to light that Key was killed by a man who solicited her for sex, Alexander's case remains unsolved. Advocates openly called for authorities to investigate both as possible hate crimes. In both cases, the Chicago Police Department misgendered and deadnamed the victims, prompting outrage from local advocates.

Unfortunately, the institutional practice of deadnaming and misgendering transgender victims of homicide is not unique to the Chicago Police Department. The Jacksonville Sheriff's Office, for example, infamously deadnamed and misgendered three different transgender murder victims, Celine Walker, Antonia 'Antash'a' English, and Cathalina James, all within the span of a few months. When pressed to change their practices, a department spokesman claimed they were only following institutional policy. Unfortunately, many other agencies adopt similar policies (Waldron and Schwenke, 2018); in other instances, they do not have official policies for dealing with transgender victims and thus choose to default to using names provided on government-issued identification as they would any other victim. Of course, it can be difficult for transgender people to obtain documents in ways that reflect their preferred identity, especially in states with policies otherwise hostile to transgender people.

Selena Reyes-Hernandez

Selena Reyes-Hernandez, a 37-year-old transgender woman, was shot to death in Chicago in May 2020. Reyes-Hernandez was shot by Orlando Perez, who, according to police reports, asked her 'if she was a girl', to which she told him that she was transgender. He left and returned with a handgun and a dark face covering, hopped her fence, walked through her open door, and shot her in the head before fleeing. A statement from the Assistant State Attorney described his subsequent actions as: 'he thought that was enough, so he ran out. But he kept seeing her face, and it kept bothering him and he was mad as hell, so he went back there to do it again.' He then moved Selena's car before returning back to her property and firing several additional bullets into her already lifeless body lying on the floor, enacting a process referred to as 'overkill', signifying the dehumanisation of the victim (Lantz, Faulkner, and Mills, 2024). In a clear example of a hate crime, Perez openly admitted that he killed Reyes-Hernandez for no other reason than the fact that she was transgender. When he left her house the first time, he could have left her to go on with her life, while he went on with his own, never contacting each other again. Instead, he felt compelled to not only return and kill her, but to return a second time to further desecrate her body. Unfortunately, Reyes-Hernandez's family did not recognise her transgender status, choosing to bury her under her deadname. Like many of the other victims described to this point, the local media, police, and medical examiner all deadnamed and misgendered her as well.

The unfolding of events between Perez and Reyes-Hernandez is most consistent with what Kelley and Gruenewald (2015) refer to as a 'mistaken identity' homicide, wherein the offender(s) initially believe the victim to be cisgender, but then learn that the victim is transgender and use violence as an extreme reaction to what is perceived as an affront to their masculinity. This reaction is also consistent with Messerschmidt's (1993, 2012) structured action theory (see also, Goffman, 1959), which posits that violence can result from perceived challenges to one's gender – or to gendered power structures at large – wherein actors experience incongruity between the construction of events as anticipated, relative to reality. When faced with such incongruities, some individuals may perceive violent action as a mechanism for rectifying this conflict, allowing them to reaffirm their own masculinity and, by extension, traditional hegemonic power structures; the symbolic nature of the violence, in this instance, represented Reyes-Hernandez's need to not only terminate his interaction with Perez figuratively – by leaving, for example – but to terminate it in a dramatic and tragic fashion as a way to counter his presumed sexual attraction to her as well. In this case, Perez perceived Reyes-Hernandez's gender identity as being so offensive that he engaged in premeditated murder, leaving and returning with a gun to shoot her, not just once, but twice.

Additional commonalities across bias-motivated incidents

While we have highlighted a number of commonalities across transphobic homicides to this point (e.g., homelessness), several warrant greater discussion. One of the most common, and unfortunate, patterns across bias-motivated incidents is the propensity for law enforcement and the media to misgender and/or deadname transgender victims; this is also evidenced in our quantitative analyses. As detailed above, this practice removes agency from the victim and contributes to further dehumanisation of transgender victims, implicitly feeding into the framing of transgender people as somehow the instigators of their own victimisation, or otherwise 'deserving' of violence (Merry, 2006; Wodda and Panfil, 2014). This informal practice should be the subject of considerable policy effort moving forward (see Lantz et al., 2024 for an extended discussion).

Unfortunately, such policies are not simply a matter of respect for transgender victims; they also fundamentally impact the efficacy and outcomes of case investigations. Recent research by Lantz et al. (2024) shows that cases involving police deadnaming are significantly less likely to be cleared and to result in the arrest of the offender, relative to those cases that do not involve deadnaming. Specifically, they found that the 'probability of arrest is decreased from roughly 60% to 48% when law enforcement engages in deadnaming; in other words, the most likely outcome shifts from cleared to not cleared' (Lantz et al., 2024: 14). Indeed, in several of the cases described above, including Tyianna Alexander, Antonia English, and Cathalina James, law enforcement publicly deadnamed or misgendered the victim and failed to solve or clear the case with the arrest of a suspect. Several of these cases were suspected of being hate crimes, but the motivation could not be confirmed without the identification of a suspect.

We also find that transgender women involved in survival sex work are particularly likely to be the victims of hate-motivated homicide. For transgender women, especially transgender women of colour, who are subject to the combined forces of transphobia, institutionalised racism, and various other marginalising forces, sex work can provide a necessary avenue for survival (Sevelius, 2013; Westbrook, 2022). The illegal nature of sex work in many places, however, including the United States, means that sex workers are also uniquely exposed to violence and victimisation. As Westbrook (2022) details, transgender women in sex work also experience unusually high levels of violence even compared to other women in sex work, noting that some men seek out transgender women because of their own desires, but then respond to their own internalised feelings of shame with violence toward these women. Finally, it cannot be ignored that most of the cases we highlight involve transgender women of colour. Research examining various facets of violence toward transgender people has noted poor police responses to such violence. It is worth considering these patterns within the context of Christie's 'ideal victims' (1986: 18), wherein more ideal victims tend to have a greater proximity to whiteness (Mills, 1997). Most of the cases we highlight, and most of the cases in our data, involve Black or Hispanic victims, who are more commonly stereotyped as crime perpetrators rather than crime victims. As such, law enforcement and other authorities may view these victims as less worthy of help or justice.

These patterns also point to a broader need to understand the problem of violence toward transgender people through an intersectional lens. The problem of bias-motivated violence toward transgender people is multifaceted: it is rooted in transphobia, to be sure, but it is also motivated by homophobia, racism, hegemonic masculinity, and is inextricably linked to a number of other social problems, including gun violence, survival sex work, and housing insecurity. Crenshaw (1989) famously applied the metaphor of the highway intersection to explain the unique hardships experienced by Black women; many of the transgender people in our data occupied uniquely dangerous social positions, existing at the crossroads of not only racialised and gendered discrimination, but a host of other discriminatory and marginalising forces as well. An unhoused Black transgender woman, for example, of which there were many in our data, may face the risk of victimisation not only because they are Black, but because they are a woman, because they are transgender, because they are unhoused, or because of any combination of these factors. Moving forward, it is critical that research on this topic approach the issue with the appropriate complexity, attending to these compounding forces as a fundamental component of such violence.

Discussion

The issue of bias-motivated homicides targeting transgender people is one of critical importance. Yet, we lack even basic research on the topic, in part because of existing data limitations, especially in the American context. In this context, the purpose of the current research was to present a descriptive examination of bias-motivated transgender homicide using a newly collected dataset on the topic. The results suggest several important patterns.

First, while some homicides targeting transgender people are clear and evident hate crimes, like the murder of Selena Reyes-Hernandez, not all such homicides are motivated by bias. Further, a non-trivial number of such homicides are speculated to be hate crimes, be it by local advocates, family, or friends of the victim, but are never conclusively labelled as such for a number of reasons, including the lack of legal protections for gender identity within applicable hate crime legislation and ineffective policing (e.g., deadnaming), among other factors. Drawing attention to these crimes is important, especially given the large body of research showing that the consequences of such incidents extend to the larger community with shared characteristics. Wenger, Lantz, and Gallardo (2022), for example, found that just knowing someone who has been the target of bias-motivated violence is associated with increased individual depression and broader impacts throughout the community (see also Iganski, 2001; Lantz, Wenger, and Mills, 2024).

Second, this research suggests the need to attend to the dangerous nature of sex work for transgender people in America, given that transgender women of colour engaging in survival sex work are especially likely to be the target of fatal hate crimes (see also, Lantz, Faulkner, and Mills, 2024). While research is limited, the work that has been done on the subject has found transgender women are disproportionately involved in such sex work, relative to cisgender people; these disproportionate participation rates are in part the product of higher rates of employment discrimination, as well as related factors (Nadal, Davidoff, and Fujii-Doe, 2014; Weitzer, 2009; Westbrook, 2022). Of course, sex work is also illegal in most places in the United States, meaning that working in this sphere is also associated with high levels of violence and very little protection (Cohan et al., 2006; Valera, Sawyer, and Schiraldi, 2000). Thus, if we wish to address bias-motivated violence toward transgender people, it is critical that we recognise the complex relationship between being transgender and being involved in sex work, as well as the elevated risk of interpersonal violence and victimisation among all sex workers; this should be considered an important point for policy efforts as we work to address violence against transgender populations.

Conclusion

Alexa Ruiz, one of the victims highlighted above, was accused of using a mirror to look at women in the women's restroom and was ultimately killed for her gender identity; while police found no proof of this 'peeping' allegation, those who knew Ruiz knew she carried a mirror. They also knew why: she would hold it up and use it to see who was behind her, because she was scared of what might happen to her if she was not watching her own back. Unfortunately, Alexa Ruiz's fears were justified, as are those of the many transgender people who live in contexts that are hostile to, or do not recognise, their existence. Taken together, our analysis points to many themes associated with fatal bias-motivated victimisation of transgender people, including the prevalence of homelessness, the dangerous nature of survival sex work, and the inextricable influence of toxic masculinity and traditional gender norms. It also cannot be ignored that most of the cases of bias-motivated violence in our data involve firearms; a factor that may be unique to the American context and is worth further exploration moving forward. But what stands out most are the many barriers to effectively identifying and labelling many of these cases as hate crimes. As we note, many instances of targeted violence toward transgender people happen in contexts which do not extend legal protections according to victim gender identity; even the most blatant anti-transgender hate crimes will not be labelled as hate crimes in those jurisdictions unless federal hate crime charges are involved. But even in those states where hate crime laws do protect gender identity, it is critical that we begin to address the fundamental inadequacies of the criminal justice system for responding to such policies. Antiquated institutional policies rooted in traditional understandings of gender inhibit the identification and recording of transgender deaths, and police practices of deadnaming and misgendering victims, a common theme among almost all the hate crime victims in our data, further limit the effectiveness of the criminal justice system in responding to these cases. If we wish to address bias-motivated violence toward transgender people moving forward, fatal or otherwise, it is critical that our policy efforts recognise the complexity of the issue, including the need to recognise transgender people in our existing legislation.

Notes

1 We use the phrases 'hate crime,' 'bias crime,' and 'crimes motivated by bias' interchangeably throughout this work.

2 Specifically, we use firth penalized logistic regression to adjust for the imbalanced nature of our dependent variable, given that confirmed bias murders are infrequent. This method is particularly effective for datasets with imbalanced outcomes, as it introduces a correction factor into the likelihood function (Suhas et al., 2023). This adjustment helps mitigate bias, ensuring that the results more accurately represent the true relationships between predictors and outcomes.

3 Specific estimates of the prevalence of homelessness and housing insecurity vary, with research conducted by the UCLA Williams Institute finding that 8% of transgender adults reported homelessness in the past year, compared to 3% prevalence rates among cisgender and genderqueer sexual minority adults and 1% prevalence rates among cisgender straight adults (Wilson et al., 2020). Research using the National Survey on LGBTQ Youth Mental Health, on the other hand, estimates lifetime prevalence rates to be higher, such that 38% of transgender girls/women, 39% of transgender boys/men, and 35% of nonbinary individuals report experiencing homelessness at some point in their life (The Trevor Project, 2022).

References

American Medical Association (AMA) (2019). AMA adopts new policies on first day of voting at 2019 Annual Meeting. Chicago: American Medical Association. https://www.ama-assn.org/press-center/ama-press-releases/ama-adopts-new-policies-first-day-voting-2019-annual-meeting

Athens L. H. (1980). *Violent criminal acts and actors*. Boston, MA: Routledge and Kegan Paul.

Badgett, M., Lau, H., Sears, B., and Ho, D. (2007). *Bias in the workplace: Consistent evidence of sexual orientation and gender identity discrimination*. Los Angeles: The Williams Institute.

Balzer, C. (2009). Every third day the murder of a trans person is reported. *Liminalis: Journal for Sex/Gender Emancipation and Resistance*, *3*, 147–159.

Bufkin, J. L. (1999). Bias crime as gendered behavior. *Social Justice*, *26*(75), 155–176.

Christie, N. (1986). The ideal victim. In E. A. Fattah (Ed.), *From crime policy to victim policy* (pp. 17–30). London: Palgrave Macmillan

Cohan, D., Lutnick, A., Davidson, P., Cloniger, C., Herlyn, A., Breyer, J., Cobaugh, C., Wilson, D., and Klausner, J. (2006). Sex worker health: San Francisco style. *Sexually Transmitted Infections*, *82*(5), 418–422.

Colliver, B. (2021). 'Not the right kind of woman': Transgender women's experiences of transphobic hate crime and trans-misogyny. In I. Zempi and J. Smith (Eds.), *Misogyny as hate crime* (pp. 213–227). Abingdon: Routledge.

Colliver, B., and Silvestri, M. (2022). The role of (in) visibility in hate crime targeting transgender people. *Criminology & Criminal Justice*, *22*(2), 235–253.

Crenshaw, K. (1989). Demarginalizing the intersection of race and sex: A Black feminist critique of antidiscrimination doctrine, feminist theory, and antiracist politics. *University of Chicago Legal Forum*, *1*(8), 139–167.

Davies, K., Tetzlaff-Bemiller, M. J., and Drake, D. (2017). *Changes in homicide patterns and implications for research: Proceedings of the 2017 Meeting of the Homicide Research Working Group*. Memphis, Tennessee. https://hrwg1991.org/wp-content/uploads/2021/04/2017-HRWG-Proceedings-LHC-5.8.2020.pdf

Dinno, A. (2017). Homicide rates of transgender individuals in the United States: 2010–2014. *American Journal of Public Health*, *107*(9), 1441–1447.

Fitzgerald, K. J. (2017). Understanding racialized homophobic and transphobic violence. In S. E. Weissinger, D. A. Mack, and E. Watson (Eds.), *Violence against black bodies: An intersectional analysis of how Black Lives continue to matter* (pp. 53–70). Abingdon: Routledge.

Goffman, E. (1959). *The presentation of self in everyday life*. New York: Doubleday.

Gruenewald, J. (2012). Are anti-LGBT homicides in the United States unique? *Journal of Interpersonal Violence*, *27*(18), 3601–3623.

Iganski, P. (2001). Hate crimes hurt more. *American Behavioral Scientist*, *45*(4), 626–638.

Kelley, K., and Gruenewald, J. (2015). Accomplishing masculinity through anti-lesbian, gay, bisexual, and transgender homicide: A comparative case study approach. *Men and Masculinities*, *18*(1), 3–29.

Lantz, B., and Faulkner, L. (2024). Female hate crime offenders: The theoretical and policy implications of an under-researched phenomenon. In J. Garland, J. Smith, and I. Zempi (Eds.), *Hate crime perpetrators: New perspectives from theory, research and practice, Vol I* (pp. 189–209). London: Palgrave Macmillan.

Lantz, B., Faulkner, L., and Mills, J. M. (2024). A descriptive account of the nature and extent of transgender homicide in America, 2010 to 2021. *Journal of Interpersonal Violence*, *39*(1–2), 341–368.

Lantz, B., and Malcom, Z. T. (2025). Hate crimes. In A. D. Madden (Ed.), *Across the aisle: Today's crime and punishment issues* (pp. 149–160). London: Bloomsbury Academic.

Lantz, B., Mills, J. M., Faulkner, M., and Wenger, M. R. (2024). Deadnamed and denied justice: The role of deadnaming and other factors in transgender homicide clearance. *Homicide Studies*, *29*(3). https://doi.org/10.1177/10887679241294085
Lantz, B., Wenger, M. R., and Mills, J. M. (2024). The individual impacts of hate crime victimization. In J. Hawdon and M. Costello (Eds.), *Research handbook on hate and hate crimes in society* (pp. 59–81). Cheltenham: Edward Elgar Publishing.
Lantz, B., and Wouters, S. R. (2024). Are group settings intoxicating? Groups, alcohol, and the situational dynamics of; violence. *Criminal Justice and Behavior*, *52*(6). https://doi.org/10.1177/00938548241307320
Lenning, E., Brightman, S., and Buist, C. L. (2021). The trifecta of violence: A socio-historical comparison of lynching and violence against transgender women. *Critical Criminology*, *29*(1), 151–172.
Lombardi, E. L., Wilchins, R. A., Priesing, D., and Malouf, D. (2002). Gender violence: Transgender experiences with violence and discrimination. *Journal of Homosexuality*, *42*(1), 89–101.
Luckenbill, D. F. (1977). Criminal homicide as a situated transaction. *Social Problems*, *25*(2), 176–186.
Merry, S. E. (2006). *Human rights and gender violence: Translating international law into local justice*. Chicago: University of Chicago Press
Messerschmidt, J. W. (1993). *Masculinities and crime: Critique and reconceptualization of theory*. Lanham, Maryland: Rowman & Littlefield.
Messerschmidt, J. W. (2012). *Gender, heterosexuality, and youth violence: The struggle for recognition*. Lanham, Maryland: Rowman & Littlefield.
Mills, C. W. (1997). *The racial contract*. Ithaca, NY: Cornell University Press
Nadal, K. L., Davidoff, K. C., and Fujii-Doe, W. (2014). Transgender women and the sex work industry: Roots in systemic, institutional, and interpersonal discrimination. *Journal of Trauma & Dissociation*, *15*(2), 169–183.
Perry, B. (2001). *In the name of hate: Understanding hate crime*. New York/London: Routledge.
Sevelius, J. M. (2013). Gender affirmation: A framework for conceptualizing risk behavior among transgender women of color. *Sex Roles*, *68*(11–12), 675–689.
Suhas, S., Malo, P. K., Kumar, V., Issac, T. G., Chithra, N. K., Bhaskarapillai, B., Reddy, Y. C. J., and Rao, N. P. (2023). Treatment strategies for serotonin reuptake inhibitor-resistant obsessive-compulsive disorder: A network meta-analysis of randomised controlled trials. *The World Journal of Biological Psychiatry: The Official Journal of the World Federation of Societies of Biological Psychiatry*, *24*(2), 162–177.
The Trevor Project. (2022). Homelessness and housing instability among LGBTQ youth. https://www.thetrevorproject.org/wp-content/uploads/2022/02/Trevor-Project-Homelessness-Report.pdf
Tomsen, S., and Mason, G. (2001). Engendering homophobia: Violence, sexuality and gender conformity. *Journal of Sociology*, *37*(3), 257–273.
Valera, R. J., Sawyer, R. G., and Schiraldi, G. R. (2000). Violence and post traumatic stress disorder in a sample of inner city street prostitutes. *American Journal of Health Studies*, *16*(3), 149–155.
Waldron, L., and Schwencke, K. (2018). Deadnamed. *ProPublica*. https://www.propublica.org/article/deadnamed-transgender-black-women-murders-jacksonville-police-investigation
Weitzer, R. (2009). Sociology of sex work. *Annual Review of Sociology*, *35*(1), 213–234.
Wenger, M. R., Lantz, B., and Gallardo, G. (2022). The role of hate crime victimization, fear of victimization, and vicarious victimization in COVID-19-related depression. *Criminal Justice and Behavior*, *49*(12), 1746–1762.

Wenger, M. R., Lantz, B., and Pupo, J. A. (2024). Constrained choice? The role of co-offenders and structural context in the decision to escalate interpersonal violence. *Crime & Delinquency*, *71*(9). https://doi.org/10.1177/00111287241259471
Westbrook, L. (2022). Violence against transgender people in the United States: Field growth, data dilemmas, and knowledge gaps. *Sociology Compass*, *16*(6), e12983.
Whittle, S., Turner, L., Al-Alami, M., Rundall, E., and Thom, B. (2007). Engendered penalties: Transgender and transsexual people's experiences of inequality and discrimination. *The Equality Review*. Press for Change and Manchester Metropolitan University. http://www.pfc.org.uk/pdf/EngenderedPenalties.pdf
Wilson, B. D., Choi, S. K., Harper, G. W., Lightfoot, M., Russell, S., and Meyer, I. H. (2020). *Homelessness among LGBT adults in the US*. Los Angeles: The Williams Institute.
Wodda, A., and Panfil, V. R. (2014). Don't talk to me about deception: The necessary erosion of the trans panic defense. *Albany Law Review*, *78*, 927.
Xavier, J. (2000). Final report of the Washington transgender needs assessment survey. Washington, DC: Administration for HIV and AIDS, Government of the District of Columbia.

9

A CROSS-SECTIONAL STUDY ON TRANSPHOBIA, COMPASSION, AND CRIME PERCEPTION IN GERMANY[1]

Kristin Weber, Aileen Krumma, Anika Radewald, Rowenia Bender, Aaron Bielejewski, and Deliah Wagner

Introduction

In the 1960s, Harold Garfinkel conducted a series of interviews with Agnes, who we would today describe as a trans woman. Garfinkel emphasised how Agnes tried to 'pass' and hide her gender status, which resulted in her minimising social contact and going out of her way to avoid drawing attention to herself. The environment of 1960s Los Angeles did not have the vocabulary to let Agnes be fully recognised, and 'normal society' operated based on broad assumptions about the natural order:

> For normals, the presence in the environment of sexed objects has the feature of 'a natural matter of fact'. This naturalness carries … the sense of its being right and correct, i.e., morally proper that it be that way. Because it is a natural matter of fact, for the members of our society there are only natural males and natural females. The good society for the member is composed only of persons who are either one sex or the other. Hence the bona fide member of the society … finds the claims of the sciences like zoology, biology, and psychiatry strange.
>
> *(Garfinkel, 1967: 123)*

Decades later, the transgender community[2] has not only gained visibility but also formed a more interconnected and supportive network, with transgender people able to find others to share their experiences with and to be open about their identity and sense of self. A transgender identity is not necessarily a 'discreditable identity' (Goffman, 1963: 42ff.) or one that can only be disclosed in specific environments.

DOI: 10.4324/9781003564928-11

Increasing visibility has led to greater academic interest (cf. Stryker, 2017) and to identification of the many ways in which gendered assumptions permeate institutions ranging from the church (Crasnow, 2021) to the justice system (Greene, 2023). The strategies which transgender people employ to 'do gender' vary but are no longer limited to simply 'blending in' (Marques, 2019).

The political discourse over transgenderism has itself been fragmented, with human rights-based approaches sharing the aisle with outright demonisation. Positioning the transgender community as a political threat has become a cornerstone of politics in many arenas, leading to new rounds of globally enacted symbolic legislation: for example, a bill proposed in the Texas state legislature in March 2025 would establish 'gender identity fraud' as a crime, essentially criminalising being transgender (Galbraith, 2025). The defence of 'binary gender' has subsumed various antifeminist and traditionalist perspectives to become both a significant political issue but also one often framed in terms of 'common sense' (Geertz, 1975), even as scholars continue to explore how 'doing gender in a way that does not reflect biological sex can be perceived as a threat to heterosexuality' (Schilt and Westbrook, 2009: 442).

Hostility to the transgender community is not limited to the US context. Friedrich Merz, Chancellor of Germany, has also expressed his views on the 'gender question': During a political debate on 9 February 2025, when asked his opinion on Donald Trump's plan to officially only recognise binary gender in the US, Merz responded, 'this is a decision, that I can understand' ['*Das ist eine Entscheidung, die ich nachvollziehen kann*'] (Mendgen, 2025).

The use of the transgender community as a *Feindbild* – a constructed public enemy and a scapegoat, literally meaning 'image of the enemy' – parallels increasing public awareness and displays of support. Increasing visibility, not only of the broader LGBTIQA+ community, but especially of transgender people, has also triggered a backlash both in rhetoric and discourse as well as through direct violence. Pride events in Germany have increasingly become targets of aggressive protests by far-right groups (Whittle, 2024; Die Sachsen News, 2024).

Even as legal protections for transgender people become a major focus in public discourse, it remains unclear to what extent different segments of the public, political actors, and media institutions frame transgender people as a legitimate social concern. It is also uncertain whether they are instead dismissed as a 'problem category' shaped by claims-makers in public debate (cf. Spector and Kitsuse, 1977). While some narratives emphasise transphobia as a human rights issue, others position transgender identities as a political controversy, shaping how hate crimes against transgender individuals are perceived and whether they are taken seriously. Despite signs of acceptance, transgender people still experience difficulty accessing healthcare (James et al., 2016), are subject to a variety of intrusive and often changing laws covering the use of restrooms (Schilt and Westbrook, 2015), and face discrimination, if not outright bans, in many social spaces, professions, and institutions. Complicating the issue is terminology, not just in terms of transgender issues (Stryker et al., 2008) but also in how hate crime is conceptualised and understood both among scholars and the general public (cf. Colliver, 2021).

At the same time, public attitudes are not static. Changes in gender orders do not follow a simple linear trajectory, but they result from long-term political and civic engagement (Bereswill and Ehlert, 2023). It remains to be seen whether increasing visibility and greater public contact with transgender communities will, over time, chip away at stereotypes and foster broader acceptance. If so, this could have significant implications for legal frameworks, media portrayals, and everyday interactions shaping the lived experiences of transgender people.

This study contributes to the broader examination of hate crime trends across different contexts and communities. By focusing specifically on transphobic hate crimes in Germany, we connect to similar patterns of identity-based violence documented globally, while applying theoretical frameworks of intergroup contact and diversity beliefs to this specific context. Our findings have implications for understanding the mechanisms behind public perceptions of hate crimes more generally, as explored in other chapters of this collection.

Research on transphobic hate crime in Germany

Hate crimes are taking place every day – sometimes visibly but mostly invisibly for the majority of the society. These crimes are defined by three key elements in Germany: (1) the presence of a criminal act;[3] (2) the perpetrator's prejudice-based motivation, which targets individuals based on 'assumed or actual' characteristics such as nationality, ethnicity, origin, skin colour, religion, gender, gender or sexual identity, sexual orientation, social status, political views, external appearance, or disability (Kugelmann, 2015: 12); and (3) the broader impact of these offences, not only on the direct victims but also on the entire affected group (Coester, 2008; Kugelmann, 2015). Beyond the physical and psychological harm inflicted on victims, hate crime carries a *symbolic message* with far-reaching consequences. This not only affects those directly targeted but also instils fear and insecurity within their social environment and among individuals who share their characteristics or identify with the affected group (Bender and Weber, 2023).

As a result, hate crime extends its harm beyond immediate victims, undermining entire communities and eroding social cohesion. By attacking individuals based on their identity, such crimes threaten fundamental democratic values and principles, ultimately destabilising society as a whole (Bender and Weber, 2023, 2025; Coester, 2017; Perry, 2014). Since 2001, hate crimes in Germany have been documented by the Criminal Police Reporting Service

(CPRS).[4] These offences fall under the broader classification of politically motivated crime and are further categorised into right-wing, left-wing, foreign ideology, religious ideology, or other forms of political extremism. Within the hate crime category, a total of 16 subcategories[5] exist, providing a more detailed classification of the specific forms of hate crime offences.

When examining the development of hate crime in Germany over the past few years, official police crime statistics reveal the following changes: In 2016, hate crime incidents reached a record high, nearly doubling from 5,376 cases in 2001 to 10,751 cases (BMI and BKA, 2020). This upward trend continued peaking in 2023 with 17,007 recorded hate crime offenses (BMI and BKA, 2024). This marks a 47.63% increase compared to the previous year (2022: 11,520 cases; Weber et al., 2025).

The CPRS has undergone significant changes affecting the classification of reported hate crimes related to gender and sexuality. In February 2020, the police created 'gender/sexual identity' as a subcategory to register hate crimes against LGBTIQA+ people but mostly to make a clear distinction between homophobic and transphobic crimes (Ponti, 2023). Two years later, the category of 'gender-related hate crimes/crimes related to sexual identity' was removed and replaced by the broader category of 'gender-related diversity' (BMI and BKA, 2024). These adjustments affect how such offences are recorded and analysed. This highlights a gap in the recording of gender- and sexuality-related offences, making it challenging to assess their development over time. This also indicates that Germany, particularly its law enforcement agencies, has only recently begun to prioritise criminal acts against LGBTIQA+ people. Meanwhile, members of this community and advocacy organisations have been reporting an increase in such offences for years (Ponti, 2023).

Between 2022 and 2023, crimes related to the category 'gender-related diversity' increased significantly, rising from 417 to 854 offences, marking an increase of 104.8% (BMI and BKA, 2023: 11). Criminal acts targeting 'sexual orientation'[6] also saw a notable rise. From 2021 (870 cases) to 2022 (1,005 cases), the number of cases increased by 15.52%, followed by a sharp rise of 49.15% in 2023 (1,449 cases). In contrast, the years 2019 (576 cases) and 2020 (578 cases) showed only a marginal increase of 0.35% (BMI and BKA, 2020, 2023, 2024). Different studies explored the low reporting behaviour of members of the LGBTIQA+ community and other individuals who experienced hate crimes (Bender and Weber 2023; Deutscher Bundestag, 2021; Ponti, 2023). A study by the European Union Agency for Fundamental Rights (FRA) states, that

> 51% of victims of harassment and 33% of victims of physical or sexual attack indicated that they considered the incident too minor or not serious enough to merit reporting it to the police.
>
> *(FRA, 2020: 47)*

The reasons for this behaviour include fear of homophobic or transphobic reactions from the police (FRA, 2020). Only 13% of LGBTIQA+ people in Germany reported experiencing physical or sexual violence to the police (FRA, 2020: 48). The Association of Lesbian and Gay Police Officers estimates that 80–90% of hate crimes against LGBTIQA+ people remain unreported, highlighting a significant dark figure of unrecorded offences (Deutscher Bundestag, 2021).

Significant research gaps in Germany remain regarding the scope, manifestations, and underlying factors of queer-hostile violence. There is also a lack of empirical data on perpetrators and their motivations as well as on how law enforcement and the judiciary respond to these hate crimes (Ponti, 2023). Our study aims to bridge these critical research gaps.

In the international research landscape, a greater number of studies focus on the predictors of transphobic attitudes that contribute to prejudice or criminal behaviour. The following section presents key findings from these studies.

Predictors of hate crime against transgender people

Criminal acts committed against people based on certain group characteristics, such as gender/sexual identity, are referred to as hate crime (Bender et al., 2024). Violence against transgender people because of their gender identity can therefore be seen as acts of transphobic hate crime. In this study, in order to ensure suitable response rates, we did not ask directly about actual propensities for violence, but instead about the support for police action against transphobic violence. This serves as an indicator of transphobic hate crime acceptance, with lower levels representing more transphobic hate crime acceptance.

The majority of transgender people have already experienced forms of harassment in public. This includes insults as well as physical and sexual abuse (Turner et al., 2009). Transphobic hate crimes are mostly driven by prejudice against the victim's transgender identity (Turner et al., 2009). Previous research has found that more negative attitudes towards the protection of minority groups, such as transgender people, were associated with lower levels of blame and punitive recommendations for the perpetrator in cases of hate crime (Cabeldue et al., 2018). Further studies suggest that the propensity for aggression and violence towards transgender people is related to transphobic attitudes (McGonigal et al., 2023).

Based on these associations, we assume that transphobic attitudes are related to less support for police action against transphobic violence as an indicator of advocacy of transphobic hate crime. In order to be able to derive possible implications that reduce hate crime against transgender people, it should therefore also be understood how transphobic attitudes arise. Therefore, a number of factors potentially influencing transphobic attitudes will also be considered.

(Positive and negative) intergroup contact

Intergroup contact can effectively reduce negative stereotyping, prejudice, and discrimination. In 1954, Allport introduced the contact hypothesis, proposing that repeated contact with other social groups group can – in suitable circumstances – foster more positive attitudes towards members of that group. Subsequent research has consistently supported this theory (e.g., Brown et al., 2007; Dovidio et al., 2017; Pettigrew et al., 2011; Pettigrew and Tropp, 2006). Studies show that direct, incidental, and indirect contact with members of other groups contribute to diminishing negative attitudes and prejudices (Brown and Paterson, 2016; De Coninck et al., 2021; Lemmer and Wagner, 2015; Pettigrew et al., 2007). Additionally, more frequent contact with individuals from different social groups leads to lasting positive attitude shifts (Brown et al., 2007; Lemmer and Wagner, 2015).

Improved empathy, perspective-taking, and positive affect toward the other group mediate the effects of contact (Pettigrew et al., 2011; Pettigrew and Tropp, 2008). Research further demonstrates the universality of these effects across nations, genders, and age groups (Pettigrew et al., 2011), highlighting the broad applicability of intergroup contact.

Contact, which is experienced as positive, enhances future interactions, reinforcing their impact (Schäfer, 2020). However, negative contact exerts a stronger influence, intensifying biases, eroding trust, and reducing willingness for future engagement (Aberson, 2015; Graf et al., 2014; Meleady and Forder, 2019; Schäfer et al., 2021). Although positive contact is more frequent, negative interactions shape attitudes more profoundly (Graf et al., 2014; Schäfer et al., 2021).

Klocke et al. (2019) show that German schoolteachers with more contact with LGBTIQA+ people are more likely to integrate diversity topics into lessons and intervene more frequently against discrimination. Similarly, Hatch et al. (2022) demonstrate that negative attitudes and limited contact with LGBTIQA+ people reinforce prejudice over time. Based on this, we presume that positive contact is negatively related and negative contact positively related to transphobic attitudes.

For the present model, we also assume direct correlations between positive and negative contact and hate crime against transgender people. Previous literature has already shown that contact experiences are associated with discriminatory behaviours (e.g., violence based on sexual identity), with positive contact experiences predicting more supportive behaviours and past negative contact experiences predicting more discriminatory behaviours (Hutchison and Rosenthal, 2011; Pettigrew, 1998; Reimer et al., 2017). We therefore assume that positive contact is positively and negative contact negatively related to the support for police action against transphobic violence.

Political orientation

Beyond contact, the study by Klocke et al. (2019)[7] also examined teachers' *political orientation*, finding that left-leaning teachers address sexual and gender diversity more often than conservatives, who are less likely to teach these topics or intervene in cases of discrimination. We presume that an increasing right-wing political orientation is positively associated with transphobic attitudes.

Political orientation appears to have a direct influence on hate crime, with increasingly right-wing political attitudes being associated with less support for increased punishment for hate crime offences (Cramer et al., 2017). This study therefore also focuses on the direct effect of political orientation on hate crime against transgender people, assuming that increasing right-wing political orientation is associated with less support for police action against transphobic violence.

Diversity beliefs

Stronger pro-diversity beliefs are related to lower transphobic attitudes (Schudson and van Anders, 2022) and reduced discriminatory behaviour towards minorities (Kauff and Wagner, 2012). Therefore, we assume that diversity beliefs are negatively associated with transphobic attitudes and positively with the support for police action against transphobic violence.

Demographic variables

Gender is considered a predictor of transphobic attitudes, with men showing stronger transphobic attitudes on average than women (Dierckx et al., 2017). Existing evidence on the impact of education is mixed (Dierckx et al., 2017; Mizock et al., 2017) and remains unexamined in Germany. Accordingly, we explore education as a factor, assuming men and the less educated show stronger transphobic attitudes. Socio-economic and demographic characteristics have shown no correlation with the extent of victimisation by hate crime in previous European studies (Van Kesteren, 2016), which is why no direct correlations between education and gender and support for police action against transphobic violence are assumed in the present study.

The present study

Considering the presented empirical findings and theoretical derivations, we sought to identify predictors of transphobic attitudes in a representative German sample (HaSteX; Bender et al., 2024).[8] The hypotheses were tested in a path model using the statistics software R Studio Version 2024.09.0 (Posit Team, 2022) and the lavaan package for structural equation modelling (Rosseel, 2012), as described in the following section.

The selection of predictors for our model – particularly political orientation, contact experiences, and diversity beliefs – was guided by prior research demonstrating their significant relationships with attitudes toward marginalised groups. Political orientation was included as a key predictor based on consistent findings in German contexts showing its strong relationship to views on gender diversity (Klocke et al., 2019). Our operationalisation of demographic variables followed established international standards, with education coded using the International Standard Classification of Education to ensure comparability across studies.

Sample and procedure

The Survey on Perceptions of Hate Crime, the Penal System and Sex Work (HaSteX) was conducted as a cross-sectional survey, representative of the German population in terms of age, region, gender, and education (Bender et al., 2024). Data were collected by Ipsos from July to August 2024 using an online questionnaire.

From the original, representative HaSteX sample of N = 3,652 people who stated that they did not identify with the male or female gender were excluded due to a lack of meaningfulness and simplification of the analyses (n = 3). Furthermore, individuals were excluded if they had missing values in variables relevant for the analysis (n = 259). Univariate outliers were excluded on the basis of standardised residuals above 3 (n = 59). Following Leys et al. (2019), 21 cases were excluded from the analysis as they were identified as multivariate outliers with $p < 0.001$ by the Mahalanobis distance.

After exclusion, this resulted in a final sample of N = 3,310 participants for further data analysis. Within this sample, 1,664 identified as female (50.3%) and 1,646 as male (49.7%).The participants were on average 48.43 years old (SD = 15.32; age range 18–75). The level of education was coded using the International Standard Classification of Education (ISCED, Federal Statistical Office, 2020) from level 1 (primary education) to level 8 (doctorate or equivalent). Level 1 and 2 respondents were categorised as having a low level of education, while levels 3 and 4 were coded as having a medium level of education and levels 5 to 8 as having a high level of education (Wagner et al., 2024). The education of 1,200 respondents was classified as a high level of education (36.25%), while 1,607 reported a medium level of education (48.55%) and 503 respondents reported a low level of education (15.2%).

Materials

Political orientation. We assessed political orientation by means of self-placement on a left-right political spectrum (Breyer, 2015). Participants were asked to indicate their own political views in social questions on a seven-point scale (1 = left, 4 = centre, 7 = right).

Positive/negative intergroup contact. With two questions, participants were asked how often they personally had direct positive and direct negative contact with transgender people, consistent with the intergroup contact framework outlined above. The frequency of positive/negative contact could be assessed on a seven-point scale (1 = never, 4 = occasionally, 7 = very often). In order to obtain the variance in the dependent variables, people who stated that they had never had contact with transgender people in general were also assigned a value of 1 (never).

Diversity beliefs. Participants' diversity beliefs were surveyed using six items (e.g., 'I value cultural diversity in Germany because it benefits the country'; Kauff et al., 2019; Meyer and Schermuly, 2012; Nakui et al., 2011). Agreement with the items was indicated on a seven-point scale (1 = strongly disagree, 4 = neither, 7 = strongly agree). For the analysis, each participant's score was the mean of six items.

Transphobic attitudes. Attitudes towards transgender people were assessed using two items. Participants were asked to indicate their agreement with the following statements on a seven-point scale (1 = strongly disagree, 4 = neither, 7 = strongly agree; Zick et al. (2023):

1 I think it's silly for a man to prefer to be a woman or, conversely, for a woman to prefer to be a man.
2 Transgender people should try not to stand out so much.

The mean value of agreement with the two items was included in the analysis.

Support for police action against transphobic violence. Participants were asked to what extent they agreed with the following statement: 'The police should take consistent action against verbal and physical attacks against transgender people'. Participants rated the statement on a seven-point scale (1 = strongly disagree, 4 = neither, 7 = strongly agree). As this variable relates to the assessment of criminal behaviour towards people based on their gender identity, the variable was used in the following study as an indicator for hate crime against transgender people.

Results

First, we present bivariate correlations and descriptive statistics for all measures in our analysis in Table 9.1.

TABLE 9.1 Bivariate correlation

		Correlations							
	M(SD)	*Education*	*Gender*	*Diversity beliefs*	*Positive contact*	*Negative contact*	*Political orientation*	*Transphobic attitudes*	*Support for intervention*
Education	2.21 (0.69)	1							
Gender	1.5 (0.5)	−0.03	1						
Diversity beliefs	4.65 (1.53)	0.14 ***	0.04	1					
Positive contact	2.35 (1.76)	0.03	0.02	0.23 ***	1				
Negative contact	1.61 (1.29)	0.0	−0.08 ***	0.04	0.47 ***	1			
Political orientation	3.87 (1.36)	−0.1 ***	−0.06 **	−0.33 ***	−0.07 ***	0.19 ***	1		
Transphobic attitudes	3.57 (1.88)	−0.07 ***	−0.18 ***	−0.4 ***	−0.11 ***	0.22 ***	0.5 ***	1	
Support for intervention	5.6 (1.66)	0.06 **	0.11 ***	0.29 ***	0.05 *	−0.19 ***	−0.3 ***	−0.38 ***	1

Note: N = 3,310. ***p < 0.001. **p < 0.01. *p<0.05. Gender: 1 = male, 2 = female. Support for intervention = Support for police action against transphobic violence.

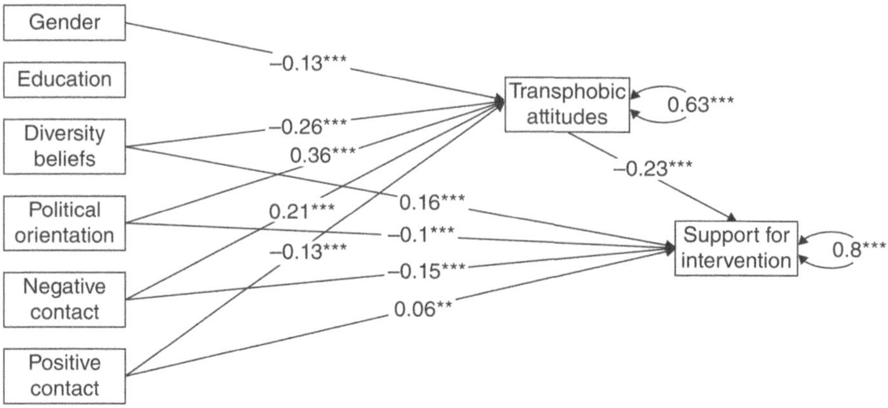

Note. N = 3,310. $\chi^2(2)$ = 8.797, *p* = 0.995, CFI = 0.997, SRMR = 0.008, RMSEA = 0.032, *p* = .05 = .894, *CI*[0.013; 0.055].
Gender: 1 = male, 2 = female. Support for intervention = Support for police action against transphobic violence.

FIGURE 9.1 Path model of the significant correlations

The highest correlation was found between transphobic attitudes and the support for police action against transphobic violence ($r = 0.38$, $p < 0.001$).

Path analysis

We tested our hypotheses in a path analysis[9] with gender, education, intergroup contact, diversity beliefs, and political orientation as predictors; transphobic attitudes as a mediator; and the support for police action against transphobic violence as a dependent variable. The calculated path model (Figure 9.1) showed a good fit to the data, $\chi^2(2) = 8.797$, $p = 0.995$, CFI = 0.997, SRMR = 0.008, RMSEA = 0.032, $p = .05 = 0.894$, *CI*[0.013; 0.055], and explained 36.6% ($R^2 = 0.366$) of the variance of the transphobic attitudes and 19.6% of the variance of the support for police action against transphobic violence ($R^2 = 0.196$). Figure 9.1 shows the path model with statistically significant standardised coefficients ($p < 0.05$) only.

Direct effects

Transphobic attitudes

The findings regarding direct effects on transphobic attitudes mostly confirmed our hypotheses: the results indicated that participants with stronger diversity beliefs scored lower in transphobic attitudes. With regard to gender, the results showed that women had less transphobic attitudes than men. More frequent negative intergroup contact was associated with stronger transphobic attitudes. This effect was stronger than the rather small effect of positive contact, which indicates that more frequent positive contact may lead to lower transphobic attitudes. The strongest association with transphobic attitudes was shown by the political orientation, whereby an increasingly right-wing political orientation was related to more transphobic attitudes. Contrary to our hypothesis, the participants' education showed no correlation.

These findings align with our theoretical framework based on intergroup contact theory. The stronger effect of negative contact compared to positive contact supports previous research showing that negative interactions have more profound impacts on attitude formation (Graf et al., 2014; Schäfer et al., 2021). Additionally, the significant relationship between political orientation and transphobic attitudes reflects the increasing politicisation of transgender issues in German public discourse, as discussed in our introduction.

Support for police action against transphobic violence

Transphobic attitudes showed the highest association with support for police action against transphobic violence, indicating that more transphobic attitudes are associated with stronger disapproval of police intervention in group-based violence against transgender people. For the other variables, we observed only very small direct effects on the support for police action against transphobic violence. These results should therefore be interpreted with caution. More frequent positive contact with transgender people was associated with a stronger endorsement of consistent intervention in group-based violence against transgender people, while more frequent negative contact was associated with more rejection of such intervention. Furthermore, a more right-wing political orientation and lower diversity beliefs were associated with a stronger rejection of intervening in hate crimes against transgender people.

Indirect and total effects

Table 9.2 shows the indirect, standardised effects via transphobic attitudes. Total effects consider both the direct and indirect effects of the individual predictors on the dependent variables. The total standardised effects of the analysed variables are shown in Table 9.3.

Support for police action against transphobic violence

With the exception of the effect of education, all effects of the predictors on the support for police action against transphobic violence were also mediated via transphobic attitudes. However, we observed only very small indirect effects on the support for police action against transphobic violence via transphobic attitudes. The role of transphobic attitudes for the support for police action against transphobic violence is therefore hardly dependent

TABLE 9.2 Indirect effects in the path analysis

	B	*SE*	*Z*	*p*	β
Support for intervention ~					
Education	0.0	0.01	−0.34	0.737	0.0
Gender	0.1	0.01	6.96	<.001***	0.03
Diversity beliefs	0.07	0.01	9.13	<.001***	0.06
Positive contact	0.03	0.0	6.55	<.001***	0.03
Negative contact	−0.06	0.01	−9.02	<.001***	−0.05
Political orientation	−0.1	0.01	−9.97	<.001***	−0.08

Note: N = 3,310. $\chi^2(2) = 8.797$, $p = 0.995$, CFI = 0.997, SRMR = 0.008, RMSEA = 0.032, $p = 0.05 = 0.894$, *CI*[0.013; 0.055]. Gender: 1 = male, 2 = female. Support for intervention = Support for police action against transphobic violence.

on the predictors in our model. The results of the indirect effects should be interpreted with caution.

Gender showed a positive indirect effect via transphobic attitudes as well as a positive total effect on the support for police action against transphobic violence. Therefore, men were slightly less likely to support police interventions against transphobic violence via more transphobic attitudes, but these effects were very small and therefore negligible.

Positive contact and diversity beliefs had minor indirect effects via transphobic attitudes. Positive contact also showed a negligible total effect, while diversity beliefs positively influenced the support for police action against transphobic violence, indicating greater support for police intervention in hate crimes against transgender people.

We found very small and negligible negative indirect effects for negative contact as well as political orientation. Yet, both negative contact and political

TABLE 9.3 Total effects in the path analysis

	b	*SE*	*Z*	*p*	β
Support for intervention ~					
Education	0.0	0.01	−0.34	0.737	0.0
Gender	0.1	0.01	6.96	<.001***	0.03
Diversity beliefs	0.23	0.02	11.62	<.001***	0.22
Positive contact	0.08	0.02	4.82	<.001***	0.08
Negative contact	−0.26	0.02	−11.07	<.001***	−0.2
Political orientation	−0.23	0.02	−9.68	<.001***	−0.19
Transphobic attitudes	−0.2	0.02	−11.11	<.001***	−0.23

Note: N = 3,310. $\chi^2(2) = 8.797$, $p = 0.995$, CFI = 0.997, SRMR = 0.008, RMSEA = 0.032, $p = .05 = 0.894$, *CI*[0.013; 0.055]. Gender: 1 = male, 2 = female. Support for intervention = Support for police action against transphobic violence.

orientation showed negative overall effects on the support for police action against transphobic violence. With increasing right-wing orientation and more frequent past negative contact with transgender people, participants indicated less support for police intervention in hate crimes against transgender people.

Transphobic attitudes nevertheless had the greatest overall effect on the support for police action against transphobic violence.

Conclusion and discussion

The aim of the study was to deepen the understanding of the dynamics of transphobic attitudes in relation to hate crime against transgender people and to analyse predicators for this in more detail. The present study showed an overall rejection of group-based violence, specifically a high level of agreement with police intervention in cases of violence against transgender people among participants ($M = 5.6$). Surprisingly transphobic attitudes were neither totally agreed nor completely rejected ($M = 3.57$). Although trans-hostile statements are not clearly rejected, the majority of participants at least agree that consistent action should be taken against trans-hostile acts of violence.

The queer community, and the transgender community in particular, has not always been seen (internally or externally) as such, i.e., as a distinct and unified community, but rather more as individual cases (Stryker et al., 2008). Even though this has changed, the results of this study, and political events in Germany, suggest that their recognition and need for support remains lacking. In December 2024, the governing coalition in Germany proposed the Violence Assistance Act, which focused on an improved support system for group-based violence, especially for vulnerable groups like woman and transgender people (SPD and BÜNDNIS 90/DIE GRÜNEN, 2024). In February 2025, the Act was adopted in a modified form. One of the main changes was the exclusion of transgender people (Bundesregierung, 2025). As part of the election campaign in February 2025, the Christian Democratic Union (CDU), the party of Friedrich Merz, declared that it would abolish the 'self-determination law'. This law allows transgender people to change their name and registered gender in official documents (CDU/CSU, 2024). This suggests that not only is the need for support for transgender people not fully seen and recognised, but also the visibility of the community as such is inadequate and could even be further constrained.

The insufficient belief in diversity in German society is linked to transphobic attitudes, as our study shows. Men especially, particularly those with a right-wing political orientation and disbelief in diversity, show tendencies to transphobic attitudes, regardless of levels of education. In our study, people with transphobic attitudes demonstrate little support for interventions in cases of group-based violence against transgender people. What may seem obvious uncovers deeper realisations when focusing on the predictors of that attitude.

The connection between transphobic attitudes and the rejection of violence against transgender people shows the threat that transphobic attitudes can pose. Violence against individual members of a minority group symbolises the violence, rejection, and degradation of the entire community.

Our results indicate that positive contact with transgender people was mentioned more frequently ($M = 2.35$), but negative contact ($M = 1.61$) is more decisive for transphobic attitudes. Personal contact is crucial for breaking down prejudices (Bender and Weber, 2023; 2025; Coester, 2008, 2017; Perry, 2014). However, this contact needs to be actively strengthened, especially given the role of the media in constructing 'images of the enemy', which are often exploited by right-wing parties. Far-right narratives deliberately fuel hostility, which is why it is not only important to strengthen the rights of transgender people, but also to increase their visibility and ensure that transgender people have a public voice. Instead of simply having conversations *about* them, they must be given a platform to speak for themselves. Better access to information and real interactions with transgender people can shape attitudes and ultimately encourage the rejection and repudiation of violence. To conduct this, we should think about the visibility of transgender people throughout the media in German society and how we talk about transgender people.

Despite our efforts to obtain a representative sample, we acknowledge potential limitations in our methodology. Self-reported measures of contact with transgender people may be subject to social desirability bias, and our cross-sectional design limits causal inferences. Future longitudinal studies could strengthen our understanding of how attitudes develop over time, particularly in response to political and social changes in Germany.

When violence against a particular group is tolerated, it not only endangers this community but also normalises violence in general: 'Violence is always an outgrowth of milder states of mind' (Allport, 1954: 57). Violence against marginalised communities is never an isolated act – it erodes social cohesion, threatens democratic values, and ultimately harms society as a whole.

Notes

1 The project was financed by funds from the budget approved by the Saxon state parliament.

2 The community of trans people includes a diversity of gender and sexual identities, like lesbian, gay, bisexual, transsexual, transgender, intersex, asexual, and queer, which are subsumed as LGBTIQA+ (in German: *lesbisch*, *schwul*, *bi- und transsexuell*, *intersexuell*, queer, *asexuell*, and *weitere Geschlechtsidentitäten*).

3 Criminal acts can occur as insults, vandalism, online and offline hate speech, discrimination, physical and psychological violence, manslaughter, murder.

4 In German: Kriminalpolizeilicher Meldedienst in Fällen politisch motivierter Kriminalität. For a critical perspective on this system see Schellenberg, 2024; Weber and Bender, 2025.

5 The categories are: antisemitic, antiziganist, xenophobic, disability, anti-Christian, anti-German, misogynistic (since 2022), gender diversity (since 2022), social status, hate crime, Islamophobic, anti-male (since 2022), racism, sexual orientation, other ethnicity, other religion (BMI and BKA, 2024).
6 This subcategory has existed since 2001. In this category, criminal acts against queer, gay, lesbian, bi-, trans-, and intersexual people are gathered (Ponti, 2023). Since 2020, crimes against transgender people were collected in the additional subcategory 'sexual identity' (although 'gender identity' would be a better category; see Ponti, 2023: 115).
7 Klocke et al. (2019) used an online survey of 1,162 teachers.
8 A detailed description of the sample, the survey procedure and all HaSteX variables contained in the dataset can be found online: https://www.zkfs.de/wp-content/uploads/2024/12/HaSteX_Data_Handbook_english.pdf
9 Due to a lack of normal distribution of the data in the dependent variables, bootstrapping with 1,000 draws was used in the calculation in order to obtain robust results.

References

Aberson, C. L. (2015). Positive intergroup contact, negative intergroup contact, and threat aspredictors of cognitive and affective dimensions of prejudice. *Group Processes & Intergroup Relations*, *18*(6), 743–760. https://doi.org/10.1177/1368430214556699
Allport, G. W. (1954). *The nature of prejudice*. New York: Addison-Wesley
Bender, R., Radewald, A., Wagner, D., Bielejewski, A., Weber, K., Krumma, A., Führer, J. L., and Asbrock, F. (2024). *Datenhandbuch: Survey zur Wahrnehmung von Hasskriminalität, Strafvollzug und Sexarbeit (HaSteX)*. Chemnitz: Zentrum für kriminologische Forschung Sachsen.
Bender, R., and Weber, K. (2023). Vorurteilskriminalität – Viktimisierung durch vorurteilsmotivierte Gewalt. In D. Bolesta, J. L. Führer, R. Bender, A. Bielejewski, A. Radewald, K. Weber, and F. Asbrock (Eds.), *Panel zur Wahrnehmung von Kriminalität und Straftäter: innen (PaWaKS): Ergebnisse der ersten bis dritten Erhebungswelle*. Chemnitz: Zentrum für kriminologische Forschung Sachsen.
Bender, R., and Weber, K. (2025). Die Erforschung von Vorurteilskriminalität – eine Übersicht mit Ausblick. In U. Kemmesies, P. Wetzels, B. Austin, C. Büscher, A. Dessecker, S. Hutter, and D. Rieger (Eds.), *Motra-Monitor 2024*. Wiesbaden: Motra.
Bereswill, M., and Ehlert, G. (2023). Diskriminierung aufgrund des Geschlechts und der sexuellen Orientierung. In *Handbuch Diskriminierung* (pp. 581–595). Wiesbaden: Springer Fachmedien Wiesbaden.
Breyer, B. (2015). Left-right self-placement (ALLBUS). *Zusammenstellung sozialwissenschaftlicher Items und Skalen* (ZIS). https://doi.org/10.6102/zis83
Brown, R., Eller, A., Leeds, S., and Stace, K. (2007). Intergroup contact and intergroup attitudes: A longitudinal study. *European Journal of Social Psychology*, *37*(4), 692–703. https://doi.org/10.1002/ejsp.384
Brown, R., and Paterson, J. (2016). Indirect contact and prejudice reduction: Limits and possibilities. *Current Opinion in Psychology*, *11*, 20–24.
Bundesministerium des Innern für Bau und Heimat (BMI and BKA) (2020, 18 May). *Politisch motivierte Kriminalität im Jahr 2020 – Bundesweite Fallzahlen* (Fact sheet). https://www.bmi.bund.de/SharedDocs/downloads/DE/veroeffentlichungen/2021/05/pmk-2020-bundesweite-fallzahlen.pdf?__blob=publicationFile&v=4
Bundesministerium des Innern und für Heimat und Bundeskriminalamt (BMI and BKA) (2024, 21 May). *Politisch motivierte Kriminalität – Bundesweite Fallzahlen 2023* (Fact

sheet). https://www.bmi.bund.de/SharedDocs/downloads/DE/veroeffentlichungen/nachrichten/2024/pmk2023-factsheets.pdf?__blob=publicationFile&v=3

Bundesministerium des Innern und für Heimat (BMI and BKA) (2023, 21 April). *Politisch motivierte Kriminalität im Jahr 2022 – Bundesweite Fallzahlen* (Fact sheet). https://www.bmi.bund.de/SharedDocs/downloads/DE/veroeffentlichungen/nachrichten/2023/05/pmk2022-factsheets.pdf?__blob=publicationFile&v=4

Bundesregierung (2025, 14 February). *Bundesrat beschließt Gewalthilfegesetz*. Die Bundesregierung informiert. https://www.bundesregierung.de/breg-de/bundesregierung/gesetzesvorhaben/gewalthilfegesetz-2321756

Cabeldue, M. K., Cramer, R. J., Kehn, A., Crosby, J. W., and Anastasi, J. S. (2018). Measuring attitudes about hate: Development of the hate crime beliefs scale. *Journal of Interpersonal Violence*, *33*(23), 3656–3685. https://doi.org/10.1177/0886260516636391

CDU/CSU (2024). *CDU CSU election programme. Summary*. https://www.politikwechsel.cdu.de/sites/www.politikwechsel.cdu.de/files/downloads/wahlprogramm-cdu-csu-kurzfassung-englisch.pdf

Coester, M. (2008). *Hate crimes: das Konzept der hate crimes aus den USA unter besonderer Berücksichtigung des Rechtsextremismus in Deutschland*. Berlin: Peter Lang.

Coester, M. (2017). Das Konzept der Vorurteilskriminalität und Folgen für die polizeiliche Praxis. In C. Kopke and W. Kühnel (Eds.), *Demokratie, Freiheit und Sicherheit* (pp. 167–182). Frankfurt: Nomos/Die Deutsche Nationalbibliothek.

Colliver, B. (2021). *Re-imagining hate crime: Transphobia, visibility and victimisation*. Palgrave Macmillan

Cramer, R. J., Laxton, K. L., Chandler, J. F., Kehn, A., Bate, B. P., and Clark, J. W. (2017). Political identity, type of victim, and hate crime-related beliefs as predictors of views concerning hate crime penalty enhancement laws. *Analyses Of Social Issues and Public Policy*, *17*(1), 262–285. https://doi.org/10.1111/asap.12140

Crasnow, S. J. (2021). The legacy of 'gender ideology': Anti-trans legislation and conservative Christianity's ongoing influence on US law. *Religion and Gender*, *11*(1), 67–71.

De Coninck, D., Rodríguez-de-Dios, I., and d'Haenens, L. (2020). The contact hypothesis during the European refugee crisis: Relating quality and quantity of (in) direct intergroup contact to attitudes towards refugees. *Group Processes & Intergroup Relations*, *24*(6), 881–901.

Deutscher Bundestag (2021, 24 February). *Grüne: Hass und Hetze gegen LSBTI-Menschen bekämpfen*. https://www.bundestag.de/dokumente/textarchiv/2021/kw23-pa-inneres-lsbti-844444

Dierckx, M., Meier, P., and Motmans, J. (2017). 'Beyond the box': A comprehensive study of sexist, homophobic, and transphobic attitudes among the Belgian population. *DiGeSt. Journal of Diversity and Gender Studies*, *4*(1), 5–34.

Die Sachsen News (2024, 17 August). Neo-Nazis gather for Christopher Street Day in Leipzig. https://www.diesachsen.de/en/social/neo-nazis-gather-for-christopher-street-day-in-leipzig-2947932

Dovidio, J. F., Love, A., Schellhaas, F. M. H., and Hewstone, M. (2017). Reducing intergroup bias through intergroup contact: Twenty years of progress and future directions. *Group Processes & Intergroup Relations*, *20*(5), 606–620. https://doi.org/10.1177/1368430217712052

European Union Agency for Fundamental Rights (FRA) (2020). *EU-LGBTI II: A long way to go for LGBTI equality*. Luxembourg: Publications Office of the European Union. https://doi.org/10.2811/582502

Federal Statistical Office (Statistisches Bundesamt) (2020). Bildungs-finanzbericht 2020. https://www.statistischebibliothek.de/mir/servlets/MCRFileNodeServlet/DEHeft_derivate_00062770/1023206207004_korr08072021.pdf

Galbraith, A. (2025, 6 March). 'Identity fraud': Proposed Texas state law would make identifying as transgender a felony. *Salon.* https://www.salon.com/2025/03/05/identity-fraud-proposed-texas-state-law-would-make-identifying-as-transgender-a-felony/

Garfinkel, H. (1967). *Studies in ethnomethodology.* New Jersey: Prentice Hall

Geertz, C. (1975). Common sense as a cultural system. *The Antioch Review, 33*(1), 5–26.

Goffman, E. (1963). Stigma: Notes on the management of a spoiled identity. *American Journal of Sociology, 56*(25), 11.

Graf, S., Paolini, S., and Rubin, M. (2014). Negative intergroup contact is more influential, but positive intergroup contact is more common: Assessing contact prominence and contact prevalence in five central European countries: Influential negative but more common positive contact. *European Journal of Social Psychology, 44*(6), 536–547. https://doi.org/10.1002/ejsp.2052

Greene, J. (2023). Gender bound: Making, managing, and navigating prison gender boundaries, 1941–2018. *American Journal of Sociology, 128*(4), 993–1030.

Hatch, H. A., Warner, R. H., Broussard, K. A., and Harton, H. C. (2022). Predictors of transgender prejudice: A meta-analysis. *Sex Roles, 87*(11), 583–602.

Hutchison, P., and Rosenthal, H. E. (2011). Prejudice against Muslims: Anxiety as a mediator between intergroup contact and attitudes, perceived group variability and behavioural intentions. *Ethnic and Racial Studies, 34*(1), 40–61.

James, S. E., Herman, J. L., Rankin, S., Keisling, M., Mottet, L., and Anafi, M. (2016). *The report of the 2015 U.S. transgender survey.* Washington, DC: National Center for Transgender Equality.

Kauff, M., Stegmann, S., van Dick, R., Beierlein, C., and Christ, O. (2019). Measuring beliefs in the instrumentality of ethnic diversity: Development and validation of the Pro-Diversity Beliefs Scale (PDBS). *Group Processes & Intergroup Relations, 22*(4), 494–510. https://doi.org/10.1177/1368430218767025

Kauff, M., and Wagner, U. (2012). Valuable therefore not threatening: The influence of diversity beliefs on discrimination against immigrants. *Social Psychological and Personality Science, 3*(6), 714–721.

Klocke, U., Latz, S., and Scharmacher, J. (2019). Empirische Arbeit: Schule unterm Regenbogen?. *Psychologie in Erziehung und Unterricht, 66*(2), 131–156.

Kugelmann, D. (2015). *Options for efficient law enforcement in cases of hate crime: Fact sheet on the legal opinion.* Berlin: Federal Anti-Discrimination Agency.

Lemmer, G., and Wagner, U. (2015). Can we really reduce ethnic prejudice outside the lab? A meta-analysis of direct and indirect contact interventions. *European Journal of Social Psychology,* 45(2), 152–168. https://doi.org/10.1002/ejsp.2079

Leys, C., Delacre, M., Mora, Y. L., Lakens, D., and Ley, C. (2019). 'How to classify, detect, and manage univariate and multivariate outliers, with emphasis on preregistration. *International Review of Social Psychology, 32,* 1. https://doi.org/10.5334/irsp.289

Marques, A. C. (2019). Displaying gender: transgender people's strategies in everyday life. *Symbolic Interaction,* 42(2), 202–228.

Meleady, R., and Forder, L. (2019). When contact goes wrong: Negative intergroup contact promotes generalized outgroup avoidance. *Group Processes & Intergroup Relations, 22*(5), 688–707.

Mendgen, A. (2025, 6 March). Wie die Union zum dritten Geschlecht steht. *RND.* https://www.rnd.de/politik/friedrich-merz-und-das-dritte-geschlecht-wo-die-union-in-der-gender-debatte-steht-YB3BW4NMCRFE3MJEW4OETW7QIQ.html

Meyer, B., and Schermuly, C. C. (2012). When beliefs are not enough: Examining the interaction of diversity faultlines, task motivation, and diversity beliefs on team performance. *European Journal of Work and Organizational Psychology, 21*(3), 456–487. https://doi.org/10.1080/1359432X.2011.560383

McGonigal, P. T., Chan, E., Eyer, M. M., and Scalora, M. J. (2023). Two sides of the same coin: The role of aggression proneness and disgust in the prediction of homophobic and transphobic attitudes. *Violence And Gender*, *10*(1), 65–69. https://doi.org/10.1089/vio.2022.0006

Mizock, L., Hopwood, R., Casey, H., Duhamel, E., Herrick, A., Puerto, G., and Stelmach, J. (2017). The transgender awareness webinar: Reducing transphobia among undergraduates and mental health providers. *Journal of Gay & Lesbian Mental Health*, *21*(4), 292–315. https://doi.org/10.1080/19359705.2017.1320696

Nakui, T., Paulus, P. B., and Van der Zee, K. I. (2011). The role of attitudes in reactions toward diversity in Workgroups 1. *Journal of Applied Social Psychology*, *41*(10), 2327–2351. https://doi.org/10.1111/j.1559-1816.2011.00818.x

Perry, B. (2014). Exploring the community impacts of hate crime. In N. Hall, A. Corb, P. Giannasi, and J. Grieve (Eds.), *The Routledge international handbook on hate crime* (pp. 47–58). New York/London: Routledge.

Pettigrew, T. F. (1998). Intergroup contact theory. *Annual Review of Psychology*, *49*(1), 65–85.

Pettigrew, T. F., Christ, O., Wagner, U., and Stellmacher, J. (2007). Direct and indirect intergroup contact effects on prejudice: A normative interpretation. *International Journal Of Intercultural Relations*, *31*(4), 411–425. https://doi.org/10.1016/j.ijintrel.2006.11.003

Pettigrew, T. F., and Tropp, L. R. (2006). A meta-analytic test of intergroup contact theory. *Journal of Personality and Social Psychology*, *90*(5), 751–783. https://doi.org/10.1037/0022-3514.90.5.751

Pettigrew, T. F., and Tropp, L. R. (2008). How does intergroup contact reduce prejudice? Meta-analytic tests of three mediators. *European Journal of Social Psychology*, *38*(January), 922–934. https://doi.org/10.1002/ejsp.504

Pettigrew, T. F., Tropp, L. R., Wagner, U., and Christ, O. (2011). Recent advances in intergroup contact theory. *International Journal of Intercultural Relations*, *35*(3), 271–280. https://doi.org/10.1016/j.ijintrel.2011.03.001

Ponti, S. (2023). Queerfeindliche Hasskriminalität in Deutschland. In Institut für Demokratie und Zivilgesellschaft (Ed.), *Wissen schafft Demokratie. Schwerpunkt Antifeminismus & Hasskriminalität*, Band 13, Online-Ausgabe. Jena (pp. 112–125). https://www.idz-jena.de/fileadmin/user_upload/PDFs_WsD13/WsD13_Sarah_Ponti.pdf

Posit Team (2024). RStudio: Integrated development environment for R (Version 2024.09.0) [Computer software]. https://posit.co

Reimer, N. K., Becker, J. C., Benz, A., Christ, O., Dhont, K., Klocke, U., Neji, S., Rychlowska, M., Schmid, K., and Hewstone, M. (2017). Intergroup contact and social change. *Personality and Social Psychology Bulletin*, *43*(1), 121–136. https://doi.org/10.1177/0146167216676478

Rosseel, Y. (2012). lavaan: An R package for structural equation modeling. *Journal of Statistical Software*, *48*(2), 1–36. https://doi.org/10.18637/jss.v048.i02

Schäfer, S. J. (2020). Understanding the effects of positive and negative intergroup contact. https://doi.org/10.18445/20200113-093234-0

Schäfer, S. J., Kauff, M., Prati, F., Kros, M., Lang, T., and Christ, O. (2021). Does negative contact undermine attempts to improve intergroup relations? Deepening the understanding of negative contact and its consequences for intergroup contact research and interventions. *Journal of Social Issues*, *77*(1), 197–216.

Schellenberg, B. (2024). *Politisch motivierte Kriminalität und Hasskriminalität. Das polizeiliche Definitionssystem. Wissenschaftliche Begutachtung und Vorschläge für die Weiterentwicklung*. Bündnis 90/Die Grünen Hamburgische Bürgerschaftsfraktion, Landtagsfraktion Bayern. Landtagsfraktion Thüringen

Schilt, K., and Westbrook, L. (2009). Doing gender, doing heteronormativity: 'Gender normals' transgender people, and the social maintenance of heterosexuality. *Gender & Society*, *23*(4), 440–464.

Schilt, K., and Westbrook, L. (2015). Bathroom battlegrounds and penis panics. *Contexts*, *14*(3), 26–31.

Schudson, Z. C., and Van Anders, S. M. (2022). Gender/sex diversity beliefs: Scale construction, validation, and links to prejudice. *Group Processes & Intergroup Relations*, *25*(4), 1011–1036. https://doi.org/10.1177/1368430220987595

Spector, M., and Kitsuse, J. I. (1977). *Constructing social problems*. New York: Routledge.

SPD and BÜNDNIS 90/DIE GRÜNEN (2024). *Entwurf eines Gesetzes für ein verlässliches Hilfesystem bei geschlechtsspezifischer und häuslicher Gewalt* (Drucksache 20/14025). Deutscher Bundestag. https://dserver.bundestag.de/btd/20/140/2014025.pdf

Stryker, S. (2017). *Transgender history: The roots of today's revolution*. London: Hachette UK.

Stryker, S., Currah, P., and Moore, L. J. (2008). Introduction: Trans-, trans, or transgender? *WSQ: Women's Studies Quarterly*, *36*(3), 11–22.

Turner, L., Whittle, S., and Combs, R. (2009). *Transphobic hate crime in the European Union*. London: Press for Change.

Van Kesteren, J. (2016). Assessing the risk and prevalence of hate crime victimization in Western Europe. *International Review Of Victimology*, *22*(2), 139–160. https://doi.org/10.1177/0269758015627046

Wagner, D., Azevedo, F., Bender, R., Bielejewski, A., Führer, J., Radewald, A., Weber, K., and Asbrock, F. (2024). Datenhandbuch Panel zur Wahrnehmung von Kriminalität und Straftäter:innen (PaWaKS). Zentrum für kriminologische Forschung Sachsen e.V. https://osf.io/7kum4

Weber, K., Bender, R., and Asbrock, F. (2025). Vorurteilsmotivierte Gewalt. Forschungsstand und Folgen für die Betroffenen. In O. Decker, F. Kalkstein, J. Kiess, and P. Kocyba (Eds.), *Demokratie in Sachsen 2024: Jahrbuch des Else-Frenkel-Brunswik-Instituts. Überland*. Leipzig: Edition überland Verlagsgesellschaft mbH.

Westbrook, L., and Schilt, K. (2014). Doing gender, determining gender: Transgender people, gender panics, and the maintenance of the sex/gender/sexuality system. *Gender & Society*, *28*(1), 32–57.

Whittle, H. (2024, 24. January). Germany's trans community battles right-wing falsehoods. *Deutsche Welle*. https://www.dw.com/en/germanys-trans-community-battles-right-wing-falsehoods/a-68065874

Zick, A., Küpper, B., & Mokros, N. (Eds.). (2023). *Die distanzierte Mitte. Rechtsextreme und demokratiegefährdende Einstellungen in Deutschland 2022/23*. [Commissioned by Friedrich-Ebert-Foundation, edited by Franziska Schröter]. Dietz.

SECTION III

Space, Place, and Transphobia

10

OCCUPATIONAL HAZARDS: THE SILENT VIOLENCE EXPERIENCED BY TRANS WOMEN AT WORK

Katie McBride

Introduction

The workplace is often framed as a site of opportunity, self-determination, and inclusion, yet for trans women, it remains a key arena of systemic exclusion and marginalisation. While employment has historically been positioned as a means of affirming gender identity, most notably through the 'real-life test' (Irving, 2008), workplaces continue to operate as sites of cisnormative enforcement rather than genuine inclusion. Despite performative diversity rhetoric, trans employees experience disproportionately high levels of discrimination, job insecurity, and economic precarity (Whittle et al., 2007). This chapter examines how the pursuit of workplace belonging becomes a form of *cruel optimism* (Berlant, 2011), where trans women invest in institutions that ultimately constrain them. Drawing on Butler's (1990) theory of gender performativity and Žižek's (2008) concept of symbolic violence, it explores how trans employees navigate professional environments that demand adherence to rigid gender norms while offering minimal material protections. Beyond insufficient workplace protections, trans employees now face heightened exposure through media harassment, as exemplified by Sodha's (2025) article in *The Guardian/Observer*. This piece deliberately names and shames trans staff members like Dr Beth Upton through misgendering and characterising trans women's identities as potential sexual perversions. Sodha (2025) frames workplace accommodations for trans women as threats to cisgender women's safety, further stigmatising trans employees. This media-driven harassment extends workplace harm beyond organisational boundaries into the public sphere, creating additional layers of vulnerability for trans employees. Central to this discussion is the role of HR processes, which frequently

DOI: 10.4324/9781003564928-13

function as mechanisms of institutional silencing rather than sites of redress (Spade, 2015). By analysing workplace discrimination as both an individual and structural harm, this chapter interrogates the interplay between economic necessity, social legitimacy, and systemic exclusion, illustrating how trans women are compelled to persist in environments where silence is not a choice but a condition of survival, personally, socially, and institutionally enforced through the threat of exclusion, precarity, and violence.

Methodology

This chapter draws on evidence gathered through a qualitative research project that examined the experiences of hate and harm encountered by transgender individuals (McBride, 2019). This project utilised an in-depth ethnographic approach, including multiple interviews. Participants, who self-identified under the broad umbrella of transgender identities, were recruited through snowball sampling, enabling the inclusion of diverse voices from across England and Wales. The qualitative methodology captured the lived experiences of participants, focusing on their identities and the harms they faced across their life-course. Interviews were designed to elicit detailed, rich narratives, resulting in the generation of 'thick descriptions' (Ponterotto, 2006). These interviews were further complemented by participatory life-story narratives (Baum et al., 2006; Singh et al., 2013), which allowed participants to reflect on their experiences within broader social and structural contexts.

The 11 participants included trans women of varying ages, socio-economic status, and professional backgrounds, three of whom comprise the case studies discussed in this chapter. Their lived experiences reflect a spectrum of harms faced in workplace environments. Their narratives illuminate the pervasive impact of neoliberal policies, offering critical insights into how trans individuals navigate discrimination and systemic exclusion. By centring these voices, this research provides a nuanced understanding of the lived realities of trans individuals, grounding theoretical analysis in authentic experiences.

The term trans here has been defined as referring to a gender identity differing from the gender assigned at birth. Ultimately, the research which informed this chapter was interested in exploring the experiences of people who identified their gender as something outside of society's normative notions of gender as a fixed and binary concept consisting of either 'man' or 'woman'. To varying degrees, all had engaged in processes of transition that included social, hormonal, and/or medical procedures in seeking, exploring, and/or achieving a material body and a life that aligned with a felt sense of personally defined gender that was authentic to their sense of self.

Theoretical backdrop

Critical Hate Studies provides a theoretical framework for understanding the broader experiences and systemic harms of hate. Rooted in the work of James and McBride (2021), this field examines hate as a phenomenon shaped by and contributing to societal power dynamics. Rather than focusing solely on individual acts of hate or violence, this framework expands the scope to include the structural and systemic conditions that facilitate the perpetuation of hatred, discrimination, and violence. James and McBride argue that understanding hate through a critical lens requires recognising its function within a broader socio-economic and political order, particularly in relation to neoliberalism, which exacerbates inequalities and fuels hostile attitudes towards marginalised communities. This perspective allows for a deeper examination of how hate impacts individuals not only through direct acts of violence but also through the cultural, economic, and institutional systems that marginalise and dehumanise them. By applying Critical Hate Studies, we gain insight into the complex ways in which hate is experienced and institutionalised.

Honneth (1996) asserts that recognition is essential to human development and self-fulfilment. He suggests that the denial of recognition, particularly the denial of respect, esteem, and love, inflicts a particularly insidious form of harm. This harm is especially evident in environments where individuals are systematically excluded or devalued. Yar (2012) expands on Honneth's theory, arguing that the lack of recognition in various social contexts, such as the workplace, leads to psychological and social harms. In the workplace context, respect signifies the basic acknowledgment of trans women as legitimate employees, deserving equal treatment and opportunities. Esteem, meanwhile, signifies recognition of their value as skilled, competent, and contributing members of a team. Yet, despite the central importance of these forms of recognition, they are frequently withheld from trans women, often leaving them with a pervasive sense of exclusion and disempowerment.

This lack of recognition is compounded by systemic violence, a concept theorised by Žižek (2008) as the broader socio-political manifestation of violence. In a neoliberal capitalist context, where productivity, self-sufficiency, and competition are prioritised, trans women face an exacerbated form of systemic violence. Neoliberal capitalism frames success as the result of individual effort and merit while obscuring the structural barriers that make success difficult for those who are marginalised. Within this framework, trans women are not only pressured to conform to cisnormative workplace expectations but are also discouraged from seeking institutional support or advocating for their rights. The fear of being labelled as 'social scroungers', a term weaponised within neoliberal discourse, creates a chilling effect, leading to further silencing of trans women's voices and experiences. Further, the concepts of being 'fit to work' and 'professionalism' often code trans identities, amongst others, as deviant, marking them as incongruent with the ideal employee profile.

At the same time systemic violence (Žižek, 2008) operates at the level of language and ideology. This can be further understood through the related media studies concept of 'symbolic annihilation' (Tuchman, 1979), which addresses how underrepresentation and misrepresentation in media discourse reinforce marginalised groups' lack of social power. As Tuchman (1979: 533) explains

> the very underrepresentation of women, including their stereotypical portrayal, may symbolically capture the position of women in American society, their real lack of power. It bespeaks their 'symbolic annihilation' by the media ... just as representation in the media signifies social existence, so too underrepresentation and (by extension) trivialization and condemnation indicate symbolic annihilation.

For trans women, this symbolic annihilation operates alongside symbolic violence, creating a dual erasure both in media discourse and workplace interactions.

Symbolic violence manifests in subtle forms of discrimination, such as microaggressions, misgendering, and exclusionary language. These actions, while less overt than physical violence, are no less harmful. They serve to reinforce cisnormative standards, implicitly delegitimising trans identities and experiences. The insidious nature of symbolic violence lies in its ability to shape social interactions and perceptions of identity in ways that normalise transphobia. In the workplace, symbolic violence operates through normative systems that continuously undermine the validity of trans women's identities, making it difficult for them to assert their personhood or occupy space authentically. As a result, many trans women are compelled to modify their self-expression or remain silent in the face of discrimination, further entrenching their marginalisation in workplace culture that rarely recognises or affirms their identities.

Berlant's (2011) concept of cruel optimism aptly captures the paradox trans women face in professional settings. According to Berlant, cruel optimism occurs when individuals invest in something that promises fulfilment, such as the hope for inclusion, only to find that this very hope becomes a self-defeating investment. For trans women, this paradox is evident in their pursuit of acceptance within workplaces that demand an adherence to cisnormative standards, which ultimately exclude them. This dynamic is particularly troubling because trans women often persist in hostile workplace environments not out of misplaced personal desire but due to seeking a 'liveable' life (Butler, 2006). Neoliberal workplaces seduce individuals into believing that acceptance and even success can be 'earned' through conformity to even the most hostile norms. Trans women find themselves caught in a system that simultaneously marginalises them while demanding their participation. By internalising the neoliberal ethos of individual responsibility (Howard and Vajda, 2017), they align their aspirations with meritocratic narratives that inherently exclude their identities. This creates a cycle where the hope for inclusion becomes both a burden and a means of survival, perpetuating marginalisation even as they pursue acceptance. The cruel optimism at work forces trans women to conform to unattainable standards, entrenching their exclusion within neoliberal professional cultures.

Workplaces in context for trans people

Neoliberalism positions work as a primary site where individuals cultivate self-discipline and achieve their authentic selves through paid labour (Catlaw and Marshall, 2018). Work is thus celebrated as a space for self-actualisation, autonomy, and fulfilment. The intention here is not to ignore the way that work can provide a mechanism to mitigate the psychological distress caused by societal discrimination (Sánchez and Vilain, 2009). Indeed, Cederstrom and Fleming (2012) highlight a growing emphasis on 'authenticity' in the workplace, where employees are encouraged to integrate personal identities into their professional roles. On the face of it, this shift represents an invitation to trans women to express their gender traits more freely but the confines of expectations which align with cisnormative ideals means that, in fact, trans women engage in a sustained form of emotional labour, where individuals sustain 'deep acting' to blur the lines between their professional and personal selves (Hochschild, 1985). This is something that Cederstrom and Fleming (2012) critique as an exploitative, commodification of workers' sense of self for organisational benefit.

Silence often functions for trans individuals as a strategic response to perceived or real harm, as trans employees adopt self-censorship to avoid drawing attention or being singled out as different from colleagues. Grant et al. (2011) underscore this, revealing that many gender non-conforming individuals engage in such strategies, which, in turn, exacerbate the psychological toll of unsupportive work environments. Whittle et al. (2007) found that 42% of trans workers feared living in their preferred gender role would jeopardise their employment, with 25% reporting job changes due to harassment or bullying.

Trans individuals face significant workplace discrimination, impacting employment stability and mental health through hiring biases, overt stigmatisation, and violence (Enogieru et al., 2024). Trans employees frequently endure discrimination and harassment but remain in their positions due to financial precarity and the perceived possibility of future inclusion (Sears et al., 2024). Trans women, especially those who do not conform to cisnormative standards, are overrepresented in insecure, low-wage positions (Kinitz et al., 2024), with discrimination and rejection undermining self-worth and feelings of belonging (Fischer and Bolton Holz, 2007). Recent research found that 50% of transgender workers face harassment, with 7% experiencing physical violence and 6% sexual assault due to their gender identity (Enogieru et al., 2024). These hostile environments not only normalise exclusion but implicitly sanction violence by failing to implement protective measures (Spade, 2015).

This pervasive hostility pressures trans women to suppress their gender expression to avoid job loss or economic instability, a dynamic exacerbated by neoliberalism's emphasis on individual responsibility for navigating hostile environments. Expectations to conform to rigid gender norms and uphold professional standards often stifle authentic self-expression, limiting access to career growth and stable employment. In these contexts, workplaces become sites of 'silent violence', where exclusion and harm operate invisibly behind façades of neutrality or inclusivity. Berlant's (2011) concept of cruel optimism captures this paradox: the pursuit of stability, recognition, and belonging becomes a self-defeating investment, as trans employees are pressured to assimilate into hostile workplaces that ultimately exclude them.

Faced with systemic discrimination, trans employees frequently engage in self-silencing as a strategy for professional survival (Knoll and van Dick, 2013). Over 70% of transgender employees modify their self-presentation, altering their dress, voice, and behaviour, to minimise conflict and avoid discrimination (Sears et al., 2024; Ragins, 2008). This form of 'covering', as Hewlin (2009) describes, reflects neoliberalism's demand for personal adaptability, where success depends on erasing difference rather than transforming hostile environments. The expectation that trans women must conform to cisnormative standards fosters alienation, psychological distress, and career stagnation (Knoll and van Dick, 2013). This 'conformity imperative' (Tamar de Waal, 2020) positions trans women in a state of 'conditional belonging', where acceptance hinges on invisibility and compliance rather than genuine inclusion. Research on trans workers' employment trajectories shows that 'stealth' strategies, deliberately avoiding disclosure of gender identity, lead to long-term stress, burnout, and disengagement from career opportunities (MacDonnell and Grigorovich, 2012). The failure of inclusion policies to address these hidden forms of exclusion only further reinforces Berlant's (2011) cruel optimism, where the hope for workplace belonging is continually thwarted by demands for self-erasure.

This section has laid the groundwork for understanding how systemic structures and neoliberal ideologies shape the experience of trans women in the workplace, often leading them to navigate environments that are hostile and unsupportive. To further illustrate these dynamics, the next section presents case study examples from the data, which reveal the manifestations of these harms through trans women's lived experiences.

Case studies: Navigating discrimination and violence in neoliberal workplaces

Bird's story: Symbolic violence and cruel optimism

Bird's story reveals how symbolic violence, administrative exclusion, and neoliberal norms work together to marginalise and silence trans women in professional environments. Bird's experience exemplifies the complex administrative and social barriers that middle-aged trans women might encounter when attempting to access meaningful employment. Despite her pursuit and achievement of relevant qualifications and aspirations to work in the beauty industry, Bird was continually shut out from opportunities due to discrimination. During one job interview, Bird encountered overt prejudice based on her appearance. She recalls the moment:

> I went in for the job, yeah. I walked in, his arms ... as soon as he saw me, he was like this. Dead. And he just, kind of looking around the room and he was talking. Like no way. And I looked at him, I said, 'I ain't got this job', I said, 'There was no point me coming, was there?' I said, 'You're only doing it because you've got to'. He said, 'What do you mean?' I said, 'Well, you're not allowed to be seen to be discriminating in any way, are you? So, if you go through the motions ... there's no point me sitting here and talking to you.' The interviewer confirmed her fears, responding, 'Well, if you dress like a man, you might get a job.'
>
> *(Bird, trans woman, 51)*

This interaction exemplifies the operation of symbolic violence, where structural discrimination is masked by performative compliance with anti-discrimination policies (Spade, 2015). This moment exemplifies cruel optimism as Bird's commitment to professional success was built on the illusion that employment was a meritocratic and neutral process when, in reality, systemic discrimination dictated her exclusion (Berlant, 2011). The concept of symbolic violence (Žižek, 2008), helps explain how, in a neoliberal social economy, marginalised individuals are led to believe that their exclusion results from their own personal inadequacy rather than structural oppression. Žižek's (2008) concept further explains this experience as Bird was led to believe in the neutrality of hiring policies only to encounter an invisible yet entrenched form of exclusion that was legitimised through administrative processes. This highlights Spade's (2015) theory of administrative violence, where seemingly neutral workplace policies (such as hiring practices) reinforce cisnormative standards that marginalise trans identities. By recognising the futility of the interview process, Bird confronted this façade of neutrality, stating, 'You're only doing it because you've got to.' This illustrates the subtle ways workplace cultures silence and invisibilise structural violence, forcing marginalised individuals to internalise their exclusion.

Bird's immediate response was one of intense emotional and physical reaction:

> I just flipped. I flipped, and I-, I shouldn't have done it but I hit him … I can't explain it. It was like this veil come over, yeah? And it switched. And I just hit him. And then he just hit the wall and slid down the wall.

This moment of violence exemplifies the cumulative harm caused by sustained rejection and dehumanisation. Lloyd (2019: 26) argues that late capitalist structures establish conditions for harm, where 'an inability to articulate an alternative presents a form of violence' on those trapped in precarity. Bird's participation in the interview process, despite her awareness of systemic bias, exemplifies cruel optimism, hope for inclusion despite repeated evidence of exclusion. Following the incident, Bird was overwhelmed with grief: 'And I just sat on the step, the kerb outside, and I cried. Cos I … it hurt, yeah. It really upset me.'

This emotional reaction underscores the deep internalisation of symbolic violence and the psychological toll of repeated rejection and exclusion (Strauss et al., 2020). The pain Bird experienced was not merely a reaction to the immediate event but the cumulative impact of long-term structural marginalisation and trauma (Auerbach, 2025, forthcoming).

Harvey (2005) explains how neoliberal workplaces emphasise self-sufficiency and competition while ignoring structural inequalities. Within this framework, trans individuals like Bird are expected to conform to rigid cisnormativity, including dress codes and gender presentation, to be considered employable and embody a 'liveable' life (Butler, 2006, 2009). Bird's experience exemplifies how these exclusions not only limit professional opportunities but also retraumatise trans women who are left to navigate these systems of silence and exclusion. To avoid the trauma of exclusion, Bird, akin to other trans people, was expected to follow the gender presentation of cisnormativity to be accepted into the workplace. Despite repeated instances of discrimination, Bird continued investing in workplace structures that ultimately failed her.

Jenny-Anne's story: Institutional betrayal and forced silence

Many organisations still lack basic understanding of what it is to be trans and therefore cannot recognise or take action to prevent the various forms of discrimination faced by trans employees (Collins et al., 2015). In workplaces where heteronormative values and practices are reinforced, trans workers experience social isolation, discrimination, and transphobic attitudes, which can manifest as overt hostility or exclusion from colleagues, clients, or supervisors, and in some cases, lead to job loss (Davidson, 2016; Hadjisolomou, 2021). Indeed, despite her prior status as an established successful professional in her long-standing career, Jenny-Anne suffered workplace harassment, discrimination, and eventual dismissal as a result of her trans identity.

In the early stages of her private transition, Jenny-Anne was outed by a police officer to her workplace, and this triggered a trail of incidents which undermined her professional standing, as her gender presentation became the primary basis for professional judgment, overshadowing her achievements. Driving home from a support group meeting, Jenny-Anne was stopped at a road closure. The officer questioned her credibility as both an employee and a representative of her workplace by asking: 'Are you allowed to drive a company vehicle dressed like that?'

This interaction exemplifies how symbolic violence operates across both social and professional boundaries, where broader societal perceptions of gender deviance are reinforced through informal (and formal) policing. This interplay between external authority and workplace culture reflects how respectability politics are omnipresent, striking opportunistically to reinforce social norms and hierarchies (Bockting et al., 2013).

The officer's subsequent disclosure to Jenny-Anne's employer led to an onslaught of workplace harassment, including veiled suggestions that she should leave her job and notes left on her desk taunting her, reinforcing her outsider status (Nadal, 2018). This discrimination, in the form of informal microaggressions, was rendered invisible through the normalisation of such behaviours within workplace 'banter' culture which simultaneously served as acts of silencing of Jenny-Anne's gender and professional identities (Watson et al., 2024). Here, workplace cultures do not overtly sanction trans identities but instead rely on covert and complicit workforce tactics to marginalise and destabilise those who fail to conform to cis and heteronormative expectations embedded within workplace cultures (Budge et al., 2010). Stigmatisation plays a significant role in perpetuating workplace exclusions. According to Paine et al. (2024), transgender and nonbinary individuals often face stigmatisation in professional environments, leading to discrimination and adverse mental health outcomes. This stigma manifests in microaggressions, misgendering, and exclusionary behaviours that reinforce feelings of alienation. For Jenny-Anne, the cumulative impact of these behaviours resulted in professional isolation and distress. Jenny-Anne was eventually dismissed, despite securing her company's largest-ever order.

Trans individuals often face the challenge of carefully navigating how openly they can express their identity to prevent harassment or job loss (Dietert and Dentice, 2009). Jenny-Anne's professional success was rendered irrelevant by perceptions of her gender which exemplifies Schilt and Connell's

(2007: 596) argument that 'open gender transitions' expose and challenge the hidden mechanisms that reinforce occupational sex segregation. Trans women who transition at work often lose access to high-status roles, as they are perceived to no longer fit within traditional gendered divisions of labour. It is important to note that while some trans people prefer to keep their identity private and 'pass' in workplace settings, there exists a significant group who would prefer this option but cannot access it. As Costello (2016: 91) explains, 'Trans* people also note that the medical claim that doctors can in fact normalize bodies to the sex/gender binary is overstated. Medical interventions may reduce trans* visibility, but only to a degree.' Many trans women lack what Janet Mock (2014, 2017) terms 'cis-passing privilege', either because they transitioned at work, because their transgender status is known within the workplace, or because their physical characteristics render passing impossible despite medical interventions. This lack of choice regarding visibility creates additional vulnerabilities in workplace settings, as these individuals cannot strategically manage disclosure in the way that more privileged trans people might.

After a lifetime of hiding her trans gender identity, in the wake of her dismissal Jenny-Anne's strategy shifted when interviewing for new roles to one of pre-emptive self-disclosure. She explained: 'I didn't want to get a new job, only to find they found out about my private life, and I got fired or made redundant or whatever' (Jenny-Anne, trans woman, 71).

This demonstrates the emotional labour trans individuals must undertake to navigate cisnormative workplace expectations (Hochschild, 1985). Although her employer initially expressed acceptance ('I don't see it's any problem, it's in your private life'), Jenny-Anne's experience highlights the superficial nature of support that trans individuals often encounter in the workplace. The expectation that she confine her gender identity to her 'private life' exemplifies what Tamar de Waal (2020) describes as 'conditional belonging,' where trans individuals are implicitly required to suppress their authenticity in order to maintain employment. This dynamic underscores how symbolic violence operates, as trans individuals are expected to conform to cisnormative standards to secure their place within professional environments. While structural and managerial support can alleviate some of these challenges, Jenny-Anne's experience illustrates the limitations of such support when it demands that trans employees compartmentalise their gender identity. Without genuine acknowledgement of their lived experiences, these environments exacerbate economic inequalities and minority stress, leaving trans individuals vulnerable to both administrative and cultural harm. As Spade (2015) argues, administrative violence is perpetuated through seemingly neutral policies that enforce cisnormative standards, systematically excluding and retraumatising trans employees.

Julie's story: Sexual violence and the burden of silence

Julie's account of sexual assault during a work trip to Europe provides a harrowing example of how trans women are subject to heightened risks of violence and systemic neglect (Lombardi, 2002). The incident occurred shortly after her public, and professional, transition. She was attending a work conference which involved navigating her first flight outside of the UK as Julie, with her passport which aligned with her gender identity. Initially, she felt a sense of success and relief after negotiating the official surveillance hurdles of international travel: 'I was feeling a bit pleased with myself, because I'd made the whole journey to [European country], not a problem whatsoever.'

However, this confidence was quickly shattered when 'Ian', a colleague from another office who had been drinking heavily, appeared at her hotel room door late at night. Julie recalls,

> There was a knock at the door ... feeling a bit safe and confident, I just opened the door and there was six foot six inches of 'Ian', in just his boxer shorts, saying 'I've just come to give you a kiss goodnight'.

'Ian' forced his way into her room, placing Julie in a position of immediate physical danger. She describes her fear and helplessness: 'My biggest fear was that what if he turns nasty? Because he was twice my size. Hands the size of dinner plates ... If he decided to turn nasty, there was nothing I could do about it.'

Trapped and fearing an escalation of violence, Julie felt she had no choice but to submit to a sexual act in order to defuse the situation.

> I decided the line of the easiest route was, excuse my frankness, if I wanked him off, he'd just go away then ... he couldn't keep an erection, so ... after ten minutes, he got bored and left anyway.

Millif (2024) argues that survival strategies in violent situations are shaped by perceptions of limited control, prioritising immediate safety over justice; another silencing factor in trans women's lived experienced as victimisation intersects with shame and self-loathing. As Laura Jane Grace (2017: 74) writes in her memoir *Tranny* about her pre-transition experiences:

> If I were to say how I really feel, What I really think, people would think I was mentally ill. Cross-dressing feels like self-mutilation. I can never be anything more than a pervert dressed up in women's clothes. So sick, sick, sick. I want to black it all out. I do not care if I am alive or dead.

This internalised shame compounds the difficulty of reporting workplace victimisation, as trans women may fear confirming negative stereotypes about their identities. Similarly, in *None of the Above*, Travis Alabanza (2022: 138) discusses the intense feelings of shame while navigating public spaces as a gender-nonconforming trans non-binary femme in London, further illustrating how shame operates as both a cause and consequence of silencing.

This is an example of symbolic violence (Žižek, 2008), where power structures render violence inescapable, forcing victims to make choices that appear inevitable and unchangeable. Further, the expectation that survivors must remain silent to preserve their professional standing underscores the broader institutional culture of silent violence, wherein trans women are encouraged to endure harm rather than disrupt professional hierarchies (Clements-Nolle, Marx, and Katz, 2006). Julie's sense of terror and vulnerability were further amplified by the absence of any clear organisational recourse whilst she was abroad, leaving her to navigate the assault and the aftermath alone: '... I was upset by it, a bit humiliated, but there wasn't much else I could do about it at that point in time.'

The next morning at breakfast, Julie encountered further trauma as 'Ian' behaved as though nothing had happened. '"Ian" was laughing and joking and the world was good for him. Like nothing had happened. It was just, well, that's what we do, isn't it?'

This response highlights the normalisation of sexual violence within certain workplace cultures (Armstrong, 2015) where perpetrators face no accountability, but survivors are expected to carry the emotional burden in silence. Armstrong (2015) highlights how discourses of harassment as 'just part of the job' perpetuate the invisibility of violence, allowing organisational culture to excuse or minimise the harm.

Upon returning to the UK, Julie reported the incident to her managing director, who expressed outrage and offered to take immediate action: 'He was absolutely furious ... he wanted to ring up the [head office] and have the guy sacked on the spot'. Julie had been with the organisation for a long time and undertook her transition openly and with support. However, despite her managing director's support, Julie hesitated to pursue further action. Julie's reluctance to report her assault by 'Ian' illustrates how self-silencing functions as a crisis management strategy for trans employees. Julie experienced cruel optimism as the burden of maintaining professional harmony fell to her. Her decision to not pursue action against 'Ian' was in line with her general approach to her gender transition. Which she summarised as:

> ... it's me taking ownership of my own journey, I'm gonna do it my way, I'm gonna earn a day off. Whereas winding them up, saying you need to give me a day's pay, which no company likes doing, regardless, and you want to keep them on side. That was sort of like, the important thing, is you want them to be your friend, you don't want them to be against you
>
> *(Julie, trans woman, 52)*

Julie's internal conflict was reflective of cruel optimism, where the hope for justice and professional acceptance was constrained by her need to preserve her career and social standing. These things were at odds with each other rather than being complimentary and achievable. The tension was generative of an enduring psychological toll associated with having to weigh personal safety and justice against social repercussions (Bockting et al., 2013). This environment not only undermines trans women's comfort but also their physical and psychological wellbeing, as they are compelled to make choices that prioritise safety over authenticity, a dynamic often echoed in violence against women literature, where the need for safety frequently takes precedence over self-expression or authenticity (Herman, 1992).

Julie's story exemplifies how intersecting forms of violence, gender-based harassment, and structural neglect converge in neoliberal workplace environments. The lack of accountability for perpetrators, the complicity of managers and victims themselves, the failure of institutional policies and protections, and the expectation that survivors manage their trauma without disrupting workplace norms all reflect the ongoing challenges faced by trans women in professional spaces.

Conclusion

This chapter has demonstrated that trans women's experiences in the workplace are shaped by a pervasive form of silent violence, sustained through institutional silencing, self-silencing, and broader structural exclusion embedded in neoliberal workplace norms. Despite the promise of workplace inclusion, trans women remain subjected to discrimination, harassment, and exclusion, often under the guise of professionalism and meritocracy. Berlant's (2011) concept of cruel optimism illustrates how trans women's aspirations for belonging are systematically undermined by the very institutions that claim to offer them stability. Rather than providing safety and validation, the workplace becomes a site of precarity, where the pursuit of inclusion demands compliance with cisnormative expectations that ultimately reinforce exclusion. The neoliberal emphasis on individual responsibility exacerbates these dynamics, shifting the burden of survival onto trans employees rather than addressing the structural inequalities that shape their workplace experiences.

Institutional betrayal, as evidenced in case studies of trans women being outed, denied support, or subjected to sexual violence, reveals that exclusion is not merely an unfortunate byproduct of workplace culture but an actively maintained system of regulation. The expectation that trans employees must engage in covering (Ragins, 2008; Hewlin, 2009) and other self-silencing strategies to maintain employment underscores the deep-rooted mechanisms of compliance that reinforce their marginalisation.

The situation for trans women in the workplace has demonstrably worsened in recent years, as evidenced by the cases of Dr Beth Upton and nurse 'Rose,' who faced not only workplace discrimination but also public humiliation through media exposure. The legal protection now afforded to 'gender critical' beliefs as a protected characteristic has created additional barriers, as workplaces must now navigate competing rights claims that often privilege cisnormative perspectives. This deteriorating climate requires renewed attention to both structural reforms and cultural interventions that can create genuinely inclusive environments beyond performative diversity initiatives.

Ultimately, this chapter challenges the notion that workplace inclusion can be meaningfully achieved without structural transformation. The narratives of trans women reveal that harm is not an anomaly but a fundamental feature of professional environments designed to privilege cisnormativity. Berlant's (2011) cruel optimism provides a critical lens for understanding why trans employees continue striving for acceptance within systems that repeatedly fail them. Without institutional accountability and a shift away from neoliberal frameworks that prioritise corporate reputation over worker protection, diversity initiatives will remain symbolic gestures rather than vehicles of substantive change.

References

Acker, J. (1990). Hierarchies, jobs, bodies: A theory of gendered organizations. *Gender and Society*, *4*(2), 139–158.

Alabanza, T. (2022). *None of the above: Reflections on life beyond the binary*. Edinburgh: Canongate Books.

Armstrong, L. (2015). 'Who's the slut, who's the whore?': street harassment in the workplace among female sex workers in New Zealand. *Feminist Criminology*, *11*(3), 285–303.

Auerbach, S. (2025, forthcoming). *Trans and non-binary people's encounters with the harms of work* (PhD thesis). University of Plymouth.

Baum, F., MacDougall, C., and Smith, D. (2006). Participatory action research. *Journal of Epidemiology and Community Health*, *60*(10), 854–857.

Bell, M. P., Özbilgin, M. F., Beauregard, T. A., and Sürgevil, O. (2011). Voice, silence, and diversity in 21st-century organizations: Strategies for inclusion of gay, lesbian, bisexual, and transgender employees. *Human Resource Management*, *50*(1), 131–146.

Berlant, L. (2011). *Cruel optimism*. Durham, NC: Duke University Press.

Bockting, W. O., Miner, M. H., Swinburne Romine, R. E., Hamilton, A., and Coleman, E. (2013). Stigma, mental health, and resilience in an online sample of the US transgender population. *American Journal of Public Health*, *103*(5), 943–951.

Britton, D. (2004). *At work in the iron cage: The prison as gendered organization*. New York: New York University Press.

Budge, S. L., Tebbe, E. N., and Howard, K. A. S. (2010). The work experiences of transgender individuals: Negotiating the transition and career decision-making processes. *Journal of Counseling Psychology*, *57*(4), 377–393.

Butler, J. (1990). *Gender trouble: Feminism and the subversion of identity*. New York: Routledge.

Butler, J. (2006). *Precarious life* (2nd ed.). New York: Routledge.

Butler, J. (2009). Performativity, precarity and sexual politics. *Revista De Antropologia Iberoamericana*, *4*(3), i–xiii.
Catlaw, T. J., and Marshall, G. S. (2018). Enjoy your work! The fantasy of the neoliberal workplace and its consequences for the entrepreneurial subject. *Administrative Theory and Praxis*, *40*(2), 99–118.
Cederstrom, C., and Fleming, P. (2012). *Dead man working*. London: Zero Books.
Clements-Nolle, K., Marx, R., and Katz, M. (2006). Attempted suicide among transgender persons: The influence of gender-based discrimination and victimization. *Journal of Homosexuality*, *51*(3), 53–69.
Collins, J. C., McFadden, C., Rocco, T. S., and Mathis, M. K. (2015). The problem of transgender marginalization and exclusion: Critical actions for human *resource development. Human Resource Development Review*, *14*(2), 205–226.
Connell, R. W. (1995) *Masculinities*. Berkeley, CA: University of California Press.
Costello, C. (2016). Intersex and trans* communities: Commonalities and tensions. In S. Horlacher (Ed.), *Transgender and intersex: Theoretical, practical, and artistic perspectives* (pp. 83–113). New York: Palgrave Macmillan.
Davidson, S. (2016). Gender inequality: Nonbinary transgender people in the workplace. *Cogent Social Sciences*, 2(1), 1236511.
Davies, W. (2016). *The limits of neo-liberalism: Authority, sovereignty and the logic of competition*. London: Sage.
Dietert, M., and Dentice, D. (2009). Gender identity issues and workplace discrimination: The transgender experience. *Journal of Workplace Rights*, *14*, 121–140.
Duggan, L. (2012). *The twilight of equality? Neoliberalism, cultural politics, and the attack on democracy*. Boston, MA: Beacon Press.
Enogieru, I., LeGrand, S., and Richardson, J. (2024). Prevalence and correlates of workplace violence: Descriptive results from the National Transgender Discrimination Survey. Occupational and Environmental Medicine, *81*(4), 178–184.
Fischer, A. R., and Bolton Holz, K. (2007). Perceived discrimination and women's distress: The roles of collective and personal self-esteem. *Journal of Counseling Psychology*, *54*, 154–164.
Grace, L. J., with Ozzi, D. (2017). *Tranny: Confessions of punk rock's most infamous anarchist sellout*. New York: Hachette Books.
Grant, J. M., Mottet, L. A., Tanis, J., Harrison, J., Herman, J. L., and Keisling, M. (2011). *Injustice at every turn: A report of the National Transgender Discrimination Survey*. Washington, DC: National Center for Transgender Equality and National Gay and Lesbian Task Force.
Hadjisolomou, A. (2021). Doing and negotiating transgender on the front line: Customer abuse, transphobia and stigma in the food retail sector. *Work, Employment and Society*, *35*(5), 979–988.
Harvey, D. (2005). *A brief history of neoliberalism*. Oxford: Oxford University Press.
Herman, J. L. (1992). *Trauma and recovery*. New York: Basic Books.
Hewlin, P. F. (2009). Wearing the cloak: Antecedents and consequences of creating facades of conformity. *Journal of Applied Psychology*, *94*(3), 727–741.
Hochschild, A. R. (1985). *The managed heart: Commercialization of human feeling*. Berkeley, CA: University of California Press.
Honneth, A. (1996). *The struggle for recognition: The moral grammar of social conflicts*. Cambridge: Polity Press.
Howard, J., and Vajda, V. (2017). Navigating power and intersectionality to address inequality. *IDS Working Paper*, *2017*(504).
Irving, D. (2008). Normalized transgressions: Legitimizing the transsexual body as productive. *Radical History Review*, *100*(1), 38–59.
James, Z., and McBride, K. (2021). Critical Hate Studies: A new perspective. *International Review of Victimology*, 27(2), 243–267.

Kinitz, D. J., Ross, L. E., MacEachen, E., and Gesink, D. (2024). 'How can you worry about employment and survival at the same time?' Employment and mental health among precariously employed cisgender and transgender sexual minority adult men in Toronto, Canada. *Culture, Health and Sexuality*, *27*(7), 884–899.

Kish-Gephart, J. J., Detert, J. R., Treviño, L. K., and Edmondson, A. C. (2009). Silenced by fear: The nature, sources, and consequences of fear at work. In B. M. Staw and A. P. Brief (Eds.), *Research in Organizational Behavior*, *29*, 163–193. Greenwich, CT: JAI Press.

Knoll, M., and van Dick, R. (2013). Authenticity, employee silence, prohibitive voice, and the moderating effect of organizational identification. *The Journal of Positive Psychology*, *8*(4), 346–360.

Lloyd, A. (2019). *Labour markets and identity on the post-industrial assembly line*. London: Routledge.

Lombardi, E. L., Wilchins, R. A., Priesing, D., and Malouf, D. (2002). Gender violence: Transgender experiences with violence and discrimination. *Journal of Homosexuality*, *42*(1), 89–101.

MacDonnell, J. A., and Grigorovich, A. (2012). Gender, work, and health for trans health providers: A focus on transmen. *ISRN Nursing*, *2012*, 1–12.

McBride, K. (2019). *A critical analysis of harms experienced by transgender individuals* (PhD thesis). University of Plymouth.

Milliff, A. (2024). Making sense, making choices: How civilians choose survival strategies during violence. *American Political Science Review*, *118*(3), 1379–1397.

Mock, J. (2014). *Redefining realness: My path to womanhood, identity, love & so much more*. New York: Atria Books.

Mock, J. (2017). *Surpassing certainty: What my twenties taught me*. New York: Atria Books.

Nadal, K. L. (2018). *Microaggressions and traumatic stress: Theory, research, and clinical treatment*. Washington, DC: American Psychological Association.

Paine, E. A., Abad, M. V., Barucco, R., Chang, Y.-W. Y., Navalta, T. V., Vance, T. A., Ehrhardt, A. A., and Bockting, W. O. (2024). 'Too much trouble': Transgender and nonbinary people's experiences of stigmatization and stigma avoidance in the workplace. *Work and Occupations*, *52*(2), 204–244.

Ponterotto, J. G. (2006). Brief note on the origins, evolution, and meaning of the qualitative research concept 'thick description'. *The Qualitative Report*, *11*(3), 538–549.

Ragins, B. R. (2008). Disclosure disconnects: Antecedents and consequences of disclosing invisible stigmas across life domains. *Academy of Management Review*, *33*(1), 194–215.

Rhode, D. L. (1997). *Speaking of sex: The denial of gender inequality*. Cambridge, MA: Harvard University Press.

Rundall, E., and Vecchietti, V. (2010). (In)visibility in the workplace. In S. Hines and T. Sanger (Eds.), Transgender identities: Towards a social analysis of gender diversity (pp. 127–152). Abingdon: Routledge.

Salzinger, L. (2003). *Genders in production: Making workers in Mexico's global factories*. Berkeley, CA: University of California Press.

Sánchez, F. J., and Vilain, E. (2009). Collective self-esteem as a coping resource for male-to-female transsexuals. *Journal of Counselling Psychology*, *56*(1), 202–209.

Sears, B., Mallory, C., Castleberry, N., et al. (2024). *Workplace experiences of non binary employees*. Los Angeles, CA: Williams Institute, UCLA School of Law.

Schilt, K., and Connell, C. (2007). Do workplace gender transitions make gender trouble? *Gender, Work and Organization*, *14*(6), 596–618.

Singh, A. A., Richmond, K., and Burnes, T. R. (2013). Feminist participatory action research with transgender communities: Fostering the practice of ethical and empowering research designs. *International Journal of Transgenderism*, *14*(3), 93–104.

Sodha, S. (2025, 9 February). No woman should be forced to change her clothes in front of a trans colleague. *The Guardian*.

Spade, D. (2015). *Normal life: Administrative violence, critical trans politics, and the limits of law* (2nd ed.). Durham, NC: Duke University Press.

Strauss, P., Cook, A., Winter, S., Watson, V., Wright Toussaint, D., and Lin, A. (2020). Associations between negative life experiences and the mental health of trans and gender diverse young people in Australia: Findings from Trans Pathways. *Psychological Medicine*, *50*(5), 808–817.

Tamar de Waal, T. (2020). Conditional belonging: Evaluating integration requirements from a social equality perspective. *Journal of Intercultural Studies*, *41*(2), 231–247.

Tuchman, G. (1979). Women's depiction by the mass media. *Signs*, *4*(3), 528–542.

Valian, V. (1999). *Why so slow?: The advancement of women*. Cambridge, MA: MIT Press.

Watson, D., Benozzo, A., and Fida, R. (2024). Trans people in the workplace: Possibilities for subverting heteronormativity. *Work, Employment and Society*, *38*(3), 744–765.

Whittle, S., Turner, L., Al-Alami, M., Rundall, E., and Thom, B. (2007). *Engendered penalties: Transgender and transsexual people's experiences of inequality and discrimination*. Wetherby: Communities and Local Government Publications.

Williams, C. (1995). *Still a man's world: Men who do 'women's' work*. Berkeley, CA: University of California Press.

Wilkinson, A., Dundon, T., Donaghey, J., and Freeman, R. (2015). Employee voice: charting new terrain. In J. Budd and P. Gollan (Eds.), *The future of employee voice* (pp. 1–13). Cheltenham: Edward Elgar.

Yar, M. (2012). Critical criminology, critical theory and social harm. In S. Hall and S. Winlow (Eds.), *New directions in criminological theory* (pp. 73–91). London: Routledge.

Žižek, S. (2008). *Violence: Six sideways reflections*. New York: Picador.

11

'A STORM IS COMING': DECONSTRUCTING DOXXING

Marta Pérez-Fernández and Grayson Bartels

Introduction

Marginalised communities and hate groups alike find community online. Studies have found that, due to the difficulty in finding in-person community, many transgender people find community online (Herrmann et al., 2024; Shapiro, 2004). As relates to this chapter, transgender refers to people whose gender does not align with the gender they were assigned at birth. Often, these online communities are spaces of emotional support, encouragement, and access to information (Selkie et al., 2020). Thus, 'queer cyberspaces' can be 'revelatory', allowing queer and trans users to 'forge systems of belonging beyond existing life worlds' (Robards, et al., 2020: 284–286). These queer cyberspaces have a constancy often lacking in the tumultuous, rapidly-evolving, often precarious physical life experiences of trans people (Cavalcante, 2016). They are particularly important for queer and trans people, who are at higher risk of harassment in their physical lives (Cannon et al., 2017).

Online spaces, however, are not always safe havens (Galpin, 2022). Despite their potential as spaces of refuge and community-building, these presumed safe spaces for minoritised groups can become sites of vulnerability and harm. Trolling and doxxing are two features of online harassment trans people face. This chapter aims to first explore and contextualise them by explaining why doxxing is a tool often used against trans people. It goes on to argue that misconceptions about the degree of 'reality' of online space heavily contribute to perceptions of online harm as less 'real' than offline harm. This research emerged from direct experience of doxxing; one of us was doxxed and subsequently withdrew from online presence while the other became more deeply engaged. Bartels (2024) was warned by an anonymous

DOI: 10.4324/9781003564928-14

doxxer via Twitter (now X) that 'a storm is coming'. After weathering this storm, we began examining the difficulties in conceptualising online harm as real and consequential.

Relevant online terminology

Before delving into doxxing, it is worth acknowledging some of the legal and criminological terms used for online harms and the limited scope that will be covered in this chapter. Lusthaus (2024: 381) suggests the broad definition that 'cybercrime is crime that makes use of digital technology in a significant way' so it moves beyond binary categories, as he believes the interdisciplinary 'study of cybercrime should be about comprehending what is happening to crime in the present technological period'. Lusthaus (2024) concisely explains the historical delineation of cybercrime in terms of the two main categories predominantly used at this time: cyber-dependent and cyber-enabled crimes. What we discuss here would be considered cyber-enabled crime, or more specifically social media offences. In England and Wales, the Crown Prosecution Service (2024) lists trolling, online threats, disclosure of private sexual images without consent, online harassment, grooming, stalking online, and virtual mobbing as social media offences. Most relevant to this chapter are online harassment, virtual mobbing, trolling, and online threats, as these directly connect to the lived experiences of trans people navigating digital spaces.

Methodology

Despite the brief discussion above, we are not advocating for an expansion of punitive measures against cybercrimes; rather, we wish to go beyond the conventional understanding of online offences and the space(s) they are assumed to occupy, as the 'criminality of online harms may have little to do with the seriousness of harm inflicted' (Price, 2021: 241). To do this, we utilise queer(ing) criminology and zemiology as methodology; frameworks that allow room for both deconstruction and reconstruction of the distinctly harmful phenomena of transphobic doxxing. More than this work being about anti-LGBTQIA+ issues, we use 'queer' as a verb to 'challenge and subvert phenomena that are viewed as stable and determined' (Woods, 2013: 30). This subversion of the perceived stability of categories such as 'online' and 'offline' provides the analytical foundation for our arguments, enabling us to illuminate how these supposedly distinct categories actually intersect in the lived experiences of trans people facing doxxing.

Recently, criminologists have tried to contend with the challenges the digitisation of space has posed. Often, however, criminology presents 'correctives to the negative outcomes, and unintended consequences of extant policies, or as supplements to fill the gaps in our current knowledge' (Campbell, 2025: 72), rather than providing a framework that allows us to reimagine the impact of this digitisation. Zemiology is an extension of critical criminology that seeks to centre harm in its analysis (Hillyard et al., 2004). This different scope allows for power structures and institutions to be dynamically explored as important actors, and for agency to be given to individual or collective harm. Here, digital zemiology is not simply social harms explored in an online space, but an understanding of the tangle of humans and technology as parallel to the relationship between co-constituted humans and reality (Elias, 2025). Digital zemiology shifts the focus from socially mediated to digitally mediated harm, recognising that humans and technology are inseparable, and this interconnection is crucial to understanding harms in the digital space.

Defining doxxing and trolling

As the centrality of online spaces in our daily lives has grown, so has our exposure to various tactics of online harassment. The *Oxford English Dictionary* (2023) reports the earliest known use of 'dox' as a verb in the 2000s, originating from 1990s hacking culture (Douglas, 2016). Though several definitions persist, doxxing is essentially 'a complex process in which personal information is assembled from multiple channels and publicly distributed online without consent from the person to whom the information belongs' (Eckert and Metzger-Riftkin, 2020: 273). Douglas' (2016: 199) typology identifies and distinguishes three types of doxxing – deanonymising, targeting, and delegitimising – to explain how doxxing is a distinct privacy violation 'often with the intent to humiliate, threaten, intimidate, or punish the identified individual'. Bartels (2024) uses his experience to illustrate all three: deanonymising, when anonymous accounts connected his identity to photographs of him circulating online; targeting, when the doxxer disclosed his place of work; and delegitimising, when the doxxer weaponised his transness to make false suggestions about him. Building on Douglas (2016), Anderson and Wood (2022: 206) identify 'seven mutually non-exclusive motivations for doxxing: extortion, silencing, retribution, controlling, reputation-building, unintentional, and doxxing in the public interest'. Whilst most definitions mention that doxxing typically has malicious intent, Anderson and Wood's (2022: 209) categories of 'unintentional' and 'in the public interest' provide examples of when it might be done with non-malicious intent. Crucially, that does not mean the doxxing causes no harm, as harassment almost always follows (Eveleth, 2015).

Trolling 'can be likened to a form of cyberbullying and involves the sending or submission of provocative emails, social media posts, or 'tweets' (Twitter/X messages) with the intention of inciting an angry or upsetting response from its intended target or victim' (Harmer and Lumsden, 2019: 5). Although trolling was originally apolitical, its pervasive nature has rarely been addressed. In fact, trolling has long been an identity and subculture as well as a social media phenomenon, shaping internet discourse and influencing offline discourse and idea dissemination (Phillips, 2016; 2018). Increasingly, trolling has contributed to the rise of right-wing white supremacist conservative ideologies, as both have become normalised on sites like 4chan (Phillips, 2018). This is exemplified by mid-2010s events like The Fappening, which involved illegally acquiring and distributing nude images of celebrities; and #Gamergate, a 'hateful campaign to delegitimise and harass women and their allies in the gaming community', both occurring in 2014 (Massanari, 2017: 334).

Subsequently, as trolling has been linked to inciting hate, incel-friendly spaces like Kiwi Farms, right-wing accounts like Libs of TikTok, anti-trans-rights activists, and trans-exclusionary radical feminists (TERFs) have engaged in trolling behaviours towards trans people (Peng, Whyke and Gu, 2024; Collins and Tenbarge, 2022; Galpin, 2022). Trolling attempts to hijack and disrupt normative interactions and communication practices and also to 'oust' the victim from participation in public forums of debate – yet another commonality with doxxing (Harmer and Lumsden, 2019: 5). When trans Twitch streamer Clara Sorrenti spoke out about anti-trans legislation in 2022, Kiwi Farms users found her and her family's phone numbers and addresses. So began a threat campaign, which eventually forced her to flee the country, with the explicit aim of driving her away from posting online – 'It was particularly bad because I'm trans' (Collins and Tenbarge, 2022). Crucially, trolling has become a defining trait of social media behaviour; it has fundamentally changed how we perceive online space and contributes to our understanding of online and offline as distinct spaces.

Trans people and online space

As established in the introduction, many studies have explored how and why trans people, in particular, form communities online; communities that help build trans people's identities as places of discovery, validation, exploration, and information-sharing (GLSEN, CiPHR, and CCRC, 2013; Robards et al., 2020). Many trans people have reported disclosing their gender identity online first due to online spaces' relative safety (Yokotani and Takano, 2021). Herrmann et al.'s (2024: 3511) study of online queer and trans youth echoes many other studies, showing that '34% had come out online first, and nearly 90% presented themselves in another gender (role) online', as well as demonstrating that these youth felt 'significantly more understood and accepted online than in most offline domains'. Gender identity is built by individual private feelings as well as feedback from others – it is experienced through community (Cipolletta, 2011; Faccio, Bordin, and Cipolletta, 2013), but in this 'search for gender identity, transgender people are often alone'

(Cipolletta, Votadoro and, Faccio, 2017: 1542). Online spaces therefore provide an avenue for gender identity development that is not necessarily otherwise accessible. These spaces are characterised by self-disclosure and confession of intimate problems, facilitating the establishment and maintenance of social ties (Cipolletta, Votadoro and, Faccio, 2017: 1543).

Access to and rejection from spaces is one of the ways queer people conceptualise their fear of violence and discrimination, as queer people articulate their visibility according to the *safety* they feel in the space they are in (Klett-Davies, 2022), 'displaying (trans)gender tends to be highly contextual, depending on trans people's perceptions of (un)safe places' (Marques, 2022: 540). Safety is partially built through the people occupying the space (Marques, 2022). These spaces shape queer expression in return, as 'people learn to (re)do gender in "appropriate" ways according to the specific situated social interactions in which they participate, and that are interpreted by others as either legitimate or illegitimate' (West and Zimmerman, 1987, 2009, cited in Marques, 2022: 540–541). Trans people's 'access to power, prestige and resources will then be expressed in the uses that they can (or cannot) make of time and space' (West and Zimmerman, 1987, 2009, cited in Marques, 2022: 541), and they therefore have different possibilities of mobility (Browne and Lim, 2010; Hines, 2010; Lubitow et al., 2017).

Queer community spaces can function as 'counterpublics'; groups that form in opposition to the grand overarching co-created intended 'public' of mainstream discourse (Warner, 2002; Fraser, 1992). In a 'queer counterpublic, for example, no one is in the closet: the presumptive heterosexuality that constitutes the closet for individuals in ordinary speech is suspended' (Warner, 2002: 120). However, counterpublics can also produce forms of exclusion, as they can form in opposition to social justice movements, exemplified by the TERF movement populated largely by white, cis women (Galpin, Gwenffrewi, and Stokoe, 2023). The way a space is populated, the social norms that emerge, and the subsequent outsider policing of these norms is crucial to trans safety, and therefore trans expression, online.

Trans people and doxxing

Trolling tactics can enable doxxing; they rely on processes of heightened visibility. Both trolling and doxxing are features of online transphobic harms: often, for trans people, trolling turns to doxxing, or doxxing becomes trolling. As discussed above, trolling is a 'deliberate, highly performative (even choreographed) provocation of targets' (Phillips, 2018: 14–15). Its motivations differ from doxxing as it is typically done just to derive pleasure from the victim's suffering or discomfort, but they both prioritise exploitability when choosing targets.

Lee (2022) outlines a rationale of doxxing. Firstly, perpetrators rationalise their actions by framing them as morally righteous (Lee, 2022). Transphobes, and their subset of TERFs, have used doxxing to police and punish trans people online. Media can function as a modern shaming mechanism (Ellis, 2021), and deconstructing the term *account*-ability implies the need for a capacity to make an account, or an archive, of behaviour (Ericson, 1995). Attempts to police transgender identity, what Bettcher (2014) calls 'reality enforcements', can function as a problematic 'accountability' mechanism to punish those who fail to follow prescribed gender binaries (Marques, 2022; Namaste, 2000; Westbrook and Schilt, 2014; Shuster, 2017; Webster, 2024). TERFs in particular perceive transness as a personal and political affront, viewing trans women as conforming to stereotypical womanhood and trans men as opportunistically entranced by male privilege (Hines, 2020; Peng, Whyke, and Gu, 2024). This allows them to rationalise their policing as a feminist act.

Secondly, perpetrators (re)define doxxing by discursively minimising its effects (Lee, 2022). Sites like X/Twitter have often been cited as particularly fertile ground for doxxing, as they facilitate discussions in bad faith, acting as a cover for online torment to call into question trans people's experiences or legitimacy (Zanghellini, 2020). This is a 'particularly traumatic form of engagement for those historically disbelieved and delegitimised groups such as the trans community' (Gwenffrewi, 2022: 513). Delegitimisation of trans people is often structural and institutional (Yelin and Clancy, 2023); for instance, Haimson et al. (2021) show how queer and trans social media users are 'more likely than their cisgender peers to have their posts/content removed by moderation, despite adhering to community or platform guidelines', potentially leading trans users to rely less on 'official resources for complaint or appeal when online harassment occurs' (Aldridge et al., 2024: 483).

Although 'doxxing can happen to anyone, at any time, for nearly any reason' (Eveleth, 2015: 49), Black and LGBTQIA+ people are disproportionately affected by online harassment (Eckert and Metzger-Riftkin, 2020; Powell, Scott, and Henry, 2018). The UK 2017 National LGBT Survey of 108,000 people found 2 in 5 had experienced an incident such as verbal harassment or physical violence within the last 12 months, and more than 9 in 10 of the most serious incidents went unreported (Government Equalities Office, 2018). This lack of support bolsters perpetrators' capacity to define their doxxing as something they can get away with.

Thirdly, perpetrators construct a negative 'other', and, finally, victimise themselves in comparison (Lee, 2022). These constructions are inherent to the TERF mindset (Peng, Whyke, and Gu, 2024). For trans people, the deanonymising aspect of doxxing (Douglas, 2016) takes on an added dimension of harm: the exposure of being associated with a legal name that might not align with their gender identity. It is not only about fallout from a potential mismatch – for transphobes, the fact of pointing out this potential mismatch is cause for humiliation. Doxxing in general may not require malicious intent, but in this context, malicious intent is a prerequisite. This is why we propose that doxxing can be experienced as a hate crime in progress, operating in an online space.

Understanding harms in online spaces

There are multiple baseline underpinnings to our mischaracterisation of the harms of doxxing. These are rooted in our inability to imagine non-physical spaces, such as the internet, as real and consequential.

Online is a real space

Borders, and boundaries, are particularly important to queer and trans people – the queer or 'sexualised self is always a spatial self' (Hubbard, 2018: 1296). Through the reaction to and reproduction of attempts to control queerness (Holzberg, Madörin, and Pfeifer, 2021), 'sexual identities, behaviours and discourses are also shaped within borders [which do not only operate as] a divide but a "cultural terrain" that disciplines and produces the queer, the troublesome and the confines of the normative' (Klett-Davies, 2022: 4). The concept of 'body borders' helps illustrate the spatial negotiations inherent to queerness; intersecting queer geographies and border studies, body borders emphasise the body as a space determined and delineated by inside and outside forces and structures (Pereira-Garcia et al., 2024). Body borders encapsulate 'physical and symbolic borders such as lines of distinction and places of regulation, meeting, and transition' (Rieber, 2003; Yachin et al., 2015 in Pereira-Garcia et al., 2024: 3). Within their borders, bodies become a physical terrain or property to be defended from threats, which 'can be physical, but also symbolical or socially constructed', such as trans- or queerphobia (Yachin et al., 2015 in Pereira-Garcia et al., 2024: 4). The negotiations inherent to articulating transness in the physical, offline world have parallels to the attempts to articulate online behaviours offline.

The online space, despite occurring in a non-physical dimension, certainly exists and is experienced, shaped, and inhabited by its users; it is 'a place, somewhere to be, to go, to have been, and to leave' (Nicolazzo, Jones, and Simms, 2022: 44). To better conceptualise the territoriality of online space, typologies of digital space have been proposed. Kellerman (2016) suggested that outlining the distinct elements of online spaces that lack familiar terrestrial boundaries would be crucial to our understanding. It is, 'by its very definition and use, a relationally created spatial location' (Nicolazzo, Jones, and Simms, 2022: 44). Ife et al. (2019) highlight the functional dimension of cyberspace, arguing that how people behave and interact online is determined by each online space's intuitive purpose – what would, in offline space, be considered a sense of place.

The shape of online space can be difficult to grasp; some believe it to be shaped by algorithms, while some map out its discursive and structural similarities to offline structures of power and their segmentation of space (Nicolazzo, Jones, and Simms, 2022). Some highlight that online space is a terrain subject to 'electronic redlining' and barriers to access (Baynes, 2004). Surveillance in online spaces, and indeed, the spaces themselves, are sometimes cited as becoming 'de-territorialised' (Galič, Timan, and Koops, 2017). Crucially, 'cyberspaces can embody different place-based characteristics depending on the user', further complicating our understanding of their shape (McNealey and Ghazi-Tehrani, 2024: 533). Regardless of the shape of online space, it is a non-physical space. Our understanding of 'spatiality' tends to be physically constructed – a visible territory occupying a physical space, corporeally accessible.

Online does not have the borders we associate with a traditional delineation (and therefore, validation) of space, but it does have borders (Nicolazzo, Jones and Simms, 2022: 65); websites, domains, and communities all build themselves into bordered spaces which often have barriers to entry and usually distinct codes of social behaviour (Phillips, 2016; Gangadharan et al., 2021). Time also operates differently online, both by archiving a person's temporal history nonlinearly, and by the common experience of 'IRL time' stopping while 'online time' continues (Nicolazzo, Jones, and Simms, 2022: 65).

Non-physical spaces like the internet have been conceptualised, as demonstrated above, but their degree of *reality* has not necessarily permeated our collective understanding. Our nascent obsession with the metaverse exemplifies the difficulty in conceptualising how important, and how real, online space is to us (Dolata and Schwabe, 2023; Cheng et al., 2022). The offline world is often colloquially referred to as the 'real' world, for instance. This misconception leads to an inability to address the consequential nature of online space. In this chapter we instead invite a line of thinking that integrates online and offline experiences along a continuum of reality, rather than a spectrum between unreality and reality. Online spaces may not be physical, but they are *real.*

The relationship between online and offline

The most important border in online spaces is the porous one between online and offline. This increased porosity is due to increased online use; as online spaces become more populated, many elements of traditional society make their imprint online, and what was once a reproduction of offline space becomes real in its own right instead of being treated as an echo of offline space

(McNealey and Ghazi-Tehrani, 2024). This blending of online and offline worlds is 'often not fully acknowledged and understood', and has 'reshaped societal norms, behaviours, and interactions, which impact everything from social connections to work practices' (Munk et al., 2024: 14). Some seek to link online and offline spaces by citing connection 'through the users' bodily presence in material spaces, geographic location tracking, time stamped posts, and user identity verification policies' (Eckert et al., 2021: 81). The difference between them could be likened to two different substances filling a similar volume container. Offline space is a liquid; online space is a gas. Both fill the space, but they operate differently. Importantly, 'technology complicates our metaphors of space and place, including the belief that audiences are separate from each other' (Marwick and boyd, 2011: 115).

Meyrowitz (1985) argued that context, rather than psychological traits, is most crucial to people's reactions, theorising that 'electronic media eliminated walls between separate social situations' (Marwick and boyd, 2011: 115). For example, online spaces are associated with a perception of a "lack of consequences", which is often used to explain the difference between offline and online behaviours. There is an understanding that anonymity promotes this, as the physicality of consequences is represented by being known online by your offline peers or social group. This has led to the idea that offline harm is an escalation of online harm, obscuring our capacity to process and weigh online harm as consequential in itself.

Our difficulty with acknowledging that online space is as real as offline space makes legislating online spaces extremely difficult. Technology is advancing too rapidly for legislators to keep up, but this is not the only problem; the issue is how technology radically changes our relationship to space by creating a shared non-physical space that is as real as our physical space. In England and Wales, the Online Safety Act 2023, for example, is a new set of laws that claim to protect children and adults online by primarily imposing new duties on providers of services (social media companies and search engines), placing the onus of responsibility for service users on the platforms themselves. The Act treats online as a distinct space, owned by service providers, to be regulated by those providers and by the government. It does not mention doxxing. It highlights that 'providers' safety duties are proportional to [...] the risk of harm to individuals' (Department for Science, Innovation & Technology, 2024), but this approach to risk overlooks the unique ways crime and victimhood are processed online (McNealey and Ghazi-Tehrani, 2024). The Act regulates online services by perceiving them as content hosts, not systems, but the latter would require holding platforms responsible for their governance and moderation, and their amplification of content (Nash and Felton, 2024). This myopic approach showcases a variety of misunderstandings; the porosity of the border between the online and offline worlds, the *reality* of the harm caused by online threats, and the narrowing of risk to potential physical consequences.

Harm in online spaces: Non-corporeal harm as real harm

What does this mean for doxxing? As previously discussed, online spaces have varying levels of moderation, and existing in online spaces tends to include self-moderation just as transness includes self-regulation (Hines, 2010). When it comes to discussing or conceptualising the online from the offline, we are prone to mistranslations. Legally, online and offline spaces are treated as different and distinct; the degree of harm is measured in offline consequences. It has been argued that 'platforms can and have been used in ways such that, while no one individual crosses the threshold of criminality, the consequences are both severe and widespread' (Price, 2021: 240–241). 'Contextual elements of risk perception are traditionally studied in geographic space', rather than online space, and our considerations of context must adapt accordingly (McNealey and Ghazi-Tehrani, 2024: 530). Our misunderstanding of the 'reality' of online space extends to a misunderstanding of the gravity of online harm, reflected in institutional and legal responses.

Firstly, the reality of online threats, their meaningfulness, is consequential. Online threats, like online relationships, may be 'ethereal' (Cipolletta, Votadoro and Faccio, 2017: 1543), but they are no less important than offline threats. 'Physical' effects of doxxing often include contacting a trans person's workplace, landlord, family, and friends, or threats of physical harm by transphobes. This perceived distance between the discursive effect and corporeal effect of threat is paralleled in the misunderstanding of online space as less real or consequential than offline space.

Instead, the threat and coercion of doxxing and the severe potential offline consequences it entails ought to be considered in terms of the harm they cause, regardless of whether the threat carries out into the physical space (Price, 2021). There is immense violence in the forced collision of online and offline space caused by the threat doxxing represents. Research reports that 'UK hate crime statistics show a sharp increase in transphobic crimes since 2015 [...] Online abuse is also rising, and many trans people fear for their safety' (Chikha, 2021 in Gwenffrewi, 2022: 513). This context is crucial when understanding the weight of threat.

In attempting to conceptualise threat, March, Hasty, and Olivett (2024) discuss the need for a measure of how sensitive one is to the potential of harm from innocuous elements. Highlighted sensitivity factors include psychological, contextual, and whether one has been harmed before (March, Hasty, and Olivett, 2024). Doxxing is in no way innocuous, but it posits itself as 'between' harmful and harmless; it is discursive, after all (Peng, Whyke, and Gu, 2024; Lee, 2022) so can cause harm while remaining difficult to punish. We argue instead that threat is harm in itself, and the harms of doxxing 'lie in not only actualising "virtual" potentialities for harm but in exponentially increasing the future potential for harm' (Anderson and Wood, 2022: 197).

Threat of harm can change a trans person's behaviour offline; as the human body exists in both physical and non-physical space, physical consequences (such as consequences caused by psychological trauma) can result from non-physical threats (Blackwell et al., 2017; Worsley et al., 2017). This demonstrates the liminality of online space and the dangers of treating online and offline as mutually exclusive, or totally distinct, spaces.

Secondly, what about online harm in itself? Online consequences are equally weighty. Doxxing, as discussed above, can take many forms and include various social media offences. The harm caused is similarly multi-layered. Non-consensual filming of a trans person, for example, 'violates privacy and often incites hate speech' (Munk et al., 2024: 17). Online environments are characterised by their pervasiveness and omnipresence; this 'enables perpetrators to extend their control, erasing any safe space for victims and affecting their sense of physical, psychological, and symbolic space' (Munk et al., 2024: 14).

The "self-surveillance" employed by online media users has become a significant element of navigating an online presence, particularly for vulnerable groups who are most subject to being monitored (Dubrofsky and Magnet, 2015), and who, accordingly, make context-informed decisions when facing potential antagonistic interactions online (Eckert et al., 2021). Doxxing heightens the elements of surveillance and self-policing trans people already operate within when creating their gender expression, narrowing the negotiation of their gender identity. Given the relationship between trans people's gender expression and the space they inhabit, it follows that attacking those spaces destroys that expression.

Trans people often choose online space for its malleability, regardless of the degree of anonymity they pursue when online (Nicolazzo, Jones, and Simms, 2022). An online space is often an intentionally curated one, yet doxxing forces transness to the forefront of trans people's navigation of online spaces. A trans person being harassed out of a specific online space ought to be treated similarly to them being harassed out of a specific offline one, such as when using a public bathroom, and the threat of exposure to harassment operates similarly (Galpin, 2022). A trans person being less likely to engage in online spaces, and changing their online behaviour as a consequence of harassment, is a serious harm caused by doxxing. It exemplifies the dangerous assumption that trans people will be punished for transgressing perceived gender boundaries (Marques, 2022) even in a space whose boundaries are malleable by design; that, therefore, there is little safety to be found. This is true for trans people seeking queer community online, but also for trans people seeking online spaces that are not centred around trans and queer community-building (Yelin and Clancy, 2023).

Aside from this, online visibility in itself is a significant weight, especially when that visibility has not been consented to (Colliver, 2021; Yelin and Clancy, 2023). Non-consensual visibility is a feature of many trans people's experiences offline. Online, this public visibility is multiplied by coefficients; the weight is exponential, compounded by the destruction of curated safety, and operates as an intimidation tactic within and outside the online space (Colliver, 2021; Price, 2021). Thus, doxxing has the potential to change how trans people move through space, online and offline – it changes the thickness of their body border, forcing a non-consensual re-negotiation of gender identity, movement, and presentation. These are harms, and they are consequential, regardless of our inability to conceptualise them as such.

Conclusion

This chapter has discussed the widespread inability to address online harm effectively. The digital zemiology framework, characterised by an analytical recentring of harm and an integration of power structures as important actors, allows for a reconstruction of doxxing as a mechanism of punishment for perceived transgressions; one that is often used by transphobes against transgender people. Unlike offline space, online space is uniquely malleable and non-physical: we have explored the *reality* of this space and its importance for marginalised groups, particularly for transgender people. However, the reality of online space is often overlooked, as legislators and the public tend to conceptualise offline space as uniquely 'real', and online/offline spaces as separate. This impacts how online harm is perceived, often as a potential precursor to offline harm, rather than as harm in itself.

In order to address online harm effectively, the liminality and porousness of borders between online and offline space must be dynamically understood. Legislation, however, remains attached to sharply distinct categorisations of harms, and those harmed. For example, the Online Safety Act (2023: 17) mentions discrimination based on 'gender reassignment' but not based on transgender identity, reflecting broader institutional failures to recognise the complexity of trans experiences. Future legal frameworks must move beyond treating online platforms merely as content hosts and instead hold them accountable as systems that shape and amplify harmful content. Additionally, law enforcement and support services require training to understand the interconnected nature of online and offline harms, particularly as they affect vulnerable populations.

The consequences of online doxxing are severe and can impact many elements of how trans people seek community and move through space. We posit that doxxing ought to be treated according to the harm it causes, rather than being minimised as merely 'virtual' or preliminary to 'real' harm. This reconceptualisation requires both institutional change and broader cultural shifts in how we understand the reality and consequentiality of digital spaces. Only by recognising online harm as equally valid and damaging as offline harm can we begin to adequately protect marginalised communities who have found refuge, community, and identity in digital spaces.

References

Aldridge, Z., et al. (2024). Social media creations of community and gender minority stress in transgender and gender-diverse adults. *Social Sciences (Basel)*, *13*(9), 483.

Anderson, B., and Wood, M. A. (2022). Harm imbrication and virtualised violence: Reconceptualising the harms of doxxing. *International Journal for Crime, Justice and Social Democracy*, *11*(1), 196–209.

Bartels, G. (2024). 'Seriously, don't leave your flat'… I was doxxed. In T. Munk and M. Kennedy (Eds.), *Victimisation in the digital age: An online/offline continuum approach* (pp. 205–219). Abingdon: Routledge.

Baynes, L. M. (2004). Deregulatory injustice and electronic redlining: The color of access to telecommunications. *Administrative Law Review*, *56*(2), 263–352.

Bettcher, T. M. (2014). Trapped in the wrong theory: Rethinking trans oppression and resistance. *Signs: Journal of Women in Culture and Society*, *39*(2), 383–406.

Blackwell, L., et al. (2017). Classification and its consequences for online harassment: Design insights from HeartMob. *Proceedings of the ACM on Human-computer Interaction*, *1*(CSCW), 1–19.

Browne, K, and Lim, J. (2010) Trans lives in the 'gay capital of the UK'. *Gender, Place and Culture: A Journal of Feminist Geography*, *17*(5), 615–633.

Campbell, E. (2025). Techno-digital policing and speculative fictions: Towards a criminology of the future. *Crime, Media, Culture*, *21*(1), 69–95.

Cannon, Y., et al. (2017). Transition, connection, disconnection, and social media: Examining the digital lived experiences of transgender individuals. *Journal of LGBT Issues in Counseling*, *11*(2), 68–87.

Cavalcante, A. (2016). I did it all online: Transgender identity and the management of everyday life. *Critical Studies in Media Communication*, *33*(1), 109–122.

Cheng, R., et al. (2022). Will Metaverse be NextG internet? Vision, hype, and reality. *IEEE Network*, *36*(5), 197–204.

Cipolletta, S. (2011). Self-construction and interpersonal distances of juveniles living in residential communities. *Journal of Constructivist Psychology*, *24*(2), 122–143.

Cipolletta, S., Votadoro, R., and Faccio, E. (2017). Online support for transgender people: An analysis of forums and social networks. *Health & Social Care in the Community*, *25*(5), 1542–1551.

Collins, B., and Tenbarge, K. (2022, 2 September). Anti-trans stalkers at Kiwi Farms are chasing one victim around the world. Their list of targets is growing. *NBC News*. https://www.nbcnews.com/tech/internet/cloudflare-kiwi-farms-keffals-anti-trans-rcna44834

Colliver, B. (2021). *Re-imagining hate crime: Transphobia, visibility and victimisation*. Cham, Switzerland: Springer.

Crown Prosecution Service (2024). *Cybercrime – prosecution guidance*. London: CPS.

Department for Science, Innovation & Technology (2024). *Online Safety Act: Explainer*. London: UK Government. https://www.gov.uk/government/publications/online-safety-act-explainer/online-safety-act-explainer#how-the-act-tackles-misinformation-and-disinformation

Dolata, M., and Schwabe, G. (2023). What is the Metaverse and who seeks to define it? Mapping the site of social construction. *Journal of Information Technology*, *38*(3), 239–266.

Douglas, D. M. (2016) Doxing: a conceptual analysis. *Ethics and Information Technology*, *18*(3), 199–210.

Dubrofsky, R. E., and Magnet, S. A. (2015). *Feminist surveillance studies: Critical interventions* (pp. 1–18). New York: Duke University Press.

Eckert, S., and Metzger-Riftkin, J. (2020). Doxxing, privacy and gendered harassment. The shock and normalization of veillance cultures. *Medien & Kommunikationswissenschaft: M & K*, *68*(3), 273–287.

Eckert, S. et al. (2021). A hyper differential counterpublic: Muslim social media users and Islamophobia during the 2016 US presidential election. *New Media & Society*, *23*(1), 78–98.

Elias, J. (2025). Towards a digital zemiology. *Justice, Power and Resistance*, *8*(1), 1–17.

Ellis, J. R. (2021). *Policing legitimacy: Social media, scandal and sexual citizenship*. Cham: Springer International Publishing.

Ericson, R. V. (1995). The news media and account ability in criminal justice. In P. Stenning (Ed.), *Accountability for criminal justice* (pp. 135–161). Toronto: University of Toronto Press.

Eveleth, R. (2015). How to deter doxxing: Newsroom strategies to prevent the harassment that can follow public posting of personal information. *Nieman Reports*, *69*(3), 46–49.

Faccio, E., Bordin, E., and Cipolletta, S. (2013). Transsexual parenthood and new role assumptions. *Culture, Health & Sexuality*, *15*(9), 1055–1070.

Fraser, N. (1992). Rethinking the public sphere: A contribution to the critique of actually existing democracy. In C. Calhoun (Ed.), *Habermas and the public sphere* (pp. 109–142). Cambridge, MA: MIT Press.

Galič, M., Timan, T., and Koops, B.-J. (2017). Bentham, Deleuze and beyond: An overview of surveillance theories from the panopticon to participation. *Philosophy & Technology*, *30*(1), 9–37.

Galpin, C. (2022). At the digital margins? A theoretical examination of social media engagement using intersectional feminism. *Politics and Governance*, *10*(1), 161–171.

Galpin, C., Gwenffrewi, G., and Stokoe, A. (2023). Transfeminist perspectives: Beyond cisnormative understandings of the digital public sphere. *The European Journal of Women's Studies*, *30*(4), 502–515.

Gangadharan, S., et al. (2021). *Digital exclusion: A politics of refusal*. Chicago: University of Chicago Press.

GLSEN, CiPHR, and CCRC (2013). *Out online: The experiences of lesbian, gay, bisexual and transgender youth on the internet*. New York: GLSEN.

Government Equalities Office (2018). *National LGBT survey research report*. GEO Research Report: RR001, 1–301.

Gwenffrewi, G. (2022). J. K. Rowling and the echo chamber of secrets. *TSQ: Transgender Studies Quarterly*, *9*(3), 507–516.

Haimson, O. L., et al. (2021). Disproportionate removals and differing content moderation experiences for conservative, transgender, and Black social media users: Marginalization and moderation gray areas. *Proceedings of the ACM on Human-computer Interaction*, *5*(CSCW2), 1–35.

Harmer, E., and Lumsden, K. (2019). Online othering: An introduction. In K. Lumsden and E. Harmer (Eds.), *Online othering: Exploring digital violence and discrimination on the web* (pp. 1–33). Palgrave Studies in Cybercrime and Cybersecurity. Cham: Springer International Publishing.

Herrmann, L., et al. (2024). How social is social media for transgender and gender-diverse youth? Association of online social experiences with internalizing mental health problems. *European Child & Adolescent Psychiatry*, *33*(10), 3503–3516.

Hillyard, P., et al. (2004). *Beyond criminology: Taking harm seriously* (1st ed.). Winnipeg: Pluto Press.

Hines, S. (2010). Queerly situated? Exploring negotiations of trans queer subjectivities at work and within community spaces in the UK. *Gender, Place and Culture: A Journal of Feminist Geography*, *17*(5), 597–613.

Hines, S. (2020). Sex wars and (trans) gender panics: Identity and body politics in contemporary UK feminism. *The Sociological Review*, *68*(4), 699–717.

Holzberg, B., Madörin, A., and Pfeifer, M. (2021). The sexual politics of border control: An introduction. *Ethnic and Racial Studies*, *44*(9), 1485–1506.

Hubbard, P. (2018). Geography and sexuality: Why space (still) matters. *Sexualities*, *21*(8), 1295–1299.

Ife, C. C., et al. (2019). Bridging information security and environmental criminology research to better mitigate cybercrime. *arXiv*, 1–38. https://arxiv.org/pdf/1910.06380v2

Kellerman, A. (2016). *Geographic interpretations of the internet* (1st ed.). Cham: Springer.

Klett-Davies, M. (2022). Border regimes: Homophobia and LGBT place making in six ordinary cities in Europe. *Religions*, *13*(1), 1–16.

Lee, C. (2022). Doxxing as discursive action in a social movement. *Critical Discourse Studies*, *19*(3), 326–344.

Lubitow, A., et al. (2017). Transmobilities: Mobility, harassment, and violence experienced by transgender and gender nonconforming public transit riders in Portland, *Oregon. Gender, Place and Culture: A Journal of Feminist Geography*, *24*(10), 1398–1418.

Lusthaus, J. (2024). Reconsidering crime and technology: What is this thing we call cybercrime? *Annual Review of Law and Social Science*, *20*(1), 369–385.

March, D. S., Hasty, C., and Olivett, V. (2024). The threat sensitivity scale: A brief self-report measure of dispositional sensitivity toward perceiving threats to physical harm. *Scientific Reports*, *14*(1), 11304–11304.

Marques, A. (2022). Displaying (trans)gender in space and time: Deconstructing spatial binaries of violence and security in the UK and Portugal. In M. Blidon and S. D. Brunn (Eds.), *Mapping LGBTQ spaces and places: A changing world* (pp. 539–553). Cham: Springer International Publishing,

Marwick, A. E., and boyd, d. (2011). I tweet honestly, I tweet passionately: Twitter users, context collapse, and the imagined audience. *New Media & Society*, *13*(1), 114–133.

Massanari, A. (2017). Gamergate and the Fappening: How Reddit's algorithm, governance, and culture support toxic technocultures. *New Media & Society*, *19*(3), 329–346.

McNealey, R. L., and Ghazi-Tehrani, A. (2024). Risky digital behavior or risky digital places? Victimization risk perception and evaluation on the internet. *Journal of Crime & Justice*, *47*(4), 530–544.

Meyrowitz, J. (1985). *No sense of place: The impact of electronic media on social behavior*. New York: Oxford University Press.

Munk, T., et al. (2024). Navigating the online-offline continuum: Exploring victims, spaces, and dangers. In T. Munk and M. Kennedy (Eds.), *Victimisation in the digital age: An online/offline continuum approach* (pp. 14–32). Abingdon: Routledge.

Namaste, V. K. (2000). *Invisible lives: The erasure of transsexual and transgendered people*. Chicago: University of Chicago Press.
Nash, V., and Felton, L. (2024) Treating the symptoms or the disease? Analysing the UK Online Safety Act's approach to digital regulation. *Policy and Internet*, *16*, 818–832.
Nicolazzo, Z., Jones, A. C., and Simms, S. (2022) *Digital me: Trans students exploring future possible selves online* (1st ed.). New Brunswick, NJ: Rutgers University Press.
Online Safety Act (2023). c. 50.
Oxford English Dictionary (2023). Dox (v.).
Peng, A. Y., Whyke, T. W., and Gu, F. (2024). Coping with gender-critical voices from within: A sociocognitive approach to Sussex's Twitter (X) crisis responses. *Discourse & Communication*, *18*(3), 433–451.
Pereira-Garcia, S., et al. (2024). 'It is not even my body': Trans persons experiencing body borders. *Gender Issues*, *41*(1).
Phillips, W. (2016). *This is why we can't have nice things: Mapping the relationship between online trolling and mainstream culture*. Cambridge, MA: The MIT Press.
Phillips, W. (2018). *The oxygen of amplification: Better practices for reporting on extremists, antagonists, and manipulators online*. New York: Data & Society Research Institute.
Powell, A., Scott, A. J., and Henry, N. (2018). Digital harassment and abuse: Experiences of sexuality and gender minority adults. *European Journal of Criminology*, *17*(2), 199–223.
Price, L. (2021). Platform responsibility for online harms: Towards a duty of care for online hazards. *The Journal of Media Law*, *13*(2), 238–261.
Rieber, A. J. (2003). Changing concepts and constructions of frontiers: A comparative historical approach. *Ab Imperio*, *1*, 23–26.
Robards, B., et al. (2020). *Tumblr as a space of learning, connecting, and identity formation for LGBTIQ plus young people: Platform and cultures* (pp. 281–292). Ann Arbor, MI: University of Michigan Press.
Scheuerman, M., Branham, S., and Hamidi, F. (2018). Safe spaces and safe places: Unpacking technology-mediated experiences of safety and harm with transgender people. *Proceedings of the ACM on Human-Computer Interaction*, *2*(CSCW), 1–27.
Selkie, E., et al. (2020). Transgender adolescents' uses of social media for social support. *Journal of Adolescent Health*, *66*(3), 275–280.
Shapiro, E. (2004). 'Trans'cending barriers: Transgender organizing on the internet. *Journal of Gay & Lesbian Social Services*, *16*(3–4), 165–179.
Shuster, S. M. (2017). Punctuating accountability: How discursive aggression regulates transgender people. *Gender & Society*, *31*(4), 481–502.
Warner, M. (2002). *Publics and counterpublics*. New York: Zone Books.
Webster, L. (2024). 'We are detective: Transvestigations, conspiracy and inauthenticity in 'gender critical' social media discourses. *ELAD-SILDA*, *9*.
West, C., and Zimmerman, D. H. (1987). Doing gender. *Gender & Society*, *1*(2), 125–151.
West, C., and Zimmerman, D. H. (2009). Accounting for doing gender. *Gender & Society*, *23*(1), 112–122.
Westbrook, L., and Schilt, K. (2014). Doing gender, determining gender: Transgender people, gender panics, and the maintenance of the sex/gender/sexuality system. *Gender & Society*, *28*(1), 32–57.
Woods, J. B. (2013). 'Queering criminology': Overview of the state of the field. In D. Peterson and V. R. Panfil (Eds.), *Handbook of LGBT communities, crime, and justice* (pp. 15–41). New York: Springer.
Worsley, J. D., et al. (2017). Victims' voices: Understanding the emotional impact of cyberstalking and individuals' coping responses. *SAGE Open*, *7*(2).

Yachin, S. E. (2015). Boundary as an ontological and anthropological category. In S. V. Sevastianov, J. P. Laine, and A. Kireev (Eds.), *Introduction to border studies* (pp. 62–79). Vladivostok, Primorsky Krai: Far Eastern Federal University.
Yelin, H., and Clancy, L. (2023). 'I have a folder in my email called hate mail': Academic public engagement, digital hate and the unequally distributed risks of visibility. *New Formations*, *110*(110), 187–206.
Yokotani, K., and Takano, M. (2021). Differences in victim experiences by gender/sexual minority statuses in Japanese virtual communities. *Journal of Community Psychology*, *49*(6), 1598–1616.
Zanghellini, A. (2020). Philosophical problems with the gender-critical feminist argument against trans inclusion. *SAGE Open*, *10*(2).

12

MICROAGGRESSIONS, PREJUDICE, AND HARM: PERCEPTIONS AND EXPERIENCES OF TRANSGENDER AND GENDER NON-CONFORMING INDIVIDUALS ON GRINDR

Ioannis Dimitrakopoulos

Introduction

In the 1970s, Pierce (1970) introduced microaggressions to describe subtle, daily discrimination faced by racial minorities (Freeman and Schroer, 2020). Sue et al.'s (2007) work defined microaggressions as brief verbal, behavioural, or environmental indignities that communicate hostile racial slights. While these foundational studies primarily centred on racial dynamics, subsequent researchers have expanded the theory to encompass other marginalised identities. For example, Croteau and Morrison (2022) and Arijs et al. (2023) explored the application of microaggression theory in relation to transgender and gender non-conforming identities (TGNC), referring to individuals whose gender identity does not conform to the sex assigned at birth or binary gender standards (Arijs et al., 2023); while Nadal et al. (2016) investigated its relevance to LGBTQ+ communities. In their work, Nadal et al. (2016) broadened the concept to include heterosexist microaggressions and indignities experienced by LGBTQ+ individuals. This expansion has spurred further research into lateral microaggressions within the LGBTQ+ community, as highlighted by studies such as Reed (2020) and Tran, Sullivan, and Nicholas (2022). Additionally, Reiheld (2020) has noted that microaggressions can target socially devalued traits beyond traditionally recognised marginalised identities, such as non-idealised body types. This flexibility in application demonstrates the theory's utility in addressing a wide range of biases, whether rooted in traditional social hierarchies or emerging social norms. As acknowledged through the framework of microaggressions (Freeman and Schroer, 2020), they can be perceived as deaths by a thousand cuts (Beaumont, 2024), reflecting upon their cumulative effect and signifying their importance in

DOI: 10.4324/9781003564928-15

understanding issues of prejudice beyond the concepts of criminalised discrimination and hate.

While microaggressions have focused on examining issues of heterosexism, only a few studies have examined issues related to within-group microaggressions (Reed, 2020; Tran et al., 2022) regarding TGNC individuals within queer settings. Considering how studies have unravelled the prevalence of harmful behaviours within the cyber settings of queer dating apps (e.g., Rodriguez et al., 2016; Chow, 2021), it is critical to examine potential threats and harm(s) caused within these settings. This chapter aims to reveal such harms by examining perceptions and experiences of microaggressions on Grindr to expand on the conceptualisations of within-group microaggressions, the harm of microaggressions, and how seemingly minor incidents may contribute significantly to the establishment of prejudice.

Microaggressions and their relationship to hate crime models

These subtle, yet pervasive acts of microaggression differ significantly from overt hate crimes, manifesting instead in daily language and behaviours that implicitly convey stereotypes and bias. Despite these distinctions, they contribute significantly to the cumulative harm experienced by marginalised communities. Hate crime models, traditionally focused on explicit and criminal acts, often overlook the broader spectrum of everyday and experienced prejudice (e.g., McClure, 2020; Schweppe and Tong, 2021; McBride and James, 2022); for instance, how the singular focus on transphobia eliminates broader issues of multifaceted vulnerabilities (Spade, 2010). Despite this, it should be stated that the prevalence of hate crimes targeting transgender individuals remains alarmingly high. In England and Wales, the Home Office (2023) reported 4,732 hate crimes against transgender individuals in the 2022/2023 period. While such explicit forms of discrimination and hate crime have profound impacts, this chapter focuses on less overt instances – those that fall outside the legal definitions of hate crimes, but nevertheless perpetuate everyday prejudice and bias.

Nadal et al. (2019) have noted that microaggressions can be ingrained within a societal structure that systemically marginalises specific identities. This positioning of microaggressions, similar to hate crime models, broadens the framework for understanding harm. Mason-Bish and Duggan (2020) noted that microaggressions can be pervasive, yet legally ambiguous, and often further victimise individuals by contributing to a social system that allows aggression. Research emphasises that the cumulative effect of microaggressions often leads to significant harm, even when individual incidents appear trivial (McClure, 2020; Freeman and Schroer, 2020). In this sense, two primary characteristics underscore the significance of microaggressions (McClure, 2020). First, their cumulative nature results in a profound impact on individuals over time, as repetitive instances of subtle discrimination can erode well-being and enhance systems of oppression (Freeman and Schroer, 2020). Second, the implicit nature of microaggressions often obscures their harmful intent, making them harder to detect and address. For example, Collins and Clément (2012) have observed that recipients may struggle to recognise microaggressions as prejudice, which allows perpetrators to evade accountability while dismissing the harmed as overly sensitive.

Beaumont (2024) titled the cumulative impact of these microaggressions as a 'death by a thousand cuts'. This metaphor captures the profound sociological harm inflicted by repeated microaggressions, which foster an environment of othering and invalidation. Philosophical perspectives further contextualise this harm. Freeman and Stewart (2021) identify collective forms of harm, such as existential harm, where individuals' autonomy in expressing their identity is denied. Kapusta's (2016) conceptualisation can further elaborate on this by linking such harm to the refusal to treat individuals with dignity and respect, thereby infringing upon their fundamental right to self-expression. Overall, as Wiltgren (2022) highlighted, this subtlety perpetuates systemic prejudice, which can be articulated as hinting at potential barriers to addressing and dismantling prejudice or hate.

Microaggressions targeting transgender and non-binary individuals

Transgender and non-binary individuals face unique forms of microaggressions linked to their gender identities. Misgendering and dismissive behaviours are among the most common manifestations (e.g., Nadal et al., 2012; Colliver, 2021; Croteau and Morrison, 2022; Griffiths and Armstrong, 2023). Scholars have demonstrated a direct correlation between such microaggressions and adverse mental health outcomes, prevalent among transgender and non-binary individuals, including diminished self-esteem and feelings of alienation (Nadal et al., 2014; Hollingsworth et al., 2017). More specifically, and regarding transgender individuals, Nadal et al. (2012) developed a taxonomy of transgender microaggressions, identifying 12 distinct themes, namely: (1) 'use of transphobic and/or incorrectly gendered terminology'; (2) 'assumption of universal transgender experience'; (3) 'exoticisation'; (4) 'discomfort/disapproval of transgender experience'; (5) 'endorsement of gender normative and binary culture or behaviours'; (6) 'denial of the existence of transphobia'; (7) 'assumption of sexual pathology/abnormality'; (8) 'physical threat or harassment'; (9) 'denial of individual transphobia'; (10) 'denial of bodily privacy'; (11) 'familial microaggressions'; and (12) 'systemic or environmental microaggressions'. Building on this work, Croteau and Morrison (2022) introduced the Non-Binary Gender Microaggression (NBGM) Scale, which categorises microaggressions into five subscales: (1) negation of identity, (2) inauthenticity, (3) deadnaming, (4) trans exclusion, and (5) misuse of gendered terminology. Both frameworks illustrate how transgender and non-binary individuals are systematically subjected to discriminatory behaviours that invalidate their identities and reinforce societal marginalisation.

Microaggressions in online dating

With microaggressions frequently occurring within dating apps (Rodriguez et al., 2016; Chow, 2021; Tran et al., 2022), this chapter aims to unravel issues of microaggressions against TGNC individuals. Unlike traditional public spaces, the privacy afforded by online dating settings may paradoxically enable subtle forms of prejudice. For example, Tran et al. (2022) emphasise how lateral prejudice manifests as microaggressions, often questioning gender authenticity or expressing discomfort with gender non-conforming identities. Generally, common microaggressions in online dating include misgendering, anti-effeminacy, fetishisation, and exclusionary behaviours (e.g., Sánchez et al., 2016; Murgo et al., 2017; Bonner-Thompson, 2017; Hale and Ojeda, 2018). For example, concepts of 'no fems', 'only masc', or 'trans only' can represent some of the most infamous examples of microaggressions on dating apps (including Grindr), often expressed either within users' bios or even directly expressed as a preference towards other users (e.g., Rodriguez et al., 2016; Kindr, 2018; Chow, 2021). Griffiths and Armstrong (2023) highlighted that whilst dating apps can offer some connectivity with the queer community, they can also become a space where these agents may experience micro-insults and micro-invalidation or fetishisation. According to their findings, it can be articulated that prejudice within dating platforms may contribute to a form of lateral violence where even LGBTQ+ community members reinforce binary norms or exoticise transgender individuals and gender non-conforming identities. Such behaviours can therefore restrict TGNC individuals from safely exploring relationships and expressing their identities.

Grindr, a popular LGBTQ+ dating platform, exemplifies the prevalence of microaggressions in online spaces. For example, as noted by Grindr's Kindr initiative (Kindr, 2018), users frequently express racialised, gendered, or sizeist prejudices under the guise of 'preferences'. In this sense, Grindr, among other dating apps, can be perceived as a setting where microaggressions and discrimination may take place on an interpersonal level. These behaviours contribute to an environment where marginalised individuals feel dehumanised and excluded, reinforcing broader societal biases. In this sense, for TGNC individuals, microaggressions represent a unique form of harm that intersects with broader issues of gender identity, self-expression, and social inclusion. Whether occurring in public spaces, workplaces, or digital environments such as online dating platforms, these acts perpetuate feelings of exclusion and alienation, contributing to both individual and collective harm. Importantly, the environments where these microaggressions occur, including spaces such as LGBTQ+ dating platforms, reveal how systemic biases and lateral prejudices can infiltrate and even be upheld within marginalised communities, as also suggested by Overton and Hepple (2022).

Methodology

This chapter draws upon data collected through an online survey and semi-structured interviews conducted with current and former Grindr users residing in England and Wales. Data collection spanned a 12-month period from October 2022 to October 2023. Of the 15 TGNC participants who contributed, 6 self-identified as transgender, 7 as non-binary, 1 as a crossdresser, and 1 as genderqueer. All participants were over 18 years of age and resided in England and Wales at the time they completed the online survey and participated in interviews. The data presented in this chapter are drawn from a larger study (Dimitrakopoulos, 2025) conducted as part of the researcher's doctoral thesis, which examined microaggressions and their resultant harms among gay men, MSM, and queer individuals (N=100). The broader research explored issues such as femmephobia, body shaming, and bottom-shaming in the context of interactions on Grindr, a leading queer dating and social app (Grindr, n.d.; Miles, 2021).

Participants were given the opportunity, via the online survey, to narrate their experiences through both closed-ended and open-ended sections, allowing them to describe their personal encounters or opt for participation in an interview. For the purposes of this chapter, the focus is on the 15 participants mentioned, most of whom shared their experiences through both closed-ended and open-ended sections of the survey (N=13). Of these participants, two provided additional responses through interviews and written responses in the survey. Recruitment was primarily conducted through social media, though the researcher also visited various cities and queer venues across England to promote the study. The selection of cities was informed by the most recent Census national survey data (Office for National Statistics, 2023). Social media and apps were primarily used for the recruitment methods, which allowed the researcher to recruit more hard-to-reach populations (e.g., Neville, Adams, and Cook, 2015; Filice et al., 2019), such as TGNC individuals.

Given the limited number of participants, the analysis presented in this chapter focuses on qualitative data. The data presented here were analysed exclusively through thematic analysis, guided by Braun and Clarke's (2006) contributions. This analysis identified three principal themes, which are: (1) degradation, (2) dehumanisation, and (3) ostracisation and monitoring. Although generalisability is limited by the sample size, the chapter aims to contribute to the ongoing discussion and conceptualisation of the experiences of TGNC individuals. It specifically addresses the intersection of microaggressions and broader issues of misogyny within online spaces, particularly in interactions involving other gay men, MSM, and queer individuals on Grindr.

Findings and themes

Through an analysis of participant narratives, themes emerged that reflect the mechanisms of prejudice and marginalisation, revealing the layered impact of microaggressions. The current analysis builds on existing literature by conceptualising these harms not merely as psychological but as social and existential, illustrating how such interactions perpetuate systemic inequalities and reinforce social and cultural marginalisation.

1 Degradation - Transphobic and misogynistic insults, rejection of identity, and harm through assumptions

A central theme identified by participants was the rejection of, and assumptions regarding, non-conforming gender identities and the degrading effects associated with insults and misrecognition experienced during interactions on Grindr. This section explores these interactions under the theory of microaggression, specifically related to subtle dismissals or denials of the identities of transgender and non-binary people. The findings demonstrate the cumulative impact of micro-insults, which are more overt forms of disrespect (Sue et al., 2007). Participants reported frequent encounters in which their identities, known or perceived as non-conforming, were questioned, denied, or confronted by other users. This aligns with previous research documenting the rejection of TGNC identities (Nadal et al, 2012, 2016; Croteau and Morrison, 2022; Griffiths and Armstrong, 2023).

Participants reported both intentional and unintentional micro-insults rooted in stereotypes about gender presentation. Intentional micro-insults occur when users knowingly reject or devalue a person's identity. For instance, Participant A (transgender male – FtM, 21 years old) explained:

> a lot of cis-men tend to assume that I am feminine or that I want to be feminine ... I get a lot of people in my messages. They tend to say stuff like 'Ohh princess' or like 'hey girl' ... and they get really upset when you're like, 'I'm not feminine'.

Here, the participant perceives an intentional disregard for his identity as others impose cis-normative assumptions, which they then enforce as if they were factual. As the participant further elaborated, such incidents can have an effect on him concerning the way he is perceived and understood within the community as a person. In his words:

> either you're blind or you're purposefully trying to make me feel bad cause a lot of the people, with like 'only smooth and only fem' in their bios, they tend to target trans men, and it's very transphobic because they kind of put

> trans men in this little box where they have to be essentially just boyish girls if that makes sense.

Unintentional micro-insults, by contrast, are rooted in presumptive stereotypes about gender presentation and are often based on assumptions. This is exemplified by Participant B (non-binary, 32 years old), who explained:

> I am sort of small, very skinny, tiny shoulders and I think in a gay man environment it feels sort of just instinctually understood by everyone in the room, what my type is. The gay catalogue of types is like, 'fem, bottomie, submissive'[1] and what that means is that the people who approach me need to be toxic masculine ... Everyone just understands that without saying anything, which is so fucking irritating.

Such microaggressions, often based on one's body type or aesthetic presentation, demonstrate how deeply embedded stereotypes can automatically dictate social expectations and interactions. In this sense, it can be articulated that such microaggressions, intentional and unintentional, can reinforce the social status of non-acceptance towards individuals and groups who deviate from the gender binary dogmas. These microaggressions act as a direct affirmation of gender dogmas, having an immediate effect on both the individual and the group.

Issues regarding presentation and assumptions can be understood as common experiences of transgender, non-binary, and perceived transgender individuals. As Participant B noted, appearance, particularly the perceived feminine body, can lead to assumptions regarding how one would be treated, and at times, according to the experiences of the participants, this treatment would be mainly negative. In this regard, another participant, who was born intersex, stated that the development of their body has led users on Grindr to perceive them as transgender or assume that they are transitioning. This has opened the individual to further negative experiences, particularly motivated by transphobia, and to issues regarding microaggressions. In their words:

> Because of chromosomal intersex identity, I have a curved figure more associated with femininity. This leads people on Grindr to assume I'm a bottom and feminine, both largely incorrect and simply on the basis of the perceived femininity of my body. (Participant C: gender queer – intersex, 21 years old)

Such narratives reveal how microaggressions reinforce binary gender expectations, marginalising gender non-conforming individuals based on appearance, expectations, and assumptions. While aspects of negative or demeaning views towards feminine characteristics among gay men and MSM settings are well-documented (e.g., Taywaditep, 2002; Rodriguez et al., 2016; Sánchez et al., 2016; Murgo et al., 2017; Hale and Ojeda, 2018), here the degrading aspect focuses on the denial of one's identity through misgendering language (Nadal et al., 2012, 2016) and on the assumptions that reinforce heteronormative beliefs (Nadal et al., 2012; Croteau and Morrison, 2022). In both cases of intentional or unintentional microaggressions, the role of assumptions and binary understandings of communication is prevalent, either by calling a transgender man a 'princess' or by expecting individuals to be more feminine due to their appearance. Such issues were also found by Griffiths and Armstrong (2023) with some participants of theirs expressing how often Grindr users make assumptions about gender non-conforming individuals by applying heteronormative cultural understandings associated with femininity, submissiveness, and gender identity. Overall, degradation can be perceived as a foundational effect of microaggressions leading to further issues of existential harm (Freeman and Stewart, 2021) and reinforcing power dynamics of acceptance and non-acceptance or of conformity – considering that Participant A further explained how some users would try and persist in making TGNC individuals conform to the expected or given sex/gender identity.

2 *Dehumanisation through sexual objectification, fetishisation, and threats of sexual violence*

Another prevalent theme among participants is dehumanisation through objectification and fetishisation, where TGNC individuals are perceived primarily as objects for sexual gratification, rather than as autonomous beings. The analysis draws upon the concept of 'exoticisation' in microaggression theory (Nadal et al., 2012, 2016), where transgender and non-binary bodies are sexualised based on fetishised and stereotyped attributes, stripping them of humanity (Cudd, 2006). According to scholars and as previously explored, this form of microaggression, whereby transgender and non-binary individuals are treated in a dehumanising manner or are treated as objects of pleasure, is often due to assumptions of sexual preferences, similar to concepts found in previous studies, such as Griffiths and Armstrong (2023).

The process of objectification can often be deeply rooted in systemic prejudices, where the value of an individual is reduced to an object of pleasure. As Cudd (2006) explains, oppressed groups are often seen as tools to satisfy the desires of the dominant group. Participant B (non-binary, 32 years old) illustrates this dynamic:

> just from looking at me [everyone] understood that they are allowed to treat me kind of like an asshole [literally – treat them as a sexual part of male-on-male intimacy] ... it's like a very dehumanising experience ... In my case,

> I guess because of fem, sissy, like gender ambiguous bottom, is read very distinctly as having no bodily autonomy as being very interested in and, like selflessly [serving] the needs of masc men and so on.

This objectification assigns submissive roles to individuals based on stereotypical assumptions about femininity and queerness, positioning them as passive objects of desire within a hierarchy that privileges dominant, masculine traits. In alignment with previous studies showing that non-binary and transgender individuals are perceived as sexual objects (Nadal et al., 2012, 2016; Griffiths and Armstrong, 2023), the participant here explains further how dehumanising these experiences are and how, due to stereotypical gender associations, they are perceived as submissive bodies with 'no bodily autonomy', or, as they described: 'The "type" assigned, roughly "slim-small-femme who bottoms for bigger-manlier-daddy types-and-demands-nothing-like-respect-in-return"'.

Participants' experiences also reflect threats to bodily autonomy that go beyond verbal objectification to include unsolicited, and often invasive sexual comments. As Participant A (transgender man – FtM, 21 years old) recounts:

> I've had times where people have been so unbelievably transphobic to me, where I've debated de-transitioning … I'll get messages saying, 'Ohh you look really fertile. I bet you'd look gorgeous if I made you have a baby'.

Such fetishistic remarks disregard the individual's autonomy and reinforce harmful stereotypes about presumed reproductive capacities ascribed to bodies which were assigned female at birth, further reinforcing misogynistic issues (Walker, 2022) and reflecting broader patriarchal norms that establish the oppression of women and femininities by reducing them to mere objects of pleasure or reproduction. These microaggressions can reinforce oppressive social structures, as detailed by Freeman and Schroer (2020) and Cudd (2006). Furthermore, beyond the objectifying and dehumanising aspects of this narrative, the participant also spoke of an instance that happened to another transgender man, a friend of his, where a user on Grindr deceived the friend to meet for a date and at the same time created a group chat sharing pictures of them and invited people to join the user at an unsolicited orgy while also using the prompts 'look how breedable'.

As the participant said, his friend did not go on the date as he found out about the Grindr group chat via a mutual acquaintance that was randomly added. However, the effects and fear of being raped or abused due to an objectified characteristic were still significant. The interviewed participant highlighted that this experience had broader fear impacts, too, stating that he would not have been 'as resilient' as his friend and that these events are frequent experiences of transgender men on Grindr. While such events are beyond any 'micro' spectrum, it can be proposed, following Cudd's (2006) conceptualisation, that these events are the threats of acts of violence experienced by oppressed communities, which reinforce their oppression and the harms of the oppressed. In this sense, these forms of violence can sometimes be enough to, by the threat of such an act alone, reinforce similar emotional impacts of the violence itself. As such, it is posed that in the above account from the participant, the use of objectifying language relating specifically to fertility is, in of itself, a 'micro' aggression, due to the fear of potential physical and sexual violence it reinforces. These issues can have significant implications on one's identity; for example, Participant A stated that he had considered 'detransitioning' so he could avoid these interactions and behaviours, as in his lived experience the threat of such violence was significantly more prevalent now compared to before transitioning. In his words:

> And sure, I dealt with similar comments when I presented as female, but not to the extent that I got on this app. Like I get it way more now than I did before. Just because people know that I'm trans. It's very, unsettling.

While such experience provides some insights into the participant's experience and perception of threat according to sex/gender, it is imperative to note that such issues of objectification are found to be significant within such apps, particularly Grindr, considering Bonner-Thompson's (2017) conceptualisation of Grindr as a 'meat-market'.

3 Ostracisation and monitoring through rejection and control of non-heteronormative identities

Finally, a significant theme is the ostracisation of TGNC individuals within dating spaces, where norms that favour masculinities and heteronormative ideals (Connell, 2005; Connell and Messerschmidt, 2005; Hale and Ojeda, 2018) participate in forming an exclusive hierarchy that marginalises non-conforming identities. Issues of unacceptance, isolation, and the concept of difference are widely known within studies of hate, prejudice, and bias – including microaggressions (e.g., Bell and Perry, 2014; Jefferson, 2015; Freeman and Schroer, 2020). In various studies regarding microaggression, one of the most prominent effects of such subtle forms of prejudice is being marginalised and feeling isolated (Williams, 2019; Wesselmann et al., 2021; Johnson and Johnson, 2022). In the case of lateral forms of prejudice, a marginalised group becomes further marginalised within a community to which they are believed to belong, while further revealing issues related to conformity and discipline.

Participants reported that masculine presentations are often idealised (e.g., Sánchez and Vilain, 2012; Rodriguez et al., 2016) on platforms such as

Grindr, marginalising individuals who deviate from these norms. As Participant D (non-binary, 25 years old) observed:

> Some people seem to only prefer masculine men and will ignore anyone who they see as less than macho. Others come to Grindr only to find trans women, sissies, twinks, and crossdressers. They seem to only want to surround themselves with people that can make them feel as straight as possible in the heteropatriarchal sense.

This first aspect of the discussion can be associated with previous research, particularly showing how transgender individuals may be perceived under a concept of deviation from ideals and almost be seen as unattractive or undesired by other individuals in the Grindr community. Particularly, such results were also present in research by Colliver (2021), showing how transgender people may be perceived as less attractive or respected once they transition. Similarly, as Participant E also mentioned: 'There is a group of people on grindr who will not sleep with trans men as they do not view them as "real" men' (transgender man – FtM, 22 years old).

This favouritism illustrates how cis-normative ideals of masculinity create an insular social space that perpetuates exclusion, even within queer communities. Such articulation can be further supported by responses provided by the participants in the online survey, supporting that masculinity is favoured within the community's understanding and norms (N=10/15), while the other five participants discussed how gender non-conforming individuals would be often favoured or valued under the concept of fetishisation, as discussed in the above narrative.

Additionally, such dynamics often lead to exclusion, fetishisation, or outright rejection based on perceived gender as it relates to sexual positioning. For instance, as Participant E shared,

> There is a large group of cis gay men who can't understand how a trans man could be a vers top. Most of the messages around this focussed on shaming me for not having a penis and suggesting I'm stupid for not understand[ing] how gay sex works.

Such biases, as also discussed in previous studies (Nadal et al., 2012, 2016; Griffiths and Armstrong, 2023), not only exclude transgender individuals from normative dating interactions but further reinforce harmful stereotypes about gender identity and sexual behaviour. This exclusion perpetuates a sense of otherness that limits belonging, even within queer spaces, marking TGNC individuals as divergent or 'lesser'. These narratives underscore the broader impact of microaggressions, both in perpetuating patriarchal norms and in enforcing a rigid social hierarchy that valorises certain identities over others.

While these narratives provide a foundational understanding of alienation, it is important to note that the majority of the examined population agreed that such incidents, especially microaggressions related to gender expression, can result in feelings of isolation (N=13/15). Further to this issue of ostracisation, participants also discussed the issue of monitoring, where they may consider changing their appearance or aspects of themselves, either to avoid microaggressions or to be accepted. In particular, while the majority of them agreed to issues of monitoring (N=13/15), Participant A also discussed in the interview how users or '*chasers*' often do not block or stop messaging the non-conforming individual but rather continuously try to make them conform to the ideals, expectations, or fetishes, by consistently messaging them and harassing them. In this sense, the participant elaborated how the combined feeling of isolation and the monitoring often leads them to consider changing or conforming to feel accepted or desired within a setting that treats them as lesser. Even though conformity and monitoring have not been widely discussed through the examinations of microaggressions, these issues can be traced in the policing of masculinities and ideals, as discussed by Rodriguez et al. (2016), as well as in the conceptualisation of microaggressions as disciplinary techniques put forward by Reiheld (2020). In this context, microaggressions and their effects can be further understood through the lens of monitoring, discipline, and conformity, where a dominant notion of what is considered acceptable is reproduced and reinforced when individuals deviate from these idealised identities (Dimitrakopoulos, 2025).

Concluding remarks

According to the presented data, the reported microaggressions experienced by transgender, non-binary, and gender non-conforming individuals on Grindr serve to reaffirm and complement existing research on this topic (Nadal et al., 2012, 2016; Croteau and Morrison, 2022). While not all typologies of microaggressions were present in the narratives, the findings still highlight lateral prejudice within LGBTQ+ online dating settings, focusing on themes of denial of identities, fetishisation, and monitoring. These insights expand existing concepts by providing experiential insights into how micro-insults – both intentional and unintentional – contribute to dehumanisation and marginalisation, revealing how the rejection of gender identity fosters an environment of exclusion and alienation. Likewise, objectification and fetishisation exacerbate the dehumanisation of TGNC individuals, reducing them to mere categories, while ostracisation highlights the dynamics of control and favouritism within the queer community, where heteronormative ideals subtly dictate belonging and social hierarchy.

Microaggressions perpetuate hierarchical gender norms that subordinate non-conforming identities, denying respect for chosen identities and reinforcing patriarchal binaries. Issues regarding misgendering and objectification not only cause alienation and degradation but can also lead to existential harm by undermining autonomy and a sense of self (Freeman and Stewart, 2021). Such issues reinforce societal rejection of non-conforming individuals, signalling inferiority and devaluing agency. As Kapusta (2016) argues, these acts deny dignity and the right to affirm one's identity, while objectification reduces individuals to tools for gratifying a privileged group (Cudd, 2006). These dynamics further entrench power structures that prioritise cis-normative identities while marginalising femininities and subordinated masculinities (Connell and Messerschmidt, 2005; Hale and Ojeda, 2018). In this sense, according to the presented data, two extremes can be identified regarding perceptions of gender non-conformity and microaggressions; individuals within such settings may be perceived as either objects of hate or objects of pleasure, further perpetuating oppression and causing existential harm.

Beyond existential harm, these findings suggest that microaggressions act as disciplinary mechanisms that punish deviation from normative ideals and may enforce conformity (Reiheld, 2020). For example, addressing a transgender man as a 'princess' reflects both a denial of identity and an attempt to reinforce cis-normative assumptions. Fetishisation similarly disciplines individuals by framing their identities as valuable only in objectifying terms. Such microaggressions perpetuate a cycle where cis-normative ideals are solidified by subordinating those who deviate from accepted norms while hinting at issues of conformity. In this sense, the aim of discipline is not merely to punish the agent deviating from accepted norms, but rather to conform them or to mould them into the object that would benefit the accepted and idealised group.

Although many of these incidents fall below the threshold of criminality, they still cause significant harm. Despite being perceived as 'micro', these actions create substantial barriers to challenging hate. Perry (2009) argues that non-criminal actions still cause harm to both individuals and society by perpetuating prejudice and reinforcing oppressive environments. Similarly, subtlety plays a critical role in the harm caused by microaggressions. As Sue et al. (2007) explain, perpetrators may not recognise the prejudice in their actions, while victims may feel unable to challenge them due to their perceived insignificance (McClure, 2020). This dynamic not only perpetuates hostility but also normalises marginalisation in cultural and social contexts. By associating non-conforming individuals with subordinated or inferior identities, such actions exacerbate social exclusion and foster environments where prejudice can thrive. These findings underscore the importance of recognising microaggressions as significant barriers to addressing broader issues of hate and hostility.

Limitations and future directions

In a final account, as mentioned previously, the presented data and findings are part of a larger study focusing upon microaggressions and the resultant social harm among gay men, MSM, and queer individuals on Grindr. Due to the sample number utilised for this chapter, any generalisation would not be applicable nor be able to draw solidified conclusions over the experiences of microaggressions by transgender men, non-binary individuals, and gender non-conforming people. In addition, due to the number of participants, there were insufficient data to allow an analysis of intersecting identities and the effects of microaggressions on multiple aspects of one's identity. However, this chapter aimed to provide some foundational insights into their lived experiences and how microaggressions may manifest on micro scales and within communities – similar to issues of lateral forms of violence or within-group discrimination (Reed, 2020; Tran et al., 2022).

These initial findings highlight the scope for further investigation into how microaggressions and general hostility may contribute to issues of conformity, either by transgender people considering detransitioning or non-binary or gender non-conforming individuals considering adapting their identities and appearance to binary concepts as a direct result of experiencing microaggressions. Furthermore, the aspect of objectification, particularly regarding issues of transgender men being perceived as 'breedable' or 'fertile' by chasers, and the resultant fear of abuse or issues of unreported sexual abuse derived from fetishisation, would potentially provide significant insights into the conceptualisation of transphobic and misogynistic microaggressions and hate crimes. Additionally, considering the multifaceted aspect of identities and vulnerabilities (Spade, 2010), future studies should focus on aspects of intersecting identities, further elaborating on issues of multiple stressors and existential harms. Moreover, as this chapter touched upon, the Kindr (2018) policy, an initiative introduced by Grindr to tackle prejudice, could be the focus of future studies in regards to examining its effectiveness – as well as other relevant policies regarding dating apps – while also considering how meso- or macro-scale initiatives, such as raising social awareness or legal reformation, as discussed by Cudd (2006), may contribute to minimising overt prejudice at a micro-level. Lastly, an aspect that can be further examined to expand the current understanding of microaggressions is the harm-oriented approach (Freeman and Stewart, 2021), particularly the social harm derived from these interactions and behaviours. Similar to the social impact of hate, microaggressions and implicit or explicit prejudice can cause significant harm to groups and communities. They do not only perpetuate oppression, marginalisation, and power imbalances but also function as disciplinary techniques, punishing or pressuring identities that deviate from dominant or socially accepted norms.

Note

1 Referring to a concept related to sexual positioning and stereotypical heteronormative/binary gender associations. Often, within such settings, a person who is a bottom – performing a passive sexual role – would be associated with femininity and submissiveness, in comparison to someone who is a top (Reilly, 2022).

References

Arijs, Q., Burgwal, A., Van Wiele, J., and Motmans, J. (2023). The price to pay for being yourself: Experiences of microaggressions among non-binary and genderqueer (NBGQ) Youth. *Healthcare*, *11*(5), 742. https://doi.org/10.3390/healthcare11050742

Beaumont, S. (2024). *Death by a thousand cuts: Gender microaggressions and gendered violence in Aotearoa New Zealand* (PhD thesis). Te Herenga Waka-Victoria University of Wellington. https://doi.org/10.26686/wgtn.25182413

Bell, J. G., and Perry, B. (2014). Outside looking in: The community impacts of anti-lesbian, gay, and bisexual hate crime. *Journal of Homosexuality*, *62*(1), 98–120. doi.10.1080/00918369.2014.957133

Bonner-Thompson, C. (2017). 'The meat market': Production and regulation of masculinities on the Grindr grid in Newcastle-upon-Tyne, UK. *Gender, Place & Culture*, *24*(11), 1611–1625. https://doi.org/10.1080/0966369x.2017.1356270

Braun, V., and Clarke, V. (2006). Using thematic analysis in psychology. *Qualitative Research in Psychology*, *3*(2), 77–101. doi.10.1191/1478088706qp063oa

Chow, J. (2021). No fats, no fems, no problems? Working out and the gay muscled body. *Sexualities*, 136346072110183. https://doi.org/10.1177/13634607211018331

Collins, K. A. and Clément, R. (2012). Language and prejudice: Direct and moderated effects. *Journal of Language and Social Psychology*, *31*(4), 376–396. https://psycnet.apa.org/doi/10.1177/0261927X12446611

Colliver, B. (2021). 'Not the right kind of woman': Transgender women's experiences of transphobic hate crime and trans-misogyny. In E. Zempi and J. Smith (Eds.), *Misogyny as Hate Crime* (pp. 213–227). London: Routledge.

Connell, R. W. (2005). *Masculinities* (2nd ed.). Cambridge: Polity Press.

Connell, R. W., and Messerschmidt, J. W. (2005). Hegemonic masculinity: Rethinking the concept. *Gender & Society*, *19*(6), 829–859. https://doi.org/10.1177/0891243205278639

Croteau, T. A., and Morrison, T. G. (2022). Development of the nonbinary gender microaggressions (NBGM) scale. *International Journal of Transgender Health*, 1–19. https://doi.org/10.1080/26895269.2022.2039339

Cudd, A. E. (2006). *Analyzing oppression*. New York: Oxford University Press.

Dimitrakopoulos, I. (2025). Direct Harms of Microaggressions and Discipline Among Grindr Users: An Analysis of the Social Harm of Femmephobia and Sizeism. *Sexuality & Culture*. https://doi.org/10.1007/s12119-025-10470-w

Filice, E., Raffoul, A., Meyer, S. B., and Neiterman, E. (2019). The influence of Grindr, a geosocial networking application, on body image in gay, bisexual and other men who have sex with men: An exploratory study. *Body Image*, *31*, 59–70. https://doi.org/10.1016/j.bodyim.2019.08.007

Freeman, L., and Schroer, J. W. (2020). *Microaggressions and philosophy*. Milton: Taylor & Francis Group.

Freeman, L., and Stewart, H. (2021). Toward a harm-based account of microaggressions. *Perspectives on Psychological Science*, *16*(5), 1008–1023. https://doi.org/10.1177/17456916211017099

Griffiths, D. A., and Armstrong, H. L. (2023). 'They were talking to an idea they had about me': A qualitative analysis of transgender individuals' experiences using dating apps. *The Journal of Sex Research*, *61*(1), 1–14. https://doi.org/10.1080/00224499.2023.2176422

Grindr (n.d.). About Grindr. https://www.grindr.com/about

Hale, S. E., and Ojeda, T. (2018). Acceptable femininity? Gay male misogyny and the policing of queer femininities'. *European Journal of Women's Studies*, *25*(3), 310–324. http://eprints.lse.ac.uk/100829/3/Accepted_Manuscript_Gay_Misogyny_Hale_Ojeda.pdf

Heap, V., and Waters, J. (2019). *Mixed methods in criminology*. Abingdon; New York: Routledge.

Hollingsworth, D. W., Cole, A. B., O'Keefe, V. M., Tucker, R. P., Story, C. R., and Wingate, L. R. (2017). Experiencing racial microaggressions influences suicide ideation through perceived burdensomeness in African Americans. *Journal of Counseling Psychology*, *64*(1), 104–111. https://doi.org/10.1037/cou0000177

Home Office (2023). Hate crime, England and Wales, 2022 to 2023. *GOV.UK*. https://www.gov.uk/government/statistics/hate-crime-england-and-wales-2022-to-2023/hate-crime-england-and-wales-2022-to-2023

Jefferson, T. (2015). What is racism? Othering, prejudice and hate-motivated violence. *International Journal for Crime, Justice and Social Democracy*, *4*(4), 120–135. doi: 10.5204/ijcjsd.v4i4.261

Johnson, N. N., and Johnson, T. L. (2022). Microaggressions: An introduction. In Management Association (Ed.), *Research anthology on racial equity, identity, and privilege* (pp. 105–121). Palmdale, PA: IGI Global. https://doi.org/10.4018/978-1-6684-4507-5.ch006

Kapusta, S. J. (2016). Misgendering and its moral contestability. *Hypatia*, *31*(3), 502–519. https://doi.org/10.1111/hypa.12259

Kindr (2018). Kindr Grindr. https://www.kindr.grindr.com/

Kraska, P. B., Brent, J. J., and Neuman, W. L. (2021). *Criminal justice and criminology research methods*. New York: Routledge.

Mason-Bish, H., and Duggan, M. (2020). Some men deeply hate women, and express that hatred freely: Examining victims' experiences and perceptions of gendered hate crime. *International Review of Victimology*, *26*(1), 112–134. https://doi.org/10.1177/0269758019872903

McBride, K., and James, Z. (2022). Hateful subjectivities: Using intersectionality to inform a Critical Hate Studies perspective. In J. Healy and B. Colliver (Eds.), *Contemporary intersectional criminology: Examining the boundaries of intersectionality and crime*. Bristol: Bristol University Press.

McClure, E. (2020). Escalating linguistic violence: From microaggressions to hate speech. In L. Freeman and J. Weekes Schroer (Eds.), *Microaggressions and philosophy* (pp. 121–145). New York: Routledge.

Miles, S. (2021). Let's (not) go outside: Grindr, hybrid space, and digital queer neighborhoods. In A. Bitterman and D. B. Hess (Eds.), *The life and afterlife of gay neighborhoods* (pp. 203–220). The Urban Book Series. Cham: Springer. https://www.ncbi.nlm.nih.gov/pmc/articles/PMC7978649/pdf/978-3-030-66073-4_Chapter_9.pdf

Murgo, M. A. J., Huynh, K. D., Lee, D. L., and Chrisler, J. C. (2017). Anti-effeminacy moderates the relationship between masculinity and internalized heterosexism among gay men. *Journal of LGBT Issues in Counseling*, *11*(2), 106–118. https://doi.org/10.1080/15538605.2017.1310008

Nadal, K. L., Erazo, T., and King, R. (2019). Challenging definitions of psychological trauma: Connecting racial microaggressions and traumatic stress. *Journal for*

Social Action in Counseling & Psychology, *11*(2), 2–16. https://doi.org/10.33043/jsacp.11.2.2-16

Nadal, K. L., Skolnik, A., and Wong, Y. (2012). Interpersonal and systemic microaggressions toward transgender people: Implications for counselling. *Journal of LGBT Issues in Counseling*, *6*(1), 55–82. doi.10.1080/15538605.2012.648583

Nadal, K. L., Whitman, C. N., Davis, L. S., Erazo, T., and Davidoff, K. C. (2016). Microaggressions toward lesbian, gay, bisexual, transgender, queer, and genderqueer people: A review of the literature. *The Journal of Sex Research*, *53*(4–5), 488–508. https://doi.org/10.1080/00224499.2016.1142495

Nadal, K. L., Wong, Y., Griffin, K. E., Davidoff, K., and Sriken, J. (2014). The adverse impact of racial microaggressions on college students' self-esteem. *Journal of College Student Development*, *55*(5), 461–474. https://doi.org/10.1353/csd.2014.0051

Neville, S., Adams, J., and Cook, C. (2015). Using internet-based approaches to collect qualitative data from vulnerable groups: Reflections from the field. *Contemporary Nurse*, *52*(6), 657–668. https://doi.org/10.1080/10376178.2015.1095056

Office for National Statistics (2023). Sexual orientation: Age and sex, England and Wales. https://www.ons.gov.uk/peoplepopulationandcommunity/culturalidentity/sexuality/articles/sexualorientationageandsexenglandandwales/census2021

Overton, L., and Hepple, J. (2022). Intersections of LGBTQ+ social spaces using gender analysis and the social model. In J. Healy and B. Colliver (Eds.), *Contemporary intersectional criminology in the UK: Examining the boundaries of intersectionality and crime* (pp. 204–219). Cambridge: Policy Press. https://doi.org/10.1332/policypress/9781529215946.003.0013

Perry, B. (2009). 'There's just places ya' don't wanna go': The segregating impact of hate crime against Native Americans. *Contemporary Justice Review*, *12*(4), 401–418. https://doi.org/10.1080/10282580903342888

Pierce, C. (1970). Offensive mechanisms. In C. Pierce and F. B. Barbour (Eds.), *The Black seventies: An extending horizon book* (pp. 265–282). Boston, MA: Porter Sargent Publishers.

Reed, J. A. (2020). *Intra-discrimination in the LGBT community: A phenomenological study* (PhD thesis). Ohio University. https://etd.ohiolink.edu/acprod/odb_etd/ws/send_file/send?accession=ohiou1585657089817672&disposition=inline

Reiheld, A. (2020). Microaggressions as a disciplinary technique for fat and potentially fat bodies. In L. Freeman and J. W. Schroer (Eds.), *Microaggressions and philosophy* (pp. 205–225). Milton: Taylor & Francis Group.

Reilly, A. (2022). The rise of the bottom: Counterdiscourse to challenge heteronormativity within the gay community. In V. Karaminas, A. Geczy, and P. Church Gibson (Eds.), *Fashionable masculinities: Queers, pimp daddies and lumbersexuals* (pp. 112–122). New Brunswick, NJ: Rutgers University Press.

Rodriguez, N. S., Huemmer, J., and Blumell, L. E. (2016). Mobile masculinities: An investigation of networked masculinities in gay dating apps. *Masculinities & Social Change*, *5*(3), 241–267. https://doi.org/10.17583/mcs.2016.2047

Sánchez, F. J., Blas-Lopez, F. J., Martínez-Patiño, M. J., and Vilain, E. (2016). Masculine consciousness and anti-effeminacy among Latino and white gay men. *Psychology of Men & Masculinity*, *17*(1), 54–63. https://doi.org/10.1037/a0039465

Sánchez, F. J., and Vilain, E. (2012). 'Straight-acting gays': The relationship between masculine consciousness, anti-effeminacy, and negative gay identity. *Archives of Sexual Behavior*, *41*(1), 111–119. https://doi.org/10.1007/s10508-012-9912-z

Schweppe, J., and Tong, K. (2021). What is a hate crime? *Cogent Social Sciences*, *7*(1). https://doi.org/10.1080/23311886.2021.1902643

Spade, D. (2010). Introduction: Transgender issues and the law. *Seattle Journal for Social Justice*, *8*(2), Article 1. https://digitalcommons.law.seattleu.edu/sjsj/vol8/iss2/1

Sue, D. W., Capodilupo, C. M., Torino, G. C., Bucceri, J. M., Holder, A. M. B., Nadal, K. L., and Esquilin, M. (2007). Racial microaggressions in everyday life: Implications for clinical practice. *American Psychologist*, *62*(4), 271–286. https://doi.org/10.1037/0003-066x.62.4.271

Taywaditep, K. J. (2002). Marginalization among the marginalized. *Journal of Homosexuality*, *42*(1), 1–28. https://doi.org/10.1300/j082v42n01_01

Tran, D., Sullivan, C. T., and Nicholas, L. (2022). Lateral violence and microaggressions in the LGBTQ+ community: A scoping review. *Journal of Homosexuality*, *70*(7), 1–15. https://doi.org/10.1080/00918369.2021.2020543

Walker, R. L. (2024). Call it misogyny. *Feminist Theory*, *25*(1), 64–82. https://doi.org/10.1177/14647001221119995

Wesselmann, E. D., DeSouza, E. R., AuBuchon, S., Bebel, C., and Parris, L. (2021). Investigating microaggressions against transgender individuals as a form of social exclusion. *Psychology of Sexual Orientation and Gender Diversity*. https://doi.org/10.1037/sgd0000513

Williams, M. T. (2019). Microaggressions: Clarification, evidence, and impact. *Perspectives on Psychological Science*, *15*(1), 3–26. https://doi.org/10.1177/1745691619827499

Wiltgren, L. K. (2022). Polite exclusion: High-performing immigrant students experience of peer exclusion. *Race Ethnicity and Education*, *25*(3), 1–17. https://doi.org/10.1080/13613324.2020.1718083

SECTION IV

Discourse, Representation, and Construction

13

ISLA BRYSON AND THE BURDEN OF REPRESENTATION: INFLAMMATORY MEDIA COVERAGE OF TRANS WOMEN IN THE UK IN 2023

Gina Gwenffrewi

Introduction: The creation of a hostile climate for trans women in press coverage, 2019–2024

Over the course of the 2010s, the number of stories in the UK press about trans people quadrupled (Baker, 2019; Ipso/Mediatique, 2020), with the coverage largely hostile (Folan, 2023). Negative coverage had, however, been the norm from the outset. The Leveson Inquiry's investigation in 2011–2012 into the culture, practices, and ethics of the UK press concluded that 'there is a marked tendency in a section of the press to fail to treat members of the transgender and intersex communities with sufficient dignity and respect' (2012: 8.32). If there was a notion that the Leveson Inquiry would help to regulate and restrict the more dehumanising coverage, then this was to be quickly disabused by the subsequent output of several newspaper commentators. Only a month after the published findings by the Leveson Inquiry, an article by the *Mail*'s Richard Littlejohn in December 2012 (Pidd, 2013) typified the challenges of media regulation and political will in the UK for a more compassionate or humane coverage about trans people. Headlined 'He's not only in the wrong body ... he's in the wrong job', the column is viewed as a case study in transphobic journalism, both for its content and its potential impact. It condemned a school for allowing one of its teachers, Lucy Meadows, to remain in her post after transitioning as a transgender woman. Misgendering Meadows throughout, the article concluded, 'if he [sic] cares so little for the sensibilities of the children he [sic] is paid to teach, he's [sic] not only trapped in the wrong body, he's [sic] in the wrong job' (Greenslade, 2013). The Littlejohn article was withdrawn by the *Mail* after Meadows was found to have died by suicide in March 2013 (Pidd, 2013). In a public statement

DOI: 10.4324/9781003564928-17

following an investigation into Meadows's death, the coroner addressed the impact of the press coverage: 'Having carried out what can only be described as a character assassination, having sought to ridicule and humiliate Lucy Meadows and bring into question her right to pursue her career as a teacher ... It seems to me that nothing has been learned from the Leveson inquiry.' The coroner ended his statement by addressing the reporters present; 'And to you the press, I say shame, shame on all of you' (Pidd, 2013).

The condemnation that followed the *Mail*'s 'character assassination' of Meadows is seen by the head of Trans Media Watch, jane fae, as ushering in a brief period of more positive press coverage about trans people, including 'a temporary rowing back by the *Mail*' (fae, 2018: 202). This respite was followed by the emergence of the press's anti-trans moral panic from around 2016 (Pearce et al., 2020), ostensibly in response to coverage of Gender Recognition Act reform but escalating into 'debates' about the legitimacy and hypothesised dangers of trans people generally (McLean, 2021; Jacques, 2020). A new politicised hostility has become the default setting in coverage of trans people since then, with misgendering now seen as an important right of freedom of expression by the conservative and 'gender-critical' columnists that dominate press opinion pieces about trans people. Paul Baker's research (2019) of the emergence of the press's moral panic coverage in the 2010s reveals that: 'There were no references to the trans(gender) lobby in 2012. In contrast, 2018–19 saw 151 mentions of this term, with over 90% of such cases writing about it in a negative way (e.g. as silencing debate, peddling politically-correct fallacies, being deranged or aggressively militant).' Transgender women's legitimacy and right to be seen as women in the public sphere, and accordingly to continue using women-only facilities, became part of the intensified focus of press coverage, typified by the *Times*' opinion piece by Janice Turner titled 'Children sacrificed to appease trans lobby' (2017), ostensibly about a trans person's access to a curtained changing-room cubicle in the women's section of a clothes shop. The challenging of trans women's legitimacy has appeared to intensify across the media's political spectrum since. This is typified by the output of the columnist Sonia Sodha who, in a 2018 article, references trans women as 'trans women' (Sodha, 2018) but has since abandoned the courtesy, and now consistently refers to trans women as men, as epitomised in an article titled: 'No woman should be forced to change her clothes in front of a male colleague' (Sodha, 2025). Concerning the hypothesised threat of trans women in women-only spaces, the latter article by Sodha references 'statistics showing that voyeurism and exposure are two of the most common male sex crimes' and that identifying as trans can involve, 'a cross-dressing sexual paraphilia'. The framing of a predatory sexual threat posed by trans women is utilised here despite the absence of such behaviour from the trans woman centred and named in Sodha's article.

An ideological and political position therefore combines with the previous fear-mongering tone of transphobic articles in the early 2010s. Once caricatured as freak-like in isolated cases, trans women are now reframed as predatory and forming a militant collective, their recent relative empowerment presented as antithetical to (cis) women's rights and safety. Or as Fran Amery and Aurelian Mondon say in their definition of organised transphobia, the framing now involves an 'essentialising discourse and politics regarding trans people to construct them into an homogenous group incompatible with "our" "normal" and "good society"' (Amery and Mondon, 2024: 5). This is despite the relatively small number of trans women in the UK. According to the 2022 Census, there are 48,000 trans women, contrasted with the UK population of over 68 million people (ONS, 2021), representing just 0.07% of the population. Concerning the issue of prisons that would become so febrile in 2023, meanwhile, the latest figures show that only six trans women are held in women's prisons in England and Wales, and the same number in Scotland's only women-only prison, all of them having been risk-assessed by local case boards (Rutherford, 2023).

The Isla Bryson case

The public rhetoric that hypothesises trans women as a threat to cis women in women-only spaces intensified in 2023. As this chapter highlights, press coverage from January 2023 focused on trans woman and convicted rapist Isla Bryson. As per the guidelines of the Scottish Prison Service (SPS) at the time, Bryson was remanded in January 2023 in isolation in a women's prison while prison authorities decided on whether she was to be housed in a men's or women's prison for her full sentence (Brooks, 2023a; Elliards, 2023). A press report detailed the strict and systematic remand process for trans women prisoners:

> a case conference takes place within 24 hours of any prisoner's arrival, involving SPS staff, with NHS and psychological input and an equality and diversity officer, in order to assess risk, and that segregation decisions must be reviewed at least monthly … [an] SPS spokesperson said: 'Where there are any concerns about any risks posed by an individual, either to themselves or others, we retain the ability to keep them separate from the mainstream population until an agreed management plan is in place'.
>
> *(Brooks, 2023c)*

In confirmation that this process was followed in the case of Bryson, the chief executive of the SPS stated in a review that 'no women were put at risk of harm by Bryson's placement. The review found Bryson was kept segregated at all times during their stay at Cornton Vale, Scotland's only all-women prison ... [the chief executive added that] all decisions made about Bryson were in keeping with existing SPS policies' (Brooks, 2023a). The period of risk assessment in January lasted two days, with Bryson 'held in Cornton Vale women's prison for assessment ... on Tuesday, then moved to a male prison, HMP Edinburgh, on Thursday afternoon' (Brooks, 2023b). However, as this chapter's data reveals, the case was framed according to a broader 'trans sex predator' narrative, which had previously been prominent in 2017–2018 with the case of Karen White (Lamble, 2023). The majority of the coverage by the *Guardian*, the *Times*, and the *Mail* about the Bryson story challenges the legitimacy of trans women and GRA reform, despite the GRA's lack of causation in relation to the Bryson case. It is the combination of the Equality Act – with exemptions based on 'a proportionate means of achieving a legitimate aim' (Equality Act, 2010: 8) – and a related case-by-case risk assessment that addresses the issue of trans women's access to women's spaces, not the GRA:

> In 2014, the Scottish Prison Service (SPS) introduced its gender identity and gender reassignment policy ... It advises that where an individual is permanently living in a gender other than that assigned at birth, 'establishment allocation should usually be the new gender in which they are living' ... This is applied on a case-by-case basis and subject to a detailed and continuing risk assessment. This policy applies regardless of whether a prisoner has a gender recognition certificate (GRC), and, as both the SPS and Scottish government have stressed in recent days, there is no automatic right for a transgender prisoner to be accommodated according to their acquired gender.
>
> *(Brooks, 2023d)*

The legal implications of the Bryson furore for trans women included in February 2023 the tightening of statutory guidance concerning trans women prisoners being housed in women's prisons (Elliards, 2023; Raab, 2023). With over 90% of trans women prisoners already housed in men's prisons (Raab, 2023), the legislative adjustment made prior medical transitioning, including vaginoplasty, a prerequisite for accepting a trans woman being housed in a woman's prison, along with the absence of any record of violence against women (Raab, 2023). Yet the tightening of access did not satisfy legacy media outlets, which continued to demand a blanket ban of all trans women, an indication of the 'burden of doubt' (Puwar, 2004: 59) cast over all trans women as a historically stigmatised minority.

By the time of the Conservative Party Conference in October 2023, prominent government figures intensified their rhetoric against the legitimacy of trans people and trans rights. This is typified by the high-profile speech delivered by the Prime Minister Rishi Sunak, who presented trans people as an oppressive threat. Sunak declared, 'We shouldn't get bullied into believing that people can be any sex they want to be. They can't. A man is a man and a woman is a woman. That's just common sense' (McKeon, 2023; Sunak, 2023). Responding to the anti-trans rhetoric of the conference, the trans youth charity Mermaids stated that 'these statements further legitimise the harassment which many trans young people and their families experience every day in the media, at home, at work, school and online' (Mermaids, 2023). The liberal centrist newspaper the *Financial Times* identified 'the heavy emphasis on the subject [that] leaves the party open to criticism that it is stoking divisive, US-style "culture wars" in pursuit of electoral gains ... One [government minister] stressed the party should be "compassionate" in its approach to trans people, adding: "It's not an issue that voters notice ... it doesn't come up on the doorstep"' (Fisher et al., 2023).

It is apparent from such comments by the government minister and from polling that the anti-trans rhetoric was being manufactured for political gain rather than to address the electorate's day-to-day concerns. The polling company YouGov, for example, recorded the British electorate's list of priorities for the 2024 general election to be related to the cost of living, health, and immigration, with 0% of respondents raising the issue of trans people and their rights (YouGov, 2024). This hyper-visibility and politicisation of trans people's legitimacy is encapsulated by a statement in February 2023 from the then-Conservative Deputy Chairman Lee Anderson. Describing the factors of Brexit and the identities of the two then-leaders of the two biggest political parties as key to the Conservative Party's landslide success of the 2019 general election, Anderson adds, 'At the next election we haven't got those three things so we'll have to think of something else. It'll probably be a mix of culture wars and trans debate' (Forrest, 2023). With this declaration of intent, Anderson and the Conservative government highlight the significance of anti-minority media messaging over addressing economic issues likely to concern the majority of British people. Such a strategy reflects the findings of Reddi et al. (2023) about 'identity propaganda', namely 'narratives that strategically target and exploit identity-based differences in accord with pre-existing power structures to maintain hegemonic social orders' (Reddi et al., 2023: 2201). Manufacturing the threat of trans people and trans rights as a problem in need of a solution became an election strategy in 2023, in anticipation of the election to come.

The false frame of the media's 'gender-critical' feminism: Women's prisons as safe spaces for women at risk from infiltration by predatory trans women

A synchronous feature of the rhetoric that dehumanises trans women prisoners as sex predators is of women's prisons as safe spaces for (cis) women, facing the threat of the invasive trans woman. Two myths are perpetuated here to protect the status of normative gender and the institution of prison. A report about violence in women's prisons contradicts this 'safe space' framing, however:

> Violence in women's prisons is another serious concern, with 469 incidents per 1,000 prisoners in the 12 months to June 2023. The assault rate is more than three and a half times higher than a decade ago, and significantly exceeds that in men's prisons. This increase in violence is often linked to mental health issues and substance abuse, exacerbated by overcrowding.
>
> *(Smith, 2024)*

Concurrent with the exclusion of this kind of data about the violence of women's prisons in the 2023 coverage about trans women prisoners is the exclusion of the framing of trans women as victims. Alison Phipps notes how trans-exclusionary feminists and the right-wing promote this double-sided myth:

> There is no convincing evidence that trans women are more likely to perpetrate sexual violence than cis women are ... [but as with] other reactionary politics, trans-exclusionary feminism generates outrage through constructing all trans women as dangerous in response to isolated incidents ... This hides the fact that trans people are particularly vulnerable to sexual victimization ... The designation 'survivor', and its claim on our empathy and outrage, is withheld from trans women.
>
> *(Phipps, 2020: 102–107)*

Specific to trans-exclusionary narratives about prison, Lamble (2023: 13) highlights how in the late 2010s, in 'debates around trans prison policy in Britain, women's prisons were routinely constructed as otherwise "safe spaces" until the entrance of trans women – thereby obscuring the acute and ongoing institutional dangers and harms that all prisoners face'. Yet the prison – including women's prisons – can also be seen to constitute a site of threat and violence to those housed in its cells irrespective of the presence of trans women. 'Prisons,' Lamble posits, 'are violent institutions. People in prison and detention experience brutal human rights abuses, including physical assault, psychological abuse, rape, harassment, and medical neglect. Aside from these violations, the act of putting people in cages is a form of violence in itself' (2011: 277). The framing of trans women as a threat to women's safety in prisons, to summarise, provides an ideological function of sanitising institutional oppression and harms by the British state against women generally. The depiction of trans women prisoners as perpetrators, not as victims, is also an ideological construction with a second function. As Felicity Adams and Fabienne Emmerich note,

> Prisons are deeply gendered institutions that enforce a gender binary and perpetuate heteronormative gender performativity. Queer people challenge gender-normative and heteronormative power relations that the prison's binary structure produces. They experience magnified forms of violence within the prison including physical and sexual violence, verbal abuse, isolation and the denial of healthcare.
>
> *(Adams and Emmerich, 2021: 108)*

Anti-trans narratives in relation to prison, in other words, help to police normative notions of sex/gender and sexuality with the construction of a dangerous 'Other'. Specific to socio-economically disadvantaged trans women, the ordeal can include being housed in men's prisons where they can experience several forms of abuse:

> A study of California inmates found that 59 percent of trans women held in men's prisons were sexually abused, vs. 4 percent of non-trans prisoners. Reporting these assaults can elicit retaliation, including time in solitary confinement, which is justified by prison administrators as a 'safety measure' for the good of the trans person.
>
> *(Johnson and Meronek, 2015: 262)*

Similarly in the UK, these forms of prison security for trans women housed in men's prisons can involve 'protective regimes [that] operate on a spectrum of isolation from solitary confinement to Vulnerable Prisoner Units' (Adams and Emmerich, 2021: 112). The rights that briefly expanded in the late 2010s, enabling some trans women to be housed in women's prisons, was a result of the devastating consequences for some trans women forced into men's prisons. As noted by Adams and Emmerich, the deaths of three trans women by suicide in 2015, while they were held in men's prisons, led to the introduction of a less oppressive prison policy from January 2017 'with the promise of extending a "more flexible approach to location" and protection of those transgender prisoners who express their gender in binary terms, but also to those with more fluid gender identities and non-binary prisoners' (Adams and Emmerich, 2021: 121). This new accommodation of trans women prisoners' needs and human rights, including accommodating a stated preference to be housed in women's prisons, conditional on a case-by-case basis, lasted until the case of Karen White, in which a new and collective 'trans sex predator' narrative appears to have been incited, when the 'burden of doubt' and 'burden of representation' become the apparent driver for a return to the harsher pre-2017 policy conditions. In the Conservative government's new designation of trans women as a post-Brexit, culture-war target on which to fight an election (Forrest, 2023), a damaging broader strategy also comes into play, described by Gillian Harkins as involving 'amplification and misdirection' (Lamble, 2023: 13), with the intensified but narrow gaze upon 'the exceptionality and monstrosity of the "sex offender" figure'. As Lamble notes, it diverts attention onto 'particular identity-groups' while ignoring 'the actual distribution of risk and harm'.

Newspaper research findings: Amplifying the 'trans sex predator' narrative

This research focuses on the press outlets the *Mail*, the *Times*, and the *Guardian* due to their status. The *Times* and *Guardian* represent 'broadsheet' outlets that operate within the 'quality market' (Sparks, 1999: 47), which overall comprises about 20% of the national newspaper readership. The *Mail* represents 'mid-market' journalism between quality outlets and tabloids operating in the 'popular market'. The mid-market comprises about 25% of the national readership. According to Colin Sparks, the 'quality market' provides the closest approximation to a 'public enlightenment' function (Sparks, 1999: 53), while the 'mid-market press' such as the *Mail* 'carries at least a modicum of this sort of material.'

The content analysis used the keywords 'trans' and 'prison' in the search engine Nexis Advance UK. The search was limited to the *Times/Sunday Times* (henceforth, 'the *Times*'), the *Daily Mail/Mail on Sunday* (henceforth, 'the *Mail*'), and the *Guardian/Observer* (henceforth, 'the *Guardian*'). Articles from each of these newspapers covered the period between 1 January and 31 October 2023, in order to include the highly politicised month of the conference season of October. The research was restricted to 100 articles per paper. Only the *Times* produced that many articles with these keywords (in fact, it published 262 articles that referenced both trans people and prisons). The *Mail* published 90, and the *Guardian* published 24 (see Table 13.1).

TABLE 13.1 Key themes and characteristics of the coverage

	Trans women and UK prisons	*Anti-trans position*	*GRA/ 'self-ID' = trans sex predators*	*Isla Bryson*	*Other (e.g., Karen White)*	*Sarah Jane Baker*	*Sturgeon/ SNP = 'trans sex predators'*	*Labour = 'trans sex predators'*
Times	100	100	39	55	11	1	21	3
Mail	90	90	35	45	16	11	16	9
Guardian	24	4	13	20	7	0	4	0

Association of 'trans sex predators' in women's prisons with GRA reform: 39% (Mail), 39% (Times), 54% (Guardian)

Each of the three news outlets either explicitly claims or mentions an association between GRA reform (a.k.a. 'self-ID') and the presence of the 'trans sex predator' in women's prisons. This is in spite of GRA reform having not been passed in the UK as legislation. Equally, the decision on whether trans women are housed in women's or men's prisons is made via risk-assessment and local boards, not gender recognition certification (Brooks, 2023c). The false association is made in 39% of *Mail* articles, similarly 39% of *Times* articles, and 54% of *Guardian* articles.

Association of 'trans sex predators' in women's prisons with progressive politicians and their inclusive policies

All three outlets frame left-leaning progressive politicians as responsible for the supposed 'scandal' of trans sex predators in women's prisons. The leader of the Scottish National Party (SNP), Nicola Sturgeon, notable for her political positions on Scottish independence and trans rights, is a particular target. Twenty-one percent of *Times* articles, 18% of *Mail* articles, and 17% of *Guardian* articles incriminate Sturgeon in the 'scandal'. Three percent of *Times* articles, 10% of *Mail* articles, and 0% of *Guardian* articles also incriminate the Labour Party, highlighting the Guardian's support of the Labour Party.

Isla Bryson is one of several trans women prisoners to feature in coverage; all but one are incarcerated in men's prisons or no longer incarcerated by 2023

55% of the *Times*' articles, 50% of *Mail* articles, and 83% of *Guardian* articles reference Isla Bryson either explicitly or implicitly. However, 11% of *Times*' articles, 18% of *Mail* articles, and 29% of *Guardian* articles reference other trans women who at some point were incarcerated for violent crimes. This includes Katie Dolatowski, who was convicted of assaulting two girls in public toilets in 2018 and who was then held in 2022 at the Cornton Vale women's prison after breaching a restriction of liberty order. The reason for the returning news coverage about Dolatowski in 2023 relates to Dolatowski praising Scotland's then-First Minister and leader of the SNP, Nicola Sturgeon.

Single stories about seven other trans women in the UK either convicted in 2023 or convicted previously include Karen White, originally housed in a women's prison in 2017 but moved to a men's prison later that year after perpetrating sexual assault against two inmates, and who in a 2023 interview called for all trans women without vaginoplasty to be banned from women's prisons. Of the other seven trans women, Lexi-Rose Crawford was convicted of rape in 2019 and housed in a men's prison in England; Amy George was arrested in February 2023 for abduction and sexual assault of a girl, before being housed in a men's prison; Tiffany Scott was housed in a men's prison on a life sentence for crimes committed between 2013–2022, before being found dead in her cell in 2024 (BBC News, 2024); and Sophie Eastwood, who had been serving a life sentence since 2004 and was moved from Cornton Vale women's prison to a men's prison (Mega, 2024) following the Isla Bryson case. Related to the Eastwood story is that of Paris Green, who was imprisoned in 2013 for the murder of a man, and at the time of writing is housed in a women's prison but has expressed her fear of being moved to a men's prison as part of the SPS's review (Mega, 2023). The story about Sarah Jane Baker, who had originally served a 30-year term in a men's prison for murder, concerns her public comments at a Trans Pride event in 2023 after her release, where Baker declared her encouragement for the use of assault against trans-exclusionary radical feminists. Following her publicised declaration, Baker was re-interned in a men's prison (Ryley, 2023).

Close textual reading: Contrasting the *Mail* against the *Times* and *Guardian*

Stylistically, the coverage of the *Times* and *Guardian* are similar, and this includes the news and opinion pieces. Photographs, if used, are limited to one per article; the article's layout is restricted to the single article; and the text itself involves more words than in the *Mail*. The language itself is also less sensationalist, with less frequent emphasis of words signifying violence than in the *Mail*, as highlighted in Table 13.2.

Given the *Mail*'s position as the UK's best-selling newspaper, examples of its news coverage and opinion column will be analysed next.

TABLE 13.2 Close textual reading of six articles: Language

	News/ Opinion	*Ra*	*Vi*	*St*	*Pv*	*Dg*	*Vu*	*Pr*	*Rk*	*Fu*	*Sf*	*Bio*	*Sx C*	*Sx O*	*Pd*
M	News	6	2	2	2	2	1	1	1	1	1	0	0	0	0
M	Opinion	13	3	0	0	2	7	3	1	0	1	5	6	2	0
T	News	0	0	0	0	0	0	0	0	0	0	0	2	2	2
T	Opinion	3	3	0	0	0	0	0	0	1	1	1	2	2	2
G	News	9	0	0	0	0	4	0	0	0	2	0	0	1	0
G	Opinion	2	0	0	0	0	1	0	0	0	0	0	3	1	0

Note: Key: Ra = rape/rapist; Vi = violence; St = stalk; Pv = pervert; Dg = Danger/dangerous; Vu = vulnerable; Pr = Predator/predatory; Rk = Risk; Fu = fury/outrage; Sf = safety/safe; Bio = biological male (used to describe trans women); Sx C = sex crime; Sx O = sex offender; Pd = paedophile.

The Mail: *News article*

'Embattled Nicola Sturgeon is plunged into fresh trans prisoner row: Scottish First Minister faces calls to stop transfer of pervert who stalked a 13-year-old girl while a man to a women's prison after Isla Bryson debacle' (Lawton, 2023).

Characteristic 1: Multiple incriminating photographs

Accompanying the *Mail* article are four colour photographs including a pre-transition photo of Tiffany Scott, handcuffed in police custody and topless but with what appears to be either a blanket or torn top. Another is a pre-transition Isla Bryson, shaven-headed and with visible face and neck tattoos, seemingly glaring at the camera in what might be a mugshot. The two pre-transition photos contribute to the menacing framing of Bryson and Scott as dangerous men. A third photo, of Bryson concealing her face outside the courthouse, can be said to signify concealment and disguise. The fourth photo, of Scottish First Minister Nicola Sturgeon, implicates her centrality in the story's headline, with the delegitimising collocation 'plunged into fresh ... row'.

Characteristic 2: Implicating progressive politicians in the 'scandal' of 'trans sex predators' in women's prisons

Approximately 12 of the *Mail* articles implicate progressive Scottish-independence advocate Nicola Sturgeon with the threat of trans women prisoners in women's prisons. This includes Sturgeon's name in the headline, generally in delegitimising terms, e.g., 'Sturgeon's muddle over trans women in male prisons' (31.01.23), 'Sturgeon's madhouse' (29.01.23), 'Humiliated Sturgeon in trans row U-turn' (27.01.23), 'Sturgeon in fresh chaos over gender' (30.01.23), and 'Sturgeon's disarray over refusal to say trans rapist is a woman' (03.02.23).

The Labour Party are similarly represented in delegitimising terms in these 'trans sex predator' articles for their general support for trans rights. This includes the use of headlines such as 'If Starmer gets to No10, the rights of women in Britain could be set back decades' (22.01.23), 'Labour again in hock to extreme ideology' (21.01.23), and 'Labour's woman problem' (21.01.23). This indicates a pattern – by right-wing outlets, especially – of publicly shaming political enemies on the left by associating more progressive-leaning, pro-trans-rights parties such as the SNP and Labour with enabling harms to women and/or children.

The Mail: *Opinion article*

'The smirking rapist now sitting in a female prison proves our legal system has sacrificed vulnerable women at the shrine of trans rights'. (Bindel, 2023)

Characteristic 1: Misinformation that exaggerates the threat of trans women

The headline and the article in this opinion column utilise intensifying adjectives to emphasise the violence and the manipulative nature of trans women prisoners ('The smirking rapist') and the vulnerability of cis women prisoners to them ('sacrificed vulnerable women'). The columnist, the renowned anti-trans activist Julie Bindel, refers to Bryson via her deadname and former gender. Overall, the article references both Bryson and two other trans women prisoners – one unnamed, the other Karen White – as examples of the general danger of housing trans women in women's prisons, in a reflection of Puwar's (2004) concept of the Othering dynamic of the 'burden of representation'. The article reinforces this argument by using an ambiguous statistic, namely that 44% of prisoners who have changed gender have committed sex crimes. The article suggests that this statistic reflects the profile of trans women prisoners, but concedes this connection cannot be verified. In response to such claims by the 'gender-critical' movement in 2017, the Ministry of Justice state that they do not collect such comprehensive data on rates of types of trans prisoners' crimes, nor does the approximately '40%' statistic take into account the possibility of trans masculine people being part of the data (BBC News, 2018).

> A government survey has counted 125 transgender prisoners in England and Wales, but the Ministry of Justice says these figures are not yet a reliable reflection of the true numbers. The MoJ says 60 of them have been convicted of one or more sexual offences but it didn't identify their gender. There are likely to be more trans inmates, on shorter sentences and who are less likely to be sex offenders, who don't show up in this data.

Apart from the Bindel article's headline, the conflation of the Bryson case with trans rights generally includes such statements as 'the chilling extent to which the legal profession has fallen victim to the clamour of trans activists', and 'the fanatical pro-trans lobby continues to exert its dangerous grip on legislators'. Again, we see evidence of Puwar's (2004) concept of a 'burden of representation'. Overall, Bindel's article uses the largest range and highest frequency of delegitimising lexis of the *Mail*'s 100 articles about trans women prisoners and their purported threat to cis women prisoners.

Characteristic 2: Omission of key information

Omission, as well as lexis and insinuation, contribute to the message that trans women prisoners are dangerous to cis women prisoners. The article omits to highlight that Bryson and White are held in men's prisons, and that Bryson's temporary stay on remand and in isolation in a women-only prison was done so while her upcoming imprisonment location was being risk-assessed. The article also omits the actual low numbers of trans people in prison overall (Rutherford, 2023). An accompanying insight omitted by Bindel's article is that over 90% of trans women prisoners are held in men's prisons in the UK, and that prison authorities use risk assessment to screen trans women's access to women-only prisons on a case-by-case basis to ensure those with records of violence against women are denied access (Raab, 2023). Finally, the article makes no mention of the threat posed by cis women prisoners. Yet as the 2023 report about UK prisons reveals, violence in women's prisons is pervasive, with the assault rate being 'more than three and a half times higher than a decade ago, and significantly exceeds that in men's prisons' (Smith, 2024).

Characteristic 3: Misinformation about the militancy of trans-advocacy organisations

Bindel's article associates the threat posed by Bryson and other trans women prisoners with a tendency towards violence of trans rights advocates more generally. It is worth contrasting her claims, however, with the public statements of the trans-rights policy group, Scottish Trans, which consults on trans policy with the Scottish Government, including on the prison policy that has been in place since 2014. As the group's manager stated in response to the Bryson case, 'It is our view that anyone who has committed sexually violent crimes, and who poses a risk to women, should not be housed with women on the female estate' (Brooks, 2023b).

Conclusion

This chapter demonstrates that three major quality or mid-market newspaper outlets across the political spectrum, namely the *Guardian*, the *Times*, and the *Mail*, conflate the few available examples of trans sex predators with trans women generally to construct their hostile Othering. The news outlets achieve this by producing repeated coverage (*Times*: 55, *Mail*: 45, *Guardian*: 20) about a single incident, namely the two-day remand of Isla Bryson in isolation in a women's prison while her case was being risk-assessed, while extending the theme to other trans women prisoners despite the majority either no longer being in prison or held in men's prisons. The housing of trans women in women's prisons is presented as controversial, out of control, and/or a national scandal, although only six trans women are held in women-only prisons in England and Wales, and six in Scotland's only women-only prison, each one risk-assessed by local panels, as is consistent with the law. The omission of mentioning the tiny numbers and the rigorous risk assessments involved contribute to a distortion of the scale and threat. Frequent associations of the threat of 'trans sex predators' with broader trans women's rights such as GRA reform represent misinformation, leading to the stigmatising of trans women's rights and indeed their very presence in the public sphere due to false associations of predatory behaviour.

In terms of a call to action, this chapter references the 2012 Leveson Inquiry verdict into the culture, practices, and ethics of the UK press, in which 'there is a marked tendency in a section of the press to fail to treat members of the transgender and intersex communities with sufficient dignity and respect' (2012: 8.32). As Paul Baker's research in 2019 reveals, the press's dehumanisation of trans women has intensified since then, not only in regards to publicly shaming trans women and those who defend them but also in misrepresenting their rights (e.g., GRA reform) as being harmful to cisgender women. It is important to note that in terms of actions, the Leveson Inquiry's second stage, known informally as 'Leveson 2', was intended to establish stricter rules for the legacy press in response to the findings (Green, 2024). While some, including the Conservative government that rejected the need for a 'Leveson 2' in 2018, argue that the digitalised media landscape has made the findings of the Leveson inquiry obsolete (Green, 2024), it remains the case that the UK legacy press continues to wield significant influence on the national stage and its stricter regulation could positively affect coverage about trans people. In my own research on the legacy media's vilification of pro-trans organisations such as Mermaids and Stonewall since 2020, I call for a democratic reset that involves a more consultative role for LGBTQI+ organisations in the framing of news about LGBTQI+ issues. The very ideological bias of the UK legacy press that vilifies trans people may represent an obstacle to such a recalibration, particularly given the tendency towards self-regulation. Nevertheless, a cross-party politically imposed 'Leveson 2' remains a political goal worth pursuing, in consultation with community groups and pro-trans organisations.

References

Adams, F., and Emmerich, F. (2021). Mapping the manifestations of exclusion: Challenging the incarceration of queer people. In S. Raj and P. Dunne (Eds.), *The queer outside in law: Recognising LGBTIQ people in the United Kingdom* (107–142). London: Palgrave Macmillan.

Amery, F., and Mondon, A. (2024). Othering, peaking, populism and moral panics: The reactionary strategies of organised transphobia. *The Sociological Review*, 1–17.

Amnesty International (2024, 10 April). UK: Cass review on gender identity is being 'weaponised' by anti-trans groups.

Anthony, A. (2021, 31 January). 'We were so scared': Four people who faced the horror of AIDS in the 80s. *The Guardian*.

Baker, P. (2019, 18 November). Exclusive: Mermaids' research into newspaper coverage on trans issues. Mermaids.

BBC News (2018, 13 August). How many transgender inmates are there?

BBC News (2024, 29 February). Trans prisoner Tiffany Scott dies in jail.

Billard, T. J. (2023). 'Gender-critical' discourse as disinformation: Unpacking TERF strategies of political communication. *Women's Studies in Communication*, *46*(2), 235–243,
Billard, T. J. (2024). *Voices for transgender equality: Making change in the networked public sphere*. New York: Oxford University Press.
Bindel, J. (2023, 25 January). Trans rapist in female prison proves legal system has sacrificed vulnerable women, Julie Bindel says.' *Daily Mail*.
Braverman, S. (2023). Suella Braverman – 2023 speech to Conservative Party Conference. https://www.ukpol.co.uk/tag/2023-conservative-party-conference/
Brooks, L. (2023a, 25 January). Trans woman guilty of raping two women remanded in female prison in Scotland. *The Guardian*.
Brooks, L. (2023b, 26 January). Why Scotland's gender reform bill is sparking concern over trans prisoner policies. *The Guardian*.
Brooks, L. (2023c, 27 January). Trans rapist prison case 'must not lead to blanket rule, says campaign group.' *The Guardian*.
Brooks, L. (2023d, 9 February). Trans prisoners in Scotland to be first sent to jails matching their birth gender. *The Guardian*.
BSA 40 (2024). British social attitudes. NatCen 2024.
Caughie, P. L. and Meyer, S. (2020). *Man into woman: A comparative scholarly edition*. London: Bloomsbury Publishing Plc, 2020.
Council of Europe (2021, 23 September). Committee highlights rise in hatred against LGBTI people.
Duggan, L. (1994). Queering the state. *Social Text*, *39*, 1–14.
Elliards, X. (2023, 9 February). Isla Bryson case review finds women were 'at no point at risk of harm'. *The National*.
Equality Act (2010). *Separate and single-sex service providers: A guide on the Equality Act sex and gender reassignment exceptions*.
fae, j. (2018). The press. In C. Burns (Ed.), *Trans Britain: Our journey from the shadows* (pp. 187–204). London: Unbound.
Fisher, L., Gross, A., and Parker, G. (2023, 3 October). Tory focus on trans and gender issues sparks unease within the party. *The Financial Times*.
Folan, E. (2023, 20 February). Welcome to Terf island: How anti-trans hate skyrocketed 156% in four years. *Novara Media*.
Forrest, A. (2023, 14 February). Lee Anderson says Tories should fight election on 'culture wars and trans debate'. *The Independent*.
Green, D. (2024, 3 May). Is it time to revive Leveson 2? *Prospect*.
Greenslade, R. (2013, 22 March). Daily Mail urged to fire Richard Littlejohn after death of Lucy Meadows. *The Guardian*.
Greenslade, R. (2022a, August). JK Rowling and the echo chamber of secrets: An autoethnographic account of a trans woman's engagement with the Scottish legacy media during the Rowling furore.' *Transgender Studies Quarterly*, *9*(3).
Greenslade, R. (2022b, November). The stoning of Stonewall during the new trans panic: How the UK legacy media delegitimize an LGBT+ charity for advocating for trans rights. In S. Atkin (Ed.), *U.C.U. 6th LGBT+ Research Conference: Papers*. London: UCU.
Home Office (2022, 6 October). Official statistics: Hate crime, England and Wales, 2021 to 2022.
Human Rights Watch (2020, 17 May). Joint statement on the rights of trans people in the UK.
Hunte, B. (2022, 2 February). Britain's equalities watchdog met privately with anti-trans groups. *Vice*.
Hunte, B. (2023, 13 April). Exclusive: Senior officials quit Britain's equalities watchdog EHRC over transphobia.' *Vice*.

ILGA-Europe (2024). Annual review. 161–164.
IPSO/Mediatique (2020, 2 December). New research on reporting of trans issues shows 400% increase in coverage and varying perceptions on broader editorial standards. https://www.ipso.co.uk/news-analysis/new-research-on-reporting-of-trans-issues-shows-400-increase-in-coverage-and-varying-perceptions-on-broader-editorial-standards/
Jacques, J. (2020, 9 March). Transphobia is everywhere in Britain. *The New York Times*.
Johnson, J., and Meronek, T. (2015). Custody's long shadow: Reentry support as abolitionist work. In E. Stanley and N. Smith (Eds.), *Captive genders* (pp. 261–268). Edinburgh: AK Press.
Lamble, S. (2011). Transforming carceral logics: 10 reasons to dismantle the prison industrial complex using a queer/trans analysis. In E. Stanley and N. Smith (Eds.), *Captive genders* (pp. 269–300). Edinburgh: AK Press.
Lamble, S. (2023). Sexual peril and dangerous others: The moral economies of the trans prisoner policy debates in England and Wales.' *Sexualities*, *0*(0) 1–22.
Lawton, K. (2023, 28 January). Nicola Sturgeon faces calls to stop transfer of pervert who stalked teenage girl to women's prison. *Daily Mail*. 28 January.
Leveson Inquiry (2012).
Maddox, D., and Mitchell, A. (2024, 15 May). Pollsters warn Sunak: Stoking culture wars can't save Tories. *The Independent*.
McKeon, C. (2023, 9 October). Sunak speech gave 'green light' to attacks on transgender people, says Labour MP. *The Independent*.
McLean, C. (2021). The growth of the anti-transgender movement in the United Kingdom: The silent radicalization of the British electorate. *International Journal of Sociology*, *51*(6), 473–482
Mega, M. (2023, 2 September). Scots trans prisoner fears male jail move after claim of 'attack' on female prison officer.' *Daily Record*.
Mega, M. (2024, 11 December). Transgender killer Sophie Eastwood moved to male jail is 'chained to guard all day'. *Daily Record*.
Mermaids (2023, 5 October). Statement in response to Conservative Party conference.
ONS (Office for National Statistics) (2021). UK Census 2021, gender identity.
Pearce, R., Vincent, B., and Erikainen, S. (2020, July). TERF wars: An introduction. *TERF Wars: Feminism and the Fight for Transgender Futures. The Sociological Review Monograph Series*, *68*(4), 3–24.
Phipps, A. (2020). *Me, not you: The trouble with mainstream feminism*. Manchester: Manchester University Press.
Pidd, H. (2013, 28 May). Lucy Meadows coroner tells press: 'Shame on you'. *The Guardian*.
Puwar, N. (2004). *Space invaders: Race, gender and bodies out of place*. Oxford: Berg.
Raab, D. (2023, 27 February). New transgender prisoner policy comes into force. *GOV.UK*.
Reddi, M., Kuo, R., and Kreiss, D. (2023). Identity propaganda: Racial narratives and disinformation. *New Media & Society*, *25*(8), 2201–2218.
Rowling, J. K. (2023, April). *The witch trials of JK Rowling*. M. Phelps-Roper (Dir.). Episode 5. 54.30– 55.15.
Rutherford, N. (2023, 28 February). Isla Bryson: What is the transgender prisoners row all about? *BBC News*.
Ryley, F. (2023, 5 September). Sarah Jane Baker cleared. Now free her! *Workers' Liberty*.
Serano, J. (2024, 7 May) 'Gender ideology' is a conspiracy theory. *Medium*.
Siddique, H. (2023, 1 October). Former race lead sues EHRC for race discrimination. *The Guardian*.
Smith, A. (2024, 16 August). Prison is a disaster for women – here's what would work instead. University of Portsmouth.

Smith, M. (2023, 13 April). Trans paedophile Katie Dolatowski hails Nicola Sturgeon as 'great first minister'. *The Times*.
Sodha, S. (2018, 8 February). Should self-identifying trans women be on all-women shortlists? Our writers discuss | Shaista Aziz, Susanna Rustin, Shon Faye and Sonia Sodha. *The Guardian*.
Sodha, S. (2025, 9 February). No woman should be forced to change her clothes in front of a male colleague.' *The Guardian*.
Sparks, C. (1999). The press. In J. Stokes and A. Reading (Eds.), *The media in Britain* (pp. 41–60). London: Macmillan Press Ltd.
Speare-Cole, R. (2022, 5 April). Government's landmark LGBT+ conference cancelled. *The Independent*.
Stonewall (2023a, 9 May). EHRC 'actively harming' trans people, ignoring international recommendations, charities warn.
Stonewall (2023b, 7 November). Stonewall statement on the UK Government's failure to ban conversion practices.
Stryker, S. (2007/2017). *Transgender history*. New York: Seal Press.
Sunak, R. (2023). Rishi Sunak – 2023 speech to Conservative Party Conference.
Sunday Times. (2023, 5 February). SNP trans fiasco highlights the dangers of groupthink.
Tatchell, P. (1983). *The battle for Bermondsey*. London: Gay Men's Press.
Turner, J. (2017, 11 November). Children sacrificed to appease trans lobby. *The Times*. thetimes.co.uk/article/children-to-appease-trans-lobby-bq0m2mm95
United Nations (2024, 17 June). The United Nations calling out transphobia and the gender-critical movement in the UK. *TransLucent*.
YouGov (2024, 1 June). General election 2024: What are the most important issues for voters?
Waterson, J. (2023, 25 July). Guardian Media Group makes record revenues for news business. *The Guardian*.
White, R. M. (2024, 8 January). A commentary on Department for Education draft guidance. *TransLucent*.
Williams, Z. (2023, 1 June). Why are trans rights in prison so rarely defended? *The Guardian*.

14

'BLOODY PRONOUNS': TRANSPHOBIC ONLINE HATE SINCE THE PROPOSED AMENDMENTS TO THE GENDER RECOGNITION ACT (GRA) 2018

Joanna Ashcroft

Introduction

This research examines online abuse toward the UK's transgender community, which has suffered the greatest increase within the LGBTQ+ community. Analysing 20,833 UK tweets from January 2017 to August 2022 using Natural Language Processing (NLP), a computational qualitative analysis tool, language patterns and terms were identified. Trending analysis on topics surfaced during the language analysis phase indicated an overall increase of all the transgender topics with one showing statistical acceleration after 2018.

For this study, transgender refers to those whose gender identity, expression, or behaviour differs from that assigned at birth (Frew, Watsford, and Walker, 2021). Reliable data on gender identity is scarce, however the 2021 Census of England and Wales identified 0.5% of the population (262,000 people), answered 'No' when asked if their gender identity was different to that registered at birth, a figure now considered as having a high risk of error (ONS, 2023). Press reports state this might have overestimated the population of transgender people (Melley, 2024), while others counter the Census's household nature obscures respondents (GIRES, 2023). Meanwhile, an Ipsos survey (2022) found 3.1% of respondents identified as transgender, non-binary, gender fluid, agender, or not male or female (Ipsos, 2022), although this may reflect some self-selection bias (Olsen, 2008). Reliable figures are still unrealised, however, a working estimate of 1–2% would be reasonable, and although apparently small, the severe repercussions to both individuals and to wider society means there is an urgent need to monitor transphobic online hate to inform public and social media strategies, promote education, and aid support services.

DOI: 10.4324/9781003564928-18

Within the LGBTQ+ community, 70% experience online abuse, while 93% of transgender people fall victim to incidents including doxxing, personal photograph leaks, and serious accusations such as rape and paedophilia (Hubbard, 2020). The impacts of this abuse can mirror that of physical crime leading to shock, anger and fear, physical and mental health problems, social isolation, relationship issues, and behavioural changes, while experiencing this in the supposed 'safety' of their own home can make the situation seem inescapable for trans people (Williams, 2019).

In 2021, the UK had 19.05 million Twitter users (Strugar, 2024). Given the controversies following Elon Musk's takeover and renaming of Twitter as 'X', it should be noted that all data for this study was collected before his acquisition in October 2022 (Paul and Milmo, 2022), which is discussed further in the Twitter/X section below.

The Gender Recognition Act (GRA) and its amendments

The GRA was passed in 2004 enabling any person over 18 to apply for a gender recognition certificate (GRC), if they satisfied the following criteria:

- have gender dysphoria (evidenced by a medical or psychologist report);
- have lived in the other gender for two years;
- intend to live in that gender permanently.

The Women's and Equality Committee, in 2018, found the GRC process was humiliating, intrusive, and overly bureaucratic, and advocated in favour of self-declaration (White, 2021). Acknowledging its issues, Liz Truss, the Minister for Women and Equalities in 2020, stated the government would not change the process (Balogun, Fairbairn, and Pyper, 2024). Meanwhile, the devolved government of Scotland passed its own Gender Recognition Reform Bill introducing self-declaration (Gender Recognition Reform (Scotland) Bill, 2019) which was ultimately blocked by the UK government (Crerar and Brooks, 2023), and as recently as November 2024, Scotland's Supreme Court is considering the definition of women (Sim, 2024). The debate on transgender rights persists with anti-transgender groups continuing to argue that transgender women, in particular, are a threat to women, women's rights, and to children (Armitage, 2020).

Twitter/X

Readers will find that both the names 'Twitter' and 'X' are used in this chapter, with 'Twitter' indicating the prior situation and study period, and 'X' used after Elon Musk's takeover. At the time of writing during the original study, Twitter/X's social media policy stated that it does not allow accounts inciting hate based on: 'race, ethnicity, national origin, caste, sexual orientation, gender, gender identity, religious affiliation, age, disability, or serious disease' (X Help, 2023); and further:

> we will reduce the visibility of posts that purposefully use different pronouns to address someone other than what that person uses for themselves, or that use a previous name that someone no longer goes by.
>
> *(X Help, n.d.)*

Despite these policies, Musk's fierce advocation of free speech, his reinstatement of banned users (e.g., Andrew Tate and Tommy Robinson), the sharing of advertising revenue with 'premium users' (enabling toxic content to become lucrative), and the banning of the term 'cisgender' (Cuthbertson, 2024) expose tensions between X's policies and Musk's actions (Barrett, 2024). A salient quote here from Ed Saperia, Dean of the London College of Political Technology states: 'You might get a couple of thousand likes for noticing that David Cameron looks like Catherine the Great, but that's nothing like the engagement you'll get for attacking trans people' (Williams, 2024).

Following the US presidential election in November 2024, and the apparent rise of hate speech and discriminatory rhetoric, X has seen users migrate to the far smaller platform of Bluesky (Boyd, 2024).

Online hate

Online hate refers to hate speech via text, audio, or visual media that is abusive, harassing, or incites discrimination (Davidson et al., 2019). The incitement of hate is also classified as a criminal offence (CPS, 2022). In October 2023, the UK passed the Online Safety Act, which focuses on protecting children, women, and girls; while covering only illegal content, this excludes hateful content and misinformation from its scope (Arshad and Brasted, 2024). Ofcom, the regulator, is finalising codes and guidance for online services and platforms, but the Act applies to services accessible to UK users, and includes the criminal offence of 'threatening communications' and age restrictions for children (Department for Science, Innovation and Technlogy, 2024). The removal of the earlier proposal to cover content that was 'legal but harmful to adults' limits protection for those within the transgender community (Arshad and Brasted, 2024).

The psychology of online abuse toward transgender people mirrors real-world abuse, such as in-group/out-group behaviours (Brewer, 2007), unconscious biases (Jolls and Sunstein, 2006), political conservatism (Haslam and Levy, 2006), perceived violations of sexual and gender norms (Lehavot and Lambert, 2007), and the presumption of harm through norm violations (Gutierrez and Giner-Sorolla, 2007). Online interactions exacerbate these behaviours, including the 'halo effect', where influencer fame infers credibilty (Howard, 2019), and 'moral panic', a term popularised by Stanley Cohen (Cohen, 1973). Social media algorithms and information silos increase engagement by further promoting emotionally charged content and stimulating outrage (Walsh, 2020).

The UK still demonstrates 'binary genderism' (Nicholas, 2019), with traditional and online social media intensifying moral panic and invalidating transgender people, representing them as mentally ill or as threats to women and children (Armitage, 2020). Feminist and trans-exclusionary radical feminist (TERF) groups, viewing gender as immutable, oppose improvements in transgender rights as a threat to women's rights and spaces (McQueen, 2016). J. K. Rowling, a vocal opponent of improved transgender rights, continues her opposition through social media, her writing (D'Alessandro, 2020), and through donations, such as fundraising for Allison Bailey (Rowling, 2022), who won an employment tribunal for discrimination after tweeting her gender-critical views (Glover, 2022). Rowling portrays trans women as a threat within women's spaces and as part of a broader 'activist' movement (Gwenffrewi, 2022).

Inflammatory rhetoric, using words such as 'ideology', 'agenda', 'activists', and 'lobbyists', politicises transgender rights and is often used by right-leaning politicians (Chikha, 2021) within social and traditional media. The normalisation of far-right opinions in the US, Europe, and the UK legitimises the stigmatisation and dehumanisation of transgender people, who are seen as 'easy' or 'soft' targets (Kidd and Witten, 2007; Youngblood, 2020; GAO, 2024). Nostalgia-driven views of 'family values', bolstered by conspiracy theories and pseudoscience, reinforce far-right and religious-right beliefs in the immutability of gender based on biology or divine will (Kettell, 2024; Smith, 2024).

Harms

Online hate can be as harmful as real-world abuse, with the level of humiliation having similar repercussions to that of physical crime (Bakalis, 2018; Williams, 2019). The impact to individuals includes anger, anxiety, depression, poor self-esteem, fear, feeling dehumanised, social withdrawal, and the inability to be true to their identity (Williams, 2019; Hubbard, 2020), with resulting hazardous behaviours such as drug abuse, eating disorders, and suicidal thoughts (Henderson et al., 2022). Whereas the online world provides transgender individuals with the chance for help and support, many are reducing their time online due to the toxic environment (Craig et al., 2020; Hubbard, 2020). The witnessing of online hate can cause those sharing the same personal characteristics to also experience victimisation, thus the impacts are felt by the wider community (Chakraborti and

Garland, 2015; Davidson et al., 2019) with harm spreading far beyond the first victim (Iganski, 2003).

Driven by a combination of all these factors, abuse, harassment, and hate toward the transgender community proliferates in the responsibility-free (Teich et al., 1997) and algorithmically facilitated environments found on social media (Craig et al., 2020).

With this backdrop, this chapter provides evidence of online hate language and its increase over time.

Methods

This study comprises English language UK tweets, retweets, and replies posted in July and August 2022 for language analysis, and from January 2017 and August 2022 for trending analysis. Originally looking at the whole UK LGBTQ+ community, due to the predominance of transgender-related results and for the purposes of this chapter, the aim and objectives have been amended.

Aim

To investigate the nature of online abuse and harassment towards the transgender community and determine whether it is increasing or decreasing.

Objectives

1 To understand the language used to conduct online abuse and harassment against the UK transgender community, principally trans women, via the collection and analysis of Twitter data.
2 To establish whether abuse and harassment against the UK transgender community has been increasing or decreasing since the 2018 amendment to the Gender Recognition Act.

Approach

This section introduces the methodological approach, justification, and steps to analyse the UK Twitter dataset, the inclusion/exclusion criteria, and the ethical considerations.

This study, informed by interpretivist epistemology, used an explanatory sequential mixed-method design (Ivankova, Creswell, and Stick, 2006). Qualitative language-based analysis took place before the quantitative analysis by surfacing terms suitable for trending. The qualitative analysis was achieved using machine learning techniques (Abram, Mancini, and Parker, 2020) via a number of Python-based applications.

Language analysis

Natural Language Processing (NLP) methods were used for topic extraction, clustering, word collocation, and keywords in context (KWIC). Accredited researcher status from Twitter provided access to archival data, enhanced query abilities, and increased data allowance. Tweets were downloaded using 'seed' terms sourced from Stonewall (Stonewall, n.d.), with the transgender-related list being: trans, transgender, gender recognition, gender certificate, grc, intersex, non-binary, sexual orientation, transitioning, and transsexual.

A target dataset of 20,000 UK Tweets was determined for language discovery purposes, and data was cleaned to remove emojis and non-regular expression (regexp) characters and then stored in a SQL database. Orange, a Python based open-source machine learning application enabled Latent Dirichlet Allocation (LDA) for topic extraction, Euclidean distance was used for the hierarchical topic clustering and topic scoring. Collocated terms and KWIC were investigated using AntConc. Inclusion criteria specified English language UK tweets that were original, retweets, or replies dated 2017 to August 2022. Where identified, tweets authored by those under the age of 18 were removed, and no user identification has been exposed. Due to a lack of structured location data, a small database of UK locations was built to identify UK users. The final dataset contained 20,833 LGBTQ+-related UK Tweets.

Trending

Terms identified though the language analysis phase were counted from 2017 to August 2022 using the twarc2 Python function for precise counting (without relying on samples). The terms counted were: TERF, not a woman, not women, trans woman, trans women, mutilating children, pronouns, trans ideology, trans agenda, and jk rowling. Without being exhaustive, and missing other terms (e.g., trans men or non-binary), these were sufficient to provide trends. Sample data determined the percentage of UK tweets and all data was exported, consolidated, and imported to Python to run Ordinary Least Squares (OLS) regression tests (Dahami, 2024) on the full dataset, and data before/after the GRA amendments with an additional test for acceleration.

Ethical considerations

Approval was obtained from the University of Portsmouth Ethics Committee prior to data collection. Data was retrieved directly from Twitter's databases using secure API credentials and a VPN, before being stored on a SQL server. All non-aggregated data was deleted upon completion. Usernames of individuals have not been exposed, but celebrities, politicians, and organisations are referenced as public figures or entities.

Findings and discussion

This section documents the findings from the language analysis phase (objective 1) and the trends in abusive, hateful, or harassing terms (objective 2).

Language analysis

Analysing 20,833 tweets generated the following results illustrated as charts and diagrams in Figures 14.1 and 14.2. During analysis, it was noted that actual abuse was conflated with talk about abuse, and although salient, the results should be read in that context.

Topics

Topics were extracted, and each tweet scored for the probability of containing each topic.

Hierarchical clustering produced topic relationships, illustrated in Figure 14.2 as a dendrogram.

The topic extraction process, despite containing data for all LGBTQ+ areas, was dominated by transgender topics. Positive terms, like love and pride exist, however most are transgender topics concerning the NHS, TERFs, young people, women's spaces (e.g., changing rooms and toilets), and schools. The topic dendrogram (Figure 14.2) highlights relationships between 'children' and 'changing rooms/toilets', reflecting arguments of women-only spaces (McQueen, 2016) and a presumption of harm by transgender individuals

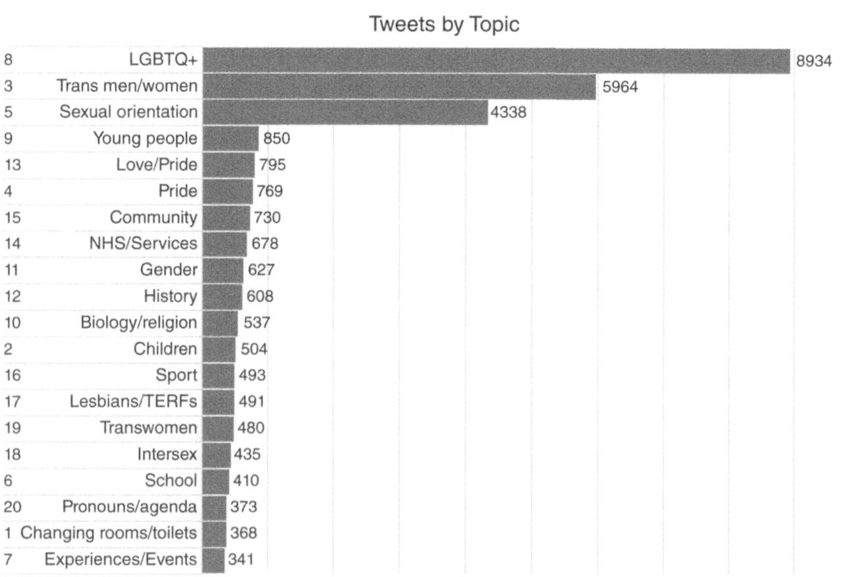

FIGURE 14.1 Tweets by topic

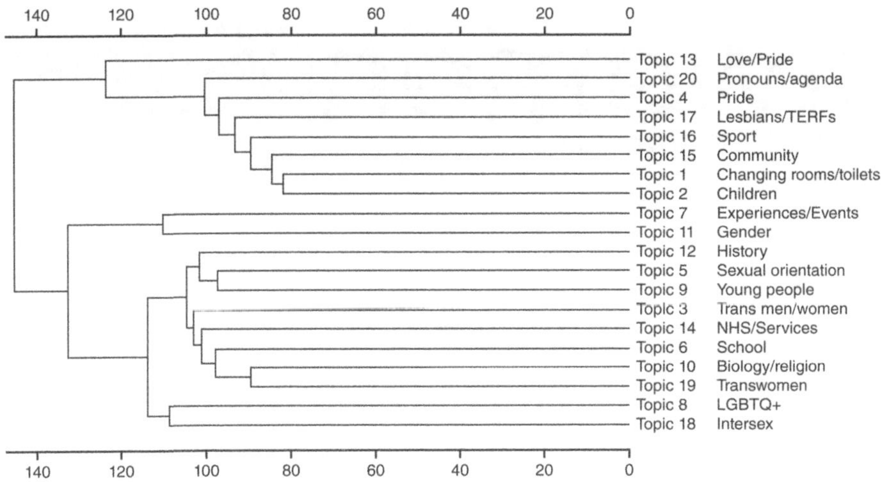

FIGURE 14.2 Topic dendrogram

(Gutierrez and Giner-Sorolla, 2007). Also indicated is a relationship between ‘trans women’ and ‘biology/religion’, echoing the TERF biological view of gender (Armitage, 2020), as well as the religious belief that gender is both immutable and divine (Norton and Herek, 2013; Kettell, 2024).

Collocation

Collocation is the likelihood of a word occurring within a parameterised number of words of a term (in this case five words either side). Collocations are illustrated below as word clouds (see Figures 14.3–14.6).

FIGURE 14.3 Collocation results for ‘transgender’

FIGURE 14.4 Collocation results for 'trans'

'Transgender' relates positively to 'pride', but negatively to themes of prisoners, offenders, and trans women in women's sports, reflecting existing literature on women-only spaces (McQueen, 2016; Armitage, 2020). The Tavistock Centre – the UK's only youth gender identity clinic – is mentioned (Andersson and Rhoden-Paul, 2022). 'Trans' has relationships to support, rights, and recognition, however also to 'exclusionary' and 'radical', referencing trans-exclusionary radical feminists (TERFs).

'Gender recognition' and 'grc' demonstrate neutral sentiment, although the word 'feminists' does appear, possibly indicating TERFs and right-wing

FIGURE 14.5 Collocation results for 'gender recognition'

FIGURE 14.6 Collocation results for 'grc'

or gender-critical feminists (Siddiqui, 2021). Both terms are mentioned in association with the gender recognition process, a gender dysphoria diagnosis, or obtaining a gender recognition certificate. Also evident is the EHRCJ (the Equalities, Human Rights and Civil Justice Committee), which advocates for self-declaration (White, 2021) and safeguarding, illustrated by the mention of Stephanie Hayden who was publicly outed as transgender (Benson, 2019).

Overall, there are positive themes of pride and culture, and discussion regarding identity exploration, healthcare, and recognition, but also negative topics surrounding biology, DNA, trans women in women's sport and spaces, and the risks trans women pose to women and children – a common TERF and far-right trope (McQueen, 2016; Armitstead, 2022).

Keywords in context (KWIC)

Using a subset of key terms, KWIC examples were selected for interest and/or representativeness.

'Trans ideology' and 'trans agenda' both infer that the transgender community are forcing their 'ideology' on society. Both terms are used with 'tiny children' and in 'schools', raising emotions and fear (Walton, 2014). Trans ideology framed as 'a men's demands movement' suggests erosion of women's rights (McQueen, 2016). Biological debate is surfaced by 'transwomen are men', 'transwomen are male', and 'transwomen are not women'. Trans women 'pose a threat' suggests a presumption of harm to others where none exists due to perceived violation of sexual and gender norms (Gutierrez and Giner-Sorolla, 2007).

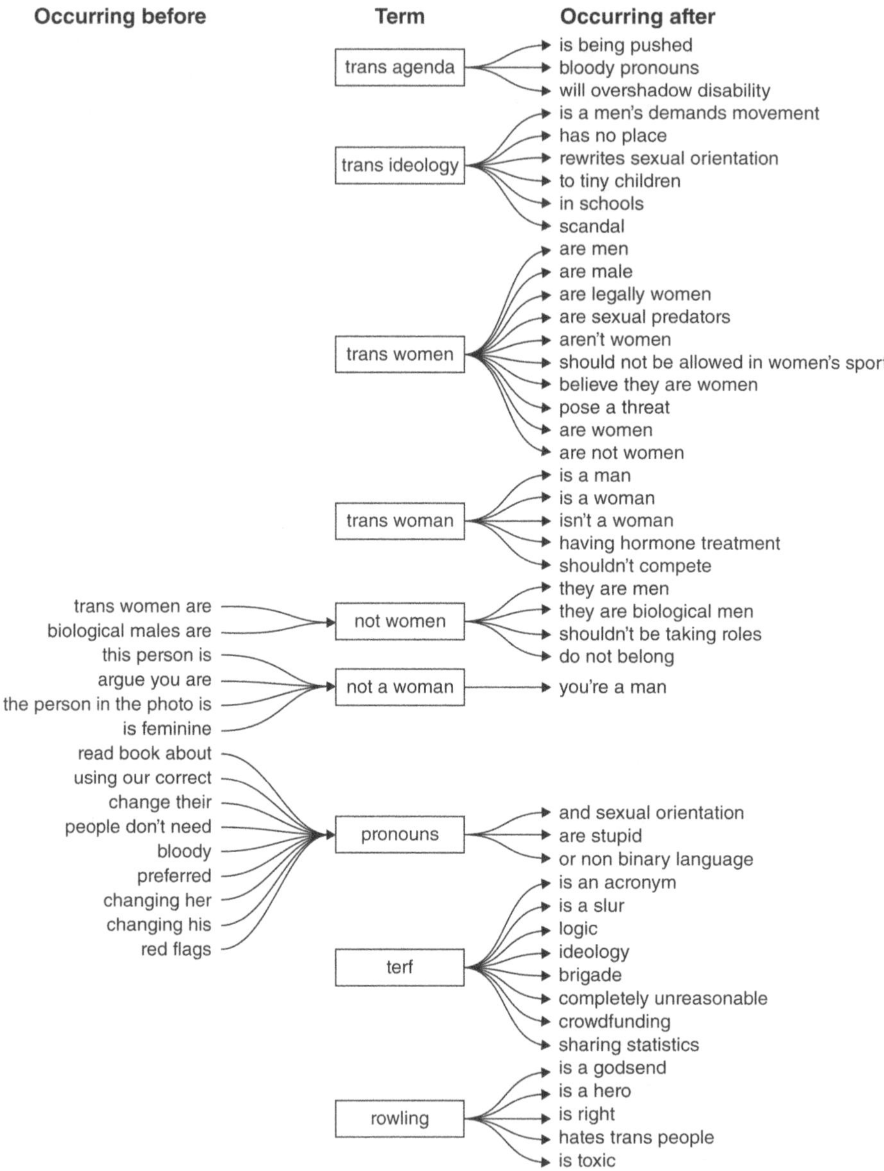

FIGURE 14.7 Keywords in context

Direct abuse includes 'this person is not a woman' and 'argue you are not a woman', which could potentially cause psychological harm to the individual and the community (see 'Harms' section above).

Negative views about 'pronouns' are illustrated with: 'people don't need pronouns', 'pronouns are stupid', and 'bloody pronouns'. Allies, describe 'terf's as a 'brigade', 'completely unreasonable', having an 'ideology' and 'crowdfunding' – referencing fundraising for lawsuits challenging pro-transgender rights (Savage and Asher-Schapiro, 2020).

Supporters of J. K. Rowling state she 'is a godsend' and 'is a hero' while her detractors say she 'is toxic'; however, these few examples only hint at her substantial influence on the stirring of anti-transgender sentiment. Rowling still boasts 14.3 million Twitter/X followers and uses her influence to support other gender-critical thinkers including Maya Forstater, who lost her job for her views, with Rowling's related post received over 321k likes (Noor, 2019; Miller, 2024; Rowling, 2024). Kathleen Stock, a previous professer at the University of Sussex, said of Rowling's involvement that likeminded women had previously been 'howling into the void' and had gained 'no traction in the media' (Phelps-Roper, 2023).

Trending

In this section, each term, or term combination, has its own chart illustrating its number of mentions (tweet count) over time, together with trend lines showing the increase or decrease over the full time period and for pre- and post-GRA amendments. The table immediately following the chart gives the slope calculations, p-value (statistical significance), and any acceleration between the latter two trend lines. The second table provides the descriptive statistics for each term including count, mean, standard deviation, minimum, and maximum. The third table for each term is the Ordinary Least Squares (OLS) regression summary which models the predicted relationship between

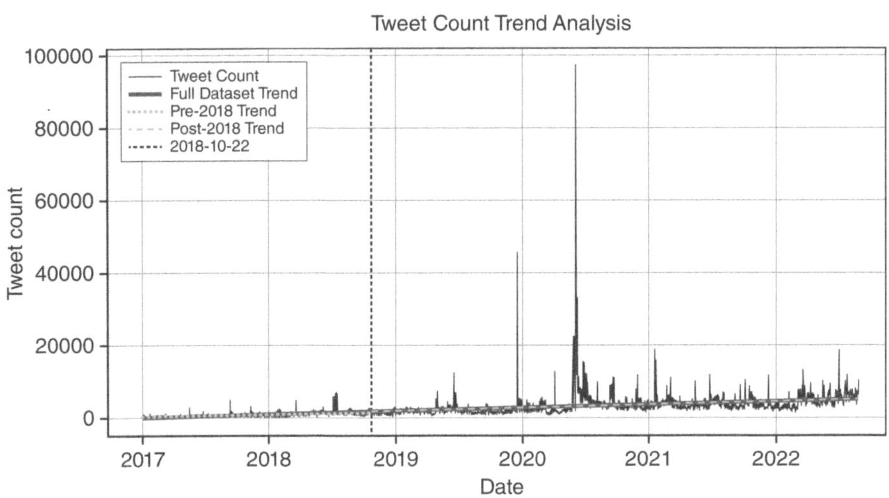

FIGURE 14.8 Trending 'terf'

TABLE 14.1 Slope comparison

Metric	*Full dataset*	*Pre-GRA*	*Post-GRA*	*Slope change (pre- vs. post-GRA)*
Slope (Tweets/Day)	2.448707	1.708609	2.448869	None
p-value trend	0.00000***	0.00000***	0.00000***	None
Acceleration test	None	None	None	2.61071

Note: *** statistically highly significant.

TABLE 14.2 Descriptive statistics

	count	*mean*	*std*	*min*	*max*
tweet_ count	2069.0	2376.02465	3437.443323	76.0	97044.0

TABLE 14.3 OLS regression results

Metric	*Full dataset*	*Pre-GRA*	*Post-GRA*
R-squared	0.181114	0.277066	0.066032
Adj. R-squared	0.1807718	0.275966	0.065369
F-statistic	457.160833	251.797041	99.546462
p-value (F-statistic)	0.00000***	0.00000***	0.00000***
Intercept	−155.937948	61.719023	1469.719967
Slope	2.448707	1.708609	2.448869

Note: *** statistically highly significant.

the variables of time (date) and volume (tweet count), with the F-statistic describing the statistical significance of the model and the p-value the statistical significance of the slope.

'TERF' originated online in 2008 (Smythe, 2018), but had very low usage until 2018 when the term saw a sharp rise. All tests for this term were statistically significant and it had the strongest rise for the whole time period. TERF accusations toward J. K. Rowling following her controversial essay and Twitter post (July 2020) (D'Alessandro, 2020; Lampen, 2020) potentially caused the mid-2020 peak.

'Not a woman' and 'not women' had a statistically significant increase for all time tests, and the post-GRA slope showed acceleration in comparison to pre-GRA. These terms have uses beyond transgender discourse; however, in the data they are seen directed at transgender women. Peaks are driven by news and media activity, e.g., the SNP being accused of imposing trans ideology on Scotland (August 2022) (Harris, 2022), J. K. Rowling's activities, and regulations for transgender athletes (October 2019) (World Athletics, 2019).

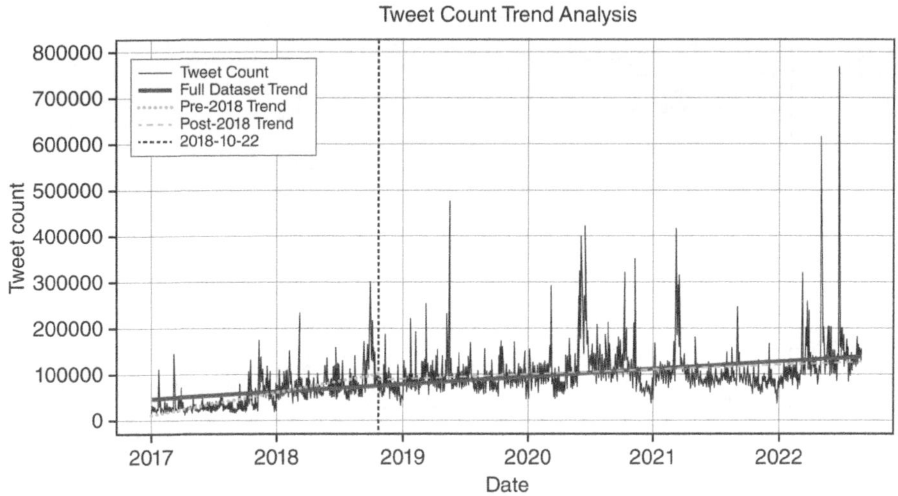

FIGURE 14.9 Trending 'not a woman' and 'not women'

TABLE 14.4 Slope comparison results

Metric	*Full dataset*	*Pre-GRA*	*Post-GRA*	*Slope change (pre- vs. post-GRA)*
Slope (Tweets/Day)	45.380387	131.548583	27.610705	None
p-value trend	0.00000***	0.00000***	0.00000***	None
Acceleration test	None	None	None	–12.42839 (sig)

Note: *** statistically highly significant.

TABLE 14.5 Descriptive statistics

	count	*mean*	*std*	*min*	*max*
tweet_ count	2069.0	90691.955534	54824.611907	11127.0	767092.0

TABLE 14.6 OLS regression results

Metric	*Full dataset*	*Pre-GRA*	*Post-GRA*
R-squared	0.244505	0.457363	0.043172
Adj. R-squared	0.244139	0.456537	0.042493
F-statistic	668.953726	553.75319	43.529334
p-value (F-statistic)	0.00000***	0.00000***	0.00000***
Intercept	43768.634902	12344.816651	87629.990328
Slope	45.380387	131.548583	27.610705

Note: *** statistically highly significant.

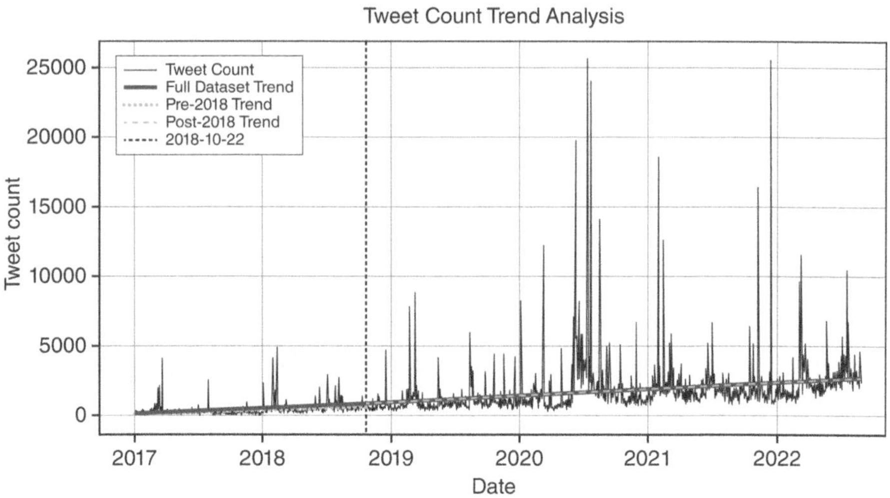

FIGURE 14.10 Trending 'trans woman' and 'trans women'

TABLE 14.7 Slope comparison results

Metric	*Full dataset*	*Pre-GRA*	*Post-GRA*	*Slope change (pre- vs. post-GRA)*
Slope (Tweets/Day)	1.320083	0.683354	1.290389	None
p-value trend	0.00000***	0.00000**	0.00000***	None
Acceleration test	None		None	3.83269

Note: *** statistically highly significant.

TABLE 14.8 Descriptive statistics

	count	*mean*	*std*	*min*	*max*
tweet_ count	2069.0	1345.763654	1759.464067	52.0	25546.0

TABLE 14.9 OLS regression results

Metric	*Full dataset*	*Pre-GRA*	*Post-GRA*
R-squared	0.200905	0.080601	0.072477
Adj. R-squared	0.200519	0.079202	0.071819
F-statistic	519.676869	57.597225	110.022151
p-value (F-statistic)	0.00000***	0.00000***	0.00000***
Intercept	−19.20208	157.831949	886.81831
Slope	1.320083	0.683354	1.290389

Note: *** statistically highly significant.

'Trans woman' and 'trans women' had a statistically significant increase for all the time tests, and although not accelerating post-GRA, had a lack of usage prior to 2018 (Roseneil et al., 2013). Peaks in the data may correlate with the activities of J. K. Rowling (July 2022) and her criticism of Police Scotland's transgender policies (December 2021) (Sachdeva, 2021), also articles about 2021 being the deadliest year for transgender people (November 2021) (Brooks, 2021), the first trans woman competing at the Olympics (July 2021) (BBC News, 2021), and a High Court judgement that it is lawful to imprison trans women in female jails (July 2021) (Siddique, 2021).

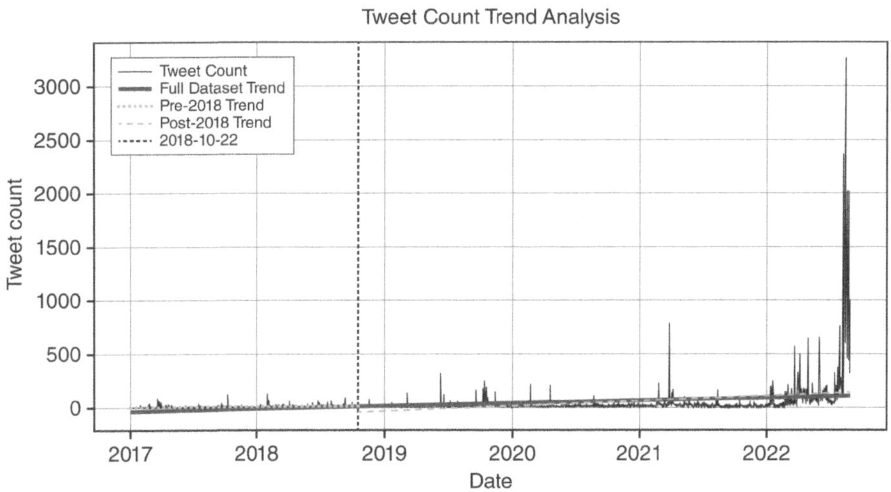

FIGURE 14.11 Trending 'mutilating children'

TABLE 14.10 Slope comparison results

Metric	*Full dataset*	*Pre-GRA*	*Post-GRA*	*Slope change (pre- vs. post-GRA)*
Slope (Tweets/Day)	0.06886	0.008129	0.1314319	None
p-value trend	0.00000***	0.00000***	0.00000***	None
Acceleration test	None	None	None	9.44047

Note: *** statistically highly significant.

TABLE 14.11 Descriptive statistics

	count	*mean*	*std*	*min*	*max*
tweet_ count	2069.0	34.283229	167.416399	0.0	3260.0

TABLE 14.12 OLS regression results

Metric	*Full dataset*	*Pre-GRA*	*Post-GRA*
R-squared	0.060379	0.018947	0.073799
Adj. R-squared	0.059924	0.017453	0.073141
F-statistic	132.8226662	12.688324	112.188479
p-value (F-statistic)	0.00000***	0.00000***	0.00000***
Intercept	−36.917755	3.368092	−47.145159
Slope	0.06886	0.008129	0.134319

Note: *** statistically highly significant.

'Mutilating children' had a statistically significant increase over all time tests but despite the peaks did not show acceleration. This term, originally used in relation to female genital mutilation (Delaleu, 2018), later shifted to transgender youth. Noticeable peaks potentially coincide with examples of this language, such as Texas Governor, Greg Abbott, describing transgender reassignment surgery as 'genital mutilation' (April 2022) (Goyette, 2022), the Australian Liberal candidate, Katherine Deves, describing transgender children as being 'surgically mutilated' (June 2022) (Henderson and Quinn, 2022), and the article targeting children's hospitals treating transgender children (August 2022) (Bond, 2022).

The term 'pronouns' is often used in discussions on transgender, non-binary, and gender-fluid individuals, and the use of pronouns in email

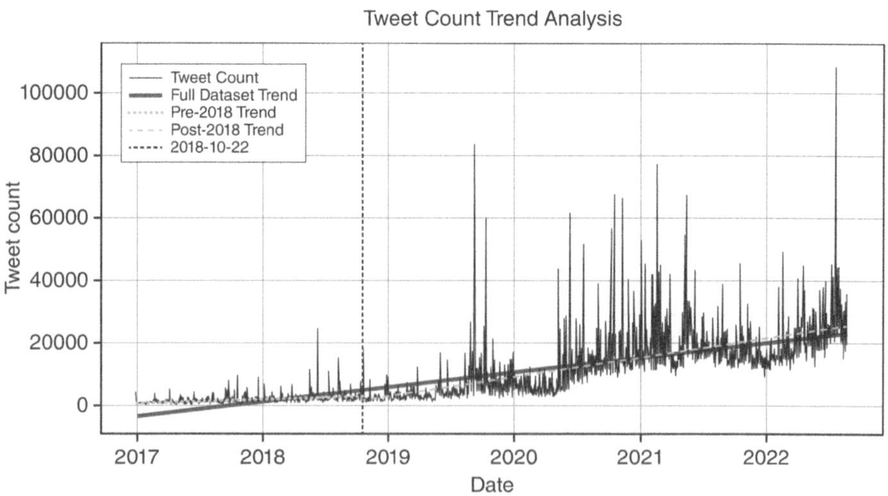

FIGURE 14.12 Trending 'pronouns'

TABLE 14.13 Slope comparison results

Metric	*Full dataset*	*Pre-GRA*	*Post-GRA*	*Slope change (pre- vs. post-GRA)*
Slope (Tweets/Day)	12.806395	3.190249	16.951341	None
p-value Trend	0.00000***	0.00000***	0.00000***	None
Acceleration Test	None	None	None	17.67829

Note: *** statistically highly significant.

TABLE 14.14 Descriptive statistics

	count	*mean*	*std*	*min*	*max*
tweet_ count	2069.0	9700.41131	10408.843033	422.0	108575.0

TABLE 14.15 OLS regression results

Metric	*Full dataset*	*Pre-GRA*	*Post-GRA*
R-squared	0.540255	0.1325	0.416435
Adj. R-squared	0.540032	0.13118	0.416021
F-statistic	2428.966347	100.348899	1004.757214
p-value (F-statistic)	0.00000***	0.000000***	0.00000***
Intercept	−3541.400944	706.204608	1471.312595
Slope	12.806395	3.190249	16.951341

Note: *** statistically highly significant.

signatures and name badges reflects inclusivity (Armitstead, 2022). However, this is far from universally popular, proved by actions of US right-wing legislators (Lavietes, 2022) and the cancellation of inclusivity policies (Armitstead, 2022). The term's frequency rose after 2018; however, the post-GRA data was not positive for acceleration. Autumnal peaks align with International Pronouns Day in October (Pronouns.org, n.d.), and there was also a peak in 2021 in line with the comedian Eddie Izzard changing her pronouns (Duffy, 2021).

'Trans ideology' and 'trans agenda' increased significantly for all the time tests; however, despite the post-GRA slope being steep, it does not show acceleration. Again, peaks in the data can be attributed to media, news, and social media events, including the SNP being accused of imposing trans ideology on Scotland (August 2022) (Harris, 2022) and J. K. Rowling's essay and Twitter posts (July 2020) (D'Alessandro, 2020; Lampen, 2020).

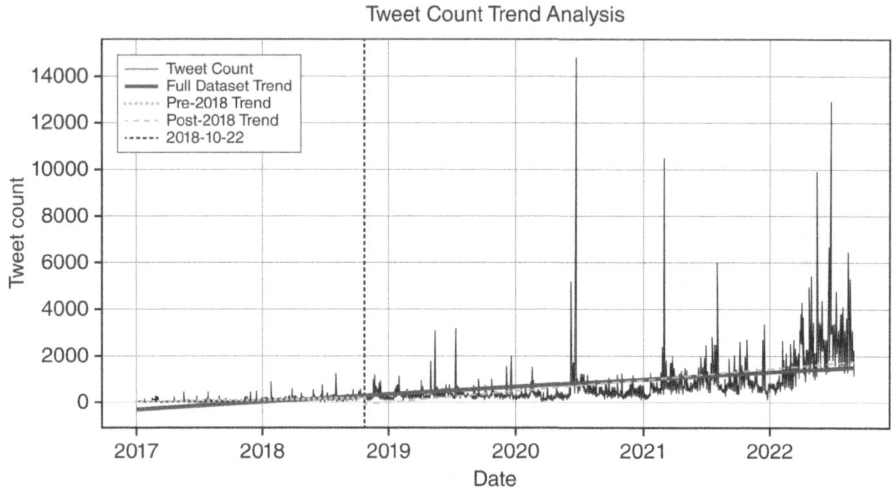

FIGURE 14.13 Trending 'trans ideology' and 'trans agenda'

TABLE 14.16 Slope comparison results

Metric	*Full dataset*	*Pre-GRA*	*Post-GRA*	*Slope change (pre- vs. post-GRA)*
Slope (Tweets/Day)	0.870966	0.296955	1.296274	None
p-value trend	0.00000***	0.00000***	0.00000***	None
Acceleration test	None	None	None	13.65805

Note: *** statistically highly significant.

TABLE 14.17 Descriptive statistics

	count	*mean*	*std*	*min*	*max*
tweet_ count	2069.0	596.007733	945.192469	8.0	14713.0

TABLE 14.18 OLS regression results

Metric	*Full dataset*	*Pre-GRA*	*Post-GRA*
R-squared	0.303048	0.286674	0.243874
Adj. R-squared	0.302711	0.285588	0.243337
F-statistic	898.770148	264.037224	454.122366
p-value (F-statistic)	0.00000***	0.00000***	0.00000***
Intercept	−304.57076	9.932901	−88.961837
Slope	0.870966	0.296955	1.29627

Note: *** statistically highly significant.

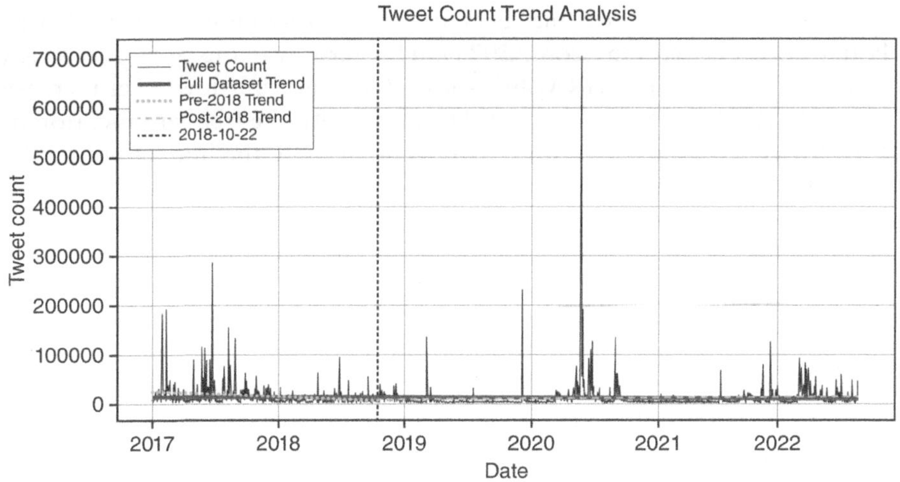

FIGURE 14.14 Trending 'jk rowling'

TABLE 14.19 Slope comparison results

Metric	*Full dataset*	*Pre-GRA*	*Post-GRA*	*Slope change (pre- vs. post-GRA)*
Slope (Tweets/Day)	−2.391584	−28.719823	3.614434	None
p-value trend	0.00000***	0.00000***	0.00000***	None
Acceleration test	None	None	None	6.58649

Note: *** statistically highly significant.

TABLE 14.20 Descriptive statistics

	count	*mean*	*std*	*min*	*max*
tweet_ count	2069.0	10314.60754	25122.191868	606.0	704191.0

TABLE 14.21 OLS regression results

Metric	*Full dataset*	*Pre-GRA*	*Post-GRA*
R-squared	0.003234	0.05912	0.003163
Adj. R-squared	0.002752	0.057688	0.002455
F-statistic	6.707388	41.282369	4.468213
p-value (F-statistic)	0.00000***	0.00000***	0.00000***
Intercept	12787.505714	22586.459015	6448.822902
Slope	−2.391584	−28.719823	3.614434

Note: *** statistically highly significant.

Lastly, we have 'jk rowling' herself – extensively known for her Harry Potter books (Biography.com, 2021). This term was the only one which showed a decrease pre-GRA, but showed a significant low-level increase post-GRA and for the full dataset. However, with the frequent mention of J. K. Rowling within this study, there is no arguing the impact her public views have had in the UK – extending far beyond this study, she continues to use her public standing to court controversy (BBC News, 2024). See the 'Online hate' and 'Language analysis' sections above for more information.

Summary

The dataset surfaces both positive sentiment and considerable hate toward the transgender community, from seemingly benign phrases like 'pronouns are stupid' through to 'agendas' and 'ideologies' underpinning a belief that any support of transgender rights threatens the democratic process and promotes misinterpretation of the law (Cowan, 2021); and then on to the alarmist, 'trans women are sexual predators' comments as demonstrated by the LGB Alliance on the Gender Recognition Reform in Scotland, with phrasing such as 'Self-ID gives predators the green light' (Ferreira, 2022). The dataset exposes the politicisation of the transgender community, a fact later illustrated during the run-up to the 2024 US presidential election where the Republicans used political attacks on transgender rights as a challenge to 'woke' politics under the premis of 'protect[ing] the children' (Cineas and Narea, 2023).

Conclusion

This conclusion covers the results of the two objectives, the limitations of the research, and suggests some recommendations.

Topic extraction revealed themes of love and pride within the LGBTQ+ community while surfacing the predominance of anti-transgender-related topics, particularly in relation to women's spaces, children, the presumption of harm, and politicised rhetoric. Topic clustering indicated a strong relationship between transgender women and biology, and between children and women's spaces. The collocation exercise surfaced subjects of self-exploration, healthcare, and recognition, while illustrating debates on biology, prisoners, women's sports, children, and the Tavistock Centre. Keywords in context revealed more explicit anti-transgender phrases such as 'trans ideology in schools', 'trans women are men', 'trans women are sexual predators', 'Rowling is a hero', along with the title of this chapter, 'pronouns are stupid'. Beyond the insults more traditionally thought of as hate (Hubbard, 2020), there is a prevalence of politically charged terms such as 'agenda' and 'ideology', with messages of danger and harm toward women and children. Overall, the language exploration exercise exposed themes indicative of far-right rhetoric – invalidating transgender people and portraying them as violent men (Doyle, 2022).

The volume of hate toward the transgender community rose in the duration of this study with all terms showing a statistically significant rise since the proposed GRA amendments and the overall time period, with the terms 'trans ideology' and 'pronouns' having two of the highest increases. The peaks in the data are frequently triggered by media articles and social media activity – with J. K. Rowling individually having the greatest impact.

Limitations

This study has a number of limitations that should be considered. Limited geographical information available in Twitter data, and volumes prorated from samples to ascertain the percentage of tweet authors provably in the UK, means the the volumes are understated. Twitter API data constraints were an obvious requirement from the platform's perspective, however means data collection was a protracted process, and additionally the use of automated text analysis means it is virtually impossible to differentiate between actual abuse and discussion about abuse, although both are salient.

Recommendations

- This research provides information on the state and nature of online transphobic hate in the UK and can support future enhancements to legislation such as the Online Safety Act through detecting, classifying, and quantifying harmful online hate (Department for Science, Innovation and Technlogy, 2024). For the victims of online hate, who suffer the repercussions (Hubbard, 2020), this study hopefully provides some context and direction for both individuals and those who support them.
- The methodology and information surfaced here can hopefully provide a starting point for future research in the field of online hate crime.

The findings of this study make clear that online transphobic hate in the UK is not a fringe phenomenon but a systemic and escalating problem, sustained by political opportunism and media amplification. Language that dehumanises and delegitimises transgender people – particularly trans women – has real-world consequences, deepening inequality and fostering environments where discrimination and violence are normalised. Confronting this harm demands more than monitoring trends; it requires robust legislative protections, proactive platform accountability, and a cultural shift that refuses to frame prejudice as 'debate'.

References

Abram, M. D., Mancini, K. T., and Parker, R. D. (2020). Methods to integrate natural language processing into qualitative research. *International Journal of Qualitative Methods*, *19*, 1609406920984608. https://doi.org/10.1177/1609406920984608

Andersson, J., and Rhoden-Paul, A. (2022, 28 July). NHS to close Tavistock child gender identity clinic. *BBC News*. https://www.bbc.com/news/uk-62335665

Armitage, L. (2020). Explaining backlash to trans and non-binary genders in the context of UK Gender Recognition Act reform. *INSEP – Journal of the International Network for Sexual Ethics & Politics*, 3(0).

Armitstead, C. (2022, 26 November). 'It's complicated – but you can't shy away from it': Everything you wanted to know about pronouns (but were afraid to ask). *The Guardian*. https://www.theguardian.com/world/2022/nov/26/pronouns-gendered-language-revolution-britain

Arshad, T., and Brasted, C. (2024). What's next for the UK's Online Safety Act and can it solve the misinformation problem?. *Hogan Lovells*. https://www.hoganlovells.com/en/publications/whats-next-for-the-uks-online-safety-act-and-can-it-solve-the-misinformation-problem

Bakalis, C. (2018). Rethinking cyberhate laws. *Information & Communications Technology Law*, 27(1), 86–110. https://doi.org/10.1080/13600834.2017.1393934

Baker, P. (2019). EXCLUSIVE: Mermaids' research into newspaper coverage on trans issues. *Mermaids*. https://mermaidsuk.org.uk/news/exclusive-mermaids-research-into-newspaper-coverage-on-trans-issues/

Balogun, B., Fairbairn, C., and Pyper, D. (2024). Gender Recognition Act reform: Consultation and outcome. *UK Parliament*. https://commonslibrary.parliament.uk/research-briefings/cbp-9079/

Barrett, P. M. (2024, 6 March). NYU Stern Center for Business & Human Rights: The threat to the election posed by Elon Musk's X. Available at: https://bhr.stern.nyu.edu/quick-take/the-threat-to-the-election-posed-by-elon-musks-x/ (Accessed: 11 November 2024).

BBC News (2021, 21 June). Laurel Hubbard: First transgender athlete to compete at Olympics. https://www.bbc.com/news/world-asia-57549653

BBC News (2024, 11 April). JK Rowling reignites row with Harry Potter stars Daniel Radcliffe and Emma Watson. https://www.bbc.com/news/entertainment-arts-68787258

Benson, O. (2019, 10 April). A number of offences of dishonesty. *Butterflies and Wheels*. https://www.butterfliesandwheels.org/2019/a-number-of-offences-of-dishonesty/

Biography.com (2021) J.K. Rowling – Books, family & facts. https://www.biography.com/authors-writers/jk-rowling

Bond, S. (2022, 26 August). Children's hospitals are the latest target of anti-LGBTQ harassment. *NPR*. https://www.npr.org/2022/08/26/1119634878/childrens-hospitals-are-the-latest-target-of-anti-lgbtq-harassment

Boyd, R. (2024, 11 December). From X to Bluesky: Why are people fleeing Elon Musk's 'digital town square'? *The Guardian*. https://www.theguardian.com/media/2024/dec/11/from-x-to-bluesky-why-are-people-abandoning-twitter-digital-town-square

Brewer, M. B. (2007). The importance of being we: Human nature and intergroup relations. *American Psychologist*, *62*(8), 728–738.

Brooks, L. (2021). 2021 has been a deadly year for transgender people. *Forbes*. https://www.forbes.com/sites/lakenbrooks/2021/11/14/2021-has-been-a-deadly-year-for-transgender-people/

Chakraborti, N., and Garland, J. (2015). *Hate crime: Impact, causes & responses*. London: Sage Publications.
Chikha, B. (2021). Combating rising hate against LGBTI people in Europe. Parliamentary Assembly, Council of Europe. https://pace.coe.int/en/files/29418/html
Cineas, F., and Narea, N. (2023). The GOP's coordinated national campaign against trans rights, explained. *Vox*. https://www.vox.com/politics/23631262/trans-bills-republican-state-legislatures
Cohen, S. (1973). *Folk devils and moral panics: The creation of the mods and rockers*. London: Paladin.
Cowan, S. (2021). Sex and gender equality law and policy: A response to Murray, Hunter Blackburn and Mackenzie. *Scottish Affairs*. https://www.academia.edu/105302565/Sex_and_gender_equality_law_and_policy_a_response_to_Murray_Hunter_Blackburn_and_Mackenzie
CPS (2022). Public statement on prosecuting homophobic, biphobic and transphobic hate crime. The Crown Prosecution Service. https://www.cps.gov.uk/publication/public-statement-prosecuting-homophobic-biphobic-and-transphobic-hate-crime
Craig, S. L., et al. (2020). Navigating negativity: A grounded theory and integrative mixed methods investigation of how sexual and gender minority youth cope with negative comments online. *Psychology & Sexuality*, *11*(3), 161–179. https://doi.org/10.1080/19419899.2019.1665575
Crerar, P., and Brooks, L. (2023, 16 January). Rishi Sunak blocks Scotland's gender recognition legislation. *The Guardian*. https://www.theguardian.com/world/2023/jan/16/rishi-sunak-blocks-scotlands-gender-recognition-legislation
Cuthbertson, A. (2024). X users are having their accounts restricted for using the term 'cisgender'. *The Independent*. https://www.independent.co.uk/tech/x-cisgender-slur-cis-elon-musk-b2545355.html
Dahami, Y. (2024). Understanding Ordinary Least Squares (OLS) and its applications in statistics, machine learning. *Medium*. https://medium.com/@dahami/understanding-ordinary-least-squares-ols-and-its-applications-in-statistics-machine-learning-ad2c13681501
D'Alessandro, A. (2020, 10 June). J.K. Rowling defends trans statements in lengthy essay, reveals she's a sexual assault survivor & says 'trans people need and deserve protection'. *Deadline*. https://deadline.com/2020/06/j-k-rowling-defends-trans-statements-essay-1202955524/
Davidson, J., et al. (2019). *Adult online hate, harassment and abuse: A rapid evidence assessment*. London: University of East London.
Delaleu, N. (2018) *Zero tolerance for female genital mutilation | News | European Parliament*. Available at: https://www.europarl.europa.eu/news/en/press-room/20180202IPR97032/zero-tolerance-for-female-genital-mutilation (Accessed: 22 November 2024).
Department for Science, Innovation and Technlogy (2024). *Online Safety Act: Explainer*. https://www.gov.uk/government/publications/online-safety-act-explainer/online-safety-act-explainer
Doyle, J. E. S. (2022, 1 April). How the far-right is turning feminists into fascists. *Xtra Magazine*. https://xtramagazine.com/power/far-right-feminist-fascist-220810
Duffy, N. (2021). Eddie Izzard opens up about her pronoun change in brilliant chat with Matt Lucas. *PinkNews*. https://www.thepinknews.com/2021/01/18/eddie-izzard-marathon-challenge-pronouns-change-genderfluid-trans-charity-marathon-matt-lucas/
Ferreira, L. (2022). LGB Alliance says it will 'get around to' helping LGB people. *openDemocracy*. https://www.opendemocracy.net/en/5050/mermaids-appeals-charity-commission-lgb-alliance-status/

Frew, T., Watsford, C., and Walker, I. (2021). Gender dysphoria and psychiatric comorbidities in childhood: A systematic review. *Australian Journal of Psychology*, *73*(3), 255–271. https://doi.org/10.1080/00049530.2021.1900747

GAO (2024). *Online extremism: More complete information needed about hate crimes that occur on the internet*. Washington DC: United States Government Accountability Office.

Gender Recognition Reform (Scotland) Bill (2019). Consultation. https://www.gov.scot/publications/gender-recognition-reform-scotland-bill-consultation-scottish-government/

GIRES (2023). Information on prevalence, incidence and monitoring. Gender Identity Research & Education Society. https://www.gires.org.uk/information-on-prevalence-incidence-and-monitoring/

Glover, J. (2022). Harry Potter author praises 'heroine' barrister who won free-speech battle. *Scottish Daily Express*. https://www.scottishdailyexpress.co.uk/news/uk-news/harry-potter-author-leads-praise-27597062

Goyette, J. (2022, 12 April). The battle between Texas and transgender children. *The Siskiyou*. https://siskiyou.sou.edu/2022/04/12/the-battle-between-texas-and-transgender-children/

Grant, W. (2021, 1 February). Three lives, one message: Stop killing Mexico's transgender women. *BBC News*. https://www.bbc.com/news/world-latin-america-55796384

Gutierrez, R., and Giner-Sorolla, R. (2007). Anger, disgust, and presumption of harm as reactions to taboo-breaking behaviors. *Emotion*, 7(4), 853–868. https://doi.org/10.1037/1528-3542.7.4.853

Gwenffrewi, G. (2022). J. K. Rowling and the echo chamber of secrets. *TSQ: Transgender Studies Quarterly*, 9(3), 507–516. https://doi.org/10.1215/23289252-9836176

Harris, T. (2022, 16 August). The SNP is using independence as a Trojan Horse to impose extreme trans ideology on Scotland. *The Telegraph*. https://www.telegraph.co.uk/news/2022/08/16/snp-using-independence-trojan-horse-impose-extreme-trans-ideology/

Haslam, N., and Levy, S. R. (2006). Essentialist beliefs about homosexuality: Structure and implications for prejudice. *Personality and Social Psychology Bulletin*, *32*(4), 471–485. https://doi.org/10.1177/0146167205276516

Henderson, A., and Quinn, T. (2022). Katherine Deves walks back her apology over 'insensitive' comments about trans children. *SBS News*. https://www.sbs.com.au/news/article/katherine-deves-walks-back-her-apology-over-insensitive-comments-about-trans-children/fdvwoxaaa

Henderson, E. R., et al. (2022). 'Words aren't supposed to hurt, but they do': Sexual and gender minority youth's bullying experiences. *Journal of Interpersonal Violence*, *37*(11–12), NP8747–NP8766. https://doi.org/10.1177/0886260520978199

Howard, J. (2019). *Cognitive errors and diagnostic mistakes: A case-based guide to critical thinking in medicine*. Cham: Springer International Publishing.

Hubbard, L. (2020). *Online hate crime report 2020: Challenging online homophobia, biphobia and transphobia*. London: Galop, the LGBT+ Anti-Violence Charity.

Iganski, P. (2003). Hate crimes hurt more. In B. Perry (Ed.), *Hate and bias crime: A reader* (pp. 131–138). New York: Routledge.

Ipsos (2022). Stonewall-gender-identity-tables-2022 https://www.ipsos.com/sites/default/files/ct/news/documents/2022-10/stonewall-gender-identity-tables-2022.pdf

Ivankova, N. V., Creswell, J. W., and Stick, S. L. (2006). Using mixed-methods sequential explanatory design: From theory to practice. *Field Methods*, *18*(1), 3–20. https://doi.org/10.1177/1525822X05282260

Jolls, C., and Sunstein, C. R. (2006). The law of implicit bias. *California Law Review*, *94*, 969–996.

Kettell, S. (2024). Navigating the secular landscape: Religious discourse on transgender rights in the United Kingdom. *Political Studies*, 00323217241273630. https://doi.org/10.1177/00323217241273630

Kidd, J. D., and Witten, T. M. (2007). Transgender and transsexual identities: The next strange fruit – Hate crimes, violence and genocide against the global trans-communities. *Journal of Hate Studies*, *6*(31), 31–63.

Lampen, C. (2020). J.K. Rowling accused of transphobia over Twitter commentary. *The Cut*. https://www.thecut.com/2020/06/j-k-rowling-accused-of-transphobia-over-twitter-commentary.html

Lavietes, M. (2022). Transgender pronoun bill advances in Tennessee's Legislature. *NBC News*. https://www.nbcnews.com/nbc-out/out-politics-and-policy/transgender-pronoun-bill-advances-tennessees-legislature-rcna26045

Lehavot, K., and Lambert, A. J. (2007). Toward a greater understanding of antigay prejudice: On the role of sexual orientation and gender role violation. *Basic and Applied Psychology*, *29*(3), 279–292.

McQueen, P. (2016). Feminist and trans perspectives on identity and the UK Gender Recognition Act. *The British Journal of Politics and International Relations*, *18*(3), 671–687. https://doi.org/10.1177/1369148116637998

Melley, J. (2024). Number of trans people may have been overestimated in census, ONS says. *BBC News*. https://www.bbc.com/news/articles/c3030519849o

Miller, L. J. (2024). J. K. Rowling's anti-trans rhetoric: Populist transantagonism. *Quarterly Journal of Speech*, *110*(3), 479–488. https://doi.org/10.1080/00335630.2024.2368562

Nicholas, L. (2019). Queer ethics and fostering positive mindsets toward non-binary gender, genderqueer, and gender ambiguity. *International Journal of Transgenderism*, *20*(2–3), 169–180. https://doi.org/10.1080/15532739.2018.1505576

Noor, P. (2019, 19 December). JK Rowling in row over court ruling on transgender issues. *The Guardian*. https://www.theguardian.com/books/2019/dec/19/jk-rowling-trans-row-court-ruling-twitter-maya-forstater

Norton, A. T., and Herek, G. M. (2013). Heterosexuals' attitudes toward transgender people: Findings from a national probability sample of U.S. adults. *Sex Roles*, 68(11–12), 738–753. https://doi.org/10.1007/s11199-011-0110-6

Olsen, R. (2008). Self-selection bias. In P. J. J. Lavrakas (Ed.), *Encyclopedia of survey research methods* (pp. 809–809). Thousand Oaks, CA: Sage Publications. https://doi.org/10.4135/9781412963947

ONS (2023). Gender identity, England and Wales: Census 2021. Office for National Statistics. https://www.ons.gov.uk/census/maps/choropleth/identity/gender-identity/gender-identity-8a/gender-identity-the-same-as-sex-registered-at-birth

Paul, K., and Milmo, D. (2022, 28 October). Elon Musk completes Twitter takeover and fires top executives. *The Guardian*. https://www.theguardian.com/technology/2022/oct/27/elon-musk-completes-twitter-takeover

Phelps-Roper, M. (2003). The witch trials of J.K. Rowling. *The Free Press*. https://open.spotify.com/episode/5r8SZLhLsgroLqPC1owm0m?si=f818f9363eff4a1f&nd=1&dlsi=40a3e364e965467f

Pronouns.org (n.d.). International Pronouns Day. https://pronouns.org/day

Roseneil, S., et al. (2013). Changing landscapes of heteronormativity: The regulation and normalization of same-sex sexualities in Europe. *Social Politics: International Studies in Gender, State & Society*, *20*(2), 165–199. https://doi.org/10.1093/sp/jxt006

Rowling, J. K. (@jk_rowling). (2022). If you believe in freedom of speech and/or think lesbians' careers shouldn't be imperilled by a lobby group whose CEO says same sex attraction is akin to 'sexual racism', you might fancy helping Allison out. (I've already put my money where my mouth is). *Twitter*. https://x.com/jk_rowling/status/1518629810557394944

Rowling, J. K. (@jk_rowling). (2024). *X (formerly Twitter)*. https://x.com/jk_rowling

Sachdeva, M. (2021). Harry Potter fans criticise JK Rowling after author posts new 'transphobic' tweet. *The Independent*. https://www.independent.co.uk/arts-entertainment/books/news/harry-potter-jk-rowling-transphobic-terf-b1974984.html

Savage, R., and Asher-Schapiro, A. (2020). Crowdfunding drives wave of UK lawsuits over trans rights. *Openly*. https://www.openlynews.com/i/?id=83473607-73b1-480e-93aa-8d793936810b

Siddique, H. (2021, 2 July). Lawful to imprison trans women sex offenders in female jails, judge rules. *The Guardian*. https://www.theguardian.com/society/2021/jul/02/trans-women-with-sex-offence-convictions-in-female-jails-lawful-rules-judge

Siddiqui, S. (2021). Feminism, biological fundamentalism and the attack on trans rights. Institute of Race Relations. https://irr.org.uk/article/feminism-biological-fundamentalism-attack-on-trans-rights/

Sim, P. (2024). Supreme Court to hear case on definition of a woman. *BBC News*. https://www.bbc.com/news/articles/ckgv8v5ge37o

Smith, C. (2024, 31 October). The Far-right campaign to regulate gender harms all Americans. Center for American Progress. https://www.americanprogress.org/article/the-far-right-campaign-to-regulate-gender-harms-all-americans/

Smythe, V. (2018, 28 November). I'm credited with having coined the word 'Terf'. Here's how it happened. *The Guardian*. https://www.theguardian.com/commentisfree/2018/nov/29/im-credited-with-having-coined-the-acronym-terf-heres-how-it-happened

Stonewall (n.d.). List of LGBTQ+ terms. https://www.stonewall.org.uk/resources/list-lgbtq-terms

Strugar, M. (2024, 21 January). Top 25 surprising Twitter statistics UK edition [2024]. *Cyber Crew*. https://cybercrew.uk/blog/twitter-statistics-uk/

Teich, A., et al. (1997). Anonymous communication policies for the internet: Results and recommendations of the AAAS Conference. In *Anonymous communications on the internet. American Association for the Advancement of Science Conference* (pp. 71–77). California: University of California, AAAS

Walsh, J. P. (2020). Social media and moral panics: Assessing the effects of technological change on societal reaction. *International Journal of Cultural Studies*, *23*(6), 840–859. https://doi.org/10.1177/1367877920912257

Walton, G. (Ed.) (2014). *The gay agenda: Claiming space, identity, and justice*. New York: Peter Lang.

Wendling, M., and Epstein, K. (2025, 20 January). Trump makes 'two sexes' official and scraps DEI policies. *BBC News*. https://www.bbc.com/news/articles/czx84en1yp4o

White, R. (2021). House of Commons Women and Equalities Committee come out strongly for self-declaration of gender in a report full of interesting detail. *Old Square Chambers*. https://oldsquare.co.uk/house-of-commons-women-and-equalities-committee-come-out-strongly-for-self-declaration-of-gender-in-a-report-full-of-interesting-detail/

Williams, M. (2019). *Hatred behind the screens: A report on the rise of online hate speech*. Cardiff: HateLab, Cardiff University and Mishcon de Reya.

Williams, Z. (2024, 5 September). Racism, misogyny, lies: How did X become so full of hatred? And is it ethical to keep using it? *The Guardian*. https://www.theguardian.

com/technology/article/2024/sep/05/racism-misogyny-lies-how-did-x-become-so-full-of-hatred-and-is-it-ethical-to-keep-using-it

World Athletics (2019). *Eligibility regulations for transgender athletes. Book of rules: Competition.*

X Help (2023). X's policy on hateful conduct. https://help.x.com/en/rules-and-policies/hateful-conduct-policy

X Help (n.d.). How X handles abuse and harassment. https://help.x.com/en/rules-and-policies/abusive-behavior

Youngblood, M. (2020). Extremist ideology as a complex contagion: The spread of far-right radicalization in the United States between 2005 and 2017. *Humanities and Social Sciences Communications*, 7(1), 49. https://doi.org/10.1057/s41599-020-00546-3

15

CONCLUDING THOUGHTS: INTERSECTING IDENTITY, RISK, AND HARM FOR TRANS COMMUNITIES

Jane C. Healy

Introduction

This edited collection set out to explore contemporary debates surrounding transphobic hate crime and harms towards transgender and other gender non-conforming people. With a focus on understanding transphobic hate, criminal justice, and policy responses; spaces and places where transphobia manifests; and examining discourse, representation, and construction of transgender identities, the chapters herein evidence a diversity of research from across the social sciences. This collection contributes to the growing canon of academic research into experiences of transphobic hate crime and provides important insights at a time of unprecedented political, social, and direct threats to trans people's lives.

This collection comes at a relevant time, where gender identity has become a divisive political tool, contributing to a global social climate in which transgender people have become targets for suspicion, discrimination, and hate. Transgender communities' access to various aspects of social life have been misconstrued as being in direct opposition to cisgender, 'sex-based' rights, as Colliver et al. points out in Chapter One. Predominantly, transgender women are the focal point of such discussions, and as such, many of the chapters herein also focus on trans women's experiences. The evidence shows how transgender communities are constructed as homogenous groups, resulting in overly simplistic and reductive perspectives by agencies and practitioners across social and justice spheres.

The main themes addressed throughout this collection include: manifestations of transphobic hate; transphobic hate and criminal justice policy; transphobia within the criminal justice system itself; spaces and places of

DOI: 10.4324/9781003564928-19

transphobia; and media and online discourses, representations, and constructions of transgender identities. Within this collection, they have been developed and engaged with utilising empirical data and conceptual augmentation. Fundamentally, through each of these themes runs a thread which we describe as the *justice void* for trans and gender non-conforming people. This justice void operates where structural, systemic, political, social and cultural barriers and tropes exist which block equal and equitable access for trans communities and maintains their marginalisation. Below we address this through each of four sub-themes.

The first dominant theme from these chapters is that they proffer a conceptual and theoretical discussion of identities and hate, which in many examples, include an intersectional framework. Section one sought to understand transgender identities and experiences of transphobic hate crime; to explore the lived realities of hate as an everyday occurrence in trans people's lives. Further, the intersectional and unique experiences of transgender, non-binary, and gender-variant people expose the role of political power and academic authority as structural sources of marginalisation. This section also briefly considered the role of media representations of transgender people and their bodies as contested spaces, though this is further elaborated upon later in the collection. The discussions in this section illustrate how public discourse impacts on the regulation of transgender identities and how bodily autonomy can be extended to young transgender and gender-diverse people. In Chapter Two, Colliver deftly illustrates the denial of victimhood experienced by transgender people when their abusers are family members. This has consequential impact on their willingness to recognise the harm caused to them, and report it, as well as social and structural influence on hate crime statistics. Additionally, the hierarchical approach to hate crimes, which prioritises and recognises physical violence above other forms of harm, contributes to the justice void whereby experiences of limited or no physical harm are perceived as less impactful or of less value and meaning. Non-violent harms are marginalised and normalised, and function to challenge accepted victimhood, resulting, as Colliver states, in the institutional devaluation of trans lives.

Colliver's findings directly relate to Pickles' arguments in the following Chapter Three; that anti-trans rhetoric and trans exclusion has been reinforced through increasingly accepted and normalised gender-critical discourses in both media and political spaces, and funded through a global labyrinth of powerful players with links to far-right, pro-life, evangelical, and gender-critical agents. A pattern of stereotyping and tropism serves to de-legitimise trans people, and as Connelly points out in Chapter Four, there is a further gap in provision and discussion for young trans and non-binary people's voices to be heard and understood. The intersections of age and gender identity remain underexplored and undervalued, apart from tropisms around rights to choose to transition and age of responsibility, and trans rights are pitted as a threat to social cohesion. The thread of the justice void weaves its way through issues of age, victimisation, public and social discourses, and activism, muting trans communities and rendering them powerless in social, cultural, and political spheres.

The second theme presented herein focuses on the role of criminal justice systems and political structures in responding to transphobic hate crime. Section two examined how transgender identities and experiences of hate are dealt with through policy and the criminal justice system, drawing on international processes in the main. Case studies from Poland, Germany, the US, and the UK provide insights into the ways in which transphobic discourses are tethered to political narratives, leading to institutional manifestations of prejudice against transgender identities. The social inequalities that this perpetuates is evident through the examples drawn from within the evidence presented. For example, Gwenffrewi's Chapter Five takes us to the USA where violence against trans women is illustrated both as an individual and structural harm, drawing on the prison industrial complex as a site of conflict.

Gwenffrewi weaves the intersections of trans identities with race, ethnicity, migration status, and poverty to underscore the increased vulnerability trans communities share in their risk of over-policing and incarceration, drawing on the high-profile case of CeCe McDonald, who was imprisoned for 19 months, and subsequent media interest. CeCe's intersectional oppression, as a black trans woman in a male prison, is highlighted through a documentary that charts both her own experiences and how they were represented through media and social discourse. What our author underscores here is the complex challenges of weaving unique personal experiences within a collective transgender narrative that is presented for public consumption. From a criminal justice perspective, she illustrates how solitary confinement is justified as a means of 'protecting' trans prisoners, when ultimately it risks further harm and ill-health through its punitive and isolationist method. Hence, *justice* is undermined through restrictions of trans prisoners' rights, which are excused and defended by institutional authorities, adding to our *void*.

Comparatively, in Chapter Six, Singh highlights the importance of fair jury selection (and real and imagined contact) for restoring justice for prosecutions related to transgender victims in England and Wales. His data contributes to the ongoing *justice void* that fails to provide equity for trans communities in the courts. Likewise, Milczarek, in Chapter Seven, uses the example of Poland to demonstrate how transphobia is institutionalised, driving increasing discrimination, fear, and hostility, but also juxtaposing it to international contexts and discourse, similar to Pickles' work earlier. Again though, Milczarek identifies a dearth in legal avenues for justice as there are limited protections for transgender communities in Polish law. Relations between media, politics, and public opinion intersect and permeate all areas of life to ostracise and discriminate against transgender people.

What is evident in Lantz and Wenger's US-based Chapter Eight is the intersection of homelessness, homophobia, transphobia, racism, and risk (something Connolly also picks up on earlier in Chapter Three). The authors evidence that homeless transgender women experienced higher risk of violent homicides for presenting as something other than their 'expected' gender. Their chapter illustrates how perpetrators are driven by a desire to rectify and revalidate their own masculinities (another common theme), alongside an absence of condemnation of the actual and vicarious harm and violence towards transgender people.

Weber and colleagues' research on transphobic crimes in Germany, in Chapter Nine, underscores the extent to which trans communities are constructed and scapegoated as a threat to a functioning and stable society. Notwithstanding the changes in measuring and recording hate crimes towards trans and gender-diverse communities, their research highlights the increase in recorded crimes in recent years and predictors of transphobic attitudes through a cross-sectional representative survey of the population. They highlight how political and media rhetoric underpin the evidenced trend towards transphobic views and attitudes, which fuels far-right hostility and reinforces our justice void.

The third theme in this collection focuses on the role of place and space, with contributors drawing out the nuances of how transphobia manifests differently across different spaces, online and in workplaces. By examining a diversity of spaces and places within which experiences of transphobia, prejudice, and hate manifest, these chapters illustrate the wider environment of fear for trans and gender-diverse people, highlighting the infiltration of transphobic discourse and hate into every corner of existence.

The chapters explore the protective and avoidance strategies that are actively deployed by transgender people to protect themselves and their livelihoods, as well as online spaces where hate crimes in progress target transgender and other gender-diverse people by exposing personal details, leaving them vulnerable to attack online and in-person. In Chapter Ten, McBride draws on Žižek's (2008) concept of symbolic violence in her analysis of interviews with trans women about their experiences in the workplace, and positions her findings within neoliberalist discourses that constrict and silence trans communities. By highlighting the exclusion of trans women in the workplace and the subtle and less-than-subtle methods employed by organisations and individuals to present barriers to full engagement in workplace occupations, McBride underscores the structural barriers to societal integration for trans communities; a common feature in our justice void.

Moving from the physical environment to online spaces, in Chapter Eleven Pérez-Fernández and Bartels' contribution draws upon digital zemiology (Elias, 2025) to illustrate the ongoing harm to trans communities via doxxing. Highlighting the important space that online environments can offer trans and queer communities, in terms of safety, identity, and emotional support, the authors argue that the harm inflicted in online spaces is misunderstood, minimalised, and lacks recognition in legal and policy circles. In Chapter Twelve, Dimitrakopoulos further emphasises the impact of harm via online environments in an analysis of an online survey and interviews exploring people's experiences of the dating app Grindr. Drawing on micro-aggressions and micro-insults, this chapter highlights experiences of dehumanisation, degradation, ostracisation, and alienation that trans and gender non-conforming individuals experience from within online communities, emphasising the pervasiveness of Othering and the reinforcing of patriarchal binaries and cis-normative assumptions and stereotypes.

Online threats and abuse are impactful, regardless of whether they result in 'offline' harm or constitute a criminal act, and yet our justice void threads its way through these online worlds in underlining the lack of seriousness attended to the threats, abuse, trolling, and doxxing that occur. These chapters ultimately evidence how trans communities withdraw, self-police, and curtail their identities and expression.

The fourth and final section offers a critical discussion of the ways that transgender people are constructed and represented across several different mediums. Section four returned to media messaging and further examined online discourses, representations, and negative constructions of transgender identities. Gwenffrewi's second chapter (Chapter Thirteen) charts the creation and maintenance of negative media coverage towards trans women in which they are often seen as a predatory threat to (cis) women and girls' safety. Highlighting the UK government's contribution to discussions on a review of the Gender Recognition Act, Gwenffrewi's analysis illustrates the structural barriers being maintained against trans people's rights. Continuing from this, Ashcroft's examination of online hate as a result of the UK government's proposed amendments to the GRA in Chapter Fourteen similarly shows patterns of predatory labelling and the politicisation of trans communities. Both contributions show how the justice void is evident in powerful political, media, and social spheres.

How hate infiltrates

The ways in which transgender identities have been constructed as a threat firmly illustrate the insidious nature of the hate that follows. These chapters address conceptual discussions and debates that are central to contemporary considerations of experiences of transgender hate. In doing so, they engage with broader discourses beyond hate studies into hierarchies of victimisation. Each chapter has engaged with academic discussion within transgender studies, thus contributing to the expansion of works and evidencing the breadth and nuance of lived experience on this topic. Whilst some individual chapters explore populism, neoliberalism, or nationalism in conjunction with transgender identities, the content also explores concepts of (trans)normativity, oppression, misogyny, media responsibility, and microaggressions.

Andrea Hollomotz's (2012) continuum of disablist violence highlights how hate and harm occur along a spectrum, from low-level, non-violent incidents, to serious and extreme violent crimes. This can be experienced over time, with ongoing, repeated, and multiple incidents occurring over long periods, often escalating in severity. Structural and individual oppression are evident and impactful on all areas of life. We would argue similar patterns of inequality, exclusion, and tolerance of abuse occur with regards to transphobic harms, as these chapters illustrate. Likewise, Žižek's (2008) symbolic violence highlights subtle forms of discrimination as insipid but not insignificant in terms of impact and harm. Furthermore, the evidence herein also highlights the specific threat trans women are seen to pose as 'predatory' men and the subsequent alienation and abuse that results from this trope.

This spectrum of harm, violence, and abuse, both structurally and individually, underlines the justice void, which is evident through this collection. We understand 'void' as meaning a completely empty space, something that represents 'no thing' – as in, no justice existing or occurring, or that has existed or occurred. This conceptualisation is distinct to and goes beyond Walters et al.'s (2017) justice *gap,* which situates hate crime injustices in the drop in numbers of hate crimes in the criminal justice system; from experiencing, reporting, charging, prosecuting, and securing successful outcomes. Our void goes far beyond this important framework, in that the gaps we have identified herein exist both outside of and within our justice systems, situated across culture, politics, social, online and offline environments. The public shaming, harassment, abuse, threats, violence, and harm, occurring across all aspect of trans communities' lives, need to be heard, and can be via the contributions in this collection.

What happens next?

This innovative and contemporary collection on issues of transphobia and transphobic hate crime is vital in our contemporary society. The authors herein utilise innovative data collection and analytical techniques to better understand transphobic hate and its various manifestations. The methods deployed range from in-depth life course interviewing techniques, to mock-juror case study analysis, quantitative cross-sectional surveys, content and discourse analysis, media analysis, and mixed methods. There is a breadth of methodological expertise presented which offers practitioners practical and evidential materials, regardless of methodological preference or discipline. Fundamentally, more of this level of high-quality research and expertise is needed.

A consistent focus on harm is also evident in this collection, harm that goes beyond criminal and legal frameworks, but situates trans people in positions of vulnerability, neglect, and dismissal. The justice void, which is clearly evidenced herein, is situated within social, criminal, environmental, procedural, and institutional lenses. Trans communities are excluded, silenced, ignored, or threatened across all of these intersecting spheres, delineating them to caricatures, stereotypes, sexual perversions, and offensive tropes, all of which deny their individuality, independence, sense of safety, and joy. This collection has been a challenge to produce in that it emphasises the very real harm to our trans allies for transgressing cis-normative gender boundaries, justified and underscored by false rhetorics of protection and/or women's safety.

The justice void raises a further concern; where hate crime and other forms of legislation exist to protect transgender victims and support trans and non-gender conforming communities, these are in direct conflict with social, cultural, and political campaigns that present those same people as unworthy of recognition and respect. This raises genuine, profound concerns that legislative and policy frameworks are meaningless in practice. For trans communities, a combination of denial of victimhood and perceptions of predation and threat combine to create and maintain the justice void we present. Successfully addressing hate crimes against trans people requires a recognition and acceptance that they are victims. If the existence of trans people is threatened or denied, in legislative and policy terms, then how can they be deserving of their victimhood? We risk denying them more than just victim status, but also legitimacy and humanity.

Conclusion

It has been a pleasure to edit this book. This is the first time a collection focused on unpacking the nuances of transphobic hate crime has been collated. The collection represents a well-rounded and deep-dive analysis of some of the key contemporary issues relevant to hate and transgender studies specifically but draws upon a varied disciplinary terrain to present a comprehensive overview. It highlights the intersectional nature of harm and hurt for our trans communities, and the significant impact this has on health and well-being. At a time when transgender rights are being challenged and, in some nation states, eroded or even removed, this collection makes a comprehensive and compelling argument for greater protection and care for our transgender and non-binary communities. Rather than being a threat to our social norms, it emphasises how much our transgender communities are being threatened instead. We believe this collection stands in defiance of hatred and harm and highlights the lived experiences and humanity we all share.

References

Elias, J. (2025). Towards a digital zemiology. *Justice, Power and Resistance*, *8*(1), 1–17.

Hollomotz, A. (2012). Disability, oppression and violence: Towards a sociological explanation. *Sociology*, *47*(3), 477–493.

Walters, M., Wiedlitzka, S., & Owusu-Bempah, A. (2017) *Hate Crime and the Legal Process: Options for Law Reform*. Final Report October 2017. Sussex: University of Sussex

Žižek, S. (2008). *Violence: Six Sideways Reflections*. New York: Picador.

INDEX

Pages numbers in *italics* denote figures, those in **bold** denote tables. A letter n following a page number indicates a reference in the notes.